Across Intellectual Property

This book is an examination of topical and fundamental issues from across IP law, bringing together authors from the US, UK, Europe, Asia, Australia and New Zealand in a comparative collection aimed at a wide international audience, especially in common law jurisdictions. It takes as a starting point the work of internationally renowned Australian scholar Sam Ricketson, whose contributions to IP law and practice have been extensive and richly diverse, with a range of engagements through teaching, scholarship, practice and law reform. The book is structured in four parts, which move across IP regimes, jurisdictions, disciplines and professions, addressing issues that include what exactly is protected by IP regimes; regime differences, overlaps and transplants; copyright authorship and artificial intelligence; internationalization of IP through public and private international law; IP intersections with historical and empirical research, human rights, privacy, personality and cultural identity; and IP scholars and universities and the influence of treatises and textbooks.

GRAEME W AUSTIN is Professor of Law at Melbourne Law School and Chair of Private Law at Victoria University of Wellington. His books include *Human Rights and Intellectual Property: Mapping the Global Interface* (Cambridge University Press, 2011) and *International Intellectual Property and the ASEAN Way: Pathways to Interoperability* (edited, Cambridge University Press, 2017).

ANDREW F CHRISTIE, Professor and Chair of Intellectual Property at Melbourne Law School, has held distinguished visitor positions at the University of Cambridge, Duke University, the University of Toronto and the National University of Singapore and has been identified by *Managing IP* as one of the 'world's 50 most influential people in intellectual property'.

ANDREW T KENYON is Professor in the Melbourne Law School and has held visiting appointments at the University of British Columbia, London School of Economics, Queen Mary University of London, and University Paris 1 Panthéon Sorbonne. He researches across media law, and his publications include *Comparative Defamation and Privacy Law* (edited, Cambridge University Press, 2016).

MEGAN RICHARDSON is Professor of Law, Co-Director CMCL and Director IPRIA, Melbourne Law School, researching in intellectual property and personality rights. Recent books include *Fashioning Intellectual Property: Exhibition, Advertising and the Press: 1789–1918* (Cambridge University Press, 2012) and *The Right to Privacy: Origins and Influence of a Nineteenth-Century Idea* (Cambridge University Press, 2017).

CAMBRIDGE INTELLECTUAL PROPERTY AND INFORMATION LAW

As its economic potential has rapidly expanded, intellectual property has become a subject of front-rank legal importance. Cambridge Intellectual Property and Information Law is a series of monograph studies of major current issues in intellectual property. Each volume contains a mix of international, European, comparative and national law, making this a highly significant series for practitioners, judges and academic researchers in many countries.

Series Editors

Lionel Bently
Herchel Smith Professor of Intellectual Property Law, University of Cambridge
Graeme Dinwoodie
Global Professor of Intellectual Property Law, Chicago-Kent College of Law, Illinois Institute of Technology

Advisory Editors

William R Cornish, *Emeritus Herchel Smith Professor of Intellectual Property Law, University of Cambridge*
François Dessemontet, *Professor of Law, University of Lausanne*
Jane C Ginsburg, *Morton L Janklow Professor of Literary and Artistic Property Law, Columbia Law School*
Paul Goldstein, *Professor of Law, Stanford University*
The Rt Hon Sir Robin Jacob, *Hugh Laddie Professor of Intellectual Property, University College London*
Ansgar Ohly, *Professor of Intellectual Property Law, Ludwig-Maximilian University of Munich*

A list of books in the series can be found at the end of this volume.

Sam Ricketson (photograph by Hamish Carr)

Across Intellectual Property
Essays in Honour of Sam Ricketson

Edited by
Graeme W Austin
Melbourne Law School, Victoria University of Wellington

Andrew F Christie
Melbourne Law School

Andrew T Kenyon
Melbourne Law School

Megan Richardson
Melbourne Law School

CAMBRIDGE
UNIVERSITY PRESS

University Printing House, Cambridge CB2 8BS, United Kingdom

One Liberty Plaza, 20th Floor, New York, NY 10006, USA

477 Williamstown Road, Port Melbourne, VIC 3207, Australia

314–321, 3rd Floor, Plot 3, Splendor Forum, Jasola District Centre, New Delhi – 110025, India

79 Anson Road, #06–04/06, Singapore 079906

Cambridge University Press is part of the University of Cambridge.

It furthers the University's mission by disseminating knowledge in the pursuit of education, learning, and research at the highest international levels of excellence.

www.cambridge.org
Information on this title: www.cambridge.org/9781108485159
DOI: 10.1017/9781108750066

© Cambridge University Press 2020

This publication is in copyright. Subject to statutory exception and to the provisions of relevant collective licensing agreements, no reproduction of any part may take place without the written permission of Cambridge University Press.

First published 2020

A catalogue record for this publication is available from the British Library.

Library of Congress Cataloging-in-Publication Data
Names: Ricketson, Sam, honouree. | Austin, Graeme, editor.
Title: Across intellectual property : essays in honour of Sam Ricketson / [edited by] Graeme Austin, Andrew Christie, Andrew Kenyon, Megan Richardson.
Description: New York : Cambridge University Press, 2020. | Series: Cambridge intellectual property and information law Identifiers: LCCN 2019038233 (print) | LCCN 2019038234 (ebook) | ISBN 9781108485159 (hardback) | ISBN 9781108719216 (paperback) | ISBN 9781108750066 (epub)
Subjects: LCSH: Intellectual property. | Ricketson, Sam.
Classification: LCC K1401 .A9295 2020 (print) | LCC K1401 (ebook) | DDC 346.04/8–dc23
LC record available at https://lccn.loc.gov/2019038233
LC ebook record available at https://lccn.loc.gov/2019038234

ISBN 978-1-108-48515-9 Hardback

Cambridge University Press has no responsibility for the persistence or accuracy of URLs for external or third-party internet websites referred to in this publication and does not guarantee that any content on such websites is, or will remain, accurate or appropriate.

Contents

Notes on Contributors   *page* x

Introduction: Across Intellectual Property   1
GRAEME W AUSTIN, ANDREW F CHRISTIE,
ANDREW T KENYON AND MEGAN RICHARDSON

Part I   Across Regimes   9

1   A Matter of Sense: What Intellectual Property Rights Protect   11
ANDREW F CHRISTIE

2   Overlap and Redundancy in the Intellectual Property System: Trade Mark Always Loses   26
GRAEME B DINWOODIE

3   Rethinking the Relationship between Registered and Unregistered Trade Marks   38
ROBERT BURRELL

4   Publication in the History of Patents and Copyright: Harmony or Happenstance?   51
DAVID J BRENNAN

5   Of Moral Rights and Legal Transplants: Connecting Laws, Connecting Cultures   64
ELIZABETH ADENEY

Part II   Across Jurisdictions   77

6   People Not Machines: Authorship and What It Means in International Copyright Law   79
JANE C GINSBURG

7   Australian Legislation Abroad: Singaporean Pragmatism
    and the Role of Australian Scholarship in Singaporean
    Copyright Law   92
    NG-LOY WEE LOON

8   'The Berne Convention Is Our Ideal': Hall Caine, Canadian
    Copyright and the Natural Rights of Authors after 1886   102
    KATHY BOWREY

9   A Future of International Copyright? Berne and the Front
    Door Out   116
    REBECCA GIBLIN

10 'Trade-Related' after All? Reframing the Paris and Berne
    Conventions as Multilateral Trade Law   129
    ANTONY TAUBMAN

11 Intellectual Property, Innovation and New Space Technology   144
    MELISSA DE ZWART

12 Intellectual Property and Private International Law:
    Strangers in the Night?   158
    RICHARD GARNETT

Part III   Across Disciplines   173

13 The Challenges of Intellectual Property Legal History Research   175
    ISABELLA ALEXANDER

14 Connecting Intellectual Property and Human Rights in
    the Law School Syllabus   189
    GRAEME W AUSTIN

15 Copyright and Privacy: Pre-trial Discovery of User Identities   201
    DAVID LINDSAY

16 Resisting Labels: Trade Marks and Personal Identity   216
    MEGAN RICHARDSON

17 Trade Marks and Cultural Identity   227
    ROCHELLE COOPER DREYFUSS AND SUSY FRANKEL

18 Intellectual Property Law and Empirical Research   240
    EMILY HUDSON AND ANDREW T KENYON

Part IV Across Professions — 253

19 Intellectual Property Scholars and University
   Intellectual Property Policies — 255
   ANN MONOTTI

20 'Measuring' an Academic Contribution — 269
   MARK DAVISON

21 Language and Law: The Role of the Intellectual Property
   Treatise — 280
   DAVID LLEWELYN

22 Intellectual Property in the Courtroom:
   The Role of the Expert — 292
   PETER HEEREY

23 Copyright and the 'Profession' of Authorship — 303
   COLIN GOLVAN

Laudatio — 315

24 Sam Ricketson: Teacher, Scholar, Advocate and Law Reformer — 317
   JILL MCKEOUGH

Notes on Contributors

Elizabeth Adeney is an Associate Professor in the Faculty of Law and Business at Deakin University. She researches in intellectual property and comparative law, and her publications include the book *The Moral Rights of Authors and Performers: An International and Comparative Analysis* (Oxford University Press, 2006).

Isabella Alexander is Associate Professor in the Faculty of Law, University of Technology Sydney. She researches and teaches in intellectual property law, specialising in the law of copyright and legal history. Her books include *Copyright Law and the Public Interest in the Nineteenth Century* (Hart, 2010) and the co-edited *Research Handbook on the History of Copyright Law* (Edward Elgar, 2016, with Gómez-Arostegui).

Graeme W Austin is Professor of Law at Melbourne Law School and Chair of Private Law at Victoria University of Wellington. His books include *Human Rights and Intellectual Property: Mapping the Global Interface* (Cambridge, 2011, with Helfer) and the co-edited *International Intellectual Property and the ASEAN Way: Pathways to Interoperability* (Cambridge University Press, 2017, with Ng).

Kathy Bowrey is Professor in the Faculty of Law, University of New South Wales. She is a legal historian and sociolegal researcher whose work explores laws and practices that inform knowledge creation and the production, distribution and reception of technology and culture. Her publications include *Law and Internet Cultures* (Cambridge University Press, 2005) and the co-edited *Law and Creativity in the Age of the Entertainment Franchise* (Cambridge University Press, 2014, with Handler).

David J Brennan is Visiting Fellow in the Faculty of Law, University of Technology Sydney and a General Editor of the *Australian Intellectual Property Journal*. His primary fields of research are patent and copyright law, with a focus on their interface with other legal regimes such as contract, property, restitution, international and trade law. Recent

Notes on Contributors

publications include work on the role of the Copyright Tribunal as a maker of copyright exceptions in the context of fair use debates and on the copyright liability of an internet intermediary which facilitates the reproduction of artists' works.

Robert Burrell is Professor of Intellectual Property and Information Technology Law at the University of Oxford and Professor at the Melbourne Law School. His books include *Copyright Exceptions: The Digital Impact* (Cambridge University Press, 2005, with Coleman) and *Australian Trade Mark Law* (2nd ed., Oxford University Press, 2016, with Handler). Recent work investigates the role of rewards as an alternative to the patent system in the eighteenth and nineteenth centuries and research with psychologists into trade mark law's assumptions about consumers.

Andrew F Christie is Professor and Chair of Intellectual Property at Melbourne Law School. He has held distinguished visitor positions at the University of Cambridge, Duke University, the University of Toronto, and the National University of Singapore, and has been identified by *Managing IP* as one of the 'world's 50 most influential people in intellectual property'.

Mark Davison is Professor in the Faculty of Law, Monash University. His books include *The Legal Protection of Databases* (Cambridge University Press, 2003), *Australian Intellectual Property Law* (3rd ed, Cambridge University Press, 2016, with Monotti and Wiseman), *Shanahan's Australian Law of Trade Marks & Passing Off* (6th ed, Lawbook Co, 2016, with Horak) and *The WTO Agreement on Trade-Related Aspects of Intellectual Property Rights: A Commentary* (Edward Elgar, 2014, with Malbon and Lawson).

Melissa de Zwart is Professor and Dean at Adelaide Law School, University of Adelaide. Prior to joining academia, she was Manager, Legal Services, CSIRO, where she advised on protection and commercialisation of technology. Her research focuses primarily on digital technology, as it interacts with culture, human behaviour and new areas of innovation. She has published widely on copyright, social media, surveillance, popular culture, the internet and outer space.

Graeme B Dinwoodie is Global Professor of Intellectual Property Law at Chicago-Kent College of Law, Illinois Institute of Technology. From 2009 to 2018, he was Professor of Intellectual Property and Information Technology Law at the University of Oxford and Director of the Oxford Intellectual Property Research Centre. He remains a

Visiting Professor at the University Oxford. His books include *A Neofederalist Vision of TRIPS: The Resilience of the International Intellectual Property Regime* (Oxford University Press, 2012, with Dreyfuss).

Rochelle Cooper Dreyfuss is the Pauline Newman Professor of Law at New York University School of Law and the Co-Director of the Engelberg Center on Innovation Law and Policy. She served as reporter for the American Law Institute's Project on Intellectual Property: Principles Governing Jurisdiction, Choice of Law, and Judgments in Transnational Disputes. Her books include the co-edited *Framing Intellectual Property Law in the 21st Century* (Cambridge University Press, 2018, with Siew-Kuan Ng) and *The Oxford Handbook of Intellectual Property Law* (Oxford University Press, 2018, with Pila).

Susy Frankel is Chair in Intellectual Property and International Trade at the Faculty of Law, Victoria University of Wellington and Director of the New Zealand Centre of International Economic Law. She is an elected Fellow of the Royal Society of New Zealand and is a former president of the International Association for the Advancement of Teaching and Research of Intellectual Property (ATRIP). Her books include *Test Tubes for Global Intellectual Property Issues: Small Market Economies* (Cambridge University Press, 2015) and *Intellectual Property in New Zealand* (Lexis Nexis 2011).

Richard Garnett is Professor at Melbourne Law School. His major research interests are in conflict of laws, international dispute resolution and cross-border online conduct. He has acted as legal adviser and counsel in private international law and international commercial arbitration matters before Australian and international tribunals. His books include *Substance and Procedure in Private International Law* (Oxford University Press, 2012) and *Private International Law in Australia* (4th ed, LexisNexis Butterworths, 2019, with Mortensen and Keyes).

Rebecca Giblin is Associate Professor at the Melbourne Law School and an Australian Research Council Future Fellow. She has held visiting appointments including Columbia Law School, University of California, Berkeley and Sciences Po (Paris). Her research includes work on authorship and copyright reform and on e-lending in public libraries. Her publications include *Code Wars* (Edward Elgar, 2011) and the co-edited *What If We Could Reimagine Copyright?* (Australian National University Press, 2017, with Weatherall).

Jane C Ginsburg is Morton L Janklow Professor of Literary and Artistic Property Law at Columbia Law School and faculty director of its

Kernochan Center for Law, Media and the Arts. She is a corresponding fellow of the British Academy and a member of the American Philosophical Society and the American Academy of Arts and Sciences. Her books include *International Copyright: US and EU Perspectives* (Edward Elgar, 2015, with Treppoz) and *International Copyright and Neighbouring Rights: The Berne Convention and Beyond* (Oxford University Press, 2006, with Ricketson).

Colin Golvan AM QC is a member of the Victorian Bar practising predominantly in intellectual property and trade practices. He has appeared in the Federal Court and the High Court of Australia in intellectual property, trade practices and defamation cases. His books include *Copyright: Law and Practice* (Federation Press, 2007), *An Introduction to Intellectual Property Law* (Federation Press, 1992) and *Words and Law* (Penguin, 1990).

The Hon Peter Heerey AM QC is a former judge of the Federal Court of Australia (1990–2009) where his work at trial and appellate levels included intellectual property and competition law. He has published widely in professional and academic journals in corporations law, defamation, expert evidence, intellectual property, law and literature and federation history.

Emily Hudson is Reader in Law at the Dickson Poon School of Law, King's College London, having previously held academic posts at the universities of Melbourne, Queensland (where remains a Visiting Associate Professor) and Oxford. Her research interests include intellectual property law, personal property law and trusts and law as it relates to cultural institutions and the creative industries.

Andrew T Kenyon is Professor at Melbourne Law School and has held visiting appointments at the University of British Columbia, London School of Economics, Queen Mary University of London and University Paris 1 Panthéon Sorbonne. He researches across media law, and publications include *Comparative Defamation and Privacy Law* (edited, Cambridge University Press, 2016).

David Lindsay is Professor in the Faculty of Law, University of Technology Sydney. His expertise lies in law and technology, and he is widely published in the areas of copyright, privacy, cyberlaw and communications law. He is the General Editor of the *Australian Intellectual Property Journal*, and his books include *International Domain Name Law: ICANN and the UDRP* (Hart, 2007) and *Public Rights: Copyright's Public Domains* (Cambridge University Press, 2018, with Greenleaf).

David Llewelyn is Professor of Law (Practice) in the School of Law, Singapore Management University, and Professor of Intellectual Property Law, King's College London. His books include Intellectual Property: Patents, Copyright, Trade Marks and Allied Rights (9th ed, Sweet and Maxwell, 2019, with Aplin and Cornish), Kerly's Law of Trade Marks & Trade Names (16th ed, Sweet & Maxwell, 2018, with Mellor and others) and Invisible Gold in Asia (Marshall Cavendish, 2010). He is an IP Adjudicator in Singapore, sits as an arbitrator and practices commercial law at David Llewelyn & Co LLC.

Jill McKeough is Professor in the Faculty of Law, University of Technology Sydney. Her research examines, among other things, the digital economy; competition law; indigenous and cultural rights; freedom of information; and access to books, software, entertainment products and educational resources. Her books include *Intellectual Property: Commentary and Materials* (4th ed, Lawbook, 2007, with Bowrey and Griffith).

Ann Monotti is Professor in the Faculty of Law, Monash University and was inaugural Director of its Centre for Commercial Law and Regulatory Studies. Her books include *Universities and Intellectual Property: Ownership and Exploitation* (Oxford University Press, 2003, with Ricketson), *Australian Intellectual Property Law* (3rd ed, Cambridge University Press, 2016, with Davison and Wiseman) and *Commercialisation of Intellectual Property* (LexisNexis, 2019, with Stoianoff and Chilton).

Ng-Loy Wee Loon is Professor of Law at National University of Singapore. Her appointments include membership of the Board of Governors of the IP Academy (2007–2011), Singapore's Copyright Tribunal (since 2009) and the Singapore Domain Name Dispute Resolution Policy Panel (since 2014). Her books include *Law of Intellectual Property of Singapore* (2nd ed., Sweet & Maxwell, 2014).

Megan Richardson is Professor at Melbourne Law School, Co-Director of its Centre for Media and Communications Law and Director of the Intellectual Property Research Institute of Australia. She researches in intellectual property and personality rights and recent books include *Fashioning Intellectual Property: Exhibition, Advertising and the Press: 1789–1918* (Cambridge University Press, 2012, with Thomas); and *The Right to Privacy: Origins and Influence of a Nineteenth-Century Idea* (Cambridge University Press, 2017).

Antony Taubman is Director, Intellectual Property Government Procurement and Competition Division of the World Trade Organization.

From 2002 to 2009, he was Director, Global Intellectual Property Issues Division of WIPO (including the Traditional Knowledge Division and Life Sciences Program). He formerly headed the IP section in Australia's Department of Foreign Affairs and Trade, and practiced patent and trademark law.

Introduction
Across Intellectual Property

*Graeme W Austin, Andrew F Christie,
Andrew T Kenyon and Megan Richardson*

This book looks across the field of intellectual property law, pulling out and examining some key strands. At the same time, it acknowledges that this is a field of tremendously broad and expanding reach. At the very least, it covers the well-established but still-developing regimes of copyright, patent, designs and trade mark law. These are typically supplemented by trade secrecy, passing off and other laws which can loosely be said to protect intellectual endeavour and enterprise from proscribed forms of 'unfair competition' or misappropriation. And the law's scope of operation is also far greater, potentially covering the grant of rights over all information generated through human and even artificial intelligence. So what will intellectual property (IP) encompass in the twenty-first century and will there continue to be a common field?

The rights that diverse IP laws establish have undergone significant expansion over the last century plus, since the 'modern' field of IP law is said to have been established. They bump up against other rights that also have considerable and evolving legal support of their own, including rights of freedom of thought and speech, of access to information, of trade and competition, of artistic and cultural flourishing and of privacy and personality. Conflicts arise when different regimes that fall within the general rubric of IP intersect, creating complex issues of overlap and priority. And then there is the vexed question of the relationships between international and national laws in framing and enforcing the legal standards. In this collection, we look closely at several issues of scope that have been pressing for some time, including where to set limits on what counts as intellectual property, how to deal with overlaps between different IP regimes, how to deal with differences between jurisdictions and how to resolve conflicts in cases where what is at stake is not just about rewarding creators and innovators. We employ a variety of methods and perspectives, drawing on different jurisdictions and regimes for possible answers, bringing in extra-legal modes of analysis and drawing on insights from diverse professions.

We are inspired in this undertaking by the work of our distinguished colleague and friend Sam Ricketson, whose long career of scholarship, legal education, advocacy and law reform in Australia and internationally has made him a towering figure in the field of IP. Legal biographer Christopher Sexton, wrapping up an interview with Ricketson published in *Intellectual Property Forum* in 2004, posited that '[a]fter a quarter of a century of commitment to the research, publication, teaching and now practice of intellectual property law, he remains the pre-eminent modern pedagogue in the field' in Australia. One and a half decades later, we add to that an acknowledgement that Ricketson has achieved an international reputation among the IP law community of the highest order.

Perhaps because he draws on such a wealth of experience, Ricketson's scholarship on IP law is notable for, among other things, its breadth – it reaches across regimes, across jurisdictions, across disciplines and across professions, evincing comparisons with other legal luminaries, including William Cornish, David Vaver, Jim Lahore and Ann Dufty who helped establish IP as an academic field in the 1970s, 1980s and 1990s. Yet uncommonly even for its time, Ricketson's oeuvre deals with all key areas of IP law, and he has authored major works on both national law and international treaties. His work is informed by the practice of other disciplines, especially history, and it is engaged with beyond the academic profession, notably in the reform and the practice of IP law.

This collection of essays, by leading scholars and practitioners from a range of countries, is dedicated to Ricketson's achievements and reflect his breadth of expertise and application. The publication builds on a one-day workshop, held in December 2017 at Melbourne Law School and hosted by four of Ricketson's immediate colleagues at the University of Melbourne, now the editors of this volume. The chapters, coming out of the workshop in response to the book's theme of 'across intellectual property', are presented in the volume's four parts, which move across IP regimes, jurisdictions, disciplines and professions.

Part I Across Regimes

Uncommonly for contemporary intellectual property academics, Sam Ricketson has produced key works across the spectrum of IP regimes. In the first part of the book, five authors explore what can be learned about IP laws by looking beyond the boundaries of individual regimes.

Andrew Christie revisits a fundamental question: What is it, exactly, that IP regimes protect? His answer is that it is not quite what the conventional view holds it to be. Christie distinguishes materiality from tangibility and asserts that it is the presence of the former (perceptibility by a human sense), not the absence of the latter (perceptibility by touch), which is the defining characteristic of IP subject matter. Because they share a common defining characteristic, there is the potential for different IP regimes to provide rights in respect of the same thing. Graeme Dinwoodie considers how the courts in Europe have addressed the overlap of trade mark protection with the protection provided by the copyright, patents and designs regimes. Observing that the result is denial of trade mark protection, he supplies what the courts have failed to provide: a justification for such a result, and doctrinal principles to achieve a better outcome. This leads into the chapter by Robert Burrell, who explores the justification for having a system for registration of trade marks while also providing protection for unregistered trade marks. He suggests that, contrary to the US approach, registered trade marks could – and probably should – be provided with stronger, but narrower, protection than is provided to unregistered trade marks.

The need to understand the specifics of how individual IP regimes operate can blind one to their commonalities. David Brennan exhorts us to consider matters of shared history. From recognising the logical and chronological connections between the key copyright and patent cases on the significance of the act of publication, he postulates a synergistic development of the two laws from the late eighteenth century through to the mid-nineteenth century. Brennan suggests that the distinction drawn today between the two regimes was, at an earlier time, embryonic. Finally, Elizabeth Adeney considers the experience of transplanting legal norms from one regime to another – specifically, the adoption of civilian law-derived moral rights into the copyright statute of a common law jurisdiction (Australia). She observes an extraordinarily elaborate implementation, wherein abstract civilian law doctrines are replaced by exhaustive statutory rules. Whether such a transplantation should be considered a success remains to be seen.

Part II Across Jurisdictions

The spatial metaphor in this book's title *Across Intellectual Property* is especially apt in the context of the chapters in Part II. For a scholar to be truly *across* intellectual property requires deep engagement with the topic across geopolitical boundaries – with all that this entails, including sensitivity to geopolitical influences on domestic and international law as well as an appreciation of distinctions between discrete domestic IP jurisdictions. The subject now makes little sense without the study of substantive and enforcement obligations and disciplines that straddle international boundaries. Since the entry into force of the Agreement on Trade-Related Aspects of Intellectual Property Rights (TRIPS Agreement) in 1996, these are now firmly anchored in the international trade regime. Much of Sam Ricketson's work exemplifies scholarly engagement with IP across jurisdictions in this sense, including his 1986 text on the Berne Convention (joined in the second edition by Jane Ginsburg), the 2015 treatise on the Paris Convention and in numerous articles and reports. This understanding of the subject is reflected in the chapters in this part.

This part begins with the pressing current question of whether copyright protection requires a human author in the context of new challenges posed for IP by works created by artificial intelligence (AI). In fact, this was a question that Ricketson had studied, as Jane Ginsburg observes in her chapter. She explains how his views on whether a human author was required sprang from his detailed understanding of the disciplines imposed by the Berne Convention itself. In her chapter on the influence of Australian copyright law and scholarship on Singaporean law, Ng-Loy Wee Loon sees the various influences of public international law on thinking about domestic issues within one nation (Australia) influencing judges in another nation (Singapore) on this very same question.

The chapters by Kathy Bowrey, Rebecca Giblin and Antony Taubman each engage with the implications of the internationalization of intellectual property through public international law instruments. Situated in a particular historical context – the possibility in the late nineteenth century that Canada might leave the Berne Convention – Bowrey's chapter details how arguments derived from the universal rights of authors were advanced in order to serve commercial interests of foreign publishers. Giblin explores the geopolitical context in which the Berne Convention is now situated and the influence on that context on possibilities for change. Taubman's chapter engages with ways that the intersection of two legal jurisdictions – IP and trade – influences current understanding of the scope of international law obligations. Melissa de Zwart's chapter takes the theme of IP across jurisdictions to a new frontier, exploring the role of IP in the exploration of outer space. Her analysis exposes the combined relevance of both private intellectual property rights and public law initiatives.

As Richard Garnett's chapter explains, the internationalisation of IP is not just a matter of public international law. Private parties also have a stake in the protection and enforcement of IP rights across international borders. Cross-border disputes between private parties that involve IP rights is the province of private international law. Garnett's chapter examines the ways that IP and private international law are coming together in the context of these disputes.

Part III Across Disciplines

Sam Ricketson's scholarship is deeply informed by history, illustrating an important value of legal research that reaches beyond contemporary doctrine. The chapters in this part take aspects of Ricketson's scholarship into wider analyses within and beyond law, reflecting diverse strands of intellectual property research that have developed markedly in recent decades.

Isabella Alexander considers challenges of undertaking legal historical research in IP, taking Ricketson's historical work as a starting point. Whether conducting IP history or the history of IP law, there are challenges of research and methodology; challenges of interpretation; and challenges relating to the purpose, relevance and audience for such historical research. All of which is to underline the value in well-conducted historical research in IP and IP law.

In a turn to the present, Graeme Austin notes that human rights have increasingly reached across IP since the start of the twenty-first century, creating a large and varied body of research. Austin highlights some opportunities this presents, exploring connections between IP and human rights within the law school curriculum, connecting students with wide-ranging interests and evaluating ideas that commonly structure each domain.

Focussing more particularly on the human right to privacy, David Lindsay analyses how judicial reasoning engages with copyright and privacy law in the pre-trial discovery of allegedly copyright-infringing internet users. Approaches in the UK, Canada and Australia suggest the discretionary power to order disclosure of a user's identity is influenced by the different ways in which these common law courts understand and balance rights. Lindsay argues there is a need for judicial approaches to move beyond the relatively unstructured multi-factorism that has been seen in rights-based analysis in these cases to consider more explicitly the values and interests underlying the rights in question.

Likewise, in her chapter, Megan Richardson argues that considerations of privacy and personality should be taken more seriously when assessing one aspect of trade mark law which has been surprisingly little considered to date – namely, the registration of a person's name or likeness as a trade mark without that person's consent. Her historical analysis focused on the late nineteenth and early twentieth centuries suggests that practical differences in the protection offered to celebrity and non-celebrity names and images continues to this day.

Rochelle Cooper Dreyfus and Susy Frankel then examine the broader question of cases in which trade marks can erode cultural identity through racial disparagement. They contrast legal approaches to disparaging marks in the United States and New Zealand and suggest the latter offers an important guide to accommodating both freedom of expression and respect for cultural identity, potentially even for US law.

Finally in this part, Emily Hudson and Andrew Kenyon examine IP scholarship's empirical turn. They consider framing questions (concerning research quality, limits and implications) that might be useful for empirical IP research, problems observed in some empirical analyses of IP law and lessons from empirical research in other disciplines. The aim is not to provide any simple checklist for IP researchers but to offer prompts to conducting, understanding and using empirical research more carefully in IP scholarship.

Part IV Across Professions

While the chapters in the earlier parts pay testament to the importance of rigorous and wide-ranging scholarship in the field of IP broadly understood, the chapters in Part IV reflect on the significant contribution that IP scholars and their scholarship can make to the practice and profession of IP law, including in ways that extend well beyond the parameters of what we might consider to be a normal academic role.

In the first chapter of this part, Ann Monotti points to the value of a rigorous and critical academic perspective when it comes to crafting university IP policies. In their chapters, Mark Davison and David Llewelyn, in very different ways, point out how well-crafted textbooks provide understanding and illumination to teachers, students and scholars and others at 'the coal face of everyday practical problems and endeavours' as Ricketson phrased it an article published in the Australasian practitioner journal *Intellectual Property Forum* in 2004. Then follow two chapters from those working at the coal face, the first from former judge of the Federal Court of Australia, Peter Heerey and the second from Queen's Counsel and art law expert, Colin Golvan, pointing to the value of expert evidence in court proceedings and appreciation of how the issue of authorship is approached from a practitioner's perspective (including that the law may understand authorship quite differently from authors themselves).

These chapters are among the most personal in the volume, testifying warmly to Ricketson's generosity and influence over many years in areas that may not be immediately evident to outside observers or indeed to universities focussed on measuring more obviously academic outputs. They reflect an older generation of IP scholars, lawyers and judges who were there when IP was being established as a field of serious scholarly and practical significance and who are still looking to make meaningful contributions to the field which they helped shape according to their own lights.

The collection concludes with a Laudatio by Jill McKeough, a more personal final paper addressing Sam Ricketson, which emphasises his gracefulness in sharing insights about IP teaching and scholarship across IP academics and his constructive support for law reform endeavours.

Acknowledgements

We heartily thank our fellow authors for enthusiastically giving their time and expertise to the project, our home institution (including the Intellectual Property Research Institute of Australia at Melbourne Law School) and Hamish Carr (Administrator of Centre for Media and Communications Law and IPRIA) for assistance with the workshop and preparation of the manuscript, our excellent editorial assistant Georgina Dimopoulos, Matt Galloway and Kim Hughes at Cambridge University Press for constructive and helpful support and advice throughout, and the proposal's reviewers and Lionel Bently as editor of the Intellectual Property and Information Law Series for some very pertinent observations and insights.

Part I

Across Regimes

1 A Matter of Sense
What Intellectual Property Rights Protect

Andrew F Christie *

1.1 Introduction

What, exactly, is the nature of the thing protected by intellectual property (IP) rights? The conventional answer to this question is that it is 'intangible' and hence has no physical existence. For example, it is said of copyright law that there is a fundamental dichotomy between the immaterial 'work' and its fixation in a physical 'copy'. The work is 'a sort of Platonic ideal that may be manifest in copies', and it is this 'conceptual, incorporeal construct to which authorial rights attach'.[1] A similar duality is held to operate in other IP laws,[2] with the result that theorists believe: 'Unlike real property law, intellectual property law posits rights in abstract objects'.[3] The problem with abstract objects, however, is that they 'do not exist'.[4]

In all his many writings on IP law, it appears that Sam Ricketson has never expressly endorsed the conventional view that IP subject matter is

---

* Sam Ricketson taught me intellectual property law as an undergraduate student at the University of Melbourne in 1983, which had the effect of igniting a lifelong passion for the subject, both as an area of practice and as a field of academic endeavour. Since then, he has been a trusted advisor, an inspiring mentor, a supportive colleague and a valued friend.
[1] Dan L Burk, 'Copyright and the new materialism' in Jessica Lai and Antoinette Maget (eds.), *Intellectual Property and Access to Im/Material Goods* (Northampton, MA: Edward Elgar, 2016), pp. 47.
[2] See, e.g., Justine Pila, *The Subject Matter of Intellectual Property* (Oxford: Oxford University Press, 2017), ch. 3.
[3] Peter Drahos, *A Philosophy of Intellectual Property* (Acton: ANU eText, 2016), p. 1. See also Pila, *The Subject Matter of Intellectual Property*, 80.
[4] Drahos, *A Philosophy of Intellectual Property*, 6. See also Pila, *The Subject Matter of Intellectual Property*, 79–80: 'Another view of types of potential relevance for IP subject matter casts them as theoretical objects having the sole or primary function of unifying all of the tokens of a given description. ... Having said that, it is difficult to accept from a legal perspective, since it implies that IP rights exist in respect of things that do not per se exist.'

intangible, abstract and non-existent.[5] That apparent lack of endorsement has motivated me to reconsider the issue.

The conclusion reached in this chapter is that the conventional view mis-states the position. In particular, while it is true that IP laws recognise something like the tangible–intangible duality, properly understood the rights granted by those laws do not attach to the 'conceptual, incorporeal construct'; rather, they attach to the corporeal thing in which that construct is 'manifest'. More specifically, while the class of things in respect of which IP protection may be granted includes intangibles, it also includes tangibles. Moreover, those things are *material*, in that they are perceptible by a human sense. Hence they do exist.

To discern what, exactly, IP rights protect it is necessary to explore how, precisely, IP laws give effect to protection. To that end, this chapter postulates the existence of four different, but related, concepts – subjects of protection, protected objects, exclusive rights and scopes of protection – and investigates the role each concept plays in effecting protection within the main IP regimes of copyright, patents, registered trademarks and registered designs. From that analysis, conclusions are drawn about how IP laws afford protection as well as about what it is they protect.

1.2 Tangibility and Materiality

While the word *intangible* is routinely used in the literature to describe IP subject matter, it is almost never expressly defined in that literature. I regard tangibility as the characteristic of being able to be perceived by the human sense of touch. In this chapter, therefore, the adjective *tangible* means perceptible by touch, while the adjective *intangible* means unable to be perceived by touch (with the noun versions of these words having corresponding meanings).[6]

A more nuanced concept is that of materiality. Materiality is the characteristic of having presence in the physical world. It is not just tangible things which have this characteristic. Something can be said to have a presence in the physical world if it is capable of perception by a human 'exteroceptor' – that is, by an organ that responds to stimuli

---

[5] The closest that Ricketson might be said to come to such an endorsement, of which I am aware, is his conception of intellectual property subject matter as 'information': Sam Ricketson, 'New wine into old bottles: Technological change and intellectual property rights' (1992) 10(1) *Prometheus* 53.

[6] This is consistent with the definitions found in general dictionaries, including in the *Oxford English Dictionary*.

originating outside the body.[7] Exteroceptors are responsible for the five basic human senses (sight, hearing, smell, taste and touch) and thermoception (perception of temperature differences).[8] Thus the adjective *material* is used herein to mean perceptible by an exteroceptor.

It will be appreciated that something which is tangible is, by definition, material. It will also be appreciated that something which is intangible, although not perceptible by touch, is material if it is perceptible by one of the other human senses. Thus an intangible that is perceptible by hearing (aurally perceptible) or by smell (olfactorily perceptible) is material.

1.3 Subjects of Protection

The phrase *subject of protection* of an IP law is used in this chapter to mean the phenomenon to which that IP law applies – that is, the class of things in respect of which protection by the IP law may be granted. Put another way, unless a phenomenon is a subject of protection of an IP law, protection under that law is not available for it.

1.3.1 Copyright

The Berne Convention[9] lists twenty-six items as illustrative instances of the 'literary and artistic works' to which it applies.[10] The items listed are of six sorts: (1) writing ('books, pamphlets and other writings'), (2) spoken or played sounds ('addresses', 'musical compositions'), (3) performed sounds and/or movement ('dramatic works', 'choreographic works'), (4) moving images ('cinematographic works'), (5) still images ('drawing', 'photographic works') and (6) three-dimensional objects ('architecture', 'sculpture'). Other international treaties expand the catalogue of subjects of protection. The Rome Convention[11] and the WIPO Performances and Phonograms Treaty (WPPT)[12] apply to unfixed and

---

[7] *The American Heritage Medical Dictionary*, 2nd rev. ed. (Boston: Houghton Mifflin, 2007), s.v. 'exteroceptor'.
[8] Wikipedia, s.v. 'Sense', 23 January 2019, retrieved from https://bit.ly/2YJNSW4.
[9] Berne Convention for the Protection of Literary and Artistic Works, opened for signature 9 September 1886, revised at Paris, 24 July 1971, 828 UNTS 221, as amended on 28 September 1979 (entered into force 19 November 1984) (cited as Berne Convention).
[10] Berne Convention, art. 2.
[11] International Convention for the Protection of Performers, Producers of Phonograms and Broadcasting Organisations, opened for signature 26 October 1961, 496 UNTS 43 (entered into force 18 May 1964) (cited as Rome Convention).
[12] WIPO Performances and Phonograms Treaty, opened for signature 20 December 1996, 2186 UNTS 203 (entered into force 20 May 2002) (cited as WPPT).

fixed performances[13] and to fixations of sounds ('phonograms'),[14] with the Rome Convention also applying to wireless transmissions of sounds or images and sounds ('broadcasts').[15] The TRIPS Agreement[16] and the WIPO Copyright Treaty (WCT)[17] require machine-operable instructions ('computer programs') to be protected as literary works under the Berne Convention.[18]

This analysis discloses that the subjects of protection under copyright law are of two general types: (1) visually perceptible, aurally perceptible or machine-readable content that is recorded, in the sense of stored, in some form (e.g., a book or a film, a phonogram, a computer program) and (2) aurally perceptible or machine-readable content that is not recorded in some form (e.g., an improvised and unrecorded address or musical performance, a broadcast). The former type of subject matter is tangible, while the latter is intangible. With one exception (broadcasts), these subjects of protection are perceptible by a human sense – either sight or hearing – and hence are material.

1.3.2 Patents

The Paris Convention[19] is concerned with the protection of 'industrial property', which is stated to include patents (as well as, among other things, registered trademarks and registered designs).[20] The convention makes it clear that a patent's subject of protection is an 'invention',[21] but it does not elaborate, either expressly or by implication, what is an invention. Helpfully, the TRIPS Agreement provides that 'patents shall be available for any inventions, whether products or process, in all fields of technology'.[22]

Self-evidently, a product is tangible, while a process is intangible. Whether a process is material depends on the process in question and,

---

[13] Rome Convention, art. 7; WPPT, ch. II.
[14] Rome Convention, art. 10; WPPT, ch. III.   [15] Rome Convention, art. 13.
[16] Marrakesh Agreement Establishing the World Trade Organization, opened for signature 15 April 1994, 1867 UNTS 3 (entered into force 1 January 1995) annex 1C (Agreement on Trade-Related Aspects of Intellectual Property Rights; cited as TRIPS Agreement).
[17] WIPO Copyright Treaty, opened for signature 20 December 1996, 2186 UNTS 121 (entered into force 6 March 2002) (cited as WCT).
[18] TRIPS Agreement, art. 10; WCT, art. 4.
[19] Paris Convention for the Protection of Industrial Property, opened for signature 20 March 1883, revised at Stockholm, 14 July 1967, 828 UNTS 305, as amended on 28 September 1979 (entered into force 3 June 1984) (cited as Paris Convention).
[20] Paris Convention, art. 1(2).
[21] See, e.g., Paris Convention, art. 4G(1), which begins: 'If the examination reveals that an application for a patent contains more than one invention ...'. See also art 4*bis*(1).
[22] TRIPS Agreement, art. 27(1).

in particular, on what it *processes* (i.e., on what it operates). Where the process operates on something that is not material (e.g., numbers), the process itself is not material. Patent law regards such processes as being unpatentable.[23] Thus the only processes that are inventions are those that are material. It follows that the subjects of protection under patent law are either tangible or intangible but in all cases are material.

1.3.3 Trademarks

Although the Paris Convention does not directly define the subject of protection achieved by trademark registration,[24] the TRIPS Agreement does. It states that a trademark is a 'sign ... capable of distinguishing the goods or services of one undertaking from those of other undertakings ... including personal names, letters, numerals, figurative elements and combinations of colours'.[25] The common characteristic of these items is that they are visually perceptible. Consistent with this, many jurisdictions recognise that the shape of a good or its packaging can be a trademark.[26] Significantly, the TRIPS Agreement provides that members may (but not must) require, as a condition of registration, that signs be 'visually perceptible'.[27] This makes it clear that, while typically visual in character, a trademark is not inevitably limited to that which is visually perceptible. This, in turn, allows for the possibility of a trademark being a sound or a scent – a possibility that has been adopted in a number of jurisdictions.[28]

A visually perceptible trademark may be three-dimensional (a shape) or two-dimensional (a text string or an image, or a combination thereof). The former is tangible, while the latter is intangible. Where a trademark

---

[23] See, e.g., Convention on the Grant of European Patents, opened for signature 5 October 1973, 1065 UNTS 199 (entered into force 7 October 1977) art 52(2) (cited as European Patent Convention), which identifies various non-material methods that are not to be regarded as inventions. For illustrations of Australian and US patent law to like effect, see, respectively, *Encompass Corporation Pty Ltd* v. *InfoTrack Pty Ltd* [2019] FCAFC 161 and *Alice Corporation Pty Ltd* v. *CLS Bank International*, 573 US 208, 134 S Ct 2347 (2014).
[24] Some indirect guidance is provided by arts. 6ter(1)(a) and (b), which prohibit certain marks from registration – thereby indicating some of the characteristics that marks have.
[25] TRIPS Agreement, art. 15(1).
[26] According to one international review, at least twenty-seven jurisdictions permit the registration of shape trademarks: IPO International Trademark Law and Anti-Counterfeiting Committee, 'Shape trademarks – An international perspective' (Paper), Intellectual Property Owner's Association, 3 June 2015, retrieved from https://bit.ly/2OG9BhY.
[27] TRIPS Agreement, art. 15(1).
[28] See, e.g., Australia's Trade Marks Act 1995 (Cth), s. 6 (definition of *sign*).

is a sound or a scent, it is intangible. Thus it may be concluded that the subjects of protection under registered trademark law are of two sorts: a tangible and an intangible. In all cases, the subjects are material, since they are perceptible by a human sense, either sight, hearing or smell.

1.3.4 Designs

The Paris Convention is completely silent on what is an 'industrial design'. The TRIPS Agreement is similarly unhelpful in elucidating the subject of protection provided by a design registration.[29] An understanding of that is provided by the EU Community Design Regulation.[30] It states that 'design' means 'the appearance of the whole or a part of a product resulting from the features of, in particular, the lines, contours, colours, shape, texture and/or materials of the product itself and/or its ornamentation'.[31] Non-EU countries adopt a conception of design to the same effect.[32]

Where the design relates to three-dimensional features (such as shape), it is tangible. Where the design relates to two-dimensional features (such as colour), it is intangible. In either case, however, the design is material, since those features are visually perceptible.

1.4 Protected Objects

Related to, but separate from, the subject of protection is the protected object. In this chapter, the phrase the *protected object* of an IP law is used to mean that thing which the law recognises as satisfying the requirements for protection to arise. The protected object is, therefore, the thing in relation to which the exclusive rights of an IP law are exercisable. Put another way, the protected object of an IP law is the thing against which a claim of infringement is judged.

There is a relationship between the protected object and the subject of protection, which depends on the form and the content of each. *Form* is a thing's material characteristic: *what* it is; *content* is a thing's conceptual characteristic: what it *is*. I posit that the relationship between a protected object and its subject of protection is one of three types. First, the

---

[29] The closest the agreement comes is the final sentence of art. 25(1), which states what may (but not must) be excluded from design protection.
[30] Council Regulation (EC) No 6/2002 of 12 December 2001 on Community designs OJ 2002 No. L3/1 (cited as Community Design Regulation).
[31] Ibid., art. 3(a).
[32] See, e.g., the US Patent Act of 1952, §171 ('ornamental design for an article of manufacture'); Australia's Designs Act 2003 (Cth), s. 5 ('the overall appearance of the product resulting from one or more visual features of the product').

A Matter of Sense: What Intellectual Property Rights Protect 17

Table 1.1 *Relationships of Protected Object to Subject of Protection*

FORM	Same	First order	
	Different	Second order	Third order
		Same	Different
		CONTENT	

protected object may itself be the subject of protection, in the sense that it has the same form and the same content as the subject of protection. Where that is so, I say that the relationship between the two is 'first order'. Second, the protected object may have a form different from, but a content the same as, the subject of protection – a 'second-order' relationship. Third, the protected object may be different from the subject of protection in both form and content – in which case the relationship is 'third order'. (It is to be noted that a different content inevitably results in a different form, and hence it is not possible for the protected object to have a content different to, but a form the same as, the subject of protection.)

The association of the characteristics that define the relationship between a protected object and its subject of protection is shown in **Table 1.1**.

1.4.1 Copyright

Protection under copyright law arises without the need to obtain registration or to satisfy some other substantive formality.[33] For protection to subsist, all that is necessary is that the subject of protection satisfies at least one of the 'criteria of eligibility',[34] together with any additional requirements that may be specified in national law.[35] This means that, so long as these conditions are satisfied, protection arises upon the

---

[33] The Berne Convention mandates that the enjoyment and the exercise of the rights that it provides 'shall not be subject to any formality'; see art. 5(2). While a formality is permitted under the Rome Convention, it is not substantive, it is merely that there be placed on all copies of published phonograms in commerce the symbol ⓟ, the year of first publication and the name of the owner of the rights; see art. 11.
[34] The criteria of eligibility relate to matters such as the nationality or residence of the person who created the subject of protection and the place of making or publication of the subject of protection – see, e.g., Berne Convention, arts. 3 and 4; Rome Convention, arts. 4, 5 and 6.
[35] Additional subsistence requirements that are typically found in national law, often as a result of case law, are that the subject of protection be 'original' and be fixed in a material form.

subject of protection coming into existence. Once copyright protection arises, the exclusive rights are exercisable in relation to the thing in respect of which the subsistence requirements were satisfied (i.e., the subject of protection).

This means that the protected object is the same thing as the subject of protection. Self-evidently, therefore, the protected object has both the same form and the same content as the subject of protection. Thus, under copyright law, the relationship between the protected object and the subject of protection is first order.

1.4.2 Patents

Patent protection results from registration, which requires examination and acceptance of an application. An application for a patent must both describe and define the subject of protection (the invention). Description of the invention is given by text and, usually, by images. Definition of the invention is given by text, in the form of a written 'claim'. Once granted, the exclusive rights of a patent are exercisable in relation to the invention as it is claimed.

Significantly, this means that the protected object of a patent is not the invention itself; rather, it is the claim's written definition of it. That definition is textual in form and descriptive in content. Neither of patent law's two subjects of protection – a product and a process – is textual in form or descriptive in content.[36] It follows that the relationship between the protected object and the subject of protection in patent law is third order.

1.4.3 Trademarks

An application for registration of a trademark must contain a printed (i.e., a textual and/or a graphical) representation of the sign. Once granted, the exclusive rights of trademark registration apply to the sign as represented in the registration.

Where the sign is visually perceptible, the representation of it is the same as the sign itself – and thus the protected object and the subject of protection have the same form and content. Where the sign is not visually perceptible but instead is aurally or olfactorily perceptible, the

---

[36] It is a fundament of patent law that textual material of a descriptive nature is not patentable – see, e.g., European Patent Convention, art. 52(2)(d), which states that 'presentations of information' are not inventions.

representation of the sign is a textual and/or a graphical description of its sound or scent.[37] This means that the protected object has a form and a content different from that of the subject of protection. It follows that the relationship between the protected object and the subject of protection of trademark registration is either first order (in the case of a visually perceptible trademark) or third order (in the case of a trademark that is aurally or olfactorily perceptible).

1.4.4 Designs

An application for registration of a design must contain a representation of the design, in the form of a drawing or a photograph of the product made to the design. Once granted, the exclusive rights provided by a design registration are exercisable in relation to the design as it is represented in the application.

It will be appreciated that the protected object is not the same thing as the subject of protection – the former is a two-dimensional image, while the latter is a three-dimensional product. They are, therefore, of a different form. Nevertheless, they are of the same content, as both are representations of the visually perceptible features of the shape and/or ornamentation of a product. It follows that the relationship between the protected object and the subject of protection under a design registration is second order.

1.5 Exclusive Rights

An IP law effects protection by vesting exclusive rights in a rights owner. These exclusive rights are the entitlement, to the exclusion of other persons, to undertake specific actions in relation to protected objects. The rights owner, in the first instance, is the person responsible for bringing into existence (i.e., for authoring, inventing, originating or designing) the subject of protection that the protected object represents.

---

[37] What constitutes a sufficient textual and/or graphical description of aurally and olfactorily perceptible signs varies from jurisdiction to jurisdiction. In Europe, it is necessary for the sign to be 'represented graphically': *Sieckmann v. Deutsches Patent- und Markenamt*, C-273-00 [2002] ECR I-11737, [2003] Ch. 487. In the US, a graphical representation is not required; instead, a 'detailed description' suffices: 37 CFR §2.52(e).

1.5.1 Copyright

The Berne Convention mandates various moral and economic rights that countries are obliged to make exercisable by authors in relation to some or all of its protected objects.[38] Other international treaties – in particular, the WCT, the Rome Convention and the WPPT – provide for additional economic rights[39] and for the extension of the moral rights to additional protected objects.[40] These various exclusive rights can be conceived as being of six basic types: (1) moral (to claim authorship and maintain integrity), (2) fixation (to fix, in the sense of store), (3) replication (to make a replica, in the sense of an identical copy), (4) modification (to make a variant, in the sense of a reproduction, translation, adaptation, arrangement or other alteration), (5) distribution (to transfer possession, whether permanently or temporarily, of a fixation) and (6) presentation (to make available, in the sense of performing in or communicating to the public).

The modification-type right is significant, in that it entitles the rights owner to prohibit others from producing things that are versions of the protected object – that is, things that, though not identical, are sufficiently similar to the protected object to warrant protection.[41]

1.5.2 Patents

The Paris Convention is silent on what are the exclusive rights exercisable in relation to a patented invention. The lacuna is filled by the TRIPS Agreement, which provides that a patent owner may exercise: (1) in relation to an invention that is a product, the exclusive rights of making, using, offering for sale, selling and importing for these purposes, the product and (2) in relation to an invention that is a process, the exclusive right of using the process, and the exclusive rights of using, offering for sale, selling and importing for these purposes, the product obtained by the process.[42]

---

[38] The moral rights are attribution and integrity; see art. 6*bis*. The economic rights are translation, reproduction, public performance, public communication (including broadcast), public recitation and alteration (including adaptation and arrangement); see arts. 8, 9, 11, 11*bis*, 11*ter*, 12 and 14, respectively.

[39] See WCT, arts. 6–8; Rome Convention, arts. 7, 10 and 13; WPPT, arts. 8–10 and 12–14.

[40] WPPT, art. 5.

[41] What constitutes sufficient similarity to warrant protection is a substantive legal issue beyond the scope of this chapter.

[42] TRIPS Agreement, art. 28(1).

It can be seen that the exclusive rights exercisable in relation to an invention are of three types: (1) utilisation (to use the protected object), (2) production (to make the protected object, when it is a product, or to make that which results from use of the protected object, when it is a process) and (3) distribution (sale or importation for sale of the protected object, when it is a product, or sale or importation for sale of that which results from use of the protected object, when it is a process).

Unlike copyright law – and, as is shown later in the chapter, trademark law and design law – patent law does not contain a modification-type exclusive right. That is to say, none of the exclusive rights provided by patent law is expressly stated to be exercisable in relation to things that are similar, but not identical, to the protected object. This would constitute a profound difference between patent law and the other IP laws considered here, but for the fact that the *practice* of patent law indirectly introduces a modification-type right through the action of 'claim construction' and the related principle of the 'doctrine of equivalents'.[43] As a consequence, the exclusive rights of a patent owner are, in practice, exercisable in relation to versions (equivalents) of the protected object beyond that which is defined by a literal interpretation of the claim.[44]

1.5.3 Trademarks

With one exception, the Paris Convention does not specify the exclusive rights that are exercisable in relation to the protected object of trademark registration.[45] The TRIPS Agreement, however, provides that the owner of a registered trademark may prohibit third parties from 'using' in the course of trade 'an identical or a similar sign' for goods or services that are identical or similar to those in respect of which the trademark is registered, where such use would result in a likelihood of confusion.[46]

---

[43] Put simply, claim construction is the process by which a claim is given meaning, and the doctrine of equivalents is the principle that, for the purpose of infringement at least, a claim can have a meaning wider than the meaning achieved from a literal reading of the words of the claim.
[44] A detailed discussion of claim construction and the doctrine of equivalents is beyond the remit of this chapter. For a recent judicial consideration of these concepts in UK patent law, see *Actavis UK Limited* v. *Eli Lilly and Company* [2017] UKSC 48.
[45] The exception is in respect of a 'well-known mark'. According to art. 6*bis* of the convention, the owner a well-known mark is entitled to prohibit 'use' of a sign which is 'a reproduction, an imitation or a translation' of the well-known mark, where the sign is 'used for identical or similar goods' and is 'liable to create confusion'.
[46] TRIPS Agreement, art. 16(1). Confusion is to be presumed in the case of use of an identical sign for identical goods or services.

It can be discerned from the treaties that trademark registration provides the trademark owner with one exclusive right – utilisation. Importantly, this right is expressed to be exercisable in relation to both the protected object (the trademark that is registered) and versions of the protected object (signs that are similar to the registered trademark).

1.5.4 Designs

While the Paris Convention does not identify the exclusive rights exercisable in relation to the subject matter protected by design registration, the TRIPS Agreement does. It provides that the owner of a design registration shall have the right to prevent a third party from making, selling or importing, for commercial purposes, articles bearing or embodying a design which is a copy, or substantially a copy, of the protected design.[47]

It can be seen that design registration provides the owner of a design with two rights: (1) production (making articles bearing and/or embodying the design), and (2) distribution (selling and importing articles bearing and/or embodying the design). These rights are expressly stated to be exercisable in relation to both the protected object (the registered design) and versions of the protected object (that which is substantially a copy of the registered design).

1.6 Scopes of Protection

The means by which an IP law implements protection is, conceptually, like a mathematical function – that is, a process or a relation f that associates each element x of a set X to a single element y of another set Y.[48] Thus IP law protection might be represented as being the function:

$$y = f(x),$$

where

f is the application of the exclusive rights
x is a protected object
y is an action that is within the exclusive entitlement of the rights owner

This function produces a set Y, being all actions over which the rights owner has exclusivity. This set may be conceived as demarcating a

---

[47] Ibid., art. 26(1).
[48] Wikipedia, s.v. 'Function (mathematics)', 14 February 2019, retrieved from https://bit.ly/2OJDEp8.

notional space – being the 'scope of protection' that is provided by the IP law in respect of its protected object.

The notional function $f(x)$ incorporates all the elements of infringement that an IP law requires to be satisfied for liability to arise. This chapter focusses on just one of those elements – namely, the relationship between the subject of protection and the protected object.[49]

Where the relationship between the protected object and the subject of protection is first order, they are the same thing. However, where the relationship is second order or third order, they are not the same thing; rather, the protected object is an abstracted representation of the subject of protection. This abstracted representation either has the same content in a different form (second order) or has a different content (third order). Thus the degree of abstraction increases as the order of the relationship increases.

The degree of abstraction of the protected object's representation of the subject of protection has a consequence on the scope of protection provided – namely, the greater the degree of abstraction, the greater is the scope of protection. That this is so can be understood by comparing the protection provided by trademark registration of a visually perceptible sign with that of an aurally or olfactorily perceptible sign. Where the sign is visually perceptible, the representation of the sign is the sign itself. However, where the sign is aurally or olfactorily perceptible, the representation of the sign is an abstraction – a textual and/or graphical representation of the sound or the scent. Such a representation is, conceptually, broader than the sign itself – with the consequence that the scope of protection provided for the sign is greater than in the case where the representation of the sign is the sign itself. (This consequence is consistent with, and indeed arguably explains, the courts' general wariness of sound and scent trademarks.)

The relationship between the degree of abstraction of the protected object and the scope of protection provided in respect of it can be portrayed using a spatial metaphor, as illustrated in Figure 1.1. In this metaphor, an exercise of an exclusive right in relation to a protected object is the shining of a light on the protected object. The scope of protection provided by the exercise of the exclusive right is the shadow cast by the protected object. The degree of abstraction of the protected

---

[49] Other elements of infringement, which are beyond the scope of this discussion, include the nature of the exclusive right (particularly how it applies in relation to versions of the protected object), any pre-conditions to infringement (such as non-independent creation – i.e., copying), and any exceptions and limitations to the exclusive right (e.g., fair dealing/fair use). The duration of the exclusive right might also be considered an element of the function.

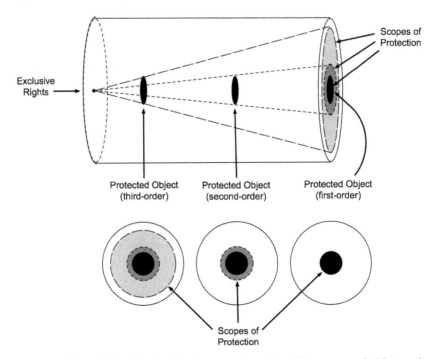

Figure 1.1: Relationship between the order of the protected object and its scope of protection

object's representation of the subject of protection is the protected object's distance from the subject of protection (which is located at the plane on which the shadow is cast). The greater the protected object's distance, the greater is the shadow cast, and thus the wider is the scope of protection.

1.7 Conclusion

The analysis in this chapter discloses the following about *how* IP laws provide protection. A legal entitlement is available to a person who is responsible for bringing into existence something that is within the specified class of phenomena to which an IP law applies (the subject of protection). The entitlement arises once specified conditions for protection are satisfied. The entitlement is the exclusive right to undertake certain actions in relation to the particular representation of the subject of protection that satisfies the conditions for protection to arise (the protected object). The scope of protection provided by the exercise of

A Matter of Sense: What Intellectual Property Rights Protect

the exclusive rights in relation to the protected object varies according to the degree of abstraction, in terms of content and/or form, that the protected object bears to the subject of protection – whereby, the greater the degree of abstraction, the greater is the scope of protection.

The analysis also discloses the following about *what* IP laws protect. Properly defined, a thing is intangible if it cannot be perceived by the human sense of touch. Not all of the subjects of protection of IP rights are intangible; many are tangible. The defining characteristic of IP subject matter is not that it is intangible but that it is material – i.e., perceptible by some human sense.[50] Since materiality is the characteristic of having presence in the material world, there need be no existential angst among IP scholars that the subject of their attention does not exist.

---

[50] As noted in the chapter, there is one exception to this: broadcasts.

2 Overlap and Redundancy in the Intellectual Property System
Trade Mark Always Loses

Graeme B Dinwoodie[*]

2.1 Introduction

It is not an uncommon complaint that the expansion in the scope of different intellectual property (IP) protection over the course of the twentieth century has given rise to unhelpful overlaps and inefficient redundancy.[1] Indeed, it is increasingly assumed that overlaps in protection will always result in too much protection, skewing the balance that

---

[*] I first met Sam Ricketson at a meeting of the International Literary and Artistic Association (ALAI) in Cambridge in 1998 where Sam elegantly described the complex provisions of international law regulating permissible exceptions and limitations in national copyright laws. The clarity and insight with which he did so would of course be no surprise to anyone who had previously read his influential scholarship. But I was immediately struck by the civility and grace with which Sam debated sometimes contentious issues and the personal warmth which he exhibited towards new colleagues in the field. It has been a delight to get to know him better over the decades that followed. Thanks to Lionel Bently, Andrew Christie, Dev Gangjee, Annette Kur, Alexander von Mulhendahl, and Luis Porangaba for helpful discussion of the issues explored in this chapter.

[1] See, e.g., Mark P McKenna, 'An alternate approach to channeling?' (2009) 51 *William & Mary Law Review* 873, 878, 884, 894 (noting that 'firms relying on these multiple forms of protection are often able to capture greater economic benefits than any of the individual regimes assume'; treating as 'a problem that different modes of intellectual property protection can serve as alternative appropriation mechanisms'; and proposing that the scope of IP rights 'should be [calibrated] with an eye towards reducing the ability of firms to leverage multiple rights to capture redundant economic benefits'); Gustavo Ghidini, 'The protection of (three-dimensional) shape trademarks and its implications for the protection of competition' in Irene Calboli and Martin Senftleben (eds.), *The Protection of Non-Traditional Marks: Critical Perspectives* (Oxford: Oxford University Press, 2018), pp. 203, 208('This disgraceful consequence of a dual protection for shapes as trademarks and designs can hardly be accepted as it represents a systemic contradiction, *and* the green light to a seriously anti-competitive situation'); Irene Calboli, 'Hands off "my" colors, patterns, and shapes! How non-traditional trademarks promote standardization and may negatively impact creativity and innovation' in Irene Calboli and Martin Senftleben (eds.), *The Protection of Non-Traditional Marks: Critical Perspectives* (Oxford: Oxford University Press, 2018), pp. 287, 295('courts across several jurisdictions have increasingly expressed concerns toward the suitability of protecting [non-traditional]

the distinct regimes have sought to achieve. In this chapter, I suggest that this is arguably a more complex question than conventional wisdom assumes. A number of different policy levers could be deployed to help mediate overlap questions and the genuine challenges of over-protection that they present. However, current EU and UK law case law appears effectively to be drifting towards a rule that when two IP regimes come into conflict, trade mark loses.[2] This is achieved most notably by an eagerness to deny protection under trade mark law to subject matter that might potentially be protected by other rights, even where there is clear marketplace distinctiveness that would conventionally trigger the concerns of trade mark law. In short, trade mark law appears to be ranking lowest in a hierarchy of IP rights. I consider a couple of metrics according to which one might develop such a hierarchy but conclude that neither supports the proposition that trade mark law (at least broadly conceived) should always be the loser. Instead, I highlight the range of policy levers that might better balance the values of trade mark protection with genuine concerns about overlapping protection.

2.2   Tension between Two Core Propositions

There exists a tension between two core propositions. First, it is clear that the different intellectual property rights – principally, but not exclusively, copyright, patent, trade mark and design right – are distinct forms of protection and that such protection can be cumulative. Indeed, in most countries, courts have usually accepted cumulation of protection unless legislation contains a clear prohibition. To intellectual property *owners*, this is a form of redundancy – but *redundancy* in the sense that that term is used by engineers rather than legal scholars, namely, duplication of critical features of a system to increase the system's reliability. Legal scholars use the term *redundant* in a far less positive sense.

The second proposition, which perhaps explains the reaction of legal scholars, is that protection under multiple intellectual property regimes usually results in over-protection. Thus defendants will frequently wish to limit overlap. The real question in many of these contests is whether

marks due to the relevant concerns for market competition and the overlaps with other forms of protection, primarily design protection').

[2] Indeed, to the extent that this preference is incompletely expressed in the case law, some scholars have sought to extend doctrines to make it more effective. See Martin Senftleben, 'A clash of culture and commerce: Non-traditional marks and the impediment of cyclic cultural innovation' in Irene Calboli and Martin Senftleben (eds.), *The Protection of Non-Traditional Marks: Critical Perspectives* (Oxford: Oxford University Press, 2018), pp. 305, 336.

you can have protection under one IP regime when there would be lesser protection under another regime to effectuate a legitimate social policy of that other regime. And, to be sure, many legislatures and some courts have, without jettisoning the general validity of the first proposition, recognised the competing force of this second assertion in enacting or adopting constraints designed to preclude multiple protection in particular settings.

It is difficult to articulate any general proposition about overlaps of protection. If one *had to*, it would probably be that there is no single generalisable way to address the overlap of different intellectual property rights – though one could no doubt articulate a number of principles that might mediate those relationships (both descriptively and normatively).

For example, when a producer has consciously made strategic choices about the acquisition of an industrial property right, that choice might make us more sceptical about a later assertion of rights with respect to subject matter that was expressly or strategically not pursued. Some of this sentiment underlies doctrines of election that have occasionally been used as a channelling device to steer producers seeking protection into one regime or another with a large degree of certainty and thus low enforcement costs. Thus for some time under US law, the prior registration of a copyright claim would absolutely preclude acquisition of a design patent (and vice versa); since 1974, however, that type of argument has failed, at least as a formal matter.[3]

Particular decisions still appear informed by estoppel-like arguments that could be conceptualised as somewhat akin to an election doctrine. Thus parts of the US Supreme Court decision in *TrafFix Devices, Inc. v. Marketing Displays, Inc.* suggest that the fact that the copying of a product feature had been (or could have been) attacked by the plaintiff as patent infringement under the doctrine of equivalents should preclude a post–patent expiration trade mark claim for copying the very same product features.[4]

---

[3] See *In re Yardley*, 493 F 2d 1389 (CCPA 1974); see generally Laura Heymann, 'Overlapping intellectual property doctrines: Election of rights versus selection of remedies' (2013) 17 *Stanford Technology Law Review* 241.

[4] *TrafFix Devices, Inc. v. Marketing Displays, Inc.*, 532 US 23 (2001) (cited as *TrafFix*). Later litigants have also sought to frame the scope of the functionality defence by reference to the scope of a hypothetical patent claim. For example, in *Fuji Kogyo Co., Ltd v. Pacific Bay International, Inc.*, 461 F 3d 675 (6th Cir, 2006) the Court of Appeals for the Sixth Circuit rejected the plaintiff's argument that because the design feature in which trade mark rights were asserted was not claimed in the relevant utility patent it should not create any inference of functionality suggested by the *TrafFix* case. The reason stated by the court was that the 'the design departure ... [was] too slight', such that the plaintiff's patent claims would (hypothetically) have covered the defendant's design under

Doctrines of election or estoppel come in lots of flavours. Some might be quite specific, based on the plaintiff having made a specific claim or filed for a particular industrial property title. But they can even be grounded in marketplace conduct from which an election can be deduced or legislatively deemed.

One might put in this category the former section 52 of the Copyright, Designs and Patents Act (UK).[5] Section 52 provided that when an artistic copyright work was applied to articles by an industrial process,[6] we should effectively treat this as an item of industrial design and restrict copyright to twenty-five years (which was the term of UK design protection). Thus after twenty-five years it would not be an infringement of the copyright in the work for third parties to make the articles and indirectly reproduce the work. Effectively, the act of industrial application of the artistic work was an election for design protection.

In any event, one could develop a typology to explain overlaps of protection based on election or estoppel, and as descriptive matter one would end up with a spectrum with multiple stopping points. But I am not going to attempt that in this chapter. I mention this example only to illustrate that a conceptual rationalisation of overlap rules, even according to a single metric, would likely encompass a fair range of propositions.

2.3 The Diminution of Trade Mark Rights in Conflicts under EU Law

In this chapter, I explore one proposition that is beginning to coalesce in EU law and suggest a number of different policy levers that can help mediate overlap questions in a better way. Somewhat simplistically stated, the proposition is: In current EU law, when two IP regimes come into conflict, trade mark loses.

Of most note, the EU and UK courts appear increasingly comfortable with front-end denial of any protection under trade mark law – even where there is clear marketplace distinctiveness – with respect to subject

---

a theory of infringement based upon the doctrine of equivalents (had the patent still been extant).

[5] Copyright, Designs and Patents Act 1988 (UK), c. 48, s. 52. Section 52 was repealed by the Enterprise and Regulatory Reform Act 2013 (UK), c. 24, s. 74, effective 28 July 2016, subject to transitional provisions allowing depletion of certain stock until 28 January 2017.

[6] See Copyright (Industrial Processes and Excluded Articles) (No 2) Order 1989 (UK) SI 1989/1070.

matter that might potentially be protected by other rights. It is a simple hierarchical approach, channelling producers into patent law, copyright law or design law.

In this section, I briefly mention a couple of the relevant cases from UK and EU law that illustrate this 'trade mark always loses' dynamic, and then consider a couple of metrics according to which one might develop a hierarchy of intellectual property rights. Neither suggests to me that trade mark law (at least broadly conceived) should always be the loser. I conclude by briefly suggesting a variety of policy levers that might balance the values of trade mark law with genuine concerns about overlapping protection.

2.3.1 *Trade Mark Always Loses: EU Case Law*

The most obvious vehicle for channelling producers away from trade mark protection is the functionality doctrine of trade mark law. That is not the only goal behind functionality case law, but it is one of them.[7]

In its judgment in *Philips*, seventeen years ago, the European Court of Justice applied one of the functionality exclusions in EU law and denied trade mark protection to the shape of the three-headed rotary shaver.[8] In referring the *Philips* case to the Court of Justice, the English court had noted the existence of a prior expired patent, a fact to which the Court of Justice was willing to give almost dispositive weight eight years later in its *Lego* decision.[9] The Court of Justice appeared to deny protection fully aware that both shapes were distinctive. So, patent law values trump trade mark protection. This is not an unusual position, and it is consistent with the approach in a number of countries.

What of copyright and design protection and their relationship with trade mark protection in Europe? Here, one problem is the 2014 *Hauck* case, where claims for copyright infringement of the Tripp-Trapp high chair succeeded in both Germany and the Netherlands. But the Court of Justice rejected a claim for an EU trade mark and gave a very broad

---

[7] Functionality doctrine in most jurisdictions has also been developed by reference to broader concerns of competition, even when conflicts with competing IP regimes are not present. See Graeme B Dinwoodie, 'The death of ontology: A teleological approach to trademark law' (1999) 84 *Iowa Law Review* 611.
[8] *Koninklijke Philips Electronics NV* v. *Remington Consumer Products Ltd* (C-299/99) [2002] ETMR 81.
[9] *Lego Juris A/S* v. *Office for Harmonisation in the Internal Market (Trade Marks and Designs) (OHIM)* (C-48/09 P) [2010] ETMR 63 (cited as *Lego*).

reading to two of the functionality provisions not at issue in *Lego*, including the exclusion of protection for shapes that give *substantial value* to the goods.[10]

The advocate general in the *Hauck* case rested his broad reading of the substantial value exclusion on the fact that its purpose 'is to demarcate the protection conferred by trade marks and that conferred by ... industrial designs and copyright'.[11] Thus, in applying that exclusion, weight should be given to the existence of other IP rights, such as design or copyright, and any actual distinctiveness is irrelevant. Thus trade mark is now relegated both to patent and to copyright and design.

The UK courts have embraced the cumulation point. A recent UK case, decided by Mr Justice Arnold and affirmed by the UK Court of Appeal, involved an effort to register a trade mark for the shape of a London taxicab.[12] The effort was rejected – and I think rightly so – on many grounds. But the reasoning on the substantial value exclusion is troubling for shape marks.

Mr Justice Arnold very much endorsed the language of the advocate general in *Hauck* and denied trade mark protection to the shape of two London taxicabs. One of those shapes had in fact been the subject of registered design protection, so denying protection to that shape fits with an estoppel rationale. But in finding *both* to fall afoul of the substantial value exclusion, Mr Justice Arnold took into account that the other *could have been*.[13]

However, almost anything can now be the subject of European design protection,[14] so on this theory, one would almost entirely exclude trade mark protection for shapes because they all can be designs under EU law. As design law grows, trade mark law has to shrink.

---

[10] *Hauck GmbH & Co* v. *Stokke A/S* (C-205/13) [2014] ETMR 60 (cited as *Hauck*).
[11] *Hauck* (Opinion of the Advocate General Szpunar, C-205/13, 14 May 2014) [70].
[12] *London Taxi Corporation* v. *Frazer-Nash* [2016] EWHC 52 (Ch), aff'd, [2017] EWCA Civ 1729.
[13] See [2016] EWHC 52 (Ch) at [214]–[215] ('upholding this objection to the validity of the UKTM would be consistent with the purpose of Article 3(1)(e)(iii) as explained by the Advocate General and the Court of Justice in Hauck, since it would prevent LTC obtaining a permanent monopoly in respect of the shape of the [taxi], rather than a 25-year monopoly by virtue of the registered design. Unlike in the case of the UKTM, the shape which is the subject of the CTM is not, and never has been, protected by a registered design. On the other hand, clearly it could have been.')
[14] See Directive No 98/71/EC of the European Parliament and of the Council of 13 October 1998 on the legal protection of designs, OJ 1998 No. L289/28, art. 1(a) ('design' means the 'appearance of the whole or a part of a product resulting from the features of, in particular, the lines, contours, colours, shape, texture and/or materials of the product itself and/or its ornamentation').

2.3.2 Justifications for an IP Hierarchy?

So what is causing this relegation of trade marks below copyright, patent and design in the European intellectual property firmament? How might one justify the imposition of a hierarchy of rights?

One might consider whether the different regimes have a different *constitutional* pedigree. This is an argument that is often raised – I think fallaciously – in the US based upon the explicit authorisation in the Copyright and Patent Clause of the US Constitution[15] and the more general basis for trade mark legislation in the Commerce Clause.[16]

This argument doesn't as a general matter have much purchase in the EU. To be sure, there are overlap cases where the presence of a fundamental EU constitutional value might cause a convergence of results under all IP regimes. Thus the Court of Justice in *Christian Dior* v. *Evora* suggested that the ability as a matter of free movement to engage in parallel importing within the EU must be the same whether the claimant asserted a right under copyright or trade mark law.[17] But that is really the vindication of a value *external to both regimes*, rather than elevating the defence available under one so that it also applies to and trumps the rules of another. The fundamental EU value of free movement of goods transcends all IP rights equally.

If constitutional principles do not guide us, an alternative explanation for formulating a hierarchy would be simply to weigh the social value of competing claims: which IP regime would it be more significant as a policy matter to vindicate?

One can see this type of approach more explicitly in US case law. Thus, in the patent/trade dress conflict in *Vornado* in 1995, the Tenth Circuit denied trade mark protection by reasoning that the ability to practise expired patents was at the core of patent law.[18] In contrast, the court characterised the consumer confusion that may arise from the copying of product configurations that are significant parts of patented inventions as a 'peripheral concern'[19] of the Trademark Act of 1946 (the Lanham Act).[20] The implication was that 'protection of traditional

---

[15] See US Constitution Art. I § 8, cl. 8.   [16] See US Constitution Art. I § 8, cl. 3.
[17] *Parfums Christian Dior* v. *Evora BV* (C-337/95) [1997] ECR I-1603.
[18] *Vornado Air Circulation Systems, Inc.* v. *Duracraft Corporation*, 58 F 3d 1498 (10th Cir, 1995), cert. denied, 516 US 1067 (1996) (cited as *Vornado*).
[19] Ibid., 1509.   [20] Trademark Act of 1946, 15 USC § 1051 et seq.

word or picture trademarks' was the core concern of trademark law.[21] In 1995, three years after *Two Pesos*,[22] and in light of the central purpose of the Lanham Act (the avoidance of consumer confusion), this was a somewhat startling conclusion that the court supported only by reference to the lack of federal trademark protection for designs when the Lanham Act was enacted.[23] But the subsequent approach of the Supreme Court in *Wal-Mart* and *TrafFix* arguably has vindicated the Tenth Circuit. In both those cases, the Supreme Court appeared willing to tolerate some more sceptical treatment of non-word marks, reciting a number of policy objectives underlying such an approach and noting in both cases the alternative availability of copyright and design patent protection.[24]

The EU and UK courts are, to my mind, doing exactly the same, as seen in both *Hauck* and the London taxicab case, discussed earlier. But they are doing so with an incomplete discussion of the policy choice they are implementing through their acts of interpretation. In particular, we should recognise that trade mark and unfair competition law pursues consumer protection objectives as well as industrial policy objectives. There is surely actionable harm that is relevant to trade mark law by permitting marketplace confusion regardless of the need of the defendant to copy so as to compete. A more nuanced approach would seek – as did some older decisions developing the functionality doctrine in the USA – to balance that core trade mark concern with the equally genuine concern about opportunistic extension of monopoly rights. There may be circumstances where the concerns of trade mark law should appropriately give way to the dictates of patent law and its finite term; clearly, there are contexts in which trade mark law elevates concerns for competition over consumer protection. But it is not clear that we need to adopt an approach that makes one policy value (and the one regime that effectuates that value) *wholly subservient* to the other.

---

[21] *Vornado*, 58 F 3d 1498, 1508 (10th Cir, 1995).
[22] *Two Pesos, Inc. v. Taco Cabana, Inc.*, 505 US 763 (1992).
[23] It is indeed unlikely that 'Congress in 1946 intended to be as expansive in its protection of product configurations as in its protection of traditional word or picture trademarks': ibid., 1508. Congressional policy had, however, evolved since 1946, as recognised by Congress in enacting the Trademark Law Revision Act, Pub L No 100-667, 102 Stat. 3935 (1988) when aware of, and content to leave undisturbed, judicial protection for product design.
[24] *Wal-Mart Stores, Inc. v. Samara Bros*, 529 US 205 (2000) (cited as *Wal-Mart*); *TrafFix*.

2.3.3 Better Balances

There are several ways in which one might doctrinally be able to achieve a better balance. For example, the courts could explicitly recognise that the scope of trade mark protection is a normative question. The Court of Justice was quite right in its *Lego* decision to recognise that the anti-competitive effects of trade mark protection there flowed not so much from the ability to stop exact replicas but from the use of the confusion standard to chill rivals in the surrounding area. Thus shape marks could be treated as 'thin' trade marks because of normative concerns about opportunistic overlaps in addition to concerns about competition.[25] This is, to my mind, what the Second Circuit did in the *Louboutin* case in the US.[26] There, the registered mark was narrowed to the colour red as used on the sole of a high-fashion shoe in contrast with the colour of the upper, enabling the Court to conclude that that mark was not infringed by a monochrome red shoe (upper and sole).[27]

We could also rethink the role of remedies in these types of cases. Consider, for example, the *Kellogg v. Nabisco* case, where the US Supreme Court declined to grant trade mark protection to the shape of the shredded wheat biscuit after the patent on the machine and process for making them had expired.[28] It is often forgotten that the court, while refusing to grant formal trade mark protection, did require the defendant to respect consumer association of the shape with the plaintiff by making efforts to differentiate its products from those of the plaintiff through labelling and advertising.[29]

Indeed, in *Lego* the Court of Justice recognised the complementary role of national unfair competition law in protecting against consumer confusion while denying EU-wide trade mark protection; it hinted that *this* was the way to balance the competing values.[30] Ideally, this would be

---

[25] Cf. *Wallace International Silversmiths, Inc. v. Godinger Silver Art Co., Inc.*, 916 F 2d 76 (2nd Cir, 1990), cert. denied, 499 US 976 (1991).

[26] *Christian Louboutin SA v. Yves Saint Laurent America, Inc.*, 696 F 3d 206 (2nd Cir, 2012).

[27] The doctrinal mechanism through which the Second Circuit explained this result – that there was no use of the plaintiff's mark by the defendant – was unsatisfying and incomplete. The court would have been better advised to pick up on the hint about scope of protection that it had dropped twenty years earlier in *Wallace*.

[28] *Kellogg v. National Biscuit Co*, 305 US 111 (1938).

[29] See Graeme B Dinwoodie, 'The story of *Kellogg Co. v. National Biscuit Co.*: Breakfast with Brandeis' in Jane C Ginsburg and Rochelle C Dreyfuss (eds.), *Intellectual Property Stories* (New York: Foundation Press, 2006), p. 220.

[30] *Lego* (C-48/09) [2010] ETMR 63, [61] ('the position of an undertaking which has developed a technical solution cannot be protected – with regard to competitors placing on the market slavish copies of the product shape incorporating exactly the same solution – by conferring a monopoly on that undertaking through registering as a

reflected in an EU-wide unfair competition regime. This would require the EU to grapple more broadly with the proper relationship between registered industrial property rights and empirically grounded unregistered claims, a thorny question often dodged by courts (including most recently by the US Supreme Court in its *Tam* case).[31] But this would be a theoretically satisfying approach – especially if we embraced a conception of unfair competition as tort-like protection grounded in proof of real social harm but offering weaker remedies than the property-based model of trade mark law that we now have in Europe.[32]

Third, one could incorporate respect for rival regimes through making defences portable. This does not typically happen. Thus, for example, the Court of Justice in *Ford* v. *Wheeltrims* held that the repair clause in design law is no defence to a trade mark infringement claim.[33] This is clearly more pro-plaintiff than most would regard as ideal. Professor David Vaver has pointedly asked, 'if IP rights overlap, why is this not true of user rights too? If the user has a right to deal fairly with a copyrighted logo, why does this not trump trade mark rights too?'[34]

This is a fair question, even if the conceptualisation of defences as user rights is more solidly grounded in Canada than in many other countries.[35] But let me suggest a watered-down version of that which meshes well with my last observation about unfair competition law. Insofar as trade mark defences in Europe turn on the defendant acting with due cause (as regards dilution claims) or in accordance with honest practices in industrial and commercial matters, perhaps the existence of a right to

---

trade mark the three-dimensional sign consisting of that shape, but can, where appropriate, be examined in the light of rules on unfair competition').

[31] *Matal* v. *Tam*, 137 S Ct 1744, 1744 n. 1 (2017); cf. *Renna* v. *County of Union*, NJ 88 F Supp 3d 310 (DNJ 2014) § 2(b) bar against registering official seals should be extended to § 43(a) action).

[32] Of course, that conception of unfair competition one is not one that is common to all member states; this is partly what has made harmonisation of unfair competition law difficult.

[33] *Ford Motor Company* v. *Wheeltrims* (Court of Justice of the European Union, C-500/14, 6 October 2015).

[34] David Vaver, *Intellectual Property Law: Copyrights, Patents, Trademarks*, 2nd ed. (Toronto: Irwin Law, 2011), p. 38.

[35] See *CCH Canadian Ltd* v. *Law Society of Upper Canada* [2004] 1 SCR 339, 2004 SCC 13. Cf. Case C-469/17, *Funke Medien NRW GmbH* v. *Bundesrepublik Deutschland*, EU: C:2019:623 at [70] (CJEU Grand Chamber 2019) ('although Article 5 of Directive 2001/29 is expressly entitled "Exceptions and limitations", it should be noted that those exceptions or limitations do themselves confer rights on the users of works or of other subject matter ... ').

engage in particular conduct under another intellectual property regime with equal claim to regulate should inform that assessment. This would require a more general elevation of 'honest practices in industrial and commercial matters' in the structure of trade mark defences, which the European Commission and Council of the EU resisted in the 2015 reforms.[36] But it might offer a less absolute and more fact-sensitive way of reconciling the competing claims of trade mark and other IP regimes.

And note that the honest practices proviso of the EU trade mark defences provision is drawn from article 10*bis* of the Paris Convention for the Protection of Industrial Property, which is the foundational treaty provision on unfair competition.[37] Do we see a theme? Especially in the US, unfair competition claims are regarded with some degree of wariness. But unfair competition claims do not need to reflect the anti–free riding impulse underlying the majority opinion (and, even more so, the rhetoric) in *International News Service* v. *Associated Press*,[38] which is now over a century old. They can be rooted primarily in a concern for misrepresentation, but that concern is plausibly engaged by the use of a distinctive product shape by a rival trader that fails to differentiate its goods from those of the plaintiff.

2.4 Conclusion

So are overlapping rights inherently problematic? It does not seem necessarily so. To be sure, there will be cases where the assertion of trade mark rights is nothing more than a ruse to circumvent the limits of patent law and restrict competition. But there may be cases where such anti-competitive effects are slight and the costs of allowing confusingly similar products substantial. In those cases, offering some limited relief might minimise the risk of consumer confusion without unduly affecting competition or undermining the patent system. In this chapter, I have suggested some of the doctrinal means of doing so, whether by developing the concept of thin marks within trade mark law or embracing a supplementary system of unfair competition. If the latter is the preferred choice, EU law would benefit greatly from trying to articulate a harmonised unfair competition law that consciously addresses the relationship

---

[36] See Directive (EU) 2015/2436 of the European Parliament and of the Council of 16 December 2015 to approximate the laws of the Member States relating to trade marks, OJ 2015 No. L336/1.
[37] Paris Convention for the Protection of Industrial Property, opened for signature 20 March 1883, 828 UNTS 305 (entered into force 7 July 1884) art. 10*bis*.
[38] 248 US 215 (1918).

between those claims and what is sought to be pursued through registered trade mark rights. A complementary tool of a weaker form of protection grounded in empirical reality and available at the EU level might allow the Court of Justice to recognise the social merits of protecting actual consumer association, which its current treatment of trade mark law as wholly subservient to patent, copyright and design laws requires it to delegate to national law.

3 Rethinking the Relationship between Registered and Unregistered Trade Marks

*Robert Burrell**

3.1 Introduction

It is really only in the past forty or so years that intellectual property (IP) has emerged as a discrete subject of scholarly enquiry. The origins of IP protection can, of course, be traced much further back, with passage of the Statute of Monopolies in 1623 and the Statute of Anne in 1709 traditionally being identified as the pivotal moments in the emergence of patent and copyright protection, respectively.[1] The intellectual history of the discipline is also much richer than some critics of this now middle-aged arrival onto the law school curriculum care to admit: specialist texts aimed at legal practitioners and the odd academic article dealing with copyright or patent law can be traced back to when the legal treatise and the law review emerged as distinct forms of publication.[2] Mention might also be made of the contributions of John Locke, Adam Smith, Immanuel Kant, Jeremy Bentham and John Stuart Mill, all of whom turned their attention to aspects of what we would now term intellectual property.[3]

---

* I first met Sam Ricketson at a conference in London in the early 1990s. His generosity towards junior scholars was and remains extraordinary and sets a standard that we should all seek to emulate.

[1] An Act concerning Monopolies and Dispensations with penall Lawes and the Forfeyture thereof (1623) 21 Jac 1, c. 3 (cited as Statute of Monopolies) and An Act for the Encouragement of Learning by Vesting the Copies of Printed Books in the Authors or Purchasers of Such Copies during the Times Therein Mentioned (1709) 8 Ann, c. 19 (cited as Statute of Anne).

[2] See, e.g., William Hands, *The Law and Practice of Patents for Inventions* (London: W Clarke, 1808); George Ticknor Curtis, *A Treatise on the Law of Copyright in Books, Dramatic and Musical Compositions, Letters and Other Manuscripts, Engravings and Sculpture as Enacted and Administered in England and America* (London: A Maxwell & Son, 1847); Emmanuel Maguire Underdown, 'The copyright question' (1886) 2 *Law Quarterly Review* 213; Simon G Croswell, 'Infringement cases in patent law' (1889) 3 *Harvard Law Review* 206.

[3] See, respectively, Justin Hughes, 'Locke's 1694 memorandum (and more incomplete copyright historiographies)' (2010) 27 *Cardozo Arts and Entertainment Law Journal* 555; Ronald L Meek, David D Raphael and Peter G Stein (eds.), *Lectures on Jurisprudence*, Vol. v: *Glasgow Edition of the Works and Correspondence of Adam Smith* (Indianapolis, IN: Liberty Fund, 1982), pp. 59, 116–17; F Kawohl, 'Commentary on Kant's essay "On the

Nevertheless, the fact remains that intellectual property has emerged as a subject of academic study in its own right only over the past few decades. In the absence of a longstanding independent intellectual history, US scholarship has dominated the field: the law and economics tradition, with its emphasis on incentivising certain behaviours, provided a ready-made set of tools for thinking about IP; a cultural willingness to engage in first-order theorising supported and reinforced by the US tenure system lent itself to the production of ground-breaking articles; and a European academy that soon became fixated on questions of harmonisation all contributed to the pre-eminence of US scholarship in the field. A highly active US academy turning its attention to the field has brought many benefits. Above all, it has allowed the discipline to mature much more quickly than would otherwise have been the case. There have also been other advantages, as IP courses have become a vehicle for exposing students to ways of thinking about law that predominate in the US, but that remain more marginal elsewhere.

There are, however, elements of US modes of thinking about IP that need to be handled with care when transplanted to different legal systems. Professor Ricketson has done as much as anyone to remind us of the importance of commonwealth countries taking their own histories and traditions seriously. In the case of trade mark law there are particular reasons for caution. The US trade mark system is unusual in that it places little weight on whether a mark has been registered. Consequently, US scholars have promoted accounts of the function of trade marks that do not differentiate between registered and unregistered marks. This chapter argues that this may distract us from an alternative model of protection. Specifically, it is argued that the justifications for having a registration system point towards registered marks providing a strong but narrow form of protection. To move to such a model would, admittedly, mark a radical departure for most countries. There are, nevertheless, good reasons for engaging in the thought experiment undertaken here. Above all, thinking about ideal models of protection can tell us something important about the direction that incremental legislative and judicial change should take.

---

injustice of reprinting books" (1785)' in Lionel Bently and Martin Kretschmer (eds.), *Primary Sources on Copyright (1450–1900)*, retrieved from www.copyrighthistory.org; John Bowring (ed.), *The Works of Jeremy Bentham*, Vol. 3: *A Manual of Political Economy* (Edinburgh: William Tait, 1838), pp. 71–2; John Stuart Mill, *Principles of Political Economy* (abridged version edited by Stephen Nathanson) (Indianapolis, IN: Hackett Publishing, 2004), p. 271.

3.2 Enforcement Costs, Clearance Costs and Trade Mark Exceptionalism

The US is unusual in having a use-based trade mark system. Although the US maintains a registration system and although that system is widely used, registration confers few benefits on trade mark owners compared to other jurisdictions. This has resulted in registration being almost entirely ignored as a feature of the trade mark system in US literature, at least until recently.[4] Trade mark rights, whether registered or unregistered, have been justified on the basis that they reduce 'consumer search costs': by providing a reliable indication of trade origin, trade marks allow consumers to identify goods that they have tried before, such that they can steer their purchases towards goods that they liked previously and away from goods they want to avoid. It is therefore said that trade marks promote market efficiency by enabling consumers to find what they want quickly and easily. This explanation is compelling, and few commentators would challenge the conclusion that the law ought to prevent uses of trade signs that would confuse consumers as to the trade origin of goods or services.[5] Providing a remedy to the businesses (i.e., trade mark owners) that would suffer from consumers being deceived is also easy enough to justify. Specifically, it is likely to lead to higher rates of enforcement than relying on state agencies or consumers themselves to bring proceedings.

None of this, however, tells us very much about the legal mechanisms we should use to prevent consumers being confused. It would be possible to build a trade mark system around a series of fact-intensive enquiries focussed on evidence that consumers were familiar with the plaintiff's mark, that they had wrongly assumed that the defendant's goods or services came from the plaintiff, and that their purchasing behaviour was influenced as a result. Such a system would have much in common with the tort of passing off and would appear to satisfy the economic case for legal intervention. Attention must also be given, however, to the cost of litigation. Passing off claims can be difficult and expensive to make out. The concern would therefore be that the cost of litigation would deter some trade mark owners from bringing claims, resulting in an

---

[4] Rebecca Tushnet, 'Registering disagreement: Registration in modern American Trademark law' (2017) 130 *Harvard Law Review* 867. Addition of pinpoint reference by RA is unhelpful. The reference is intended to refer to Rebecca's contribution, not to the point where Rebecca makes this claim.

[5] Views diverge on when consumers are likely to be confused and as to what forms of 'confusion' ought to be actionable. See Mark McKenna, 'Testing modern trademark law's theory of harm' (2009) 95 *Iowa Law Review* 63; Mark Lemley and Mark McKenna, 'Irrelevant confusion' (2010) 62 *Stanford Law Review* 413.

under-enforcement of trade mark rights and hence an increase in consumer confusion.

Concern about enforcement costs may therefore cause us to devise mechanisms that make trade mark rights easier and cheaper to enforce. For example, we might decide that the first person to use an inherently distinctive mark ought to be able to prevent third parties using a confusingly similar mark for the same or similar goods or services, without being required to demonstrate a reputation. This is the position in the US, and it is a perfectly defensible approach. However, it is not an approach that can be justified by reference to reducing consumer search costs alone.[6] On the contrary, allowing trade mark owners to enforce rights in a trade sign without requiring evidence that consumers recognise that sign as a badge of origin may at times increase consumer search costs. Specifically, this may occur if the plaintiff has used an inherently distinctive sign but has not yet established a reputation among consumers. If the defendant has begun to develop such a reputation, any forced rebranding is likely to disorient its customers and increase their search costs.[7] The current US rule thus has to be explained on the basis that it produces lower error costs in aggregate than a passing off style system. In other words, although the current rule may lead to an over-enforcement of trade mark rights in cases where the plaintiff has not yet established a reputation, on balance this is preferable to the under-enforcement of rights that a passing off-style system would produce.

One way of understanding registration is that it also serves as a means of reducing enforcement costs. Owners of registered marks are not generally required to demonstrate that the mark enjoys a reputation, evidence of actual confusion is not necessary to a finding of infringement and, as is explained later in the chapter, the system is built around broad abstract rights. Viewed through an enforcement costs lens, it is not just trade mark owners but society at large that benefits from making registered trade marks easier to enforce. Registration also brings other benefits. Most notably, the register acts as a source of public information that enables traders to discover which signs third parties have already claimed. Registration therefore helps reduce business 'clearance costs' – that is, it assists traders in choosing marks that can be used safely. Other benefits of having a registration system include communicating reliable

---

[6] See Robert Bone, 'Enforcement costs and trademark puzzles' (2004) 90 *Virginia Law Review* 2099.

[7] Joel R Feldman, 'Reverse confusion in trademarks: Balancing the interests of the public, the trademark owner, and the infringer' (2003) 8 *University of Florida Journal of Technology Law & Policy* 163.

ownership information. This facilitates the licensing and assignment of marks.[8] It might also (at least in principle) assist consumers or state agencies to identify trade mark owners.

The public benefits of trade mark registration ought to form the principal yardstick against which the desirability and the performance of the system are judged. The sorts of metrics that registries like to focus on – how many applications did they receive, how quickly were they processed and at what cost – are all well and good, but they should not cause us to lose sight of the ultimate goals of the system. Take the scope of registered trade mark rights. It has already been noted that registered trade mark rights go beyond what can be justified by reference to the goal of preventing consumer confusion. Above all, this is because registered trade marks abstract away from market reality.[9] To illustrate, when deciding whether the signs are sufficiently similar to trigger potential liability, the signs that are compared will be produced through a process of construction that serves to remove the inquiry from what occurs in the marketplace. The plaintiff's 'sign' will be the mark as registered. Thus if the plaintiff has registered a word mark, the plaintiff's sign will be that word written in any script and reproduced in any colour. The fact that the sign actually used by the plaintiff in the marketplace is this word in a pink cursive font will not limit the scope of the plaintiff's monopoly. The plaintiff's sign will then be compared with the sign used by the defendant. However, this sign will have to be isolated from a mass of other material. Extraneous matter, such as differences in the colour or shape of goods or differences in the type of packaging or general labelling employed, will be excluded from the analysis, even though these things may reduce the likelihood of confusion. Similarly, when a tribunal is assessing the similarity of goods or services, the nature of the plaintiff's goods or services will be determined by reference to the scope of the specification, not the scope of the plaintiff's use. Provided the trade mark owner has been careful to specify its products using broad terminology, its monopoly will extend beyond the goods or services it actually offers.

Registration therefore creates a sphere of exclusivity around a mark that has little to do with preventing consumer confusion per se. From the owner's perspective, this creates a degree of exclusive space for its brand. From a public policy perspective, however, this additional degree of

---

[8] Robert Burrell, 'Trade mark bureaucracies' in Graeme B Dinwoodie and Mark D Janis (eds.), *Trademark Law and Theory: A Handbook of Contemporary Research* (Northampton, MA: Edward Elgar, 2008), p. 95.
[9] The US is again the exception: the scope of protection being determined by the scope of the use, not the scope of the registration. See Section 3.3.

protection can be justified only on the basis that (1) it serves as an incentive for owners to register their marks such that the register can perform its public information function and/or (2) by reference to the need to reduce enforcement costs.[10] Justifying the contours of modern trade mark registration systems by reference to the public information function is not, however, free from difficulty. For a start there is the problem that only limited incentives seem to be required to persuade traders to register their marks. The US trade mark system is widely used – so widely used in fact that the US may be running out of some types of marks,[11] despite the fact that registration confers few advantages. The expansive set of rights given to trade mark owners in countries like Australia may therefore not be required to persuade owners to register. Then there is the problem that trade mark registers may not perform their public information function effectively. One issue is that the information may be inaccurate. There is good evidence that large numbers of invalid marks sit on trade mark registers for long periods of time. The presence of these marks on the register will increase rather than decrease business clearance costs. A second concern is that the information will always be incomplete, as owners are under no obligation to register their marks. Traders will therefore have to conduct time-consuming searches in order to determine which other signs are in use in the marketplace, precisely the sort of searches that they would have to carry out if the register did not exist. Such searches can operate from a higher starting point thanks to the register. However, it is difficult to escape the conclusion that even if registers were more carefully policed (above all, to ensure that marks that are not in use are struck off) and even if more were done to persuade owners to register, registration would only have a modest impact on business clearance costs.[12]

If the public information function provides an incomplete justification for trade mark registration, more attention needs to be paid to the enforcement costs argument. Specifically, attention needs to be given to when it makes sense to apply a presumption in favour of making rights easy to enforce and when, in contrast, owners should be put to the

---

[10] There is another possibility – namely, that registration encourages owners to invest in brands, but the argument that 'brand entrepreneurs' need to be incentivised through the trade mark system is unconvincing. See Dev Gangjee and Robert Burrell, 'Because you're worth it: *L'Oréal* and the prohibition on free riding' (2010) 73 *Modern Law Review* 282.
[11] Barton Beebe and Jeanne C Fromer, 'Are we running out of trademarks? An empirical study of trademark depletion and congestion' (2018) 131 *Harvard Law Review* 945.
[12] Burrell, 'Trade mark bureaucracies'.

trouble of proving their case in passing off.[13] A strong case can certainly be made for including 'double identity' infringement as it exists in Europe, New Zealand and Singapore[14] within the ambit of registered trade mark law. If the defendant is using the same mark for the same goods and services, there has to be a strong presumption that consumers would be confused. The model of protection employed by these jurisdictions in double identity cases also makes sense from an enforcement costs perspective. In the jurisdictions mentioned, double identity infringement attracts a form of strict liability. The defendant will avoid liability only if it can bring itself within a defence – for example, by demonstrating that its use was for the purpose of comparative advertising.[15] In the ordinary case this means that rights should be easy and cheap to enforce.

Thinking about registered trade marks in terms of double identity protection also has benefits when viewed in terms of the quality of the information communicated by the register. Another concern about the ability of the register to communicate useful information is that it can be difficult to determine what the scope of protection is likely to be. Registered trade mark protection now invariably extends to the use of 'similar' marks on 'similar' goods or services. Questions of similarity are to be judged through the application of multifactor tests whose application can be difficult to predict even for those versed in the law. Moreover, most jurisdictions have now extended protection to cases where a similar mark is used on dissimilar goods or services, but only in cases where the mark enjoys a reputation.[16] Whether this threshold has been passed will not normally be evident from the register.[17] Consequently, a trader consulting the register may struggle to form an accurate view as to what marks it

---

[13] *Passing off* is being used here as a shorthand for a fact-intensive approach to establishing whether a trade mark has been infringed. As such it would include actions under the Competition and Consumer Act 2010 (Cth) sch. 2 (Australian Consumer Law) and the Fair Trading Act 1986 (NZ).

[14] See, respectively, Directive (EU) 2015/2436 of the European Parliament and of the Council of 16 December 2015 to approximate the laws of the Member States relating to trade marks, OJ 2015 No. L336/1, art. 10(2)(a); Trade Marks Act 2002 (NZ) s. 89(1)(a); Trade Marks Act (Singapore, cap. 332, 2005 rev. ed.) s. 27(1).

[15] Comparative advertising is a defence in each of the jurisdictions mentioned: see, respectively, Directive 2006/114/EC of the European Parliament and of the Council of 12 December 2006 concerning misleading and comparative advertising, OJ 2006 No. L376/21; Trade Marks Act 2002 (NZ) s. 94; Trade Marks Act (Singapore, cap. 332, 2005 rev. ed.) s. 28(4)(a).

[16] This is true even in countries that have refused to introduce protection against dilution. See, e.g., Trade Marks Act 1995 (Cth) s. 120(3).

[17] Robert Burrell and Michael Handler, 'Dilution and trademark registration' (2008) 17 *Transnational Law and Contemporary Problems* 713.

can and cannot safely use. As things stand, the register will perform effectively only if the hypothetical trader has its hypothetical lawyer on hand to explain what the information on the register means. A system built around double identity infringement would largely avoid this problem.

The case for having registered trade mark rights confer a strong degree of protection in double identity cases is therefore solid. However, even if the protection afforded by registration were confined to these types of cases, it must be remembered that the system would still lead to liability in cases where consumer confusion is unlikely. This is most obviously true in situations where the registered owner operates at a significant geographic distance from the defendant. But there might be other cases where over-enforcement might occur, particularly if such a system retained word marks and the ability to claim graphic elements in all colours[18] and continued to permit the use of broad terminology in specifications. Nevertheless, a registration system built around double identity infringement could credibly be defended on the grounds that an enforcement costs analysis on balance favours such a system and that it brings with it the public information benefits typically claimed for trade mark registration.

The question thus becomes, how much beyond double identity can one go? To what extent should we allow actions in relation to marks that differ in some important detail? To what extent should differences in the goods or services be ignored? In deciding these questions, we need to think about the point at which the danger of over-enforcement becomes telling and the point at which the information communicated by the register becomes difficult to interpret. Whatever the answer to these questions may be, there is good reason to believe that current registration systems go much too far.

There is now widespread concern that trade mark rights are being abused, with trade mark owners adopting aggressive enforcement strategies in cases that are never going to cause confusion.[19] Less commonly acknowledged, however, is the fact that this phenomenon is underpinned by a legal regime that leaves scope for considerable uncertainty as to when marks might be held to conflict. It can be difficult for legal advisors

---

[18] Cf. Trade Marks Act 1995 (Cth) s. 70.
[19] This concern is commonly associated with media reports of 'brand bullies', but academic research supports the view that trade mark overclaiming is a significant problem. See, e.g., William T Gallagher, 'Trademark and copyright enforcement in the shadow of IP law' (2012) 28 *Santa Clara Computer & High Technology Law Journal* 453; William McGeveran, 'The imaginary trademark parody crisis (and the real one)' (2015) 90 *Washington Law Review* 713.

to provide defendants with the assurance they need in the face of cases that adopt an expansive approach to the similarity of marks and similarity of goods enquiries. Moreover, it must be remembered that the absence of evidence of actual confusion will never be determinative in cases involving a registered mark. This means that the common sense response to an allegation of infringement – the marks cannot be deceptively similar since no one has been confused – will take a defendant only so far. It is difficult to escape the conclusion that the problem of trade mark overclaiming would be less severe if protection for registered trade marks were more limited in scope. If defendants knew that plaintiffs were going to be required to plead their case in passing off, with all the evidential hurdles that entails, the willingness of defendants to stand their ground might be increased significantly.

This, however, does not lead to the conclusion that infringement should be confined to double identity cases. Protection may now extend too far, but double identity infringement alone might well be too narrow. This is particularly true if double identity infringement were to be approached in the way that it is at the moment in the EU. The Court of Justice of the EU has held that the double identity provision is to be given a narrow sphere of operation. As a consequence, the test for identity of marks 'must be interpreted strictly' and only 'insignificant differences' that would not leave an impression on consumers can be set aside.[20] This makes sense in the context of a legal system that provides a series of other broad rights but seems unnecessarily restrictive as the sole basis of liability. That is, it ought to be possible to expand protection at least somewhat further without compromising the ability of the register to communicate accurate information and without tipping the infringement scales unduly in favour of trade mark owners. For example, one might reasonably take the view that the registered trade mark action ought to extend to protect against the use of marks that differ in some small, but not entirely trivial, detail. It might therefore be possible to defend something like the current Australian test of substantial identity. Applying this test, it has been said that the word *Funship* would be substantially identical with *The Funship*,[21] and the word *Polykin* was held to be substantially identical with *Polyken*,[22] findings that are probably incompatible with an application of the EU test of 'identity'.[23]

---

[20] *SA Société LTJ Diffusion* v. *SA Sadas* Case-291/00 [2003] ECR I-2799.
[21] *Carnival Cruise Lines Inc* v. *Sitmar Cruises Ltd* (1994) 31 IPR 375, 391 (FCA).
[22] *Kendall Co* v. *Mulsyn Paint & Chemicals* (1963) 109 CLR 300, 305.
[23] The European cases are, however, far from consistent. Compare *United Airlines Inc* v. *United Airways Ltd* [2011] EWHC 2411 (Ch), [41] (UNITED AIRLINES and

It is not, however, the intention of this chapter to set out in detail how, precisely, a strong but narrow registered trade mark system might operate, since the aim is not to provide a detailed model of reform but rather to point out that the current model of registration is not inevitable.

3.3 The Direction of Reform

Our understanding of how trade mark registration operates is invariably shaped by the system with which we are most familiar. There can therefore be a tendency to assume that there is only one way in which trade mark registration can operate. However, registration can take different forms and have different aims and effects. In the present day this is most obviously seen in the way registration operates in the US. The US registration system does not serve to construct the boundaries of the trade marks owner's property right. Rather, those boundaries are constructed by how the sign is used. This is best illustrated by the way infringement is assessed. In the US, questions of infringement are determined by comparing the marks as they are used in commerce. This means that differences in the presentation of goods can be decisive. Take, for example, the analysis in *Procter & Gamble* v. *Johnson & Johnson*.[24] The question in that case was whether the defendant's use of the marks ASSURE for tampons and SURE & NATURAL for sanitary pads infringed the plaintiff's mark SURE, registered in respect of deodorant. In finding for the defendant, Leval J placed considerable weight on the visual presentation of the products. He noted, for example, that 'the Sure Anti-perspirant container is white; the word "Sure" is written in upright uniform caps going diagonally across the upper part of the container, the name bordered above and below by bold diagonal colored stripes. The color contrasts are strong. There are no pictures or distractive images on the packaging'.[25] In contrast, 'the Sure & Natural package has a pale orange and yellow background with daisies on the lower corner. The brand name is written with initial caps and smaller lower case letters horizontally across the top of the package ... its impact and appearance have little in common with Sure's packaging or presentation'.[26]

The considerations on which Leval J focussed would be regarded as largely irrelevant to an infringement analysis in most jurisdictions. In

---

UNITED AIRWAYS held identical on an application for summary judgment) with *Bayer Cropscience SA* v. *Agropharm* [2004] EWHC 1661 (Ch), [34] (serious issue to be tried as to whether PATRIOT C and PATRIOT P are identical to PATRIOT). See also Belinda Isaac and Rajiv Joshi, 'What does identical mean?' (2005) 27 *European Intellectual Property Review* 184.

[24] 485 F Supp 1185 (SDNY 1980).   [25] Ibid., 1198.   [26] Ibid.

other countries the owner's mark will be the mark *as registered*. This is the sign that will be compared with the sign that has been 'used' by the defendant. The difference flows from the nature and function of registration. Trade mark registration in the US acts like a signpost that helps identify the property, without seeking to fix its boundaries. In contrast, registration elsewhere does serve to fix the boundaries of the trade mark owner's rights; it serves more like a set of fence-posts. There is nothing necessarily wrong with this model of registration, but we must be prepared to ask questions about the quality and reliability of the fence-posts we are using. In particular, we should at least satisfy ourselves that the current model is preferable to a system in which registration gives strong but narrow rights.

The suggestion that we might move towards a model for registered trade mark protection that would be confined to something close to double identity infringement (with other types of case left to passing off) is not an idea that will gain traction anytime soon. The dominant (much broader) conception of the scope of registered trade mark rights is not merely enshrined in legislation, but also in contractual arrangements between trade mark owners and licensees. It is a conception that is normalised and reinforced by the working practices of trade mark professionals.

It is, however, important not to jump to the conclusion that the model of registration being canvassed here would be incompatible with international IP agreements. At first glance, admittedly, any attempt to limit registered trade mark rights to something close to double identity infringement would be incompatible with the TRIPS Agreement.[27] Article 16(1) of TRIPS provides, in relevant part, that 'The owner of a registered trademark shall have the exclusive right to prevent all third parties not having the owner's consent from using in the course of trade identical or *similar signs* for goods or services which are identical *or similar* to those in respect of which the trademark is registered where such use would result in a likelihood of confusion'.[28] This provision is not, however, as restrictive as it appears. This is because the TRIPS Agreement says nothing about the model of registration to be adopted. The US is perfectly entitled to maintain its signpost model of registration and there would be nothing to prevent a country from adopting a mixed model.

---

[27] Marrakesh Agreement Establishing the World Trade Organization, opened for signature 15 April 1994, 1867 UNTS 3 (entered into force 1 January 1995) annex 1C (Agreement on Trade-Related Aspects of Intellectual Property Rights; cited as TRIPS Agreement).
[28] My emphasis.

Consider, for example, the Australian infringement provisions. When a substantially identical or deceptively similar sign is used in relation to goods or services that are the same as those for which the trade mark is registered, infringement occurs under section 120(1) of the Trade Marks Act 1995 (Cth). When such a sign is used in relation to goods or services that are not the same as, but are similar or closely related to, the goods or services for which the trade mark is registered, infringement occurs under section 120(2), unless the alleged infringer can establish that its actual use of the sign was not likely to deceive or cause confusion. There is nothing in the TRIPS Agreement that would prevent Australia from adopting a fence-post approach for claims falling within section 120(1), but a signpost approach for claims falling within section 120(2). In other words, for claims falling under the latter subsection, Australian courts could switch to comparing the plaintiff's *goods* with the defendant's goods, rather than confining themselves to the mark as registered. Such a move would be broadly consistent with Tan and Foo's call for Singapore to move to a system where less attention is paid to matters of bureaucratic form.[29]

At the very least, we need to be careful in how we assess judicial creativity. Take, for example, the position in Australia. Since the passage of the Trade Marks Act 1995 (Cth), judges have taken a number of steps to build marketplace factors into the confusion analysis. This is to be seen, for example, in the way evidence of reputation has been allowed to influence the assessment of deceptive similarity,[30] in the acceptance that other extraneous factors can also be relevant to this enquiry (such as how many brands are present in the market and the extent to which third-party traders also make use of particular themes)[31] and in the way the use as a trade mark threshold has been applied.[32] The tendency has been to build space for marketplace considerations into the infringement analysis so as to limit the scope of trade mark rights. In so doing, courts have shown a desire to prevent registered trade mark rights from becoming untethered from their ultimate justification – that is, to prevent consumer confusion. They have had to do so, however, while trying to avoid disrupting the idea that the scope of protection given to registered trade marks is determined by reference to their bureaucratic form. We should therefore be unsurprised if the rules that have been developed depend on

---

[29] David Tan and Benjamin Foo, 'The extraneous factors rule in trademark law: Avoiding confusion or simply confusing?' (2016) March *Singapore Journal of Legal Studies* 118.
[30] See, e.g., *Mars Australia Pty Ltd* v. *Sweet Rewards Pty Ltd* [2009] FCA 606.
[31] *MID Sydney Pty Ltd* v. *Australian Tourism Co Ltd* (1998) 90 FCR 236; *CA Henschke & Co* v. *Rosemount Estates Pty Ltd* [2000] FCA 1539.
[32] See, e.g., *Top Heavy Pty Ltd* v. *Killin* (1996) 34 IPR 282.

the drawing of artificial lines or somewhat arbitrary distinctions. Any assessment of the merits of these developments should instead be judged against the twin yardsticks of their impact on enforcement costs and on the quality of the information communicated by the register. One way of understanding the post-1995 trend is to say that courts have compromised the quality of the information communicated by the register. For example, as Davison has noted, by allowing evidence of reputation to impact on the scope of protection, courts have undermined a system whose 'bright line is publicly available information as to who has the rights in a trade mark and what those rights are'.[33] This is unquestionably true. But before we decide that courts have taken a wrong turn, we have to bear in mind that trade marks have been dramatically extended with the result that over-enforcement of marks has become a significant problem. A trade-off that sees the trade mark rights being reined in at the expense of the quality of the information communicated by the register is by no means obviously undesirable. Better still might be a bifurcated system with a core of strong but narrow rights and an unabashed market-based approach in other cases. However, most registration systems remain a long way from this goal.

---

[33] Mark Davison, 'Reputation in trade mark infringement: Why some courts think it matters and why it should not' (2010) 38 *Federal Law Review* 231.

4 Publication in the History of Patents and Copyright
Harmony or Happenstance?

David J Brennan[*]

> *[I]n every copyright lawyer there is always a patent lawyer waiting to spring forth, fully fledged and ready to litigate, and ... the worlds of science and technology are inextricably intermingled with those of literature and the arts ... And, in truth, the origins of copyright and patents are very similar, stemming from a common desire to provide some kind of state-sanctioned incentive for creative and innovative work.*[1]

4.1 Introduction

In the second half of the eighteenth century, the principles that should distinguish the bodies of law that we know today as patents and copyright were contestable. The nuanced distinctions and categories that exist today in law – protection for inventive functionality rather than mere discovery in patents, and for original expression rather than mundane facts or mere ideas in copyright – were embryonic at best. It was, however, accepted that patent grants for newly introduced industry permitted under section 6 of the 1623 Statute of Monopolies and published literary property recognised under the 1709 Statute of Anne created exclusive rights in protected information.[2] By dint of this perception, a kinship of sorts can be seen to exist between the two species of

---

[*] Sam Ricketson taught me intellectual property and private international law at the Melbourne Law School in the early 1990s and has since been a trusted colleague. It is an honour to contribute this chapter. I thank Janice Luck, Ann Monotti, Michael Bryan and Jane Ginsburg for their comments on a draft version; responsibility for the analysis is mine.
[1] Sam Ricketson, 'Business method patents: A matter of convenience? (The Stephen Stewart Memorial Lecture 2002)' (2003) 2 *Intellectual Property Quarterly* 97, 98.
[2] An Act concerning Monopolies and Dispensations with penall Lawes and the Forfeyture thereof (1623) 21 Jac 1, c. 3 (cited as Statute of Monopolies) and An Act for the Encouragement of Learning by Vesting the Copies of Printed Books in the Authors or Purchasers of Such Copies during the Times Therein Mentioned (1709) 8 Ann, c. 19 (cited as Statute of Anne).

51

right in the minds of judges and law-makers of the era, and as such it would not be unusual that changes in one regime might trigger some reconsideration of the other. The extent of such early reciprocal development might be masked by a modern tendency to compartmentalise the two intellectual property regimes. Scholarly examinations of doctrinal matters in patent and copyright law have tended to shy away from considering matters of their shared history. This, in turn, might have understated some of the ways in which each regime influenced the other at critical stages of evolution.

This chapter seeks to address that possible understatement by making some observations about changes in the late eighteenth and mid-nineteenth centuries to aspects of patent and copyright law. It suggests that those changes might be better understood by a greater appreciation of a shared history between patent and copyright law. It will commence with the centrality of manuscript publication to the resolution of the question of literary property in the late eighteenth century and ask whether the use that Lord Mansfield made of the patent specification in the *Liardet* v. *Johnson* litigation was at least influenced by the resolution of that copyright question.[3] From there it will ask whether a reciprocal influence occurred in the mid-nineteenth century insofar as the patent law concept of a novelty-destroying prior publication came to influence what amounted to an 'abandonment' of rights in copyright because of some prior publication. It will conclude by observing that as English law entered the twentieth century, the basic contours of patent and copyright law around publication for entitlement to property and prior publication for disentitlement were – whether by accident or design – essentially the same.

4.2 Invention and the Question of Literary Property

A clear majority of the eleven common law judges of the late eighteenth century who offered their advisory opinions to the House of Lords in *Donaldson* v. *Beckett* took the position that some form of copyright existed at common law regardless of any print publication.[4] However, a narrower majority of those judges also took the position that on the passing of the Statute of Anne, which conferred merely a finite term of

---

[3] E Wyndham Hulme, 'On the history of patent law in the seventeenth and eighteenth centuries' (1902) 18 *Law Quarterly Review* 280, 284–7.
[4] *Donaldson* v. *Beckett* (1774) 4 Burr 2408, 2409-2417; 98 ER 257, 258–262 (cited as *Donaldson*). See generally: H Thomás Gómez-Arostegui, 'Copyright at common law in 1774' (2014) 47 *Connecticut Law Review* 1.

protection for print-published literary works, the action at common law in published literary works was either 'taken away' by that statute or that the author was 'precluded by such statute from any remedy, except on the foundation of the said statute'.[5] *Donaldson v. Beckett* involved whether to continue a chancery injunction made after the expiration of the finite statutory term attaching to a published book of poems titled *Seasons* by James Thomson, on the basis of the existence of a perpetual common law right.[6] The same literary work had been earlier litigated before the Kings Bench in *Millar v. Taylor* where, by a three-to-one majority headed by Lord Mansfield, the existence of the perpetual common law right in the published work had been vindicated.[7] A type of 'jury vote' taken by the Lords (both law lords and lay peers) in *Donaldson v. Beckett* was in favour of ending the injunction, effectively overturning the holding in *Millar v. Taylor* but without judicial reasoning. Therefore, the anterior issues surrounding the existence and nature of any common law copyright were not dealt with.[8] Yet because the outcome of the vote could be reconciled with the majority position of the common law judges' advisory opinions (i.e., perpetual common law copyright existed but upon print publication it was pre-empted by the Statute of Anne which covered the field), that became the received orthodoxy in English law until the passing of the Copyright Act 1911 (UK).[9] There remained, however, lingering resistance to this orthodoxy insofar as it admitted the existence of common law copyright.[10]

Lord Mansfield emerges as the central figure in the legal kerfuffle over literary property. In *Millar v. Taylor* he commenced his reasons with the observation that, notwithstanding the best efforts of the four judges, the unanimity that had existed to that date in his tenure on the Kings Bench was being upset by the dissenting judgment of Justice Yates, who rejected the existence of common law copyright.[11] In that dissent, John Harrison's invention of an improved nautical clock (chronometer) featured prominently. Harrison's clock was a breakthrough because it

---

[5] *Donaldson*, 258 (the language of the third question) and discussed by Gómez-Arostegui, 'Copyright at common law', 28–33.
[6] *Donaldson*, 257.
[7] *Millar v. Taylor* (1769) 4 Burr 2303, 2407; 98 ER 201, 257 (cited as *Millar*).
[8] *Donaldson* (1774) 4 Burr 2408, 2417; 98 ER 257, 262 and Gómez-Arostegui, 'Copyright at common law', 33–45.
[9] Mark Rose, *Authors and Owners – The Invention of Copyright* (Cambridge, MA: Harvard University Press, 1993), p. 112.
[10] *Jefferys v. Boosey* (1854) 4 HL Cas 815, 962; 10 ER 681, 739 (Lord Brougham) (cited as *Jefferys*); Charles Palmer Phillips, *The Law of Copyright* (London: V & R Stevens Sons & Haynes, 1863), p. 2.
[11] *Millar* (1769) 4 Burr 2303, 2395–2396; 98 ER 201, 250–251.

maintained sufficient accuracy at sea to permit calculation of longitudinal position. Having introduced Harrison's clock earlier in his reasons, Justice Yates returned to it, stating that 'Mr Harrison ... employed at least as much time and labour and study upon his time-keeper as Mr Thomson could do in writing his *Seasons* ... as far as value is a mark of property, Mr Harrison's time-piece is, surely, as valuable in itself, as Mr Thomson's *Seasons*'.[12] Setting out the arguments put in favour of the view that an author's common law right applied with equal force to an inventor such as John Harrison, Justice Yates concluded with the observation that '[y]et with all these arguments, it is well known, no such property can exist, after the invention is published'.[13]

The first advisory opinion delivered to the House of Lords by Baron Eyre, who like Justice Yates was against the very existence of common law copyright, also mentioned John Harrison to argue the absurdity of perpetual common law copyright:

Had Mr Harrison wrote a description of the use of his time-piece, which he could have done in a few hours, the pamphlet would have been the subject of literary property; the profits of which he might have claimed for ever: but the time-piece itself, the subject of twenty years study, might be copied in the first hour it was published.[14]

The Harrison chronometer of 1759 was an example of incremental invention or, to use the language of the eighteenth century, an 'addition'. It was arrived at by the realisation that small, high-frequency oscillators were more stable than larger mechanisms.[15] While it was a considerable technological advance, the influence of the 1644 reference in Coke's *Institutes* to *Bircot*'s case endured.[16] Under it, incremental improvement should be denied patent grant on the basis that it 'was to put but a new button to an old coat, and it is much easier to add than to invent'.[17] This rule meant that gradual technological improvements were doctrinally outside of eligible 'manner of new manufactures'. Instead, patent grants were confined to the introduction to the nation of industries and trades

---

[12] Ibid., 2361, 2387; 232, 246.   [13] Ibid.

[14] 'Literary property', *Morning Chronicle* (London), 16 February 1774, p. 2.

[15] Ed Estow, 'Icon: Harrison H4 marine timekeeper', Gear Patrol, 18 February 2014, retrieved from https://gearpatrol.com/2014/02/18/history-of-the-harrison-h4-marine-timekeeper; Dava Sobel, *Longitude: The True Story of a Lone Genius Who Solved the Greatest Scientific Problem of His Time* (New York: Walker, 1995), ch. 10.

[16] Edward Coke, *Third Part of the Institutes of the Laws of England: Concerning High Treason, and Other Please of the Crown and Criminall Causes* (London: M Flesher for W Lee and D Pakeman, 1644), p. 184; James Oldham, *English Common Law in the Age of Mansfield* (Chapel Hill: University of North Carolina Press, 2004), pp. 200–1.

[17] Coke, *Third Part of the Institutes on the Laws of England*, 184.

not hitherto practised locally. Such things as improving a clock for seafaring applications was not obviously permitted under the rule in *Bircot*'s case. In turn, given the long-standing need for the capacity to measure nautical longitude, the absence of any clear patent incentive might help to shed light on why non-patent incentives had been offered. Since 1713, a prize of up to £20,000, administered by the Commissioners for the Discovery of the Longitude at Sea, was on offer.[18] Having supplied an ingenious solution, John Harrison was denied the full prize for reasons symptomatic of the venality that can infect patronage-based systems.[19] Indeed, prior to the monarch's personal intercession on Harrison's behalf, in 1762 the Parliament itself intervened and authorised the Commissioners of the Navy to pay Harrison £5,000 upon his publishing and making known his 'Watch for Discovery of the Longitude ... so that other Workmen may be enabled to make other such Instruments or Watches for the same Purpose'.[20] Such a disclosure obligation presaged system-wide changes to patent law that Lord Mansfield would introduce. Moreover, this statutory obligation might have been in the minds of Justice Yates and Baron Eyre when they referenced Harrison's invention in their respective *Millar* v. *Taylor* and *Donaldson* v. *Beckett* opinions. The policy of the statute resembled those judges' own copyright logic: public grant should occur only upon the author causing his or her manuscript to be published.

The intellectual impacts on Lord Mansfield of the outcome in *Donaldson* v. *Beckett* and the rhetorical uses of Harrison's invention by Justice Yates and Baron Eyre are matters for speculation. However, clearly *Donaldson* v. *Beckett* represented a rejection of Lord Mansfield's *Millar* v. *Taylor* view that literary property was recognised in perpetuity by the common law, irrespective of publication. From 1774, publication emerged as the critical act which made finite a type of right which had been held to be perpetual. *Donaldson* v. *Beckett* confined the term in published literary works to those stipulated in the Statute of Anne: at least fourteen years and at most twenty-eight years, depending upon the

---

[18] An Act for providing a Publick Reward for such Person or Persons as shall discover the Longitude at Sea (1713) 12 Ann, c. 14.
[19] Sobel, *Longitude*, ch. 13. However, those advocating a re-examination of such patronage systems for possible modern revival have offered a revised historical account: Robert Burrell and Catherine Kelly, 'Public rewards and innovation policy: Lessons from the eighteenth and early nineteenth centuries' (2014) 77 *Modern Law Review* 858, 873: 'There is a case to be made that the Board of Longitude did not act entirely unreasonably in refusing to grant Harrison the full longitude prize.'
[20] An Act for the Encouragement of John Harrison, to publish and make known his Invention of a Machine or Watch, for the Discovery of the Longitude at Sea (1762) 2 Geo III, c 14; Sobel, *Longitude*, 147–9.

longevity of the author. At that time, the permissible term of a patent grant made under the Statute of Monopolies was fourteen years, although patentees at least since the 1740s had successfully petitioned Parliament to pass Private Acts to prolong patent terms, typically for an additional fourteen years.[21] In other words, in the wake of *Donaldson v. Beckett* there existed a degree of de facto harmony between the proprietary terms of a published literary work and a manner of new manufacture protected by a patent grant augmentable by Private Act.

4.3 Lord Mansfield and the Fundaments of Patent Law

In this setting of relative term equivalence between published literary works and grants of patents, Lord Mansfield gave jury instructions which reshaped the fundaments of patent law. The 1776 instructions in *Morris v. Bramson* were taken to overrule the principle in *Bircot*'s case.[22] The significance of that change was profound, so that by the end of the eighteenth century it was accepted that since *Morris v. Bramson* a patent for incremental invention was good, so long as confined to the 'addition only, and not for the old machine too'.[23] The type of improvement to a known device that John Harrison had been responsible for would now be more clearly eligible for patent grant. Then, two years after *Morris v. Bramson*, Lord Mansfield's jury instructions in *Liardet v. Johnson* shifted the whole justification for patent grants from the introduction of new types of industry to the publication in the patent specification of a technical secret:

The third point is whether the specification is such as instructs others to make it. For the condition of giving encouragement is this: that you must specify upon record your invention in such a way as shall teach an artist, when your term is out, to make it and to make it as well as you by your directions; for then at the end of the term, the public have the benefit of it. The inventor has the benefit during the term, and the public have the benefit after.[24]

Comparable to the instructions in *Morris v. Bramson*, these too brought about a re-making of the fundaments of patent law that took effect by the end of the century. The principles from *Liardet v. Johnson* and *Morris v. Bramson* ('the Mansfield-enunciated patent reforms') meant that the justification for patent grant had moved focus from a national interest in

---

[21] Thomas Webster, *Reports and Notes of Cases on Letters for Patents of Inventions* (London: Thomas Blenkarn, 1844), p. 37.
[22] (1776) 1 CPC 30, 34; 1 HPC 181, 187.
[23] *Boulton and Watt v. Bull* (1795) 2 Bl H 463, 489; 126 ER 651, 664 (Buller J).
[24] Hulme, 'On the history of patent law', 285.

newly introduced trades and industries, to a social contract: the public disclosure of specific technical secrets, including incremental improvements, became the 'consideration' for any patent grant. The written specification 'must put the public in possession of the secret in as ample and beneficial way as the patentee himself uses it'.[25]

The centrality of publication in copyright after *Donaldson v. Beckett*, and Lord Mansfield's formidable straddling of both copyright and patent jurisprudence, might help shed a clearer light on the Mansfield-enunciated patent reforms that occurred in the immediate wake of *Donaldson v. Beckett*. Lord Mansfield's *Millar v. Taylor* conception of perpetual common law copyright was emphatically not conditioned upon book publication. Rather, it was justified by the author's exertions alone. His conception was significantly – although not totally – displaced by *Donaldson v. Beckett*.[26] The outcome in *Donaldson v. Beckett* rendered the proprietary rights in an author's unpublished manuscript less certain, but certainly confined rights in published works to the Statute of Anne statutory terms. Indeed, in the latter part of the 1770s, an author's unpublished manuscript and an inventor's technical secret both had an uncertain proprietary status. Common law copyright might have still protected the manuscript while unpublished, but this was less certain after *Donaldson v. Beckett* and throughout the centuries influential viewpoints have disputed its existence. Indeed, prior to 1911 only chattel property rights in the manuscript could be asserted with complete confidence. Secrets per se, whether personal or technical, have never attracted proprietary recognition in the Anglo tradition.[27] After *Donaldson v. Beckett* it was only upon due print publication of the manuscript that a finite term of copyright was available. To use the language of the Statute of Anne, upon publication there was a property right 'for the encouragement' of 'useful books'. In patents, while the transmission of new trades or industry was traditionally required (such as by training apprentices), grants had never formally required the publication of any technical information as any quid pro quo. The written specification had been earlier introduced simply to distinguish grants from each other.[28] After the Mansfield-enunciated patent reforms it was only upon full public disclosure of the inventor's technical secret in the written specification that the patent grant was valid. To use the language of Lord

---

[25] *R v. Arkwright* (1785) 1 WPC 64, 66; 1 HPC 245, 251 (Buller J).
[26] Rose, *Authors and Owners*, 112.
[27] *Prince Albert v. Strange* (1849) 1 Mac & G 25; 41 ER 1171 and *Saltman Engineering v. Campbell Engineering* (1948) 65 RPC 203.
[28] Christine MacLeod, *Inventing the Industrial Revolution: The English Patent System, 1660–1800* (Cambridge: Cambridge University Press, 1988), pp. 51–3.

Mansfield's jury instructions in *Liardet* v. *Johnson*, the disclosure of technical knowledge was 'the condition of giving encouragement' so that 'the public have the benefit of it'.[29]

Thus by the end of the eighteenth century the basic contours of protection for literary works and inventions were the same. After *Donaldson* v. *Beckett* and the Mansfield-enunciated patent reforms, publication of the author's manuscript or the inventor's secret emerged as the crux of both regimes, and encouragement for the writing or the invention emerged as the overarching justification for both. Was this happenstance, the product of deliberate harmonisation or subliminal cross-cutting impact? It may not be possible to provide a conclusive answer. However, a reasonable deduction is that Lord Mansfield's experience in the vexed copyright question, in which John Harrison's chronometer played a cameo role, at least influenced this coincidence in the basic contours between the two. As will be suggested next, it is also possible to observe one other significant coincidence relating to publication that took shape between the two regimes in the following century.

4.4 Prior Publications in Patents and Copyright

If late in the eighteenth century concepts from the resolution of the question of literary property did inform patent law fundamentals through the medium of Lord Mansfield, perhaps patent law concepts reciprocated and gave shape to copyright doctrine in the nineteenth century. What can be seen to emerge in the nineteenth century after *Jefferys* v. *Boosey* was similarity in a more detailed feature of the patent and copyright regimes.[30] As noted earlier, at best there were murky rights in information prior to grant of patent or due print publication of copyright subject matter, with clearer rules governing patent grant and statutory copyright for finite terms. The rules relating to patents have evolved and remain part of modern law, but many of the rules governing copyright pertained to the era and were overtaken by the UK giving effect to the 1908 (Berlin) revision of the Berne Convention in 1911. So that under *Jefferys* v. *Boosey*, for a work to attract English copyright protection (as opposed to public performance rights or rights arising from the International Copyright Acts) the work's author had to be physically present in the jurisdiction when, in England, the *first* printing and publishing of the work occurred locally. Then, and only then, was the author a British 'author' for statutory copyright purposes. A valid patent grant

---

[29] Hulme, 'On the history of patent law', 285.
[30] *Jefferys* (1854) 4 HL Cas 815; 10 ER 681.

Table 1 *Hulme's Comparative Table of UK Patent Law*

Sixteenth Century	End of Eighteenth Century
Consideration of the grant the introduction of the industry. Formal disclosure of the invention waived by the Crown.	Consideration of the grant the written disclosure of the invention. No proof of working required.
Patents of addition of doubtful validity.	Patents of addition good at law.
Crucial test of monopoly prior user within the realm within the memory of man.	Crucial test of grant absolute novelty of the invention both in practice and as regards the published literature of the Art within the Realm.
Prior sale not prejudicial.	Prior sale fatal to the validity of patent.

required the support of a specification *first* disclosing the invention. By the mid-nineteenth century, first public disclosure was the critical, and comparable, legal event for creation of property rights in inventions and writings. When would an earlier publication disentitle an inventor or author to statutory rights?

Hulme concluded his influential 1897 article with a comparative table intended to highlight what were the late-eighteenth-century changes to UK patent law,[31] the content of which is reproduced above in Table 1.

The Mansfield-enunciated patent reforms were essentially the trigger for all the changes summarised in Hulme's table. The second item in the table is explained by Mansfield's jury instructions in *Morris v. Bramson*. The first, third and fourth items are changes explicable in large part by the impacts of Lord Mansfield's jury instructions in *Liardet v. Johnson*, described by Hulme as 'a landmark in the history of English patent law'.[32] Whereas the first deals with the sufficiency of the written disclosure of the invention, the third and fourth items deal with a related core requirement of patent law: that the invention so disclosed is 'novel'.

In the decades following *Liardet v. Johnson*, clear statements of principle relating to the necessity for the patent grant to be in respect of novel subject matter led to the patentee custom of separately demarcating, by 'claiming', novel features.[33] In that way it was hoped that the specification could be used both to fully disclose and to assert novelty.[34]

---

[31] E Wyndham Hulme, 'On the consideration of the patent grant, past and present' (1897) 13 *Law Quarterly Review* 313, 318.
[32] Ibid., 317.
[33] David J Brennan, 'The evolution of English patent claims as property definers' (2005) 4 *Intellectual Property Quarterly* 361.
[34] Ibid., 372–7.

(The use of the patent claim for infringement purposes came later.[35]) Thus after *Liardet* v. *Johnson*, novelty of the technology emerged as a concept defined by an assessment of the secret disclosed in the specification compared against publications prior to the grant. Lord Ellenborough's 1803 jury instruction made the point that: 'if prior to the time of his obtaining a patent, any part of that which is the substance of the invention has been communicated to the pubic ... so as to be a known thing, in that case he cannot claim the benefit of his patent'.[36] Critically, a patentee being responsible for that communication was no exception. In *Wood* v. *Zimmer* there existed evidence of the patentee disclosing his invention by product sales prior to grant. Chief Justice Gibbs, after observing that 'the question is somewhat new', stated in his 1815 jury charge:

> To entitle a man to a patent, the invention must be new to the world. The public sale of that, which is afterwards made the subject of a patent, though sold by the inventor only, makes the patent void.[37]

To similar effect Lord Brougham, who had been responsible for 1835 statutory reforms which had conferred prolongation and confirmatory patent jurisdiction upon the Privy Council, made the following comment during the course of an 1843 House of Lords appeal:

> The [Statute of Monopolies] excludes from a patent the true inventor who shall have made the invention so public that others at the time of granting the patent shall use the invention. The public have lost the consideration for the patent, namely the specification which is given.[38]

In this statement Lord Brougham concisely explained why any prior publication in patent law, including communications for which the patentee was responsible, destroyed the validity of the grant. Under the logic of *Liardet* v. *Johnson* disclosure of the secret was the inventor's payment for the grant. There could be no payment if, whether by an inventor or a third person, the secret had been prior published whether in print, by product sale or by public use. By his subsequent decision in *Jefferys* v. *Boosey*, Lord Brougham helped to ensure that this became the basis of a rule in copyright law too.[39]

---

[35] Ibid., 380–99. [36] *Huddart* v. *Grimshaw* (1803) 1 WPC 85, 86-87.
[37] *Wood* v. *Zimmer* (1815) Holt 58, 60; 171 ER 161, 162.
[38] *The Househill Coal and Iron Company* v. *Neilson* (1843) 1 WPC 673, 719.
[39] *Jefferys* (1854) 4 HL Cas 815; 10 ER 681. See generally, David J Brennan, 'The root of title to copyright in works' (2015) 4 *Intellectual Property Quarterly* 289, 308–19.

After *Donaldson* v. *Beckett* there was no doubt that, for a literary work, once the work had been (with its author's consent) printed and sold to the British public, that work had been published. At that moment any common law rights ended, and a finite statutory copyright might arise. It was the equivalent of an inventor disclosing technical secrets in the written specification supporting a patent grant. However, what was the position if the author's work had been earlier disclosed to the public in a manner other than printed publication? *Macklin* v. *Richardson* was decided in the period between *Millar* v. *Taylor* and *Donaldson* v. *Beckett*.[40] An injunction was sought to restrain the print reproduction of a dramatic work which had been publicly performed with the author's permission, but not circulated in print. By a shorthand taker sitting as a member of the audience during a performance, the defendant had obtained a copy and printed the work for sale. The defence argued that no infringement was actionable because the plaintiff's public performance prior to securing Statute of Anne copyright meant that the plaintiff had neither common law nor statutory rights. This was rejected:

It has been argued to be a publication, by being acted; and therefore the printing is no injury to the plaintiff: but that is a mistake; for besides the advantage from the performance, the author has another means of profit, from the printing and publishing; and there is as much reason that he should be protected in that right as any other author.[41]

Thus unpublished literary and dramatic matter did not lose common law copyright by its communication to the public by performance, and implicitly statutory rights remained available upon authorised print publication. This was at odds with the patent rule that was shortly to develop in the wake of *Liardet* v. *Johnson*. In *Jefferys* v. *Boosey*, Lord Brougham brought the copyright position into line with patent law by rhetorically asking: 'if [the author] makes his composition public, can he retain the exclusive right which he had before?'[42] To this, the following answer was given: 'whatever may have been the original right of the author, the publication appears to be of necessity an abandonment'.[43] The rejection of *Macklin* v. *Richardson* was done by Lord Brougham putting forward a concept of publication more expansive

---

[40] *Macklin* v. *Richardson* (1770) Amb 694; 27 ER 451.
[41] Ibid., 696; 452 (Lord Commissioner Smythe).
[42] *Jefferys* (1854) 4 HL Cas 815, 962; 10 ER 681, 739.   [43] Ibid., 965; 740.

than the circulation of printed copies. Resembling that in patent law, it comprised acts of prior public disclosure and included disclosures for which the originator was responsible. These served to divest inventor and author alike of general law rights, and to disentitle each one of statutory rights under the Statute of Monopolies and Statute of Anne respectively.[44]

By the time of *Caird* v. *Sime* in 1887, the more elastic patent rule of any prior public disclosure rendering the subject matter publici juris had taken hold in copyright. Lord Watson was in no doubt that if William Blackstone's lectures at Oxford were public communications, and if his *Commentaries on the Laws of England* were substantially the same as the lectures, 'the *Statute of Anne* could give the author no copyright in the original text'.[45] Thus by the late nineteenth century, the patent prior publication rule (which persists today) had become the copyright prior publication rule. While this aspect of English copyright law was swept away by the Copyright Act 1911 (UK), the possibility of works entering the public domain by certain public performances and exhibitions remained a contentious aspect of US copyright law for most of the twentieth century.[46]

4.5 Conclusion

The propositions that the resolution of the question of literary property could have sparked the reshaping of patent doctrines in the late eighteenth century, and that in turn those patent doctrines could have had a reciprocal influence upon an important aspect of English copyright law of the nineteenth century, are speculative. The similar patterns that emerged in each regime around a first stylised publication for entitlement purposes, and around prior disentitling publications, might have been coincidence. However, the 'cross-pollinating' roles possibly played by Lord Mansfield in the late eighteenth century and by Lord Brougham in the middle nineteenth century add a perspective from which to view the similarities. Moreover, considering such possible historical

---

[44] However, some confusion persisted: Brennan, 'The root of title to copyright in works', 312–13, discussing *Clark* v. *Bishop* (1872) 25 LT NS 908.
[45] *Caird* v. *Sime* (1887) 12 App Cas 326, 350.
[46] Paul Goldstein, *Copyright: Principles, Law, and Practice*, vol. 1 (Boston: Little, Brown, 1989), pp. 249–52, where error is suggested in the *King* v. *Mister Maestro*, 244 F Supp 101 (1963) holding that the public delivery of Dr Martin Luther King Jr's 'I Have a Dream' speech did not constitute a publication of the work such as to divest copyright in it.

connections allows research to look outside meticulously compartmentalised accounts of patent and copyright history and to consider messy truths. It is at least plausible, that when they were legal amoebas in the eighteenth and nineteenth centuries, the rights under the Statute of Monopolies and the Statute of Anne were considered to be similar enough to be treated similarly.

5   Of Moral Rights and Legal Transplants
Connecting Laws, Connecting Cultures

Elizabeth Adeney[*]

5.1   Introduction

The movement of a doctrine, principle or set of rules from one body of law into another appears to be an irresistible invitation to metaphor. The new law is 'received' or 'imported' or 'adopted' into the old law. More negatively, the old law may be seen as 'infected' by foreign material[1] or the new law may 'irritate' the recipient body.[2] Other metaphors are more focussed on the actions of the mover. The image of legal 'transplantation' has existed since early in the twentieth century, alluding at first to the horticultural act of transferring a plant, propagated elsewhere, into foreign earth.[3] In the 1960s *transplantation* took on a new range of associations as human organ transplants (the metaphor within the metaphor) became more successful.[4] With those associations came the related images of 'rejection' through 'immune reactions' in the recipient law.[5]

The movement in metaphors from horticulture to surgery involved a problematic simplification of the transplant concept since the metaphor suggested, barring any 'tissue rejection', the continued performance by the transplanted organ of its original function, without change either to itself or the receiving body. The surgical imagery has been criticised for this reason, Teubner pointing out that a legal transplant may both

---

[*] Sam Ricketson was the supervisor of my doctoral thesis on moral rights, and like all the best supervisors, he set the bar extremely high. The constant challenge throughout those years was to uncover materials on this subject that Sam had not already written about!

[1] Gunther Teubner, 'Legal irritants: Good faith in British law or how unifying law ends up in new divergences' (1998) 61(1) *Modern Law Review* 11.

[2] Ibid., 11, 20.

[3] Cairns traces the metaphor to Frederick P Walton in 1927, followed by R W Lee and Hermann Mannheim in the 1930s: John W Cairns, 'Watson, Walton, and the history of legal transplants' (2013) 41 *Georgia Journal of International & Comparative Law* 637, 688ff.

[4] Ibid., 643, noting the explicit analogy with organ transplantation in Otto Kahn-Freund, 'On uses and misuses of comparative law' (1974) 37 *Modern Law Review* 1 (delivered in 1973 as the second Chorley Lecture, London School of Economics).

[5] Teubner, 'Legal irritants', 12.

undergo and activate transformations in its new environment.[6] It may be that the older horticultural image offered the better analogy to legal development. As wine-makers know, the soil into which the vine is transplanted will affect the grapes. Conversely, judicious planting can improve soil and unwise planting may impair it.

Legal transplantation is one expression of this section's theme of traversing regimes. Every transplant connects a source with a destination in more or less complex and productive ways. The plant in question in the present chapter is the moral right of authors as conceived of in civil law countries and as transplanted into the statutes of a number of common law countries. It is part of the network of intellectual property (IP) laws connecting legal systems, lawyers and creators around the world. As is further elaborated in this chapter, Sam Ricketson in his writings has for decades both elucidated the building and functioning of this network and encouraged the propagation of new concepts in Australian law.

5.2　Forms and Purposes of Legal Transplantation

It has been asked whether legal transplants can ever function effectively in the receiving legal system. In the eighteenth century Montesquieu considered them a chancy venture.[7] In the following century, when Napoleonic imperialism prompted nationalism in subject states, it was strongly argued that legal transplantation was a flawed method of legal development. Roman law in particular was criticised for its inability to reflect the thinking of northern European populations.[8] English and

---

[6] Ibid. This insight was not new. Kahn-Freund, in introducing the surgical metaphor, had spoken of 'adjustments' to the received organ: Kahn-Freund, 'On uses and misuses of comparative law', 6. See also Alan Watson, 'Afterword', in *Legal Transplants: An Approach to Comparative Law*, 2nd ed. (Athens: University of Georgia Press, 1993), p. 116: 'Transplanting frequently, perhaps always, involves legal transformation. Even when the transplanted rule remains unchanged, its impact in a new social setting may be different. The insertion of an alien rule into another complex system may cause it to operate in a fresh way' (notes omitted).
[7] Charles de Secondat, Baron de Montesquieu, *De l'Esprit des Loix* (Geneva: Barrillot et fils, 1748), bk 1, ch. 3 ('Des loix positives').
[8] Jacob Grimm, *Deutsche Rechtsaltertümer* (Berlin: Akademie-Verlag, 1956), p. xvii, complaining that: Roman law 'is not indigenous, has not been bred or grown on our soil; in significant fundamentals it is contrary to our way of thinking and therefore cannot satisfy us. ... it casts no light on our history and our history casts no light on it' (my translation).

Scandinavian law were admired as more fruitfully aligned with the cultures of their people.[9]

In the twentieth century doubts continued to be raised about the wisdom of legal transplantation. While Alan Watson pointed out the frequency and success of transplants,[10] Kahn-Freund counselled caution, arguing that some transplants should not be contemplated without a detailed knowledge of the source legal culture.[11] These positions do not necessarily conflict, much depending on whether an idea on the one hand, or a system-specific elaboration of that idea on the other – supported by untransplantable legal or political culture – is sought to be adopted.

Without insisting too much on the horticultural metaphor (since metaphors in the law should not be allowed to assume a life of their own), transplants take, roughly speaking, at least three different forms.

The first is the transplantation of substantial parts of a legal system to rule a subjugated country. Such was the movement of English law into Australia, New Zealand, India and North America and of Roman law into central Europe. This type of transplantation often accompanies the movement of a whole culture or population or demographic group from one part of the world to another. For better or worse, it is generally an act of legal imperialism.

The second is the transplantation of rules and principles which seem to work well in their country of origin, in the hope that their effects will be duplicated in their receiving country and will solve identified problems there.[12] Such a transplant is motivated by internal concerns in the receiving state; in this sense the recourse to foreign laws is an indigenous development. In other senses this is a problematic form of legal growth since a law or set of laws will inevitably operate differently in different legal cultures. Success will depend on how ambitious the transplant is, how similar it is to existing legal structures, and how carefully it is bedded down.

The third form of transplantation – and the most relevant here – is that which is mediated through a multilateral treaty. This form of

---

[9] Ibid., xviii: 'England, Sweden, Norway and other countries, which have not been immediately exposed to [Roman law] ... certainly have the retention of indigenous laws to thank for many valuable advantages in their community life' (my translation).

[10] Watson, *Legal Transplants*, 95–6.

[11] Kahn-Freund, 'On uses and misuses of comparative law', 27.

[12] Some would call the suggested incorporation of the 'fair use' concept into Australian copyright law a transplant of this kind. For discussion of the suggestion see Australian Law Reform Commission (ALRC), Copyright and the Digital Economy, Report No. 122 (2013), chs 4 and 5.

transplantation has been common over the last century, with the material to be transplanted not sourced directly from the law of another state. Rather, the principles to which the source laws give effect are formulated in an agreed form, often after long periods of negotiation, with member states agreeing to enact counterpart provisions in their own domestic laws. The purpose may be harmonisation of world or regional law, for the better functioning of the world community. More precisely, in the case of the main IP treaties, the purpose is the softening of the effect of jurisdictional boundaries and the enabling of cross-border litigation. A secondary purpose is the exportation of social norms, in this case a heightened respect for the act of authorship.

Such treaties are driven by the exporters of law. The transplant is to a greater or lesser degree imposed by the source states on the newer state parties in return for the benefits of treaty membership. But due to negotiating pressures even older state parties, which have participated at the negotiation stage, find themselves bound by provisions that are not necessarily in the form they would have chosen. This is the case with moral rights law.

5.3   From Source Countries to Treaty, the Intermediate Step

The legal transplantation of moral rights into Australia was initiated by their adoption, in article 6*bis*, into the Berne Convention for the Protection of Literary and Artistic Works (Berne Convention),[13] achieved largely through the work of the Italian delegation at and before the 1928 Rome Revision Conference. The formulation of article 6*bis* at Rome was crucial to the future success of the rights. At this point the antecedents of article 6*bis* were already well established in France, Germany, Italy and other European states. However, each of these countries had constructed the moral right differently, so that there was no one doctrine or rule to export. In France it was initially a creature of jurisprudence and was perpetual;[14] in Germany it was developed doctrinally and legislatively and had limited duration.[15] Jurists in these countries conceived of it as a single 'droit moral' or 'authorial personality right'.[16]

---

[13] Berne Convention for the Protection of Literary and Artistic Works, opened for signature 9 September 1886, 828 UNTS 221 (entered into force 5 December 1887), as amended.
[14] Henri Desbois, *Le droit d'auteur en France*, 3rd ed. (Paris: Dalloz, 1978), p. 470.
[15] KUG of 9 January 1907 § 25, LUG of 19 June 1907 § 29.
[16] The jurist Josef Kohler in Germany had classified it as an *Individualrecht*, Otto von Gierke as a *Persönlichkeitsrecht*. The French jurist André Morillot used the term *droit moral*.

Across Europe it was composed of a variety of prerogatives expressed in wording that was individual to each national legal system.

The formulation chosen by the Berne negotiators was a reworking of the source concepts. A singular and inclusive concept had fragmented, and some of its component prerogatives – for example, the right of withdrawal,[17] the right to release the work to the public[18] or the right to continue making changes to the work[19] – had been discarded. The negotiators had committed themselves to certain core values, fixing the rights in an apolitical form and making no assumptions about a recipient country's administrative or legal structures.

The values on which all parties could agree were the essential independence of the moral rights from the economic rights, the fact that they would remain with the author despite any copyright transfer, that the author should have a right to be associated by name with his or her work and that certain 'derogatory' alterations to the work, 'prejudicial' to the author's honour or reputation, should be actionable. The notions of *honour* and *reputation* were an elaboration, for the benefit of the common law countries, of the broad and unfamiliar civil law concept of an author's 'intellectual' or 'moral' interests.[20] The duration provision was a compromise between continental European and common law positions, allowing considerable flexibility.[21] Means of redress were thrown open to be determined by individual member states according to their existing legal systems.[22]

In combining brevity with some detail, article 6*bis* of the Berne Convention stood halfway between doctrine and regulation. The fact that its wording has never been adopted in France or Germany for their authorial rights indicates how little it reflected their ways of imagining the rights. To them it was not an improvement or a clarification. But to the common law countries it was the essential precondition to the acceptance of rights of whose virtues those countries' legislators remained to be convinced.

The fixation of moral rights in treaty form created for member states an obligation to the international community not to deviate from these principles in their treatment of foreign, if not domestic, authors. Moreover, rules of treaty interpretation require that attention be given to more than the bare words of the agreement, including, in some cases,

---

[17] Italy, Decree 1950 of 7 November 1925, art. 15.
[18] Poland, Law of 29 March 1926, art. 58.   [19] Hungary, Law LIV of 1921, art. 3.
[20] Sam Ricketson, *The Berne Convention for the Protection of Literary and Artistic Works: 1886–1986* (London: Centre for Commercial Law Studies, Queen Mary College: Kluwer, 1987), pp. 461–2 [8.98].
[21] Ibid., 462 [8.98].   [22] Ibid., 102 [3.28].

Of Moral Rights and Legal Transplants 69

supplementary means of interpretation such as the preparatory work for the treaty.[23] Since statutes which give effect to treaty obligations are to be interpreted in Australia in ways not inconsistent with those obligations,[24] the input of civil law countries during treaty formation remains of relevance to domestic courts. There remains, in other words, an attenuated but active connection between the transplant and the originating legal cultures, despite the intervention of the treaty. Moreover, the capacity of the transplant to mutate once incorporated in domestic law is greatly restricted.

5.4   The Final Step: Connecting Moral Rights to Australian Copyright

In Australia, moral rights came into force in late 2000, when the final act of connection between the existing Australian law and the legal transplant took place. Events of the preceding decades had prepared legal, artistic and commercial communities for the introduction of those rights. Interest groups had been repeatedly consulted,[25] discussion papers issued,[26] reports prepared,[27] bills drafted.[28] Legislators had before them the example of UK moral rights law and, to the extent that it was relevant, US law as well as the laws of European countries. Overseas experts had given reasoned expression in Australia to their support for moral rights.[29] Sam Ricketson too, among others, had published several articles pointing out Australia's international obligations to provide for

---

[23] Vienna Convention on the Law of Treaties, opened for signature 23 May 1969, 1155 UNTS 331 (entered into force 27 January 1980) arts. 31, 32.
[24] *Polites* v. *Commonwealth* (1945) 70 CLR 60, 77 (Dixon J) and 79 (McTiernan J).
[25] At, inter alia, the Australian Copyright Council, Australia Council National Symposium on Moral Rights (29-30 November 1979), the Moral Rights Consultation Forum (18 August 1998) and the Legal and Constitutional Legislation Committee Discussion (18-19 August 1997).
[26] Copyright Law Review Committee (CLRC), *Discussion Paper – Moral Rights* (Canberra: Australian Government Publishing Service, 1984); Commonwealth of Australia, Discussion Paper – Proposed Moral Rights Legislation for Copyright Creators (1994); Australian Copyright Council, Moral Rights Bill. A Discussion Paper (2000).
[27] CLRC, *Report on Moral Rights* (Canberra: Australian Government Publishing Service, 1988); Senate Legal and Constitutional Legislation Committee, Consideration of Legislation Referred to the Committee, Copyright Amendment Bill 1997 (1997).
[28] Copyright Amendment Bill 1997 (Cth); Copyright Amendment (Moral Rights) Bill 1999 (Cth).
[29] David Vaver, 'Authors' moral rights and the Copyright Law Review Committee's report: W[h]ither such rights now?' (1988) 14 *Monash University Law Review* 284; Jane C Ginsburg, 'Moral rights in a common law system' in Peter Anderson and David Saunders (eds.), *Moral Rights Protection in a Copyright System* (Brisbane: Institute for Cultural Policy Studies, Griffith University, 1992).

moral rights, the benefits of the rights and their consistency with established, but insufficient, legal principles.[30] His was a particularly persuasive voice in this debate, his previously published treatise on the Berne Convention[31] giving Australian legislators important insights into the drafting of article 6*bis*. This work both guided the domestic drafting of the rights and was likely to assist in any future interpretation of the provisions.

It is useful at this point to return to some of the questions that recur in transplantation literature: First, did the methods used to effect the transplantation involve alterations to the basic concepts of moral rights? Second were the receiving legal structures affected by the transplant? Finally, how effective was the transplant in achieving the ends it was meant to achieve?

5.5   Distortions to Moral Rights?

At first sight, the moral rights provisions in Australia are extraordinary by civil law or even Berne standards. No country in the world has elaborated them to the extent that this country has. The abstract doctrines of their source countries have been replaced by an exhaustive set of statutory rules. Taking the key concepts from article 6*bis* of the Berne Convention, the legislators reimagined them in an Australian legal context and gave them the characteristics of Australian statutory rights. Certain rights would be given; those rights would be elaborated as fully and clearly as possible, thereby defining most of the indicia of infringement. Additional statements of infringement would also be supplied. A range of defences would be provided to screen out from infringement some desirable uses of the copyright material. Duration would be spelled out, as would the parties to exercise the rights. The rights would apply to the existing Australian categories of works, as well as to films. Wholesale carve-outs – of groups of authors or of copyright material – were avoided. Such carve-outs would have seemed unnecessarily defensive in a country where, thanks partly to Sam Ricketson's groundwork, there was little hostility to the rights.

Concepts already familiar from copyright law were used to connect the moral rights to their new environment. Existing notions of authorship,

---

[30] See especially Sam Ricketson, 'The case for moral rights' (1995) 25 *Intellectual Property Forum* 37; Sam Ricketson, 'Is Australia in breach of its international obligations with respect to the protection of moral rights?' (1990) 17(3) *Melbourne University Law Review* 462; Sam Ricketson, 'Moral rights and the droit de suite: International conditions and Australian obligations' (1990) 3 *Entertainment Law Review* 78.
[31] Ricketson, *The Berne Convention*.

developed in Australian case law, were evidently meant to be used to identify the recipients of the rights except in cases where the rights extended to 'unauthored' material. The rights were to apply, like copyright, to 'substantial parts' of works as well as to works in their entirety.[32] The attributable acts, giving rise to the need for attribution, were acts which, for the most part, were already familiar from the list of copyright prerogatives.[33] The right against 'false attribution' was able to take meaning from the falsity concept used in other areas of law.[34] The word *reputation*, taken from article 6*bis* of Berne, appeared to connect, though in as yet unclear ways, to defamation law. Any conflict with civil law or Berne concepts of reputation was left for the courts to deal with. A 'reasonableness' defence[35] in some respects resembled existing ways of softening the force of statutory rights, though it left much room for further judicial development.

Statements of purpose also needed to be made to persuade Parliament of the merits of the legislation, to guide its interpretation and to establish the normative aspects of the transplant. In Parliament it was stated that:

[This bill] is about acknowledging the great importance of respect for the integrity of creative behaviour. At its most basic, the bill is a recognition of the importance to Australian culture of literary, artistic, musical and dramatic works and of those who create them.[36]

This statement of purpose was probably the least effective aspect of the rights' introduction. Although the necessary votes were garnered, the statement failed to focus on the wrongs to be remedied by the provisions or the practical advantages to be gained by their introduction.[37]

It is clear that the acclimatisation effected by the Australian drafting has produced a set of rights differently configured within the law from those of Europe. In that sense the modes of operation of the rights have

---

[32] Copyright Act 1968 (Cth) ss. 14, 195AZH.   [33] Copyright Act 1968 (Cth) s. 31.
[34] *Meskenas* v. *ACP Publishing Pty Ltd* (2006) 70 IPR 172 [20], citing *Murphy* v. *Farmer* (1988) 165 CLR 19.
[35] Copyright Act 1968 (Cth) ss. 195AR, 195AS.
[36] Commonwealth, Parliamentary Debates, House of Representatives, 8 December 1999, 13026 (Daryl Williams, Attorney-General).
[37] State moral rights–type legislation in the US, by contrast, is much more direct in this respect. For example, the preamble to the 1987 Pennsylvania Fine Art Preservation Act goes straight to the point: '1) The careers and professional reputations of artists depend on the physical integrity of their works of fine art. ... 3) The act of altering, defacing, mutilating or destroying a work of fine art jeopardizes and can cause irreparable damage to the professional and economic interests of the artist. 4) In order to protect artists, and ultimately preserve art for the benefit and enjoyment of the public, it is necessary to afford artists certain legal rights and remedies in relation to their works of fine art': Pa Stat Ann §§ 2101–2110 (Purdon 1988).

changed. On the other hand, there is little evidence that moral rights as agreed to by the Berne negotiators have been significantly altered in Australia. Australia has given to foreign authors, for the most part, a set of actionable rights bearing an acceptable resemblance to the rights they enjoy at home. If there is an exception to this it may arise from the question of alienability and consent. Though article 6*bis* does not in terms describe a fully inalienable right, it may be argued that the negotiating parties intended it to do so. While Australia shied away at the last minute from allowing the rights to be subject to waiver, it allowed for such far-reaching consent by the rights holder as to be tantamount to an alienation of the rights.[38]

5.6 Effects on Australian Copyright Culture

But have 'irritations' been set up in the body of Australian copyright law? Have the rights prompted adaptations of or alterations or challenges to it? At one level, their introduction certainly encourages new analysis of well-established concepts. At another level, aspects of the moral rights may point towards future directions in copyright law.

One concept which the moral rights provisions have challenged is that of the 'substantial part', which introduces flexibility into questions of infringement. When the legislators incorporated substantiality into the moral rights provisions they did so independently of European or Berne influence. This inclusion was not discussed in the explanatory materials, leaving uncertainty about whether or not the legislators intended a neat overlap with substantiality for copyright purposes. Where a substantial part of a work has been taken by a copyright infringer, does the same method of calculating substantiality apply when attention turns to potential moral rights infringement in the same case? It should not do so, since 'substantial part' is measured taking into account the interests protected by the rights in question,[39] and moral rights interests diverge sharply from copyright interests.[40] The drafting of this transplant prompts a heightened awareness of the interest-dependent nature of the substantiality concept and the importance of differentiating the two sets of rights.

---

[38] Copyright Act 1968 (Cth) ss. 195AW, 195AWA.
[39] Discussion of the interests protected, and hence what value has been usurped by the infringer, is common in cases concerning non-work subject matters. See, e.g., *Network Ten Pty Ltd* v. *TCN Channel Nine* (2004) 218 CLR 273 and the associated Federal Court judgments in this litigation.
[40] For further discussion of this issue see Elizabeth Adeney, 'Moral rights and substantiality: Some questions of integration' (2002) 13(1) *Australian Intellectual Property Journal* 5.

Of Moral Rights and Legal Transplants 73

In the transplantation of moral rights into Australian law, an awkward reclassification of films occurred. Normally classified as 'subject matter other than works' under Australian law,[41] they were reclassified, for the purpose of moral rights only, as 'works', the classification that they carry in the Berne Convention.[42] This allowed them to be seen as having authors. If one were looking for an irritant which could have future consequences, this is surely a prime example. The awkwardness of the incomplete reclassification invites law reform that would include films, for copyright purposes as well, into the 'works' category. Where a film is a product of the intellect, it is difficult to see why it would be denied the 'work' status in an Act which is content to classify any and every photograph as a work.

Since moral rights are deeply personal to the author, a further effect of the transplant is that renewed emphasis is placed on the humanity and intellectuality of authorship.[43] It would be highly undesirable for a rift to open up between copyright law and moral rights law on the question of what constitutes authorship. Thus the introduction of moral rights inevitably helps to fix and maintain authorship in a form requiring 'independent intellectual effort', subsuming the tests of 'sweat of the brow' or 'industrious collection'.[44] Such subsumption is not a product of moral rights, since it predates their introduction by many decades, but the adoption of moral rights strongly reinforces the point.

Moral rights pose a further question for copyright law in having introduced the new defence of reasonableness into the Act. An act or omission may not infringe certain moral rights if it is reasonable in the circumstances.[45] The defence is notable for being both standard based and open ended,[46] and allows courts to exercise a broad discretion in their decision making. The provision is therefore a trail-blazer in Australian copyright law, where suggestions for an open-ended defence to copyright infringement have so far been ignored by government, despite

---

[41] Copyright Act 1968 (Cth) pt IV ('Copyright in Subject-Matter Other Than Works').
[42] Berne Convention, art. 2(1) (as amended by Paris text, 1971).
[43] Copyright Act 1968 (Cth) s. 190.
[44] *IceTV Pty Ltd* v. *Nine Network Australia Pty Ltd* (2009) 239 CLR 458, 474 [33] (French CJ, Crennan J and Kiefel J), citing *Sands & McDougall Pty Ltd* v. *Robinson* (1917) 23 CLR 49, 52 (Isaacs J).
[45] Copyright Act 1968 (Cth) ss. 195AR, 195AS.
[46] The ALRC has noted that standards- or principles-based provisions are increasing in Australian law: ALRC, Copyright and the Digital Economy, 99 [4.57], citing consumer protection and privacy legislation.

the perceived inadequacy of the present purpose-oriented fair-dealing defences.[47]

While not itself a transplant, 'reasonableness' rolls into one word the mechanisms that are used around the world to soften the effect of moral rights. It particularly resembles in its effects the German 'balancing of interests', setting off the interests of the author against opposing property or commercial interests.[48] In its operation it resembles the US fair use defence, listing criteria which tribunals must apply when considering reasonableness.[49] In fact two of the applicable considerations appear to have been transplanted from that source: the nature of the work and the purpose of the use. This transplantation is of the least contentious kind, however, since no more is taken than the idea of the indicative list and non-specific wording. The fair use concept with its penumbra of jurisprudence is not taken.

Most important is what effect the introduction of this open-ended defence will have on Australian copyright law in the long term. For many years the Australian government has been considering how to render the defences to copyright infringement more responsive to community expectations in the digital age. The adoption of a US-style fair use exception into Australian law has been recommended by the Australian Law Reform Commission.[50] Against this background, the pre-existence of the reasonableness defence issues a couple of challenges. First, it challenges the opposition to standard-based defences, demonstrating how such an open-ended defence might be constructed without causing perceptible problems in its legal environment. Second, its existence challenges the abovementioned preference, in the copyright context, for a US-style fair use defence over an indigenous reasonableness defence.[51]

For the most part, the Australian legislators chose in 2000 to draft the moral rights provisions in the familiar language of copyright law, evidently seeing virtue in knitting the two systems as closely together as possible. Applying the same principle of unification, a new copyright defence could be drafted in language already adopted in moral rights law. To be sure, distinctions would need to be made between what is

---

[47] As early as 1998, the CLRC recommended the replacement of the present defences: CLRC, *Simplification of the Copyright Act 1968* (1998) [2.01]–[2.03], a point reiterated by the ALRC in 2013.
[48] This jurisprudential principle applies particularly to the § 14 right of integrity: Adolf Dietz and Alexander Peukert, '§14 Entstellung des Werkes' in Gerhard Schricker and Ulrich Loewenheim (eds.), *Urheberrecht: Kommentar*, 5th ed. (Munich: Beck, 2017), pp. 372–4 [26]–[34].
[49] 17 USC §107. [50] ALRC, *Copyright and the Digital Economy*, 87 [4.1].
[51] Ibid., 87–9 [4.1]–[4.13], which strongly favours fair use.

reasonable for moral rights purposes and what is reasonable for copyright purposes, taking into account the interests protected. But this would be no more complex than differentiating substantiality in the two fields. In this way Australian law could grow from this largely indigenous seed, borrowing ideas from the fair use doctrine where desirable, but refraining from transplanting the term *fair use* which has been developed for application in a substantially different legal framework.

5.7 The Success or Otherwise of the Transplant

The previous discussion was speculative, based on little Australian moral rights jurisprudence. This in itself is surprising, given that more than eighteen years have elapsed since the Berne concept of moral rights was introduced into Australian law. Dramatically less litigation has been generated in Australia than in the source countries of France or Germany over the same period.[52] On this evidence, some might view the rights as a failed transplant.

From the point of view of authors in other Berne member states, for whom these provisions were primarily introduced, the rights are functional. The two successful litigations[53] reassure foreign authors that moral rights may be utilised in Australia; Australia is, in broad terms, compliant with its treaty obligations. The paucity of litigation also indicates that parties are arranging their position on moral rights at a sub-litigation level. A normal contract in the arts industry now contains moral rights provisions. Although most authors remain in a poor negotiating position, parties are forced to give express attention to the rights when dealing with each other.[54]

On the other hand, the development of the rights has been held back by the failure of the provisions to generate high-level judicial interpretation, litigation having occurred only at the lowest level of the federal court structure. The exercise of the rights is not a familiar part of legal practice and cannot yet produce predictable outcomes. This self-perpetuating lack of case law may be contributed to by the efficacy of the consent provisions and the relative breadth of the – still scarcely

---

[52] In Germany, more than ten published judgments in moral rights matters have appeared in the last three years alone, two of them in the highest court, the Federal Court of Justice (BGH).
[53] *Meskenas* v. *ACP Publishing Pty Ltd* (2006) 70 IPR 172; *Perez* v. *Fernandez* (2012) 260 FLR 1.
[54] On the questions raised by publishing contracts see Francina Cantatore and Jane Johnston, 'Moral rights: Exploring the myths, meanings and misunderstandings in Australian copyright law' (2016) 21(1) *Deakin Law Review* 71.

tested[55] – reasonableness defence. Litigation is also expensive, and the risk of the author having to bear the opponent's costs in an unsuccessful action is daunting. Perhaps, too, the values protected by the rights – the author's interest in name, honour and reputation – are insufficiently established in Australian creative culture for an investment in risky litigation to seem worthwhile.

5.8 Conclusion

Legal transplantation incrementally universalises law and the norms it embodies. By and large this is to be welcomed in an increasingly networked world, though the need for laws to reflect the special concerns of individual nations also remains strong. The incorporation of moral rights into the laws of most common law countries, including Australia, was an exceptionally attenuated process, effected through the substantial detachment of the rights, by international treaty, from their original legal contexts and their fixation in principles that were required to be reproduced, without deviation, in domestic laws. When the rights came to be drafted for use in Australia, much effort was put into connecting them to the copyright culture and provisions already in place. Less effort was put into articulating the practical purposes of the rights. In 2019 the rights are still a mere seedling in the vast copyright plantation of this country. Whether the digital future will see the rights grow into a sturdy protector of authorship remains to be seen.

---

[55] The concept received only limited discussion in the *Meskenas* judgment, where it was decided that the inadvertence of a failure to attribute authorship did not, in the circumstances, satisfy the test of reasonableness: *Meskenas v. ACP Publishing Pty Ltd* (2006) 70 IPR 172 [18].

Part II

Across Jurisdictions

6 People Not Machines
Authorship and What It Means in International Copyright Law

*Jane C Ginsburg**

6.1 Introduction

Artificial intelligence has invaded the legal and popular imagination. Countless colloquia,[1] news articles[2] and entertainment offerings[3] project a future in which AI will guide (if not take over) endeavors from the

---

* Many thanks for expert research assistance to Luke Budiardjo, Columbia Law School class of 2018. Thanks also to Andrew McWhorter, Columbia Law School class of 2019 for additional research. A shorter version of this essay appeared as an editorial in IIC – *International Intellectual Property and Competition Law* (February 2018).
[1] See, e.g., Common Law for the Age of AI (symposium) (2019) *Columbia Law Review*, in press; Colloquium on Artificial Intelligence, American Intellectual Property Law Association, March 2019; The Future of Work in the Age of AI (The Atlantic Festival), *The Atlantic*, 2 October 2018, retrieved from http://ageofaiwork.theatlantic.com; Surviving the A.I. Surge: Artificial Intelligence and the Practice of Law (symposium) (February 2018) *South Carolina Law Review*; Hack to the Future: How Technology Is Disrupting the Legal Profession (symposium) February 2018 *University of Miami Law Review*.
[2] See, e.g., Jake Swearingen, 'A.I. is flying drones (very, very slowly)', *New York Times*, 26 March 2019, retrieved from https://nyti.ms/2UXqAlt; Eric Niiler, 'Can AI be a fair judge in court? Estonia thinks so', *Wired*, 25 March 2019, retrieved from www.wired.com/story/can-ai-be-fair-judge-court-estonia-thinks-so; Jaclyn Peiser, 'The rise of the robot reporter', *New York Times*, 5 February 2019, retrieved from https://nyti.ms/2UJq7w1; Gabe Cohn, 'Up for bid, AI art signed "Algorithm"', *New York Times*, 22 October 2018, retrieved from https://nyti.ms/2R99M1S; Noam Scheiber, 'High-skilled white collar work? Machines can do that, too', *New York Times*, 7 July 2018, retrieved from https://nyti.ms/2NuLxtU.
[3] For examples of motion pictures, television shows, and books depicting AI-influenced futures, see, e.g., *Blade Runner 2049* (Alcon Entertainment, 2017); *Avengers: Age of Ultron* (Marvel Studios, 2015); *Interstellar* (Legendary Pictures, 2014); *Ex Machina* (Film4 & DNA Films, 2014); *Her* (Annapurna Pictures, 2013); *WALL-E* (Walt Disney Pictures, 2008); *A.I. Artificial Intelligence* (Warner Bros, 2001); *The Matrix* (Warner Bros, 1999); *Ghost in the Shell* (Production I.G., 1995); *The Terminator* (Orion Pictures, 1984); *2001: A Space Odyssey* (Metro-Goldwyn-Mayer, 1968); *Westworld* (HBO Entertainment, 2016); *Black Mirror: White Christmas* (Zeppotron, 2014); *Almost Human* (Frequency Films, 2013); *Futurama: Space Pilot 3000* (The Curiosity Company, 1999). See also Philip K Dick, *Do Androids Dream of Electric Sheep?* (New York: Doubleday, 1968); Robert A Heinlein, *The Moon Is a Harsh Mistress* (London: Dennis Dobson, 1966); Isaac Asimov, *I, Robot* (New York: Gnome Press, 1950).

79

menial to the mentally intensive. If AI will direct the legal, business and medical professions, will it also supplant authors? And if computers come to replace human authors in the generation of music, art, literature and audiovisual works, would (or should) their outputs still be 'original works of authorship' endowed with copyright protection?

In 1992 Sam Ricketson anticipated this question when he delivered the annual Manges Lecture at Columbia Law School, presciently titled 'People or Machines: The Berne Convention and the Changing Concept of Authorship'.[4] The title allowed a double meaning: either the concept of authorship in the Berne Convention[5] could accommodate both people and machines or, on the contrary, only one of those could be an author, and the holder of that status could not be the machine. As Ricketson systematically developed the inquiry, it became clear that 'People or Machines' in fact meant 'People *Not* Machines'. More than twenty-five years later, with the ensuing evolution of machines capable of generating outputs often indistinguishable from human-authored works, I suggest that conclusion remains correct, perhaps even more urgently so than in 1992.

This essay briefly recapitulates Ricketson's analysis and then considers whether subsequent technological developments warrant reconsideration of the human authorship premise underlying the Berne Convention. If that premise holds firm, the next question is whether non-human-generated outputs in fact require some form of intellectual property protection. Any such regime, it should be noted, would fall outside the Berne Convention.

6.2 People or Machines

In his 1992 article, Ricketson acknowledged that the Berne Convention did not define authorship, but contended that 'there was nonetheless a basic agreement between the contracting states as to the meaning of the term, and, because of this, it was thought unnecessary to define it ... it seems only logical to interpret "authors" and "authorship" for the

---

[4] Revised and published at (1991) 16 Columbia-VLA Journal of Law & Arts 1. Ricketson elaborated further on the theme of human authorship in his commentary 'The need for human authorship – Australian developments: *Telstra Corp Ltd v Phone Directories Co Pty Ltd*'(2012) 34(1) *European Intellectual Property Review* 54.
[5] Berne Convention for the Protection of Literary and Artistic Works, opened for signature 9 September 1886, 828 UNTS 221 (entered into force 5 December 1887), as amended (cited as Berne Convention).

purposes of the Convention as pertaining to the persons who created such works'.[6] Moreover, surveying Berne's text, Ricketson found that the leitmotiv of human authorship undergirded most of the articles of the convention.[7] Thus, with respect to copyright term: '[T]he general term of protection in article 7(1) is made dependent upon the life of the author ... and such a provision would be inappropriate in the case of non-human entities, which may have an infinite existence.'[8] Similarly, the protection of moral rights assumes human authorship: '[T]he requirements with respect to the protection of moral rights ... make no sense other than in relation to human authors.'[9]

Arguably, Berne's commitment to human authorship wavers with respect to certain subject matter, notably photographic and cinematographic works. Berne accords a lesser minimum term to photographs, twenty-five years from creation, rather than fifty years *post mortem auctoris* (pma).[10] This might suggest that the intervention of a machine in the creative process may render those works less human, and therefore less 'authored'. Ricketson observed that the 'quantum of "authorial presence" [in photographs] is ... highly variable'.[11] A proposal during the 1948 revision process to protect 'photographic works or works realized by an analogous process to photography which constitute intellectual creations, but with the exception of ordinary photographic productions' endeavoured to distinguish photographs of questionable authorship.[12] Nonetheless, the drafters ultimately abandoned the reference to 'intellectual creation' as 'unnecessary in view of the fact that this restriction was already implied by the term "literary and artistic works"'.[13] In other words, 'literary and artistic works' already incorporate a prerequisite of original human authorship. If an 'ordinary photographic production' lacks original authorship, there is no need to accumulate bases of exclusion.

In regard to cinematographic works, these are 'subject to the same general, though unstated, requirement of human authorship and intellectual creation as the other works listed in article 2(1). ... [But the provision on cinematographic works] is the one clear instance in Convention history where the concept of "authorship" has received explicit consideration, with the consequence that Union countries may treat

---

[6] Ricketson, 'People or machines', 8.   [7] Ibid., 21.   [8] Ibid., 11.   [9] Ibid.
[10] See Berne Convention, art. 7(4).   [11] Ricketson, 'People or machines', 13.
[12] Ibid. See also Marcel Plaisant, 'General report on the work of the Brussels Diplomatic Conference for the Revision of the Berne Convention, June 26, 1948' in World Intellectual Property Organization (WIPO), *Berne Convention Centenary 1886–1986*, WIPO publication No 877(E), (Geneva, 1986), p. 179.
[13] Ricketson, 'People or machines', 13.

someone other than a natural person as the author of such works'.[14] The revisions adopted at the Stockholm Revision Conference of 1967 'implicitly acknowledge that member countries are free to confer initial ownership of copyright on persons other than the author or co-authors of cinematographic films and thereby accept the position of [countries] which ... [grant] these rights to the maker of the film[, who] may very well be a non-natural person [like a corporate entity]. ... [T]his special treatment of cinematographic works serves to underscore the general principle that authorship is limited to natural persons [under the Berne Convention]'.[15]

Ricketson found further evidence of the Berne Convention's human author-orientation in its exclusion of 'productions by a collective enterprise'. These 'quite clearly fall outside the scope of the Convention, even though they may utilize high inputs of other literary and artistic works. Thus, sound recordings and broadcasts have been traditionally refused access to the magic circle of Berne protection. ... [T]he real reasons [for this exclusion] are twofold: first, the difficulty of actually identifying the human creators responsible for the production in question, and, second, doubts as to whether their contributions, if ascertainable, can really be termed "intellectual"'.[16]

Ricketson next considered the then-recent 1991 WIPO Proposal for Protection of Computer-Produced Works: Because some works produced by computers involve 'numerous' human contributions, which

merge into the totality of the works in such a way, that it is difficult or impossible to recognize each contribution and its individual author separately, ... the International Bureau proposed to the First Session of the Committee of Experts that original ownership of copyright in such a work should vest in the physical or legal entity who undertook the arrangements necessary for the creation of the work; that such works should not enjoy moral rights protection; and that their term of protection should be fifty years from the date of production or twenty-five years from this date in the case of computer-produced works of applied art.[17]

The Committee of Experts eventually 'judged that it would be premature to deal with such works in a possible protocol'.[18]

---

[14] Ibid., 15.   [15] Ibid., 16.   [16] Ibid., 22.
[17] Ibid., 28–9, quoting WIPO, 'Committee of experts on a possible protocol to the Berne Convention for the protection of literary and artistic works', presented at Questions Concerning a Possible Protocol to the Berne Convention, first session, in WIPO Doc BCP/CE/1/2, 4–8 November 1991, p. 18 (internal quotation marks omitted) (cited as WIPO Committee of Experts).
[18] Ricketson, 'People or machines', 30, quoting WIPO Committee of Experts, 16–17. The 'possible protocol' became the 1996 WIPO Copyright Treaties, which do not address

Ricketson observed that the 1991 WIPO proposal assumed that these computer-aided productions did have human authors, but that it was impossible to identify their individual contributions:

> These proposals ... would have vested [the initial ownership of rights] in a person who might well be a legal entity and whose claim to entitlement derived essentially from ownership or control of a machine – the computer. The rationale for this approach ... was the difficulty of identifying the actual human contributors to the work.[19]

But, anticipating the accomplishments of today's algorithm-driven productions, Ricketson cautioned:

> This reference to human contributors, however, may well prove fanciful as the development of expert systems and artificial intelligence increases the likelihood of the creation of purely computer-generated works. Indeed, we may already be at this stage in the case of electronic data bases where the work of compilation and assembly can be carried out in accordance with the operation of specifically designed computer programs. In such instances, the notion of human contribution becomes meaningless, unless traced back to the creator of the data base program or expert system. ... such productions ... lack the necessary requirements for recognition as works of authorship under the Berne Convention.[20]

Ricketson pushed his forceful defense of human authorship further:

> In light of the general propositions put forward concerning the concept of authorship under the Berne Convention, one might query whether there still remains much in this 'soul' [of copyright] worth protecting. ... [One might argue that we should] declare that copyright is not really concerned with the protection of the fruits of human authorship, but only concerned with the question of commercial value, however that value is embodied or arrived at ... such a change ... would make it possible to bring all new forms of technological

---

computer-generated works: World Intellectual Property Organization Copyright Treaty, opened for signature 20 December 1996, 2186 UNTS 121 (entered into force 6 March 2002) and World Intellectual Property Organization Performances and Phonograms Treaty, opened for signature 20 December 1996, 2186 UNTS 203 (entered into force 20 May 2002).

[19] Ricketson, 'People or machines', 29.

[20] Ibid. The initial WIPO proposal drew heavily from then-recent British legislation specifically extending protection to computer-generated works. The Copyright, Designs and Patents Act of 1988 (UK) c. 48 grants protection to "'literary, dramatic, musical or artistic works that are computer-generated", a term which is defined as "meaning a work generated by a computer 'in circumstances such that there is no human author of the work'. The author of such a work is then stated to be the 'person by whom the arrangements necessary for the creation of the work are undertaken'. The term of protection for such works is a fixed period of fifty years from the date of production, and they do not enjoy moral rights" Ibid., 29, quoting Copyright, Designs and Patents Act 1988 (UK) c. 48, ss. 178, 9(3), 12(3), 79(2)(c), 81(2).

creation within the broad umbrella of the Berne Convention ... rather than [adopting] tailor-made ... sui generis protection [for these new forms of creation] . ... While this suggested approach appears attractive in a pragmatic sense, I do not believe that we should move in this way ... there are powerful arguments, both in principle and necessity, in favor of retaining this human-centered notion of authorship and authors' rights.[21]

Moreover, '[t]he human-centered notion of authorship presently enshrined in the Berne Convention embodies a fundamental human right, namely that of the creator over the work he or she creates'.[22] Referencing the affirmations of the authorship right on the occasion of the 100th anniversary of the Berne Convention, Ricketson contended:

> the specific prescriptions of the Berne Convention ... derive from [the] fundamental conception of authorship as a human activity and a human right. It therefore distorts this conception to extend protection to other forms of creation that do not have identifiable human authors, ... or where the rights are initially vested in a person who may well not be a human being.[23]

6.3 'Purely Computer-Generated Works'?

Ricketson anticipated the prospect of works whose authorship would be difficult to establish, not because of a plethora of human and non-human

---

[21] Ibid., 33–4. [22] Ibid., 34.
[23] Ibid., quoting Berne Convention, art. 1; the International Covenant on Economic, Social and Cultural Rights, opened for signature 16 December 1966, 993 UNTS 3 (entered into force 3 November 1976) art. 15(1); and the declaration adopted by the Assembly of the Berne Union in 1986, reprinted in 22 Copyright 373 (1986).

Ricketson, 'People and machines', 36, urged resistance to the temptation to welcome non-human-authored works into the copyright fold in the hope that a rising tide of copyright protection not only would lift no-authorship boats but also would further elevate human-authored vessels. He rejected the 'slipstream' argument that 'stronger protection for [a broader category of non-human-created works] will automatically lead to stronger protection and increased protection for [the narrower category of human-created works]. [On this view, t]o insist, therefore, on excluding these productions from protection is simply to indulge in pedantic formalism and to deny the passing on of gains to "real authors" ... It is also a case of history repeating itself, when it is remembered that the prime movers for the adoption of the first copyright statute in the United Kingdom were the members of the Stationers' Company who used the claims of authors as a smoke screen for achieving protection of their own interests. This time, however, it could be the authors who use the industrialists and investors as the means of securing their own welfare'. He countered: 'My own view is that ... there is no obvious reason why the best way to advance these interests lies through according the latter the status of authors. ... Some aspects of [protection for non-human-created works] might be excessive or unnecessary ... and authors should benefit just as much from the slipstream effect where producers obtain strong and effective protection under a neighboring rights or sui generis regime as where this occurs as a result of the extension of authors' rights' (at 36–7).

contributors (as WIPO expected) but because of the absence of *any* human whose participation in the computer's output would be sufficiently proximate and original to constitute authorship. In other words, as generative machines become more sophisticated, copyright may face a new category of 'purely computer-generated works' which do not owe their origin to a human author.

Most commonly cited examples of computer-generated works are perhaps better described as 'computer-assisted works' – works created by a human author through the controlled outsourcing of tasks to a sophisticated machine tool.[24] Many of these works do not pose a novel authorship question: the maker of a work produced through the use of a word processor's spell- or grammar-correction feature is clearly the 'author' of the output, just as the sculptor who hires welders to execute a monumental-size version of her model remains the 'author' of the resulting piece. Moreover, even outputs that combine data inputs with a processing program may more appropriately be described as computer-assisted works (rather than truly computer-generated works) because of the persistent human control over the process of the machine's creation.[25] For example, sketches produced by 'Paul', a robotic portraitist trained to create portraits of human subjects, cannot fairly be considered truly computer-generated, even though the sketches may be physically created by a robotic arm – Paul is trained to sketch in the style of its creator and, unlike similar machines,[26] lacks the ability to create its 'own distinct artistic style' or to 'learn' to improve its processes without the intervention of a human programmer, who must precisely define the algorithmic steps necessary to create each sketch.[27] Paul is therefore more similar to one of Damien

---

[24] See, e.g., James Grimmelmann, 'There's no such thing as a computer-authored work – And it's a good thing, too' (2016) 39 *Columbia Journal of Law & Arts* 403.
[25] For example, the 'next Rembrandt' portrait created by selecting and combining features from a database of all of Rembrandt's paintings involves a great deal of sophisticated computer programming, but it is essentially a mash-up produced through persistent human supervision and direction of the inputs. See ING presents *The Next Rembrandt* (film), retrieved from www.nextrembrandt.com.
[26] For example, 'AARON' is a similar artificially intelligent visual artist which produces works after being 'fed knowledge and experience' and learning a 'set of abstract rules that specify the anatomy of the human body'. See Ana Ramalho, 'Will robots rule the (artistic) world?: A proposed model for the legal status of creations by artificial intelligence systems' (2017) 21 *Journal of Internet Law* 1, 13.
[27] 'RoBotticelli: The mechanical marvel creating extraordinary works of art', BBC News, 8 September 2015, retrieved from https://bbc.in/1OcjRWt.

Hirst's or Ai Weiwei's art workers[28] than to a truly creative computer program.

Nonetheless, the development of machines which can produce works through digital neural networks that have 'taught themselves' to combine rules of literary, musical or artistic assembly after being 'trained' on a database of pre-existing works might suggest that truly computer-generated works could be in near prospect. For example, programs exist which compose musical scores by utilising 'deep learning' algorithms to learn from examples of classical music;[29] other programs, such as Juke Deck, devise melodies and generate a full musical composition and performance in response to a user's entry of basic selection criteria like tempo and genre.[30] Google Translate employs a system that 'learns' from experience and improves its algorithm with multiple iterations of its program and which utilises a neural net that is simply 'trained' and is not programmed with specific procedural algorithms or linguistic rules.[31]

If the human intervention in producing these outputs does not exceed requesting the computer to generate a literary, artistic or musical composition of a particular style or genre, the human users do not contribute sufficient 'intellectual creation' to meet minimum standards of

---

[28] Anita Singh, 'Damien Hirst: Assistants make my spot paintings but my heart is in them all', *The Telegraph*, 12 January 2012, retrieved from https://bit.ly/2kuPDsm (noting that even though a team of assistants and art workers, and not the artist himself, generates Hirst's famous 'spot paintings', Hirst still claims that 'every single spot painting contains my eye, my hand and my heart' because he 'controlled every aspect of them coming into being'); Michael Petry, 'Artisans who turn ideas into art: Who pickled Damien Hirst's shark and painted Ai Weiwei's seeds?', *The Independent*, 28 April 2011, retreived from https://bit.ly/2ktjJwc (noting that the '100 million porcelain seeds' making up Ai Weiwei's *Sunflower Seeds* installation at the Tate Modern were 'made by hundreds of skilled people in Jingdezhen, China').

[29] For example, the 'IAMUS' program has produced works of contemporary classical music that human musicians have performed and recorded; see, e.g., Sylvia Smith, 'Iamus: Is this the 21st century's answer to Mozart?', BBC News, 3 January 2013, retrieved from www.bbc.com/news/technology-20889644.

[30] See JukeDeck.com/make, which prompts users to input basic parameters like tempo, genre, instruments, duration and climax and then creates a musical work based on the defined parameters using a neural network trained with musical examples. For a broader survey of recent efforts to implement artificial intelligence techniques in music creation, see Alex Marshall, 'From jingles to pop hits, AI is music to some ears', *New York Times*, 22 January 2017, retrieved from https://nyti.ms/2m1a6p7.

[31] According to the translation program's developers, '[t]he machine is not "analyzing" the data the way that we might, with linguistic rules that identify some of them as nouns and others as verbs. Instead it is shifting and twisting and warping the words around in the map. ... Some of the [developments in Google's translation system were] not done in full consciousness. [The researchers] didn't know themselves why they worked'. Gideon Lewis-Kraus, 'The great AI awakening', *New York Times Magazine*, 14 December 2016, retrieved from www.nytimes.com/2016/12/14/magazine/the-great-ai-awakening.html.

authorship under the Berne Convention. Offline, merely giving a command does not make one an 'author': Pope Julius II may have commissioned the painting of the ceiling of the Sistine Chapel; from a Berne perspective (at the very least), the author of the frescos remains Michelangelo. Were a future Julius IV to instruct a computer to interrogate its comprehensive database of religious art to devise and paint a sequence of Old Testament scenes, that Julius would no more be the author of the output than was his forebear.

Perhaps, then, the authors of the output would be the upstream team of human computer programmers and database designers who created the digital compendium of religious art and provided the machine-learning algorithms that enabled the computer to produce the painted sequence.[32] But if the upstream designers supply a tool without directing its use or knowing what it will be called upon to produce, attributing authorship to them seems akin to denominating the programmers of Microsoft Word the 'authors' of all works produced using that word-processing program. The Old Testament sequence Julius IV ordered may therefore be authorless.[33]

6.4 Consequences for International Copyright

But, if artificial intelligence (AI) at least in some instances, as we have seen, effaces human authorship, what of the copyright status of the outputs? Ricketson adverted to, and repulsed, copyright objectives based in 'commercial value' rather than 'protection of the fruits of human authorship'.[34] Copyright, however, reposes on two pillars (whose respective widths vary in common law and civilian systems): first (generally attributed to civil law states), the natural rights of the author, a rationale that roots exclusive rights in personal creativity and that largely underpins the Berne Convention; and second (most frequently associated with common law countries), incentives to create, to invest in creativity and to disseminate works for the general benefit of society. Protection of commercial value aligns with the latter justification for copyright. But Berne does not completely ignore this basis, as one may infer from its accommodation of producer-ownership of copyright in

---

[32] See *The Next Rembrandt*.
[33] For a detailed analysis of 'authorless' AI-aided outputs, see Jane C Ginsburg and Luke Ali Budiardjo, 'Authors and machines' (2019) 34 *Berkeley Technology Law Journal* 343.
[34] Ricketson, 'People or machines', 33–4.

cinematographic works as well as its provision of shorter terms for works of arguably borderline authorship, such as photographs and applied art.

On the other hand, acknowledging that Berne harbors incentive rationales for copyright is hardly the same thing as contending that Berne embraces a concept of copyright in which incentive/investment rationales supply the *sole* justification for exclusive rights. The latter concept entertains the expulsion of human authors and, given Berne's humanist cast, that would purge copyright of its 'soul'.

Justifications based in incentives to produce works that promote the progress of knowledge might sustain some, certainly less extensive, form of intellectual property protection. The premise underlying incentive justifications – that without a property right, desirable works will not be produced – however, requires substantiation. One must inquire whether computer-aided authorless outputs in fact need the impetus of exclusive rights, or if sufficient other incentives already exist – for example, higher up the chain, through copyright or patent protection of the software programs, patent protection of the specialised machinery to produce works of fine and applied art, copyright or (in the European Union) sui generis protection of the database the software consults, and legal and technological measures to control access to that database. This empirical investigation should be undertaken before any Berne member states beyond the Commonwealth nations that have already emulated the UK approach[35] extend copyright or sui generis protections to purely computer-generated works.

The inquiry necessarily also extends to the nature of the outputs: what kinds of computer-generated works are likely to have significant commercial applications? The market for aleatory music or art may be limited to museums and a few concert venues. Commercially relevant outputs may cluster along the 'low authorship'[36] end of the spectrum: compilations of information, rudimentary news and sports reports, corporate annual reports, virtual (fake?) book reviews for Amazon. Perhaps music-generation systems like JukeDeck would appeal to background music

---

[35] See Robert C Denicola, 'Ex machina: Copyright protection for computer-generated works' (2016) 69 *Rutgers University Law Review* 251 for a survey of national copyright laws in Ireland, New Zealand, South Africa, Hong Kong and India, emulating the Copyright, Designs and Patents Act 1988 (UK) c. 48, s. 9(3) example of denominating as the 'author' of a computer-generated work 'the person by whom the arrangements necessary for the creation of the work are undertaken' and of providing a shorter term of copyright without moral rights.

[36] See Jane C Ginsburg, 'Creation and commercial value: Copyright protection of works of information' (1990) 90 *Columbia Law Review* 1865, 1866, 1870 (defining the term *low authorship* to include 'personality-deprived information compilations such as directories, indexes, and data bases').

services who license anodyne aural ambience for supermarkets and elevators, but even if the licensees of the JukeDeck system select the output criteria, and therefore might claim the closest causal relationship to the generation of the music, the proprietors of the JukeDeck system may have the greater interest in preventing the copying of JukeDeck's rather generic outputs, lest the copyist acquire output that would enable it to forego JukeDeck's services (and compete unfairly with the client who paid for the output). In other words, the thing of value is not so much the work as access to the system that generates it.

Photographic images may furnish another area of potential commercial exploitation: given a big enough database (i.e., Google?), it may be possible for a machine-learning computer on its own to generate images – for example, of a cute kitten that doesn't exist – by searching through and combining the feline features in the database, without the human curation of the compiled elements that characterised the production of the 'next Rembrandt'. Computer-generated images could supplant the perhaps low-end market for images whose salability turns on clear presentation of the subject, rather than on the artistry of the subject's portrayal. As in the case of generic music generation, the primary interest in preventing copying would appear to reside not with the user who requests the generation of the image (assuming that user contributed no creative input of her own), but with the proprietor of the system who would lose customers for additional outputs if they could simply copy prior output.

If it is true that the most interested party is the proprietor of the system, rather than the user who requests the output, then the incentives address not so much the generation of the work as the protection of the systems that produce it. But there may already exist a variety of other incentives to develop and apply the systems. Moreover, while copyright protection offers the social benefit of obliging would-be copiers to create their own works, thus enriching the corpus of works,[37] different users of the AI systems can keep generating the same content; protecting access to and use of the system does not necessarily promote variation in the outputs.[38]

---

[37] See, e.g., Joseph P Fishman, 'Creating around copyright' (2015) 128 *Harvard Law Review* 1333, 1336–7 (arguing that copyright restrictions may encourage further creativity by requiring new creators to create around existing copyrights by generating new non-infringing ideas, and arguing that 'the creative process ... thrives best not under complete freedom, but rather under a moderate amount of restriction').

[38] Were the output protected and its proprietor the user, would instructing the machine to generate the same cute kitten picture as the machine previously produced constitute copying actionable by the prior user? What if the second user simply requested a cute kitten and the machine on its own generated the same image?

If our speculation is correct that commercial applications of AI are most likely to produce outputs which, if human generated, would have been works of low authorship, then a potential irony lurks: in some uncertain future, computers may replace human beings in the production of precisely the kinds of works, such as the 'news of the day', that the Berne Convention excludes from copyright[39] or whose doubtful level of authorship underscored the hesitation of drafters of earlier Berne texts to include within the scope of conventional subject matter.[40] In this scenario, Berne would limit its coverage to works of higher authorship, because the unworthy works' complete lack of human authorship would remove them from the convention's subject matter.

Moreover, because lack of human authorship would disqualify such outputs from Berne subject matter under article 2, other Berne members incur no obligation to protect computer-enabled authorless outputs even if their countries of origin choose to cover them by copyright.[41] One might inquire whether the outputs would nonetheless retain international protection by virtue of the Agreement on Trade-Related Aspects of Intellectual Property Rights (TRIPS Agreement),[42] because that treaty refers to 'rightholders' rather than to authors.[43] Moreover, authors' moral rights cannot be enforced under TRIPS through an intergovernmental dispute resolution proceeding;[44] this preclusion might suggest that TRIPS lacks Berne's commitment to human authorship. But TRIPS incorporates Berne articles 1 to 21[45] and does not purport to apply a lesser threshold of authorship than Berne. On the contrary, where TRIPS resolves an arguable ambiguity in Berne subject matter regarding computer programs, it does so not by distinguishing software from more traditional works of authorship but rather by insisting on its assimilation: computer programs 'shall be protected as literary works under the Berne

---

[39] Berne Convention, art. 2(8) ('The protection of this Convention shall not apply to news of the day or to miscellaneous facts having the character of mere items of press information.').

[40] See generally, Sam Ricketson and Jane C Ginsburg, *International Copyright and Neighbouring Rights: The Berne Convention and Beyond*, 2nd ed. (Oxford: Oxford University Press, 2006), ch. 8 ('Works Protected by the Convention').

[41] See Berne Convention, art. 5(1): 'Authors shall enjoy, *in respect of works for which they are protected under this Convention*, in countries of the Union other than the country of origin, the rights which their respective laws do now or may hereafter grant to their nationals, as well as the rights specially granted by this Convention' (emphasis added).

[42] Marrakesh Agreement Establishing the World Trade Organization, opened for signature 15 April 1994, 1867 UNTS 3 (entered into force 1 January 1995) annex 1C (known as Agreement on Trade-Related Aspects of Intellectual Property Rights, or TRIPS).

[43] Cf. Berne Convention, art. 9(2) (legitimate interests of author) with TRIPS art. 13 (legitimate interests of right holder).

[44] TRIPS art. 9(1).   [45] Ibid.

Convention'.[46] By the same token, with respect to databases, TRIPS pulls these arguably borderline works into the humanist Berne criteria: 'Compilations of data or other material, whether in machine readable or other form, which by reason of the selection or arrangement of their contents constitute *intellectual creations* shall be protected as such'.[47] In both cases, some instances of the covered works may fall short of the threshold of originality, but TRIPS has chosen to protect only those that conform to the criteria of human authorship, at the possible cost of leaving some software and databases unprotected.

6.5 Conclusion

The development of neural networks and other sophisticated artificially intelligent machines may soon confront copyright with the category of 'purely computer-generated works' that Ricketson hypothesised years ago. Without true human authors, these outputs fall outside the scope of international (and most national) copyright subject matter. Any protection for these outputs has nothing to do with securing the 'fruits of human authorship'. Worse, admitting these creatures to the copyright fold would, in Ricketson's conceptualisation, corrupt the soul of copyright. But some intellectual property protection for these outputs may be necessary to fulfill the instrumentalist goals that (to a greater or lesser extent) underlie copyright systems; a complete lack of protection for computer-generated outputs might discourage the development of the technologies or of the business models required to generate and commercialise these productions. But we should not simply assume that without copyright-like protection, society will be deprived of these benefits. Indeed, not all outputs necessarily require the same (or any) scope of coverage. Careful empirical analysis of the need for intellectual property protection for purely computer-generated outputs (in addition to already-protected inputs), must precede any enactment of intellectual property protection on the national or international level.

---

[46] Ibid. art. 10(1).
[47] Ibid., art. 10(2) (emphasis added). *Intellectual creation* is the standard for compilations of works under Berne Convention, art. 2(5).

7 Australian Legislation Abroad
Singaporean Pragmatism and the Role of Australian Scholarship in Singaporean Copyright Law

Ng-Loy Wee Loon

7.1 Introduction

When it was enacted in 1987, the Singapore Copyright Act was a very close copy of the Australian Copyright Act 1968 (Cth). Given the Australian provenance of the Singapore Copyright Act, Singapore courts and tribunals hearing copyright disputes naturally look to Australian decisions for guidance. They also regularly refer to Australian scholarship.

There is one Australian scholar who is by far the most frequently cited in Singapore copyright decisions: Sam Ricketson. This chapter focusses on one occasion where Professor Ricketson's scholarship played an important role in steering the copyright law in Singapore back onto the right path. The issue on that occasion was the following: can the author of a 'work' be a juristic person such as a corporate entity, or is authorship restricted to human creation? Long before the controversy arose in the Singaporean courts, Ricketson had carefully and comprehensively made the case that a work of an author must be human.[1] Key aspects of Ricketson's argument are set out in the chapter in this volume by Jane Ginsburg. My own chapter explains how, influenced by Ricketson's scholarship, Singaporean courts eventually adopted the correct view that a corporate entity could not be an author for the purposes of Singaporean copyright law.

7.2 The Structure and Provenance of Singapore's Copyright Law

First, it is helpful to explain the basic structure of Singapore's copyright law and to describe the influence of Australian legislation on the current Act. Historically, Singapore's copyright law was in substance English

---

[1] *Telstra Corporation Limited* v. *Phone Directories Company Pty Ltd* (2010) 194 FCR 142 (cited as *Telstra Corp*). Some would say there were already hints of this position given by the High Court of Australia in its decision in *IceTV Pty Ltd* v. *Nine Network Australia Pty Ltd* (2009) 239 CLR 458.

copyright law: the Copyright Act 1710 (Statute of Anne),[2] the Copyright Act 1842[3] and the Copyright Act 1911[4] were all part of the law of colonial Singapore. For more than twenty years after independence, Singapore was content to stay with the Copyright Act 1911 with some modifications. It was only in the mid-1980s that Singapore saw the need to overhaul its copyright law.

The impetus was due in part[5] to the ambition to develop Singapore's software industry. For this to happen, the policymakers reasoned that there must be adequate copyright protection for computer programs. The Copyright Act 1911 was obviously inadequate for this purpose; there was even some doubt that computer programs were protected under that Act.[6] In the law reform exercise, the usual practice of looking to the UK proved unhelpful because, at that time, the UK itself was in the midst of grappling with the revision of its copyright law mummified in the Copyright Act 1956.[7] Although there were amendments made in 1985 to clarify that computer programs were literary works for the purposes of the Copyright Act 1956,[8] it was a known fact that these amendments

---

[2] The Copyright Act 1710 (Imp) 8 Ann, c 19 (cited as Statute of Anne) became part of the law of Straits Settlements (comprising Singapore, Malacca and Penang) under the Second Charter of Justice 1826. The latter is the Letters Patent granted by the Crown to establish the Court of Judicature in the Straits Settlements. Its effect was to introduce into the Straits Settlements the entire corpus of English statute and common law as it stood on 27 November 1826, subject to the qualifier of suitability (to local conditions and customs).

[3] The Copyright Act 1842 (Imp) 5 & 6 Vict, c. 45 was an imperial legislation which extended to 'every Part of the British Dominions': see s. XXIX.

[4] The Copyright Act 1911 (Imp) 1 & 2 Geo V, c. 46 was an imperial legislation which extended 'throughout the parts of His Majesty's dominions': see s. 25(1). It came into operation in Singapore via a proclamation issued by the governor of the Straits Settlements.

[5] There was another reason – namely, pressure from the US. The Office of the US Trade Representative acting under the 'Special 301' provisions had warned that, unless Singapore updated its copyright law to provide adequate protection to US copyright works, there would be a withdrawal of the Generalized System of Preferences (GSP) status granted to Singapore under the US Trade and Tariff Act of 1984, Pub. L. No. 98-573, 98 Stat. 2948. The role of the US was revealed during parliamentary debates: see UK, Parliamentary Debates, House of Lords, 25 February 1988, vol. 50, col. 596–7.

[6] The lack of clarity on this issue was mentioned by the Singapore High Court in *Federal Computers Sdn Bhd v. Ang Jee Hai Eric* [1993] 1 SLR(R) 681.

[7] See 4 & 5 Eliz, 2 c. 74.

[8] Copyright (Computer Software) Amendment Act 1985 (UK). The effect of this amending legislation was simply to 'graft' computer programs onto literary works for the application of the Copyright Act 1956: see *Milltronics Ltd v. Hycontrol Ltd* [1990] FSR 273, 280.

were only an 'interim measure' and were 'not sufficient to deal with all the many problems facing the [software] industry'.[9]

Waiting for the UK to complete its reform exercise to see the end product would have held back Singapore's plans to spur the development of its software industry and achieve greater economic growth. Tradition yielded in the face of practicality. Thus Singapore turned its attention to another regime – Australia's.[10] The Copyright Act 1968 (Cth) (Australian Copyright Act) reflects the Anglo copyright tradition. In line with the UK Copyright Act 1956, it maintains a distinction between two broad categories: 'works' and 'subject-matter other than works'.[11] The former category comprises literary, dramatic, musical and artistic works.[12] The latter category comprises sound recordings, cinematographic films, broadcasts and published editions of works. This division is a cornerstone of the statute's architecture, with the fundamentals of copyright protection (prerequisites to satisfy, term of protection, exclusive rights, etc.) for the protected materials in each category set out in two distinct parts of the statute – Part III for 'works' and Part IV for 'subject-matter other than works'. This division can be a useful starting point to approach copyright. (I will say a little more about this division later.)

In addition, the Australian Copyright Act had been updated in 1984 to deal with the position of computer programs. This was very important to Singapore's policymakers. The Australian 1984 amendments[13] were more substantial than the English 1985 amendments. For example, the Australian amendments (but not the English 1985 amendments) included a definition of *computer program* and a provision permitting the making of a back-up copy of the computer program. The Australian amendments must have been satisfactory because the new copyright statute passed by the Singapore Parliament in January 1987 (Singapore Copyright Act)[14] was a very close copy of the Australian Copyright Act, as amended up till 1984.

---

[9] This was candidly acknowledged by William Powell, the Member of Parliament who introduced the Copyright (Computer Software) Bill, during the third reading of the bill: UK, Parliamentary Debates, House of Commons, 19 April 1985, vol. 77, col. 560.
[10] This was not the first time that Singapore had looked to Australian legislation as a model. In particular, the original version of Singapore's Land Titles Act is modelled on the South Australian legislation (the Real Property Act 1886 (SA)) that created the so-called Torrens land title registration system.
[11] There is another category of protected materials – namely, 'performances', which shall be disregarded for the purposes of this discussion. UK copyright legislation has now jettisoned this structure. See Copyright, Designs and Patents Act 1988 (UK), c. 48, s. 1.
[12] See Copyright Act 1968 (Cth) s. 10 (definition of *work*).
[13] Copyright Amendment Act 1984 (Cth).
[14] Copyright Act 1987 (Singapore, cap. 63, 2006 rev. ed.) (cited as Singapore Copyright Act).

There were of course some material differences between the two pieces of legislation right from the start, and the divergence grew over the years as each country amended its copyright legislation to meet different challenges and needs. Even when the reason to amend was the same – for example, when both countries had to implement what are substantially the same copyright provisions in their respective free trade agreements (FTAs) with the US – the outcome was not necessarily the same. Today the material differences between the two Acts include the positions taken on parallel importation,[15] on the 'fair use versus fair dealing' debate,[16] and on moral rights protection.[17] Notwithstanding the differences, anyone familiar with the Australian Copyright Act and encountering the Singapore Copyright Act for the first time will immediately see the familial resemblance, especially in their bone structure (the architecture of the statute).

7.3 The Meaning of *Author* in Singapore's Copyright Law

In Australia, the position was settled in 2010 by the Full Court of the Federal Court of Australia: the author of a 'work' must be a human being.[18] However, many years prior to this decision, Professor Ricketson had already made a very convincing case for this proposition. In this Part, I focus on two strands of his analysis. The first strand relates to the position under international law. The second relates specifically to the position under Australian law.

---

[15] Singapore has favoured parallel importation from the start, and thus the original version of the Singapore Copyright Act permitted parallel importation of all protected materials. The Australian Copyright Act, on the other hand, had some restrictions on parallel importation. These restrictions were subsequently lifted for certain types of protected works. But even today, some restrictions apply to books: see Copyright Act 1968 (Cth) s. 44A.

[16] For example, when Singapore had to amend its copyright legislation in 2004–2005 to provide for the stronger copyright protection it agreed to in its FTA with the US, it decided to supplement the 'fair dealing' provisions (modelled on Australian equivalents) with a provision that is in substance the US-style 'fair use' exception. Australia also agreed to substantially the same stronger copyright protection in its FTA with US but decided not to switch to the 'fair use' exception. This option is currently under consideration: see Commonwealth of Australia, Australian Government Response to the Productivity Commission Inquiry into Intellectual Property Arrangements (August 2017) 7.

[17] Protection of moral rights in line with article 6*bis* of the Berne Convention has been available in Australia since 2000. This is not the case in Singapore, even though it has been a member of the Berne Union since 1998. But note that Singapore will be introducing a right of attribution soon (discussed later in the chapter).

[18] *Telstra Corp* (2010) 194 FCR 142.

In international law, there is a basic assumption that the authors of literary and artistic works (other than cinematographic works) are human beings. Professor Ricketson came to this conclusion after delving into the history of the Berne Convention for the Protection of Literary and Artistic Works (Berne Convention).[19] There may be no definition of the term *author* in the Berne Convention but, in his view, underpinning a number of provisions of the Berne Convention is the premise that the word *author* refers to a natural person and does not extend to a juristic person such as an incorporation. One example is the Berne Convention's adoption of the fifty years post mortem auctoris (pma) formula as the general rule to determine the duration of protection for literary and artistic works (other than cinematographic works). This formula does not make sense when applied to corporate entities which could have an infinite existence.

However, Ricketson also noted that this tacit understanding has been breached in some national laws. He pointed to two examples of such breaches. First, the UK legislation has devised the concept of 'computer-generated works' – that is, 'works' which are created by computers in circumstances where there is no human author.[20] (To this, I would add Hong Kong as an example from Asia.) Second, the US legislation has the concept of 'deeming authorship' in its 'work for hire' doctrine where the employer – which can be and is often an incorporation – is deemed to be the author of a work created by the employee, so as to vest initial ownership of the copyright in the employer.[21] (To this, I would add China, Japan, Korea and Taiwan as examples from Asia.[22]) I think it is very important to highlight that in these examples of breach, the post

---

[19] Berne Convention for the Protection of Literary and Artistic Works, opened for signature 9 September 1886, 828 UNTS 221 (entered into force 5 December 1887), as amended (cited as Berne Convention). Sam Ricketson, *The Berne Convention for the Protection of Literary and Artistic Works: 1886–1986* (London: Centre for Commercial Law Studies, Queen Mary College, Kluwer, 1987), pp. [5.2], [7.32]–[7.33]. This view is repeated in the second edition of the work: Sam Ricketson and Jane C Ginsburg, *International Copyright and Neighbouring Rights: The Berne Convention and Beyond*, 2nd ed. (Oxford: Oxford University Press, 2006), pp. [7.02]–[7.05], [7.12], [9.40]–[9.42]. See also Sam Ricketson, 'People or machines: The Berne Convention and the changing concept of authorship' (1991) 16 *Columbia-VLA Journal of Law & Arts* 1.
[20] Copyright, Designs and Patents Act 1988 (UK) c. 48, s. 178.
[21] Copyright Act of 1976, 17 USC §201(b), read with the definition of 'work for hire' in §101 (cited as US Copyright Act). Apart from employment cases, the 'work for hire' doctrine may also apply to commissioning cases.
[22] [Copyright Law of the People's Republic of China] (People's Republic of China) National People's Congress, 26 February 2010, art. 11 (cited as China's Copyright Act); [Copyright Act], Act No 48 of 1970, art. 15 (cited as Japan's Copyright Act); [Copyright Act], Act No 432 of 1957, art. 9 (cited as South Korea's Copyright Act); [Copyright Law of Taiwan], Order No. 212, 14 May 1928, art. 16 (cited as Taiwan's Copyright Act).

mortem auctoris formula is not used to calculate the term of protection for works. Instead, these jurisdictions tag the term of protection to the creation or first publication of the 'computer-generated work' or the 'work for hire'. For instance, Taiwan's copyright legislation provides that the economic rights in a work 'authored by a juristic person' last for fifty years from the creation of the work or its public release, whichever is later.[23] This effort to avoid the grant of a potentially perpetual term of protection is a point I shall return to later.

As far as Australia is concerned, Professor Ricketson is adamant that the author of a work must be a human being. He points out that Australia considered but rejected the concept of computer-generated works.[24] Australia has also stayed away from the concept of 'deemed authorship'. Where it desires to vest initial ownership of copyright in a party other than the author – say, the employer – this is achieved without deeming the employer as the author. The law simply vests initial ownership in the employer while making clear that the (human) employee remains the author.[25] All this points to Australia adhering strictly to the assumption that only humans can be authors of works. This assumption permeates the entire structure of the Australian Copyright Act. It is also evident in the division that the Act makes between 'works' and 'subject-matter other than works'. I have earlier commented that this division can be a useful starting point to understand copyright. This is because it should prompt a newcomer to copyright to ask the question: Why this division? Is there a difference in the rationale for protecting the materials in the two categories, and what is this difference? The answer, from Australia's perspective at least, is that there are two fundamentally different types of activities involved, each deserving a different type of protection. In the first category, the law is protecting the human intellectual activity that goes into the creation of a work, whereas in the second category, the law is protecting the investment that funds the manufacture of a 'subject-matter other than works'. For this reason, Professor Ricketson has described the nature of the right in the second category as 'essentially a

---

[23] Taiwan's Copyright Act, art. 33. See also China's Copyright Act, art. 21; Japan's Copyright Act, ar.t 53(3), South Korea's Copyright Act, art. 41; and US Copyright Act, §302(c).
[24] This was rejected by the Australian Copyright Law Review Committee: see Sam Ricketson, 'The need for human authorship – Australian developments: *Telstra Corp Ltd v Phone Directories Co Pty Ltd*' (2012) 34(1) *European Intellectual Property Review* 54, 55.
[25] See Copyright Act 1968 (Cth) s. 35(4) (for employment in the news and publication sector) and s. 35(6) (for other cases of employment).

manufacturer's or investor's right'.[26] The investment activity in the second category can be undertaken by corporate entities and the Australian Copyright Act makes provision for this possibility by referring to the creator of subject-matter other than works not as author but by other labels. For instance, the label used in the case of cinematographic films is 'maker', defined as the person by whom the arrangements necessary for the production of the first copy of the film were undertaken.[27]

The Australian analysis applies equally to Singapore: the Singapore Copyright Act adopts the *post mortem auctoris* formula;[28] it does not have the concept of computer-generated works or the concept of deeming authorship; it maintains a distinction between authorship and ownership in employment cases;[29] it has the division between works and subject-matter other than works; and the creators of the former are called authors whereas creators of the latter are called by other labels like maker.[30] The position in Singapore must surely be that advocated by Ricketson: an author of a work for the purposes of the Singapore Copyright Act must be a human being. This is indeed the position in Singapore today. However, between 1999 and 2011, the waters were muddied by two High Court decisions where it was held that an incorporation was the author of a work.

In the first case that came up in 1991,[31] the claimant was a company which had commissioned an individual to design a getup for use on the packaging of the company's products. The defendant was a trader who used a very similar getup on his products. It was quite clear that the defendant had copied a substantial part of the artistic work in the getup. When the claimant company sued for copyright infringement, the defendant challenged the claimant company's locus standi to sue – rightly so, in my view. Under the rules governing ownership of copyright set out in the Singapore Copyright Act, initial ownership of copyright in the artistic work in the getup was vested in its author[32] – that is, the

---

[26] Sam Ricketson and Christopher Creswell, *The Law of Intellectual Property: Copyright, Designs and Confidential Information*, 2nd rev. ed. (Sydney: Thomson Reuters, 2015), p. [14.145].

[27] Copyright Act 1968 (Cth) s 90, read with s 22(4)(a) and (b).

[28] Singapore Copyright Act s. 28(2). Note that there are exceptions to the post mortem auctoris formula. In particular, a photograph is protected for seventy years after its first publication: see s. 28(6).

[29] Ibid., s. 30(4), for employment in the news and publication sector, and s. 30(6), for other cases of employment.

[30] Ibid., s. 88 read with s. 16(4)(a) and (b).

[31] *Alteco Chemical Pte Ltd* v. *Chong Yean Wah* [1999] 2 SLR(R) 915 (cited as *Alteco*).

[32] See Singapore Copyright Act, s. 30(2), which provides that the author shall be the copyright owner. Note that s. 30(5) sets out an exception to this rule. Section 30(5) deals with the position of commissioned works: where the commissioned work is a

individual artist who designed the getup. The claimant company had failed to obtain an assignment of this copyright from this artist. Without this transfer of title, the claimant company had no locus standi to bring the copyright infringement action. However, the High Court judge seemed reluctant to dismiss the action on this basis; after all, the defendant had clearly 'reaped where he had not sown'. The High Court judge therefore came up with what he called a 'modern' meaning of *authorship*. An author, he said, was the party who made the arrangements and paid for the creation of the artistic work.[33] In the judge's view, the claimant company fell within this meaning, and hence it was the author of the artistic work in the getup. This dispensed with the need for any assignment from the artist to the claimant company, thereby enabling the judge to conclude that the defendant was liable for copyright infringement.

The 1991 decision was criticised by academics,[34] but it was applied by another High Court judge in a case that came up about ten years later. The second case involved a horse-racing guide containing compilations (literary works) of information about horse-racing. The claimant was a company incorporated under the laws of Singapore. In its statement of claim, the company put itself forward not just as the copyright owner but *also* as the author of the literary work. The purpose of this bizarre assertion was to use the Singaporean nature of its incorporation to satisfy the requirement that the author of the work must be a 'qualified person' – that is, a national or resident of Singapore.[35] The High Court judge held that it was possible for an incorporation to be the author of a work. Other than the 1991 case, she also relied on the fact that the word *person* is defined in the Singapore Interpretation Act 1965 to include any company or association or body of persons corporate or unincorporated. But this acontextual interpretation of the word *person* is problematic. By this analysis, the non-exhaustive definition of the word *person* in the

---

photograph, portrait or an engraving, initial title to this commissioned work is vested in the commissioning party. This exception did not apply to the getup in the *Alteco* case because the artistic work in the getup was not a photograph, portrait or an engraving. As such, the initial title to copyright in the artistic work in the getup was governed by s. 30 (2), leading to the conclusion that the copyright owner was the artist who designed the getup.

[33] *Alteco* [1999] 2 SLR(R) 915, [26].
[34] See, e.g., George Wei, *The Law of Copyright in Singapore*, 2nd ed. (Singapore: SNP Editions, 2000), pp. 1391–3, and Ng-Loy Wee Loon, *Law of Intellectual Property of Singapore*, rev. ed. (Singapore: Sweet & Maxwell Asia, 2009), pp. 104–6.
[35] Singapore Copyright Act, s. 27(4).

Singapore Interpretation Act would allow an *animal* to be an author for the purposes of the Singapore Copyright Act![36]

In 2011, the Court of Appeal was presented with the opportunity to consider this issue when the second case went on appeal.[37] It was then that the law of authorship was put back onto the right path. When affirming that the author of a work must be a human being, the appellate court cited inter alia Professor Ricketson's scholarship. There was specific focus on the vital importance of having a finite term of copyright protection. The Court of Appeal delved into the history of copyright law, all the way back to the Statute of Anne. (I have mentioned earlier that this statute was part of the law of colonial Singapore.[38]) The long title of this statute sets out its objective as the following:

An Act for the Encouragement of Learning, by vesting the Copies of Printed Books in the Authors or purchasers of such Copies, during the Times therein mentioned.

The Court of Appeal noted that the Statute of Anne created a statutory right that had a limited term of protection – a maximum of twenty-eight years for new books – so that learning could be further advanced by the free access and use of the literary work upon the expiration of that period. From this perspective, the court was firmly of the view that it was 'clearly against public policy to allow copyright protection in perpetuity',[39] a potential consequence of extending the meaning of author to include incorporations. As the Singaporean courts finally recognised, an interpretation which resulted in actual or potential perpetual protection of the subject matter could not be correct. For this reason alone, and consistent with the analysis advanced by Ricketson in the Australian context, the term *author* as used in the Singapore Copyright Act cannot include corporate bodies.

7.4 Conclusion

Over the years, Australian and Singaporean copyright law have diverged, as each country has amended its legislation to meet different needs and challenges. But in more recent times, there are signs suggesting that there

---

[36] Consider the recent controversy stirred up by the 'monkey selfie' case in the US, where the People for the Ethical Treatment of Animals sought an order for a declaration that the macaque monkey in the wild was the author of the selfie photograph it took with the camera of a nature photographer. See *Naruto v. Slater*, 888 F.3d 418 (9th Cir, 2018).
[37] *Asia Pacific Publishing Pte Ltd v. Pioneers & Leaders (Publishers) Pte Ltd* [2011] 4 SLR 381 (cited as *Asia Pacific Publishing*).
[38] See n. 2. [39] *Asia Pacific Publishing* [2011] 4 SLR 381, [72].

will nevertheless be some degree of convergence between the two bodies of national law. For example, Australian law has been mentioned in Singapore's recent decision in January 2019 to introduce a right of attribution.[40] Another example – this time a reverse of the cross-fertilisation process – lies in the 'fair dealing versus fair use' debate that has resurfaced in Australia. When the Productivity Commission recommended switching over from the closed list of fair dealing exceptions to the open-ended US-style fair use exception, it made mention of the fact that countries such as Singapore have already done so (Singapore in 2005).[41]

Like family ties, the connection between Australia's and Singapore's copyright laws will not be easily broken. My prediction is that the courts and academics in Singapore will continue to look to Australian decisions and scholarship for inspiration.

---

[40] Singapore Copyright Review – Enhancing Creators' Rights and Users' Access to Copyrighted Works, Ministry of Law, 17.1.19, retrieved from https://bit.ly/2SXD2tz.
[41] Australian Government Productivity Commission (2016) Intellectual property arrangements inquiry report (20 December), retrieved from www.pc.gov.au/inquiries/completed/intellectual-property#report.

8   'The Berne Convention Is Our Ideal'
Hall Caine, Canadian Copyright and the Natural Rights of Authors after 1886

Kathy Bowrey*

---

* This research was supported by Australian Research Council Discovery Grant, DP140100172 K. Bowrey and C. Bond, *Australian Made: A History of Australian Copyright Law and Creator Success 1868–1968*. In the late 1980s I started to field inquiries from digital artists about copyright's demonization of their practice. As a property lawyer I knew nothing about copyright law. Sam Ricketson's treatises provided

8.1 Introduction

Sir Thomas Henry Hall Caine (1853–1931) was a Victorian writer whose romance novels, which often borrowed torrid themes of divine justice from biblical stories, reputably sold over 15 million copies during his lifetime. Born to a poverty-stricken working-class background in Liverpool, he identified with his father's birthplace on the Isle of Man. The location and its people provided inspiration for many of his tales. Caine was acclaimed as a British Tolstoy.[1] Adaptations of his stories were performed on the stage in London, New York, across Canada and in the Australian colonies. Caine's friends included Dante and Christina Rossetti, John Ruskin, Wilkie Collins and George Bernard Shaw. Bram Stoker served as his personal secretary and, in 1897, the then unknown author dedicated *Dracula* 'to my dear friend, Hommy-Beg'.[2] He was recognised on the streets of London and New York.[3] In many regards, Caine embodied the spirit of his times. He saw himself, and his social circle, as leaders of an honourable profession, where the literati instructed the reading public by appealing to their intellects and emotions. He was a staunch advocate for the natural rights of authors, but with respect to the USA, also a pragmatist. While '[t]he Berne Convention is our ideal … when we cannot get the Berne Convention we are willing to accept what is not immoderately retrograde'.[4]

America's history as a pirate nation has been thoroughly examined.[5] Trans-Atlantic politics have been described as especially fractious.[6] However, in the late nineteenth century Great Britain and the United States worked together to mutual advantage to secure control of the

---

a way in that led me to begin to understand this complicated and confounding body of law. Sam always contextualised the subject through its history. Reading his books led to a long-lived passion for copyright history. I still send Sam draft work. He still very generously and carefully reads it, kindly pointing me to a clearer path. I am extremely grateful for his kindness and support and for mentoring generations of Australian IP scholars that now form a friendly scholarly community. It is a wonderful gift.

[1] See Hall Caine, *The Master of Man: The Story of a Sin* (Cassell & Co, 1927 [orig. 1921]) and the favourable reviews published therein: 'Sir Hall Caine in The Master of Man has shown himself to be the English Tolstoy' (*Manchester City News*) and 'It places him to the same rank, as a great world novelist, with Zola, Hugo and Tolstoy' (*Leeds Mercury*).
[2] Bram Stoker, *Dracula*, John Paul Riquelme (ed.) (Boston/New York: Bedford/St Martins, 2002), p. 23.
[3] The leading biography is Vivien Allen, *Hall Caine: Portrait of a Victorian Romancer* (Sheffield: Sheffield Academic Press, 1997).
[4] Hall Caine, 'The copyright question', *The Gazette* (Montreal), 14 October 1895.
[5] Adrian Johns, *Piracy: The Intellectual Property Wars from Gutenberg to Gates* (Chicago: University of Chicago Press, 2009).
[6] Peter Baldwin, *The Copyright Wars: Three Centuries of Trans-Atlantic Battle* (Princeton, NJ /Oxford: Princeton University Press, 2014).

world's English language publishing markets. This chapter focusses on Caine's well-publicised 1895 tour of Canada, serving as a representative of the Society of Authors and, unofficially, on behalf of the British Parliament and Colonial Office and in consultation with his American publisher, William Appleton, who then served as chairman of the American Publishers' Copyright League. Caine's task was to prevent Canada's effective withdrawal from the Berne Convention and, as a consequence, the anticipated collapse of British-American copyright. Caine pushed forward his own interests, as well as the rights of English authors, across several continents, by successfully appealing to the ideology that undergirded the Berne Convention. In tracing Caine's strategy to advance authorial interests in the face of significant political opposition, this chapter helps document how the idea of a natural and universal right of authors was globally disseminated to advance the commercial interests of established publishers based in London and New York.

Sam Ricketson's seminal work *The Berne Convention for the Protection of Literary and Artistic Works 1886–1986*,[7] provides the conceptual framework of the inquiry. He notes that there was a 'utopian and unrealistic' inspiration that lay behind the Berne Convention – the idea of a universal copyright based on 'the conception of the author's natural right of property in his work, existing independently of, and prior to, the formal rules and sanctions of positive law'.[8] Ricketson then goes on to acknowledge that when it came to production of the convention text, this idealism was tempered by the 'pragmatic view', where principle was sacrificed in order to gain adherence to a particular proposition.[9] Caine personified both inclinations. He held a righteous belief in authorial property fortified by an astute strategic mind and, for an apprentice architect and journalist with no legal training, an audacious degree of self-confidence in negotiating legal and political affairs. He gained sufficient profile and cultural influence that, during his lifetime, he was frequently parodied in the press.[10]

---

[7] Sam Ricketson, *The Berne Convention for the Protection of Literary and Artistic Works 1886–1986* (London: Centre for Commercial Law Studies, Queen Mary College, Kluwer, 1987).
[8] Ibid., 41. [9] Ibid.
[10] Many of the newspaper articles cited in this paper were found in Caine's personal scrapbooks. Papers of Sir Thomas Henry Hall Caine (1853–1931), Manx National Heritage Library and Archives: MS 9267 Hall Caine Scrapbook. I am extremely grateful to Wendy Thirkettle for drawing my attention to these and to all the staff at Manx National Heritage.

8.2 The Universal Right of Authors

Caine expressed a philosophical view of the author's right that was commonly held by literary men and women in his lifetime. He made numerous versions of the same speech to large contingents of British, American and Canadian press who followed his tour from New York to Montreal to Toronto and to members of the National Club (Toronto), the Canadian Publishers Association, and politicians. He lectured that:

> Those rights are natural rights, that they are not primarily created by the State, that however necessary it may be to call in the help of the law for the protection of the rights of literary property, the author's right in the book he produces is a right of creation, and that by its nature should never cease, and should never be divided with another ... I am not pretending that this is the bearing of copyright from the point of history or of the law of nations. But it is the principle of copyright put down on the bed rock of natural law. Doctor Johnson put it down on this bed rock, and no man has ever been more sound on the rights of literary property.[11]

Caine acknowledged that the author's struggle was not over, yet significant progress had already been made:

> For fifty years we have been struggling – we and our great predecessors – Dickens, Thackeray, Carlyle, Lytton, and a host of others – for recognition of the principle that *a man has a right to the commercial value of the property he creates in books*. It has been a stiff fight but we have conquered all along the line. We have prevailed upon the chief nations of Europe to meet together in convention at Berne, and established once and for all the fundamental principle that without registration, simultaneous publication or any similar mummery, an author holds property in the children of his brain.[12]

Caine's attitude toward copyright echoed his religious conviction that there was a moral arc to the universe. Despite limitations in the laws of man, copyright should be judged in light of its movement toward eternal perfection. Obstacles, such as the USA not signing the Berne Convention, were smoothed over. Caine told all who would listen that we have secured 'an even greater triumph in America'[13] with recognition of British copyrights in the passing of the International Copyright Act of 1891 (the Chace Act).[14]

The Chace Act contained three significant rituals or 'mummeries' that authors had to comply with: first, registration of the title with the Library

---

[11] Caine, 'The copyright question'.
[12] Hall Caine, 'The Canadian Copyright Act' (1895) 67 *The Contemporary Review* 477, 477–8 (emphasis added).
[13] Ibid., 478.   [14] Ch. 565, 26 Stat 1106, 3 March 1891.

of Congress on or before the date of publication; second, deposit of copies was required on or before the date of publication with no grace period allowed for in the 1891 statute, although as per previous Acts, some late deposit was allowed in practice and the books had to be printed in the USA; third, a copyright notice had to be included on all copies. A report by the US Copyright Office from this time notes numerous 'inequalities of exchange' in the internationalisation of rights, including that:

> there may be an important practical difference in the ease or difficulty of compliance with obligatory formalities, depending upon whether the author is a citizen or a foreigner. It is not as easy, for example, for a foreign as for a native author to arrange for the filing of his title page at Washington before publication, and it is obviously a much less difficult matter for an American than for a foreign author to arrange to have his book type-set in the United States before the day of first publication, which may mean for the alien author the burden of a double printing of his work, abroad and in the United States.[15]

The terms were especially difficult for foreign authors unknown to American publishers to comply with. Publishers were most unlikely to arrange publication and render logistical assistance to those untested in the market, unless the author paid for the publication. Compliance posed far less of a problem, however, for writers like Caine, who had established transatlantic connections.

Rather than acknowledging this reality, Caine suggested to audiences that formalities had little to do with literary property at all:

> A book is a thing made by an author. The printing and bookbinding are the mere mechanism of a book – the mere machinery by which copies are multiplied and distributed. ... In America, nobody dares to defend the manufacturing clause on principle.[16]

This account contained many falsehoods smoothed over by one truth. Literary property statutes in both the eighteenth and nineteenth centuries reflected decades of political wheeling and dealing to support printing and akin trades. It is true that these statutes were hard to defend in terms of well-recognised nineteenth-century philosophical justifications for private property rights. There were, however, other philosophical and pragmatic justifications for literary property laws and their statutory limits.[17] Caine deftly avoided acknowledging this and further embroidered his

---

[15] Library of Congress, US Copyright Office, *Report on Copyright Legislation* (Washington, DC: US Government Printing Office (1904), pp. 28–9.
[16] Caine, 'The Canadian Copyright Act', 478.
[17] See Ronan Deazley, *On the Origin of the Right to Copy: Charting the Movement of Copyright Law in Eighteenth Century Britain (1695–1775)* (London: Hart Publishing, 2004).

appeal to the author's natural right with a significant misattribution. He implied that the natural right of author was the only sound principle on which copyright could be based because the book's 'commercial value' arose from authorial creation. This ignored the reality that commercial value was entirely dependent upon the legal conditions that determined the conditions of circulation and the efficient enforcement of copyright. This was the very reason the noted author travelled to the USA in 1895.

In this period when his most popular works were on sale in Canada, Caine derived royalties from English editions, cheaper colonial editions and authorised US editions, which were subject to an import tax if passage across the border was detected. His profit could be maximised by better calibrating these releases, in particular by more strategic assignment of American rights.

The reality was that when it came to his American copyright, Caine could rely upon his good friend, New York publisher William Appleton, to manage formalities, enforce his rights and secure his value. Indeed, part of the compromise sitting behind the Chace Act was the concession that successful British authors such as Caine would be entitled to a 20 per cent royalty on their American editions, which was twice the royalty contained in the standard British Publisher Association agreement in circulation in 1890, and much higher than the 12.5 per cent royalty on colonial reprints.[18] It is no surprise that leading British authors thought the Chace Act a 'triumph', mummeries and all.

British publishers also understood how to best exercise their American rights:

So thoroughly do the English houses understand this question, and in so many cases have they established branch houses here for publication of their own books, that a leading Boston author was tempted to remark to the head of a leading American publishing house that the chief effect of the International Copyright Act seem[s] to be to enable English publishing firms to establish branch houses here, manufacture duplicate plates, and flood the market with English books.[19]

American publishers could also copyright works by American authors in Britain and thereby assume direct control over the Canadian

---

[18] 'Canadian copyright', *The Publishers' Circular*, no. 1529 (14 September 1895): 268; Canada, Parliamentary Debates, House of Commons, 4th sess., 5th Parl., vol. xxi, 29 March 1886, 378 (Mr Edgar). The reprint royalty had barely been collected in Canada in any case. See Sara Bannerman, *The Struggle for Canadian Copyright: From Imperialism to Internationalism 1842–1971* (Vancouver: University of British Columbia Press, 2013), p. 53.

[19] Arthur Stedman, 'Literary property', *The Author*, June 1894, p. 7.

market.[20] Such was Caine's friendship with his publisher that Appleton, along with a contingent of press, met Caine when his liner docked in New York. The author and his family were guests at Appleton's estate. The publisher also introduced the author to his neighbour, President Cleveland.[21] The famous Manxman was quite defensive when the Canadian press reflected on these American connections and what they might mean.[22]

What is revealed from Caine's personal papers is that, as the Canadian press suspected, Appleton and Caine remained in close correspondence in this period so that updates could be given. Approval was sought from the American Copyright League (the US equivalent of the Society of Authors) and the American Publishers' Copyright League to the terms Caine negotiated with the Canadians.[23]

8.3 The Canadian Grievance

The Canadian legislators were operating on 'the assumption that if copyright be a printer's protection scheme in the United States, it ought to be nothing less in Canada, and inferentially in the other colonial dependencies in Great Britain'.[24]

Canadian printers and publishers had a tradition of strongly asserting their interests to confront the dominance of the British firms throughout the Empire.[25] Colonials faced many challenges. British imports were considered too highly priced and titles often unsuited to the local market. Throughout the nineteenth century, American piracies were also readily imported into Canada as well as to the Australian colonies. Further, after *Routledge v. Low*,[26] the need to register at Stationers Hall to obtain a British copyright meant there were disincentives for colonial authors to print locally, unless the work was only of local interest. The situation was not redressed until the passing of the International Copyright Act

---

[20] This situation was further clarified with the extension of Berne Convention protection to non-Union authors in the 1896 revision of the Berne Convention. See Bannerman, *The Struggle for Canadian Copyright*, 63.
[21] Allen, *Hall Caine*, p. 243.
[22] 'Mr Caine's mission', *Daily Mail and Empire* (Toronto), 21 October 1895.
[23] Papers of Sir Thomas Henry Hall Caine (1853–1931) Manx National Heritage Library and Archives: MS 09542 Correspondence (Legal).
[24] 'Canadian copyright'.
[25] Eli MacLaren, *Dominion and Agency: Copyright and the Structuring of the Canadian Book Trade 1867–1918* (Toronto: University of Toronto Press, 2011); Bannerman, *The Struggle for Canadian Copyright*. For the British perspective see Catherine Seville, *The Internationalisation of Copyright Law: Books, Buccaneers and the Black Flag in the Nineteenth Century* (Cambridge; Cambridge University Press, 2006), pp. 78–145.
[26] (1868) LR 3; HL 100; 37 LJ Ch. 454; 18 LT 874; 16 WR 1081.

1886.[27] In 1875, Canada successfully asserted the right to print cheap editions in Canada under license, to compete with pirated American editions.[28] Following the creation of the Berne Union, Canada also passed a new law to assert its copyright sovereignty in 1889.[29] However, the new copyright act was read as a denunciation of the Berne Convention. It led to an intervention by the Colonial Office and a threat to invoke the Colonial Laws Validity Act 1865[30] to strike it down. The law was never proclaimed.[31] This move only energised Canada's copyright rebellion.

It was not the case that Canadian publishers were entirely anti-Berne or anti-copyright. As Sara Bannerman notes, 'For many the Berne Convention symbolized the forward march of international law, civilization and progress'.[32] Many Canadian publishers hoped that it would mean that new opportunities would open up. As well as encouraging local publication by Canadians rather than publishing in London, they expected to be able to contract directly with British authors for exclusive rights to publish books in Canada, where they judged the title would do well in the local market. However, perhaps unsurprisingly given the royalty deal some British authors had secured, transatlantic publisher contracts had emerged that dealt with 'North American' rights as a bloc. It was complained that,

Canadian publishers are constantly endeavouring to enter into arrangements with authors and artists direct, but the English publisher looks upon us as mere colonials, steps between us and the author, and sells our market to the United States publisher.[33]

To redress this situation, as well as discussing raising tariffs on American imports, a new bill in 1895 extended the provisions of the 1875 Act. It required British authors to arrange for Canadian printing of their works within a month of first publication or thereafter be subjected to a compulsory license, subject to the author receiving 10 per cent of the retail price.[34] Most importantly, Canadian publishers would be free to set the retail price and determine how the format and content of the work was

---

[27] International Copyright Act 1886 (Imp) 49 & 50 Vict, c. 33.
[28] Copyright Act 1875, 38 Vict, c. 88; Copyright Act 1875, 38 & 39 Vict, c. 53.
[29] Meera Nair, 'The Copyright Act 1889: A Canadian declaration of independence' (2009) 90(1) *Canadian Historical Review* 1.
[30] Colonial Laws Validity Act 1865 (Imp) 28 & 29 Vict, c. 63.
[31] Bannerman, *The Struggle for Canadian Copyright*, 52.   [32] Ibid., 48.
[33] 'The Canadian Copyright Question', 3 November 1894. Unattributed clipping, Papers of Sir Thomas Henry Hall Caine (1853–1931), Manx National Heritage Library and Archives: MS 9267/2 Hall Caine Scrapbook.
[34] Caine, 'The Canadian Copyright Act', 479.

presented to the public. To Caine and the Society of Authors this was entirely contrary to the spirit of the Berne Convention.[35] It directly undermined the perceived natural rights of authors, which included the right to determine both the edition manuscript and demarcation of geographical markets.

8.4 The British Publishers' Response

British publishers feared the Canadian copyright proposal was the beginning of a race to the bottom. They complained that pricing concessions had historically been made in the Canadian market, in recognition that authorised works competed with American pirate editions. They had hoped that following the Chace Act, the trade could now prevent multiple competing editions from different sources servicing the Canadian reading public, except where British publishers controlled the terms.

Macmillan and Co argued that there were moral rights implications: Canadian publishers would be free to bring out inaccurately printed and abridged books, 'purposefully mutilated', with illustrations that the author disapproved of and found repugnant. The royalty proposed was judged inadequate and difficult to collect, especially given the poor history of revenue collection that dogged colonial editions published under the Foreign Reprints Act 1847.[36] The effects were also argued as particularly draconian for British educational and scientific works, which had notoriously slow sales and high production costs.[37] Publisher John Murray forewarned the broader implications across the Empire:

The exclusion of pirated and unauthorised reprints of copyright works from our Australian colonies and India has, even in existing circumstances, been a task requiring the utmost vigilance and care ... The circulation of legalised Canadian reprints would render this work of exclusion well-nigh impossible ... If [Canadian demands] are granted, nothing can stop the extension of the concession to other

---

[35] Whether the formalities attached to the Canadian Copyright Act 1889 contravened article 2 of the Berne Convention was an open debate, and the matter was worked around by Britain in revisions to the convention in 1896. See Bannerman, *The Struggle for Canadian Copyright*, 57, 64.

[36] Foreign Reprints Act 1847 (Imp) 10 & 11 Vict, c. 95. See Sam Ricketson, 'The Imperial Copyright Act 1911 in Australia' in Uma Suthersanen and Ysolde Gendreau (eds.), *A Shifting Empire: 100 Years of the Copyright Act 1911* (Cheltenham, UK: Edward Elgar, 2013), 52, 58; Ronan Deazley, 'Commentary on the Foreign Reprints Act 1847' in Lionel Bently and Martin Kretschmer (eds.), *Primary Sources on Copyright (1450–1900)*, retrieved from www.copyrighthistory.org.

[37] Caine, 'The Canadian Copyright Act', 76–8. Herbert Spencer had made a similar point about the detrimental effects of the proposal on educational publishing in *The Times*, 22 October 1895.

Colonies, and any one who is at all conversant with the book market can foresee what a grievous injury would thereby be caused to owners of English copyright.[38]

In short, the Canadian bill was seen as a denunciation of copyright as an imperial principle. It would herald the collapse of the Empire book market and, by extension, fatally compromise the Berne Union:

> having given pledges to America that in exchange for the copyright she gives us, we will give copyright to her throughout British dominions, one of our colonies makes demands that it shall be allowed to break down the whole principle which during fifty hard years we have so laboriously built up.[39]

Such was the degree of concern in Britain that there was public discussion of the use of an imperial veto, a matter that Caine publicly dismissed in pressing the need to come to a compromise.[40]

8.5 Caine's Compromise Proposal

As the *Canadian Bookseller* noted in the lead-up to Caine's visit:

> Newspapers are undoubtedly the great reflectors of public opinion. It is therefore most gratifying to be able to record that such newspapers in Canada that mention editorially such an obtrusive a subject as copyright are unanimous irrespective of party politics, in demanding that Canada must have the fullest right to legislate on copyright.[41]

Caine's wife scrapbooked endless articles on the subject for him. He quietly judged that concessions would have to be made. He publicly acknowledged that at this time, the US had 65 million readers, whereas Canada had only 5 million. Regardless of the imposition of an import tax, there was no way of preventing unauthorised editions flooding the Canadian market. However, he took care to discuss far more than copyright. He spoke about his famous works and plays, gave advice to budding authors, commented favourably on Canadian and American society and arranged 'at-home' interviews with his wife. He also spoke of the loyalty of Canada to Britain, drawing on paternalistic themes familiar to those who had read his novels:

---

[38] Caine, 'The Canadian Copyright Act', 73–5.   [39] Ibid., 78.
[40] Hall Caine, 'The Canadian copyright question', *St James Gazette* (London), 28 January 1896. At this time there was also public discussion of the inevitability of Canada uniting with America, led by British-Canadian historian and journalist Goldwin Smith. Caine eventually claimed Smith as a supporter. See Goldwin Smith, *Canada and the Canadian Question* (New York: Hunter Rose & Company/Macmillan, 1891); Goldwin Smith, 'The Canadian Copyright Bill' (1895) 5(6) *Canadian Monthly* 551.
[41] 'The Copyright discussion', *The Canadian Bookseller*, September 1895, 1.

Though you are independent of the old country ...You are in the position of the son, of a father who has many sons ... So the son goes off and marries himself, perhaps, to the strange woman. But because he lives under another roof he does not cease to be his father's son. He bears his father's name. He carries his father's blood. If he does wrong, the shame will be his father's no less than his.[42]

Caine was pleased with his reception. In a remarkably candid private note he informed the Colonial Office, 'How it is now. The public tired out – there is no doubt here. Colonial Office, Canadian cabinet, interested classes tired out. Therefore easy for me to do something. My task made easy'.[43] He suggested that he would continue to profile the Berne Convention as the rallying cause: 'They said it was impossible. It is done'.[44] He had devised a proposal that would satisfy American authors and American publishers; observe the Berne Convention; and satisfy Canadian publishers, authors and booksellers. He also claimed the Canadian Parliament was eager for a result.[45]

In letters to the Society of Authors, his American publisher Appleton and the American Copyright League and American Publishers' Copyright League, Caine proposed the following compromise:

- British authors would have a minimum of 60 days to arrange Canadian publication, and up to 90 days if they can show cause for the delay;
- Canadian publications must print from plates made in London or America;
- If the work is not published at all outside of Britain it remains subject to British law;
- If a Canadian Publisher applies to the Minister for a license, the author must be informed in writing;
- The Canadian publisher acts as an agent of the English or American publisher;
- The license fee is a minimum of 10% on a book not less than 25 cents with not fewer than 500 copies with royalty paid in advance;
- Serial stories published in newspapers can be protected by simply listing the name and a general description in the register in Ottawa or in London (subject to a higher fee). If the story is pirated in America the Canadian publisher must first apply for a license and allow 60 days

---

[42] Hall Caine, 'Speech to Canadian publishers and booksellers', *The Author*, December 1895, 152.
[43] Note to Joseph Chamberlain, Colonial Office, undated, c. 1895. Papers of Sir Thomas Henry Hall Caine (1853–1931), Manx National Heritage Library and Archives: MS 9267 Hall Caine Scrapbook.
[44] Ibid.   [45] Ibid.

'The Berne Convention Is Our Ideal' 113

for the author to make arrangements or pay $25 for papers in towns of under 100,000 and $500 for towns over 100,000.[46]

8.6 The Outcome for Canada

Despite his self-acclaimed success as a political deal maker, Caine's compromise proposal was not accepted. The position he advocated for, however, remained influential. Seville notes that the British resolved that copyright formalities did not conform to the Berne Convention.[47] Further, when the Berne Convention was next revised in Paris in 1896, no Canadian delegation was present, which was a significant omission. However, Britain did represent Canadian interests on the international stage in order to prevent the dominant interpretation of article 2 – that foreign authors should be protected without formalities – from appearing.[48] Britain was pragmatic in presenting a unified voice for the Empire, despite not necessarily accepting the view they advocated as a matter of copyright principle within empire.

Bannerman notes that Canada moved away from the idea of formally denunciating Berne, and amendments passed in 1900 did not include compulsory licensing.[49] However, Canadian publishers did provide one major concession in support of the national economic interest. As noted earlier, under the 1875 Act, Canadian publishers had the right to obtain a license to print British works. With the 1900 amendment they could also apply to the Minister of Agriculture for an order to exclude importation of all copies first published in the British dominions, including those printed in London.[50] In effect this facilitated the turning of independent Canadian publishers into agents of British firms, as Caine had advocated in his compromise.[51]

The Berlin Revision to the Berne Convention in 1908 did not permit copyright formalities.[52] Canada refused to allow Britain to ratify the text

---

[46] Report to the Society of Authors, for publication January 1896. Papers of Sir Thomas Henry Hall Caine (1853-1931), Manx National Heritage Library and Archives: MS 9267 Hall Caine Scrapbook.
[47] Seville, *The Internationalisation of Copyright Law*, 129–30.
[48] This led to the 1896 Interpretative Declaration and Additional Act. See Sam Ricketson and Jane C Ginsburg, *International Copyright and Neighbouring Rights*, 2nd ed. (Oxford: Oxford University Press, 2006), p. [3.06]; Bannerman, *The Struggle for Canadian Copyright*, 63.
[49] An Act to Amend the Copyright Act 1900, 63-64 Vict, c. 25.
[50] Bannerman, *The Struggle for Canadian Copyright*, 69–70.
[51] For a discussion of Macmillan Company (Canada) see MacLaren, *Dominion and Agency*, 122–40.
[52] See Ricketson and Ginsburg, *International Copyright and Neighbouring Rights*, [3.12].

on its behalf. This led to an additional protocol in 1914 that permitted Berne Union countries to restrict the protection afforded to non-union countries where they did not offer adequate reciprocal protection, such as the USA.[53] Bannerman concludes that:

> Britain's control over Canada's international copyright commitments remained firm throughout the 1886 and 1908 diplomatic conventions. Canada, without its own voice at the meetings, without control over all of the copyright laws that were in effect domestically, without the autonomous ability to denounce the Berne Convention, and without the ability to refuse its signature or (in 1896) ratification, was dragged along in international copyright affairs.[54]

8.7 Caine's Legacy

The Berne Convention was not simply an international copyright instrument that advanced legal co-operation between sovereign states based upon a shared respect for authorial labour as well as political compromises. It provided a rallying point that helped change the political narrative and distract modern colonial subjects from the reality of their political, economic and cultural subservience within the Empire.[55] This legacy endures.

Throughout his journey abroad there was relatively little public engagement by Caine with the Canadian publishers' arguments. Instead, Caine made repeated appeals to the 'common sense' of a universal right of authors, bolstered by a personal charm offensive where the author engaged and entertained his readers, winning them over and boring them into disinterest about copyright law. The complicated economic negotiations that sat behind these dynamics advanced English–American interests in tandem, ahead of the interests of authors and especially the reading public in the British dominions. This was rarely openly acknowledged by those appealing to the Berne Convention. It is only due to Caine's vanity and his wife's dedication and patience in preserving so much of his correspondence and pasting his newspaper clippings in a scrapbook that his important role in projecting an idealised picture of international copyright can be exposed today.

---

[53] Bannerman, *The Struggle for Canadian Copyright*, 66, 77–8; Ricketson and Ginsburg, *International Copyright and Neighbouring Rights*, [3.21].
[54] Bannerman, *The Struggle for Canadian Copyright*, 66.
[55] Britain was not the only empire to do this. See José Bellido, 'El Salvador and the internationalisation of copyright' in I Alexander, and T Gomez Arostegui (eds.), *Research Handbook on the History of Copyright Law* (Cheltenham: Edward Elgar, 2016), pp. 313–34.

This would not be the only occasion that authors would take centre stage to front public debates about copyright policy and continue to perpetuate the myth of the author's natural right. Caine and his compatriot's success can still be discerned today. However, more often than not, it is now the authors of the former colonies that rush to defend the imperial status quo that has defined the international book publishing industry, in vain hope of fostering local publishing and the flourishing of an independent literary identity.[56]

---

[56] For a recent example see Kathy Bowrey, 'What's really at stake in changes to copyright', Australian Broadcasting Corporation, The Drum, 3 June 2016, retrieved from https://ab.co/2koXaJm.

9 A Future of International Copyright?
Berne and the Front Door Out

Rebecca Giblin[*]

9.1 The Unamendable Treaty

The Berne Convention was always intended to be revised regularly to keep pace with technological and social change.[1] There were seven revisions in its first eighty-five years, with the longest pause being the twenty years between the Rome (1928) and Brussels (1948) Acts, at which time the world was understandably preoccupied with other matters. But progress ground to a halt in 1971. Since then, we have gone almost half a century with no substantive revision at all.

That can be attributed, in part, to the procedure involved. Revising Berne's substantive provisions requires a unanimity of votes cast, effectively giving each member a veto right and making change exponentially more difficult as membership grows. As I write there are 176 contracting parties, with three – the tiny Pacific Island nations of Tuvalu, the Cook Islands and Kiribati – joining in 2017 alone. But sheer numbers aren't the only problem. More significant is the chasm between members' interests, particularly between developed and developing nations, which has significantly affected Berne's development since the post-colonial era following World War II. In the lead up to that period, as chronicled by Sam Ricketson and Jane Ginsburg in their history of Berne, successive revisions had expanded rights and made the treaty 'increasingly less

---

[*] This work has received funding support from the Australian Research Council (FT170100011). I developed these ideas over many enjoyable hours of debate with Sam Ricketson and Jane Ginsburg in New York during late 2017 – thanks to both for their generosity of both time and ideas. Some of the ideas I touch on are developed more deeply elsewhere: see Rebecca Giblin, 'A new copyright bargain? Reclaiming lost culture and getting authors paid' (2018) 41 *Columbia Journal of Law & the Arts* 369.

[1] Sam Ricketson and Jane C Ginsburg, *International Copyright and Neighbouring Rights: The Berne Convention and Beyond*, 2nd ed. (Oxford: Oxford University Press, 2006), p. 340, citing Berne Convention for the Protection of Literary and Artistic Works, opened for signature 9 September 1886, 828 UNTS 221 (entered into force 5 December 1887) art. 17, which envisaged amendment of the treaty to introduce improvements to 'perfect' the system (cited as Berne Convention).

congenial to the interests of developing countries'.[2] By 1967, such nations made up more than 40 per cent of the membership, and they were visibly chafing at what Drahos describes as a system 'run by an Old World club of former or diminished colonial powers to suit their economic interests'.[3] The poorer nations began raising increasingly urgent questions about the impact of Berne on their development agendas, and there emerged a real risk that they would withdraw from the Berne union altogether. In a nod to the justice of their claims, the 1967 revision contained a protocol that allowed greater flexibility to developing nations, including over the making of translations and copies.[4] However, powerful publisher and author groups mobilised resistance to the reforms and the protocol was ultimately abandoned, creating a schism which threatened for years to destroy the union.[5] The wounds were sutured, barely, by the 1971 Paris Act. Its substitute appendix offered up less generous concessions that every member was, however grudgingly, then able to live with, and the union held.

In the immediate wake of these events emerged a strong view that further revision should not or could not be attempted. Koumantos, in the 'should not' camp, argued that the Berne Convention already gave authors essentially everything they needed, and that to open it up for further revision would be to peek into Pandora's box. 'Authors have no reason to ask for a revision of the Berne Convention – not even in order to complete or clarify certain points. This is because once the procedure of revision is begun once can never know what will come out of it.'[6] Ricketson was of the view that revision, however desirable, simply could not be achieved. While he did nominate a wish list of future changes to Berne in his 1987 treatise, it was combined with an observation that a revision conference in the short to medium term would be 'pointless'.[7] Later, he wrote that 'the prevailing view [after 1971] was that there would be no more revisions of the old kind, and that it would thereafter remain

---

[2] Ibid., 884.
[3] Peter Drahos with John Braithwaite, *Information Feudalism: Who Owns the Knowledge Economy?* (London: Earthscan, 2002), p. 76.
[4] Berne Convention, revised at Stockholm, 14 July 1967 (cited as Stockholm Act) annex (Protocol Regarding Developing Countries).
[5] Ricketson and Ginsburg, *International Copyright and Neighbouring Rights*, 913–14. These events have been described as a 'crisis in international copyright': see Howard D Sacks, 'Crisis in international copyright: The protocol regarding developing countries' (1969) 26 *Journal of Business Law* 128.
[6] Georges Koumantos, 'The future of the Berne Convention' (1986–1987) 11 *Columbia VLA Journal of Law & the Arts* 225, 236.
[7] Sam Ricketson, *The Berne Convention for the Protection of Literary and Artistic Works: 1886–1986* (London: Centre for Commercial Law Studies, Queen Mary College, Kluwer, 1987), p. 919.

unchanged, a kind of enduring artifact to a particular conception of authors' rights that could be taken no further in the changing circumstances of the late twentieth century'.[8]

Treaty obsolescence doesn't necessarily result in pain for treaty parties. Even if members don't wish to formally renounce their obligations, it's not uncommon for outdated parts of toothless treaties to be quietly abandoned. Berne, long regarded as 'little more than a code of polite behaviour',[9] might have met that fate had the formal linking of intellectual property and trade by the Agreement on Trade-Related Aspects of Intellectual Property Rights (TRIPS Agreement)[10] not set it on a different course. That change in fortunes came quickly. In 1988, stronger intellectual property (IP) rights were identified as a US trade priority. After that, industry and governmental discussions about an IP agreement as part of the Uruguay round of the General Agreement on Tariffs and Trade (GATT) rapidly gained momentum, and copyright was put into play as part of a complex bargain entwining such disparate areas as agriculture, textiles and access to medicines. The speed with which the copyright aspects were settled is enough to make one blink. Cornish observed that 'the allure of freer global trading under a revised GATT' was 'scarcely foreseeable in 1986',[11] and Ricketson has admitted some embarrassment for mentioning the emerging issue only in passing in his 1987 text. And yet by 1990, drafts of what would become TRIPS already incorporated Berne as the base on which additional 'Berne-plus' rights were negotiated, and the copyright text was essentially settled by late 1991. Given the pace at which events developed, it's perhaps not surprising that the parties adopted an existing text as a baseline. Additions were tacked on to resolve some of the urgent controversies of the day, such as whether to protect computer programs as literary works. But TRIPS' biggest revolution lay in enforceability. TRIPS took that 'code of polite behaviour' and gave it real teeth, rendering enforceable virtually the whole via World Trade Organization (WTO) dispute resolution mechanisms.

---

[8] Sam Ricketson, 'The Berne Convention: The continued relevance of an ancient text' in David Vaver and Lionel Bently (eds.), *Intellectual Property in the New Millennium: Essays in Honour of William R Cornish* (Cambridge: Cambridge University Press, 2004), pp. 217–18.

[9] William R Cornish, 'Foreword' in Sam Ricketson and Jane C Ginsburg, *International Copyright and Neighbouring Rights: The Berne Convention and Beyond*, 2nd ed. (Oxford: Oxford University Press, 2006), p. v.

[10] Marrakesh Agreement Establishing the World Trade Organization, opened for signature 15 April 1994, 1867 UNTS 3 (entered into force 1 January 1995) annex 1C (Agreement on Trade-Related Aspects of Intellectual Property Rights; cited as TRIPS Agreement).

[11] Cornish, 'Foreword'.

9.2 New Wine into Old Bottles

The dangers of that elevation were readily apparent even before TRIPS was formally agreed. Writing in 1992, Ricketson observed that 'the older and established regimes are now unmistakably beginning to show increasing strains when faced with the problems posed by technological progress'.[12] He saw a lesson in a cautionary biblical parable: 'Neither do men put new wine into old bottles: else the bottles break and the wine runneth out, and the bottles perish: but they put new wine into new bottles, and both are preserved.'[13] The story references the practice of storing wine in animal skins, which dried out as they aged. Those old skins could no longer expand as the fermenting wine released gas – and unfortunate explosions ensued. Ricketson was warning that copyright's skins were growing dangerously brittle, even as the world was trying to lock itself into their continued use. Heedless, world governments formally agreed to TRIPS two years later. With adoption of Berne's outdated and unamendable rules becoming a condition of unprecedented access to world trade markets, its membership exploded by more than 200 per cent from its centenary figure of eighty-six.

To be fair, at that time the full significance of the dawning information age was probably not yet fully appreciated. After all, in 1994, less than half a per cent of the world's population yet had access to the internet; little of the world's culture had been digitised and the potentialities of digital abundance yet to become apparent.[14] But by 1995, Ricketson was already warning that 'the norms now embodied in TRIP[S] (and in Berne) are in danger of becoming outdated and irrelevant in the face of the challenges posed by digital technology, the convergence of technologies and communications, and the emergence of the information superhighway'.[15] Perhaps, as he suggested, a new paradigm of copyright protection may have already been required. It was too bad, then, that the world had just doubled down on the old ways of doing things.

---

[12] Sam Ricketson, 'New wine into old bottles: Technological change and intellectual property rights' (1992) 10(1) *Prometheus* 53, 54.
[13] Matthew 9:17.
[14] Exploring the significance of the evolution from scarcity to abundance, see generally Mark Lemley, 'IP in a world without scarcity' (2015) 90(2) *NYU Law Review* 460.
[15] Sam Ricketson, 'The future of the traditional intellectual property conventions in the brave new world of trade-related intellectual property rights' (1995) 26 *International Review of Intellectual Property and Competition Law* 872, 898.

Those old ways are based on assumptions formed in the world we used to inhabit.[16] Berne and TRIPS reflect a paradigm where marginal costs of copying and distribution were so high that most works were lost within a few short years of publication. In that context there was little downside in the wholesale grant of inordinate terms that would almost certainly outlast their owners' interest, since all but the most popular would be quickly lost regardless. At the same time, formalities on exercise and enjoyment of rights were necessarily onerous and expensive, and a blanket prohibition made sense to prevent authors from being unfairly burdened.

Today those assumptions no longer hold good (at least for those of us with digital access). We have the ability to copy and distribute many kinds of work globally, instantaneously, and at a marginal price close to zero. In this paradigm, there's a real cost to the grant of broad and long rights regardless of whether their owners want them, need them, or even know they exist. Online connectivity has also changed the costs and benefits of registration so fundamentally that we have reached a point (as I have argued elsewhere) that Berne's prohibition on formalities, intended to support authors, has become a key barrier to reforms that could secure them a fairer share.[17] In sum, Berne's rules were designed for a different world and were locked in and given teeth just as realisation was beginning to dawn about the realities of this new one.

So here we are, a quarter of a century after TRIPS was agreed, almost half a century since Berne's last substantive revision, still using those same old bottles. As they detonate around us, the occasion of this Festschrift seems the ideal occasion to ask: Just what are we going to do with all this wine?

9.3 Our Options Are Limited

Currently, Berne/TRIPS severely constrain the universe of possibles. Copyright law would undoubtedly look very different if we were to design it from scratch today.[18] However, the chances of any wholesale revision of Berne are vanishingly small, given the vast number of members, the chasm between their interests, and the structure that gives even the single-most-tiny a right to veto. Indeed, that combination makes even

---

[16] For fuller development of these outdated assumptions, see Rebecca Giblin, 'A new copyright bargain? Reclaiming lost culture and getting authors paid' (2018) 41 *Columbia Journal of Law & the Arts* 369.
[17] Ibid.
[18] See generally Rebecca Giblin and Kimberlee Weatherall (eds.), *What If We Could Reimagine Copyright?* (Acton, Australia: ANU Press, 2017).

minor revisions look seemingly impossible to achieve.[19] TRIPS has proved effectively unamendable as well.[20]

That *could* change. US President Donald Trump has been repeatedly threatening to withdraw the US from the WTO, and at the time of writing, the US is deliberately undermining the organisation by refusing to fill its appeals court vacancies.[21] If the WTO fails, all bets are off. However, barring any such upheaval of global political and trading frameworks, Berne/TRIPS look set to define the outer bounds of copyright for the foreseeable future. Ricketson recently confirmed his view of past decades, writing in 2018: 'it may be accepted that revision of the Berne text presently remains highly unlikely – to quote a leading character in an iconic Australian film, "You're dreaming!"'[22]

Assuming revision won't happen, states can't simply create a new club with different rules, either: Berne's article 20 permits members to enter into other international agreements only to the extent they grant authors more extensive rights or do not derogate from what is already granted under Berne. That limits parties to 'special agreements' such as the World Intellectual Property Organization (WIPO) Copyright Treaty (WCT), which, though explicitly responding to the need 'to provide adequate solutions to the questions raised by new economic, social, cultural and technological developments',[23] could not meaningfully do so, since any amendments had to fall within Berne's existing strictures. Article 20 was perhaps taken as far as it could be with the 2013 Marrakesh Treaty,[24] which focussed on *enabling*, rather than limiting, use of works. But still, it could not go beyond the limits set out in Berne itself.

---

[19] Cf. Daniel Gervais, *(Re)structuring Copyright: A Comprehensive Path to International Copyright Reform* (Northampton, MA: Edward Elgar, 2017); Alan Story, 'Burn Berne: Why the leading international copyright convention must be repealed' (2003) 40(3) *Houston Law Review* 763.

[20] Rebecca Giblin and Kimberlee Weatherall, 'A collection of impossible ideas' in Rebecca Giblin and Kimberlee Weatherall (eds.), *What If We Could Reimagine Copyright?* (Acton, Australia: ANU Press, 2017), pp. 315, 322–3.

[21] See e.g., Rosalind Mathieson, 'US block of WTO appeals body compromises system, director says', *Bloomberg*, 9 November 2017, retrieved from https://bloom.bg/2kBeLxt; 'Disaster management: The WTO is under threat from the Trump administration', *The Economist*, 7 December 2017, retrieved from https://econ.st/2m0GB6F.

[22] Sam Ricketson, 'The international framework for the protection of authors: Bendable boundaries and immovable obstacles' (2018) 41 *Columbia Journal of Law & the Arts* 341, 353.

[23] WIPO Copyright Treaty, opened for signature 20 December 1996, 2186 UNTS 121 (entered into force 6 March 2002), preamble.

[24] Marrakesh Treaty to Facilitate Access to Published Works for Persons Who Are Blind, Visually Impaired or Otherwise Print Disabled, opened for signature 27 June 2013, WIPO Doc VIP/DC/8 (entered into force 30 September 2016).

Individual nations might derogate from Berne/TRIPS regardless, gambling that their actions won't be challenged. As Taubman has explained, TRIPS breaches don't necessarily result in enforcement action:

> Compliance with WTO standards is not like policing a parking lot, where an enforcement officer will issue a ticket and impose a penalty for non-compliance – or a speed camera that will routinely issue a penalty for any infringement. Non-compliance with TRIPS does not bring automatic penalties, and normally does not even yield a formal finding of non-compliance. The only way of reaching an official determination of non-compliance is if another country is concerned about IP protection to the extent that they are prepared to initiate a legal complaint and follow it right through to its conclusion.[25]

Naturally, political and pragmatic considerations will factor heavily in deciding whether to take such action. Despite early fears that TRIPS would unleash a tsunami of litigation, few derogations have actually attracted an enforcement response to date. For example, various developing nations have departed from Berne/TRIPS in furtherance of their development programs[26] (those hard-wrung concessions of the Berne appendix ultimately proving so unhelpful that they have been implemented virtually nowhere[27]). So far that has been without formal comebacks in the WTO. However, such tactics will work only where that overall political and pragmatic calculus suggests enforcement is not worthwhile. More fundamental reforms, those with the potential to threaten the most powerful beneficiaries of the existing framework, would be much more likely to trigger a response. That's likely one reason why we haven't yet seen any attempts at real paradigmatic reform.

A more radical option would be to renounce Berne altogether. That option is easily dismissible however, since it would mean the loss of reciprocal international protection for domestic works (and could not even re-enliven the Universal Copyright Convention, given that treaty's special clauses applying to former Berne nations).[28] It's also impossible

---

[25] Antony Taubman, *A Practical Guide to Working with TRIPS* (Oxford: Oxford University Press, 2011). pp. 13–14.

[26] Alberto Cerda Silva, 'Beyond the unrealistic solution for development provided by the appendix of the Berne Convention on copyright' (2013) 60 *Journal of the Copyright Society of the USA* 581, 598–605.

[27] See e.g., Ricketson and Ginsburg, *International Copyright and Neighbouring Rights*, 957; Margaret Chon, 'Copyright and capability for education: An approach "from below"' in Tzen Wong and Graham Dutfield (eds.), *Intellectual Property and Human Development: Current Trends and Future Scenarios* (New York: Cambridge University Press, 2011), pp. 218, 230, 233; Lea Shaver, 'Copyright and inequality' (2014) 92 *Washington University Law Review* 117, 148.

[28] Universal Copyright Convention, opened for signature 6 September 1952, 216 UNTS 132 (entered into force 16 September 1955), Appendix Declaration Relating to art. XVII.

without abandoning TRIPS and the WTO and hence losing access to vital world trading markets. While it is now thinkable (if not expected) that the WTO system might soon come to an end, in part because of the US actions described earlier, just now withdrawal is still simply not an option for virtually any member – as suggested by the fact that, at time of writing, no member ever *has*.[29]

So Berne/TRIPS are effectively unamendable, they block derogatory agreements and leaving isn't (yet) an option. Ignoring them can be a rational tactic, but would be highly perilous in the case of paradigmatic reforms that threaten to tread on powerful toes. Does this mean we're left with no options while the bottles explode around us, other than to continually lament, in any discussion of meaningful reform, 'But Berne won't let us do that'?

9.4 Berne's 'Front Door Out'

No, there is at least *one* other alternative – to take Berne's front door out.

Berne was only ever intended to regulate members' treatment of other members' nationals and so gives states an entitlement to depart from Berne minima with regard to works 'first published' within their borders.[30] However, it has long been assumed that Berne's standards are definitionally more advantageous to authors, and thus that members would rarely (if ever) choose to exercise this right. For example, Ginsburg writes:

Although neither [Berne nor TRIPS] prescribes the level of protection a member State must afford authors whose works were first published in that State, most countries, *wary of treating their own authors worse than foreign authors*, end up incorporating the international norms in to domestic legislation.[31]

Nations *should* rightly be wary of giving less preferential treatment to their own authors. But as we have seen, the world has changed almost beyond recognition since Berne's rules were put in place, and many of its underlying assumptions no longer hold good. That makes it timely to also challenge the orthodoxy that domestic Berne departure must be definitionally worse for authors. Elsewhere, I recently built the case that

---

[29] A full list of members and observers of the WTO can be found at 'Understanding the WTO: The organization: Members and observers', World Trade Organization, retrieved from www.wto.org/english/thewto_e/whatis_e/tif_e/org6_e.htm.
[30] Berne Convention, art. 5(1).
[31] Jane C Ginsburg, 'Contracts, orphan works, and copyright norms: What role for Berne and TRIPs?' in Rochelle Cooper Dreyfuss, Harry First and Diane Leenheer Zimmerman (eds.), *Working within the Boundaries of Intellectual Property: Innovation Policy for the Knowledge Society* (Oxford: Oxford University Press, 2010), p. 483.

elements of national departure from Berne minima could be the key to creating an alternative copyright bargain that could solve some of copyright's most persistent failures. I sketched a system that more clearly delineated between copyright's incentives and rewards components, envisaged use of formalities-supported reversion to better secure the rewards share to author, and – again utilising registration – permitted broader use of no-longer-wanted-but-still-copyrighted works in a system analogous to a domaine public payant.[32] That analysis showed how departures from Berne's prohibition on formalities on exercise and enjoyment of rights (and potentially its limits on exceptions and compulsory licensing) could, if carefully tailored, significantly improve authors' remuneration outcomes in ways that aren't otherwise possible, upending the assumption that Berne departure would necessarily make them worse off. And it demonstrated how, simultaneously, it was possible to reclaim much of the value and culture lost under current approaches. This cracks open a path to a real alternative – for nations to sidestep Berne's most crippling barriers by taking advantage of their right to domestically depart from its minima; to take the front door out. Doing so would mean retaining the benefits of reciprocal global protection and access to world markets, while regulating their own works and authors in ways that better reflect current realities and take advantage of copyright's non-zero-sum nature.

My 'front door out' also raises a number of mind-bending new questions, such as how would the principle of national treatment work where a nation's departure from Berne minima makes domestic authors better off, rather than worse? And what would article 19's preservation of claims to the benefit of 'greater protection ... granted by legislation in a country of the Union', mean for foreign authors where that greater protection could require departure from Berne? There's not space to address these questions here, but they're tasty fodder for chewing another day.

9.5 Could the 'Front Door Out' Be Subverted?

Of course, any solution that depends on elements of domestic departure will make crucial determination of works' country of origin – and therein raise possibilities for subversion. Article 5(4) of Berne states that a work's country of origin is the country where it is first published or, where it is published simultaneously (that is, within thirty days of first publication[33]) in multiple union countries, by the country with the shortest term. The

---

[32] Giblin, 'A new copyright bargain?' [33] Berne Convention, art. 3(4).

losers in any alternative copyright bargain involving elements of domestic Berne departure would likely seek to bypass it by manipulating the country of first publication and taking the 'back door' in to treatment as a foreign work. If they were simply first published in country B at least thirty days before publishing in country A, would that force country A to afford its own nationals' works treatment as foreign works? If so, it would seriously undermine the strategy's feasibility.

For a few compelling reasons however, it seems unlikely that article 5 could be so subverted. Berne does not specify what happens when a work's country of origin differs from an author's country of nationality.[34] It has been argued that such cases might be treatable as having two countries of origin – that is, that of first publication and that of nationality.[35] As explained by Ginsburg and Ricketson, 'the basis of the suggestion is the assumption that the Berne Convention is not to be interpreted as breaking the bonds between Union countries and their citizens, as it is only concerned with the relations of Union countries to foreign authors'.[36]

If a member *were* to adopt this interpretation and regulate its own nationals' works regardless of place of first publication, it would seem exceedingly unlikely to be challenged via WTO dispute settlement mechanisms. That is not only because of the political and pragmatic considerations canvassed earlier but also because Berne's clear intent to reserve to members the right to regulate their own nationals would make it difficult to prove both breach and damage.

There's another critical reason too why it's unlikely that any nation would push for enforcement of Berne's country of origin principles precisely as written. Recall that, when a work is simultaneously published in multiple union countries (defined in article 3(4) as occurring within thirty days of first publication), the country of origin is the one with the shortest term. When simultaneously published in union and non-union countries, the country of origin is the union country.[37] This text was designed and adopted in a 1960s world. What happens when we apply it to the one we inhabit today, by enquiring into the country of origin for works first published online? Such works are typically made accessible globally within moments, to union and non-union countries alike.

---

[34] Ricketson and Ginsburg, *International Copyright and Neighbouring Rights*, 283.
[35] Ibid., 283–4, citing Alfred Baum, 'Völkerrecht, Berne Konvention und Landesgesetze' (1950) *Gewerblicher Rechtsschutz und Urheberrecht* 437, 451; Wilhelm Nordemann, Kai Vinck, Paul W Hertin and Gerald Meyer, *International Copyright and Neighbouring Rights Law* (New York: VCH,1990), p. 75.
[36] Ricketson and Ginsburg, *International Copyright and Neighbouring Rights*, 284.
[37] Berne Convention, art. 5(4).

If online publication amounts to simultaneous first publication in every country from which it may be accessed, then a plain English reading suggests *every* union member with the shortest term will be a country of origin. That was the reasoning of a US district court in *Kernal Records v. Mosley*, which held that the online first publication of music (on an Australian website) meant that the work was simultaneously published in the US and thus ought to be treated as a local US work.[38] If every shortest-term member is the country of origin of every internet work, that means *every one of those countries of origin will have the ability to depart from its minima*. Thus a literal application of Berne's text raises the possibility of blowing the whole Berne system up. This would no doubt give pause to any copyright-exporting nations who might otherwise be tempted to argue against an interpretation permitting fellow members to regulate their own nationals. The absurdity of that literal reading also further demonstrates how unmoored Berne has become from today's realities.

A study group of the International Literary and Artistic Association (ALAI) has sought to avoid such an interpretation by arguing that Berne's article 3(3) requires the distributed copies to be in physical form:

> We infer this from the words 'manufacture of copies' … and the term 'availability of *such* copies' (emphasis supplied), which would seem to refer back to the material copies that are made available by the author or authorized intermediary distributor. … [T]he conclusion that the copies envisioned in article 3(3) are pre-existing physical copies also follows from the comparison of the first and second phrases of art 3(3): the exclusion from the definition of 'published works' of literary or artistic works communicated by wire or broadcasting casts doubt on the characterization of works 'made available' to the public over digital networks as 'published.'[39]

However, this attempted fix surfaces fresh difficulties. For one thing, article 3(3)'s own text specifies that '"published works" means works published with the consent of their authors, *whatever may be the means of manufacture of the copies*.'[40] The inclusiveness of that language cuts against ALAI's proposed technologically specific reading. For another,

---

[38] *Kernal Records Oy v. Mosley*, 794 F Supp 2d 1355, 1360 (SD Fla 2011). On appeal, the 11th Circuit was not convinced the relevant publication had in fact occurred online, but nonetheless indicated online distribution on a public website was consistent with a presumption of simultaneous worldwide availability: *Kernel Records Oy v. Mosley*, 694 F 3d 1294, 1306 (11th Cir, 2012).

[39] Country of Origin Study Group of the International Literary and Artistic Association (ALAI), 'Determination of country of origin when a work is first publicly disclosed over the internet', 14 January 2012, 2–3, retrieved from www.alai.org/en/assets/files/resolutions/country-of-origin.pdf.

[40] Berne Convention, art. 3(3) (emphasis added).

this reading would still result in numerous countries of origin, especially given growing use of print-on-demand. Further, ALAI's proposed interpretation would lead to absurdities of its own: works distributed exclusively in digital form (as is increasingly the case) would *never* be 'first published' anywhere. Their authors would be obliged to rely on article 5 (4)(c)'s rules governing unpublished works, which provide that, for most works, the country of origin is the country of the author's nationality.[41] While this would at least preserve nations' rights to regulate the works of their own nationals, it creates new difficulties for authors of non-union members, who might then lack a requisite point of attachment. It also raises further difficult questions in cases where digitally distributed works have multiple authors.[42] While the ALAI Study Group acknowledges these difficulties, it argues that 'the seemingly counter-intuitive result that a work disseminated only in dematerialized digital format is never "published" is the less problematic outcome'.[43] Ricketson and Ginsburg have separately argued that, in the case of simultaneous publication online in a number of countries, it might make sense to have a reading that designates the country of origin as the country of the author's nationality.[44]

9.6 Extending the Benefits of Domestic Departure from Berne

All this should provide considerable comfort to any nation which, looking for ways past the obstacles imposed by Berne's outdated strictures, chooses to depart from them for its own nationals (even as it flags a fresh danger emerging from Berne's obsolescence). However, that still takes us only so far. Since copyright is territorial, enacting countries could apply such systems only within their own borders. There, too, they could defeat attempts to subvert them through adoption of the contract law of foreign jurisdictions.[45] But private international law problems would inevitably plague any attempt to enforce Berne-departing copyright laws beyond their own borders. Could the potential benefits of domestic Berne departure nonetheless be extended?

---

[41] Berne Convention, art. 5(4)(c).
[42] ALAI Country of Origin Study Group, 'Determination of country of origin', 5–8.
[43] Ibid., 5.
[44] Ricketson and Ginsburg, *International Copyright and Neighbouring Rights*, p. 285.
[45] For a general discussion of private international law issues arising in the copyright context, including territorial complexities introduced by the internet, see Jane C Ginsburg and Pierre Sirinelli, 'Private international law aspects of authors' contracts: The Dutch and French examples' (2015) 39 *Columbia Journal of Law and the Arts* 171.

We have seen that article 20 prohibits international agreements that derogate from Berne's minima. Significantly, however, it does nothing to prevent nations from agreeing to each regulate their own nationals in a harmonised way that involves elements of permitted Berne departure. This opens the possibility of countries banding together to individually depart from Berne for their own nationals, where overall that would result in a better deal. Harmonised, cooperative, front door departure could potentially achieve widespread benefits of a kind currently beyond reach. For example, participants could each create appropriate domestic registries to facilitate rights clearance and payment. If designed for compatibility and then internationally shared, that could soon result in a comprehensive database of the type currently ruled out by Berne/TRIPS. Similarly, if nations with shared interests and language were to mandate harmonised author protective mechanisms, this could contribute greatly to efforts to secure their own creators a fairer share.

Weatherall and I once described the Berne/TRIPS framework as a 'hostage situation we can't see anyone walking away from'.[46] Right now, the existence of the 'front door out' does nothing to change that. It would take enormous political will to reallocate copyright's rights and responsibilities to take advantage of copyright's zero-sum nature and better reflect today's realities. Any government considering such an approach would have to face down strong resistance from trading partners and corporations with vested interests in the existing ways of doing things. It will take time before competing motivations might become strong enough to surmount such pressures. Eventually however, we may reach a point where individual nations can no longer afford the waste generated by regulating the digital world with analog rules. If and when we are finally ready to take authors' interests seriously, reclaim our lost culture and retire that despairing lament of 'but Berne doesn't let us do that' – the front door will be there.

---

[46] Giblin and Weatherall, *What If We Could Reimagine Copyright?*, 321.

10 'Trade-Related' after All?
Reframing the Paris and Berne Conventions as Multilateral Trade Law

Antony Taubman [*]

10.1 Introduction

Should trade agreements set standards for domestic protection of intellectual property (IP) rights or should they avoid such 'behind the border' regulation? How should such IP standards be construed in a trade law setting? And what does the integration of trade and IP law mean for the public policy objectives purportedly promoted by the two systems? This chapter considers these questions in the light of the incorporation of the two longstanding central pillars of the international law of IP, the Paris Convention[1] and the Berne Convention,[2] into the WTO Agreement[3] through the vector of its annex 1C, the TRIPS Agreement.[4]

The seemingly contingent meshing of IP and trade law though TRIPS, apparently an artefact of pragmatic negotiating ambitions, may belie a broader coherence resonating with the early development of multilateral IP law. Rather than reframing international IP law as trade law, the ultimate effect of integrating the Paris and Berne Conventions into TRIPS may have been to redefine international trade law, exemplifying

---

[*] This chapter presents strictly personal views which should not be taken to represent the views of the WTO, its Members or its Secretariat, and which have no bearing on matters of treaty interpretation.
[1] Paris Convention for the Protection of Industrial Property, opened for signature 20 March 1883, revised at Stockholm, 14 July 1967, 828 UNTS 305, as amended on 28 September 1979 (entered into force 3 June 1984) (cited as Paris Convention).
[2] Berne Convention for the Protection of Literary and Artistic Works, opened for signature 9 September 1886, revised at Paris, 24 July 1971, 828 UNTS 221, as amended on 28 September 1979 (entered into force 19 November 1984) (cited as Berne Convention).
[3] Agreement Establishing the World Trade Organization, opened for signature 15 April 1994, 1867 UNTS 3 (entered into force 1 January 1995) (cited as WTO Agreement).
[4] WTO Agreement, annex 1C (Agreement on Trade-Related Aspects of Intellectual Property Rights; cited as TRIPS Agreement).

the shift of focus in trade policy to the regulation of commercial activity beyond the border.

10.2 From IP-Related Aspects of Trade Law ...

What might be the essential rationale, in principle, for *a* multilateral agreement on trade-related aspects of IP rights – as conceptually distinct from *the* contingent, actual TRIPS Agreement? Reduced trade tensions and greater stability may flow from an objective, unambiguous, balanced and fair standard of what amounts to adequate and effective IP protection, which doesn't unduly intrude into domestic policy space, doesn't unreasonably curtail regulatory diversity and evolution and provides for sound public policy adapted to domestic needs and circumstances. From a trade policy perspective, given the territoriality of IP rights, the legitimacy and relevance of such standards would pivot on accepting that certain business models and mutually beneficial international commercial transactions depend on adequate and effective IP protection and the effective articulation between national IP systems – the absence of which would amount to 'distortions and impediments'[5] to legitimate international trade. Legitimate expectations of fair opportunities to compete – even notions of market access – would then extend to agreed principles, not overly prescriptive rules, on how traders can make use of and benefit from the IP system in foreign jurisdictions; bounds would be set, though, to such expectations, so as not to pre-empt appropriate domestic policy choices. This would enable reasonable, workable interoperability between domestic IP systems, sufficient for legitimate, social-welfare-enhancing[6] business models that rely on IP protection to operate effectively across borders – with scope for inclusion of forms of trading in digital products and IP licences, legitimate 'trade in bits'.[7]

Ideally, then, the task of the treaty negotiator – and then of the interpreter of treaty text – would be to translate such expectations into legal provisions that provide for clarity of trading partners' respective rights and obligations,[8] a predictable environment for IP-based transactions[9] and reduced tensions arising from the absence of an effective multilateral framework.[10]

---

[5] Ibid., Preamble.   [6] Ibid., art. 7.
[7] Nicholas Negroponte, 'Bits and atoms', *Wired*, 1 January 1995, retrieved from www.wired.com/1995/01/negroponte-30.
[8] WTO Agreement, annex 2 ('Understanding on Rules and Procedures Governing the Settlement of Disputes'), art. 3.2.
[9] Ibid.   [10] TRIPS Agreement, Preamble.

10.3 ... to Trade-Related Aspects of IP

The *actual* TRIPS Agreement, as concluded, arguably aspires to this idealised notion, while inevitably falling short of the ideal. In practice, it crystallised questions about the proper relationship between international IP and trade law and, in yoking these domains together, exemplified perceived tensions between them. As the General Agreement on Tariffs and Trade (GATT) Uruguay Round took shape, the notion of incorporating IP into multilateral trade law was opposed by developing countries, contested by international institutions, and criticised from the diverse viewpoints of IP scholars, trade economists, and anti-globalisation activists – rejected alike by supporters and opponents of liberalising the international trade system. Alongside critical perspectives concerning public policy, public welfare, human rights and IP policy, TRIPS elicited concerns that IP protection was not 'about trade': that the idea of 'trade-related aspects' – the diplomatic formula putting IP literally on the multilateral trade negotiation agenda[11] – masked 'trade-unrelated' negotiating ambitions, a matter of 'royalty collection ... forced onto the WTO's agenda',[12] 'as if a loan shark had taken control of a legitimate enforcement agency to collect on its predatory demands.'[13] A package of IP standards in a trade law setting, TRIPS has been characterised as a cuckoo's egg,[14] an uneasy marriage[15] and a shotgun wedding or marriage of convenience.[16]

TRIPS, as concluded, also effectively reframed the Paris and Berne Conventions as multilateral *trade* law, a development Sam Ricketson identifies as 'the most significant recent phase in Paris Convention history ... the transformation of its provisions into trading standards that are potentially enforceable through the dispute settlement procedures of

---

[11] See generally, Antony Taubman, 'The coming of age of the TRIPS Agreement: Framing those "trade-related aspects"' in Christophe Geiger (ed.), *The Intellectual Property System in a Time of Change: European and International Perspectives* (Strasbourg, France: CEIPI, 2016), p. 246.

[12] Jagdish Bhagwati, 'From Seattle to Hong Kong' (2005) 84(7) *Foreign Affairs*, retrieved from www.foreignaffairs.com/articles/2005-12-01/seattle-hong-kong.

[13] Ibid.

[14] Matthew Kennedy, *WTO Dispute Settlement and the TRIPS Agreement: Applying Intellectual Property Standards in a Trade Law Framework* (Cambridge: Cambridge University Press, 2016), p. 5.

[15] Arvind Panagariya, 'TRIPS and the WTO: An uneasy marriage' in Keith E Maskus (ed.), *The WTO, Intellectual Property Rights and the Knowledge Economy* (London: Edward Elgar, 2004), pp. 91–102.

[16] Antony Taubman, *A Practical Guide to Working with TRIPS* (Oxford: Oxford University Press, 2011), p. 5.

the [WTO]'.[17] Paris and Berne had been developed, negotiated and administered – perceived and analysed – over more than a century[18] as distinct multilateral treaties in their respective fields, within the discrete, technical domain of international IP law, framed by its specific institutional context.

When the elements of multilateral trade law – and proposed rules to govern commercial activities[19] – were drawn up in the immediate postwar period, IP protection was framed as a conditional *exception* to trade law disciplines[20] and as linked to restrictive business practices.[21] Later, developing countries opposed subsequent initiatives to bring into the multilateral trade law system even the most evident point of 'trade and IP' convergence, suppressing trade in counterfeit goods.[22] Linking IP and trade was generally rejected as bad trade policy and bad trade economics, as an unacceptable distortion of trade negotiating mandates, as prejudicial to development and as distorting both trade law and IP law. This past resistance made the paradigm shift of TRIPS all the more striking: positive standards for IP protection became core trade law commitments, as did the central elements of the discrete, established treaty system administered by the World Intellectual Property Organization (WIPO).

10.4 A Past Era of 'Trade-Related Aspects' of IP

Yet the conceptual and formal disjunction between the international law of trade and commerce and of IP (particularly its industrial property element) was not inevitable. IP provisions were increasingly present in the trade and commerce agreements of an earlier era of economic globalisation, the later nineteenth century. Burgeoning trade in industrial and branded goods led to increased pressure for protection of trademarks, and progressively other forms of industrial property, in foreign markets.

---

[17] See Sam Ricketson, *The Paris Convention for the Protection of Industrial Property: A Commentary* (Oxford: Oxford University Press, 2015), p. [5.20].
[18] See Ibid.; Sam Ricketson and Jane Ginsburg, *International Copyright and Neighbouring Rights: The Berne Convention and Beyond* (Oxford: Oxford University Press, 2006).
[19] Interim Commission for the International Trade Organization, *Final Act and Related Documents of the United Nations Conference on Trade and Employment* (Lake Success, New York, 1948), UN Doc E/Conf.2/78 (cited as Havana Charter).
[20] WTO Agreement annex 1A ('General Agreement on Tariffs and Trade 1994'), art. XX.
[21] Havana Charter, art. 46.
[22] Multilateral Trade Negotiations, Commercial Counterfeiting, GATT Doc MTN/NTM/W/204 (11 December 1978); Agreement on Measures to Discourage the Importation of Counterfeit Goods, GATT Doc L/5382 (18 October 1982).

Bilateral trade agreements addressed the suppression of counterfeiting of trademarks,[23] national treatment and MFN principles[24] and even substantive standards for industrial property protection,[25] alongside agreements specifically on trademarks, patents and copyright.

Access to IP protection was presented both as a practical necessity and as an element of fairness in trade, spurring momentum towards a multilateral agreement on industrial property. Citing the letter of invitation to the 1872 Vienna Conference, the first step towards the Paris Convention, Yusuf comments that trade arguments for an IP standard setting are 'perhaps as old as the international regime on [IP rights] itself',[26] noting parallels with arguments for TRIPS advanced in the 1980s. At the 1883 conference concluding the Paris Convention, the French trade minister, as host, invoked the benefits for trade; the Nordic delegate cast the Convention as 'an act of justice, conceived with a view to protecting trade and industry against competition that is unfair and sterile, and leave the field open for fair and fertile competition'.[27] The 1886 Berne Convention was conceived in the context of authors' rights, ushered into existence by Victor Hugo, with an emphasis on cultural policy.[28] Even so, copyright had for decades formed part of bilateral trade negotiations (mostly by reference to literary and artistic property).[29] The UK International Copyright Act[30] signalled 'recognition of and response to the importance of international copyright in better protecting its domestic trade as well as exploiting the overseas market beyond its own colonial borders'.[31] The well-being of the publishing industry – export potential

---

[23] E.g., Treaty of Commerce, Navigation and Trade Marks, Belgium-USA, signed 8 March 1875, 149 CTS 131 (entered into force 11 June 1875).
[24] E.g., Brazil-USA Agreement concerning Trade-Marks (1878); Treaty of Commerce and Navigation between Great Britain and Japan (1894); Treaty of Friendship, Commerce, and Navigation, between the United Kingdom and the Republic of Nicaragua (1905) (providing national treatment for 'patents for inventions, trade-marks, and designs').
[25] Treaty between the United Kingdom and China respecting Commercial Relations & c. (1902).
[26] Abdulqawi Yusuf, 'TRIPS: Background, principles and general provisions' in Carlos Correa and Abdulqawi Yusuf (eds.), *Intellectual Property and Trade: The TRIPS Agreement* (Alphen aan den Rijn, The Netherlands: Kluwer, 2008), p. 7.
[27] Actes de la Conférence Internationale pour la Protection de la Propriété Industrielle, Réunie à Paris du 6 au 28 mars 1883, 28-29
[28] Claude Masouyé, *Guide to the Berne Convention for the Protection of Literary and Artistic Works (Paris Act, 1971)* (Geneva: WIPO, 1978), p. 1.
[29] Belgium and Mexico, Traité d'amitié, de commerce et de navigation (1895); Japan and Russia, Traité de commerce et de navigation (1895).
[30] International Copyright Act 1838, 1 & 2 Vict, c. 59.
[31] Ronan Deazley, 'Commentary on International Copyright Act 1838' in Lionel Bently and Martin Kretschmer (eds.), *Primary Sources on Copyright (1450–1900)* (2008), retrieved from https://bit.ly/2lxAbM4.

and the impact of cheap imports – guided subsequent efforts by the Board of Trade to conclude bilateral copyright agreements.[32]

The 'more overtly commercial tone'[33] of the Paris Convention was evident in a preambular aspiration to assure 'complete and effective protection' to 'industry and trade' and a guarantee of fairness in commercial transactions. The 1883 text of Paris established the principles of national treatment and the right of priority: legal and practical essentials, respectively, for market access to foreign markets for traders whose business models depend on the ability to manage IP rights on an equal competitive footing with their domestic competitors – what Carvalho terms 'articulation'[34] of domestic systems. At that basic level, in enabling the practical interoperability of domestic systems, Paris can be understood as 'trade-related' even in its earliest form. IP's trade-relatedness was also exemplified in the local working issue of whether importation exhausts a patentee's responsibility to make available the patented technology. The chair of the 1880 Conference declared French legislation requiring local production to be 'barbaric' and a futile attempt at protection which caused 'serious prejudice to trade'.[35] Ricketson charts[36] how this trade issue remained contentious throughout the negotiations and at the 1886 Rome revision conference.[37] It remains contentious today,[38] precipitating a TRIPS dispute.[39]

A further trade linkage was evident in Paris and Berne standards on border enforcement of IP rights; concluded under the aegis of Paris, the 1891 Madrid Agreement for the Repression of False or Deceptive Indications of Source on Goods[40] required such goods to be seized upon

---

[32] Friedemann Kawoh, 'Commentary on the Anglo-Prussian Copyright Convention of 1846' in Lionel Bently and Martin Kretschmer (eds.), *Primary Sources on Copyright (1450–1900)* (2008), retrieved from https://bit.ly/2kovHY6.
[33] Ricketson and Ginsburg, *International Copyright and Neighbouring Rights*, 13.
[34] Nuno Pires de Carvalho, *The TRIPS Regime of Patents and Test Data*, 5th ed. (Alphen aan den Rijn, The Netherlands: Kluwer Law International, 2017), p. 92.
[35] Actes de la Conférence Internationale pour la Protection de la Propriété Industrielle, Réunie à Paris, 4–20 November 1880.
[36] See Ricketson, *The Paris Convention for the Protection of Industrial Property*, [4.09].
[37] See also Carvalho, *The TRIPS Regime of Patents and Test Data*, 278, on trade policy and protectionism in the Paris negotiations.
[38] Intellectual Property Appellate Board, Chennai, OA/35/2012/PT/MUM, Order No. 45 (4 March 2013); see also Carvalho, T*he TRIPS Regime of Patents and Test Data*, 280; and Marsoof A 'Local working of patents: The perspective of developing countries', in A Bharadwaj, V Devaiah and I Gupta (eds.) *Multi-dimensional Approaches towards New Technology* (Singapore: Springer, 2018).
[39] Brazil – Measures Affecting Patent Protection, DS199.
[40] Madrid Agreement for the Repression of False or Deceptive Indications of Source on Goods, opened for signature 14 April 1891, 828 UNTS 163 (entered into force 1 June 1963).

importation. Such provisions anticipated and overlapped with provisions in the 1947 GATT on the suppression of geographically misdescriptive trade names[41] and the future initiatives to establish a GATT Anti-Counterfeiting Code.[42] The 1925 Hague Revision Conference for the Paris Convention saw strong institutional linkages with the Economic Committee of the League of Nations (effective predecessor of the GATT and the WTO, expressly mandated to liberalise trade relations). Alongside drafting proposals on trademarks, indications of source and official emblems, the Economic Committee submitted a draft convention on unfair competition,[43] which it presented as a crucial link between trade and IP and an element of ensuring 'equitable treatment for commerce,'[44] a foundational objective of the league. The London Conference (itself chaired by a representative of the Economic Committee) concluded with a resolution calling for continued collaboration, although subsequent revision conferences lacked a comparable trade policy presence.

10.5 Paris, Berne and 'Effective and Adequate' IP Protection

Against this complex background, then, how can the Paris and Berne Conventions be construed as elements of a multilateral understanding on the linkage between trade and IP – that is, as contributions to removing distortions and impediments to legitimate forms of international trade? A partial answer can be reverse engineered from the contrasting ambitions which the Uruguay Round negotiations sought to reconcile.[45] Proponents of an agreement on trade-related aspects of IP sought to establish a minimum standard of IP protection in domestic jurisdictions, in terms of substantive standards ('adequacy') and their enforceability in practice ('effectiveness'), reflected in the reference in the TRIPS negotiating mandate to the 'need to promote effective and adequate protection of intellectual property rights', a formula influenced by the domestic legal basis for the unilateral demands made of trading partners of the United States under the 1984 Trade and Tariff Act.[46] The ensuing negotiations

---

[41] General Agreement on Tariffs and Trade 1994, art. IX.6.
[42] Christopher Wadlow, '"Including trade in counterfeit goods": The origins of TRIPs as a GATT anti-counterfeiting code' (2007) 3 *Intellectual Property Quarterly* 350.
[43] Projet de la Société des Nations sur la concurrence déloyale, Circulaire 193/1418 (15 November 1924); text at pp. 96–7, Actes de the Hague Conference.
[44] Covenant of the League of Nations, art. 23(e).
[45] Outlined in Adrian Otten, 'The TRIPS negotiations: An overview' in Jayashree Watal and Antony Taubman (eds.), *The Making of TRIPS* (Geneva: World Trade Organization, 2015), pp. 55–78.
[46] Following its amendment in 1984, 19 USC § 2242 requires the United States Trade Representative to identify foreign countries that 'deny adequate and effective protection

initially turned on three contrasting conceptions of IP's 'trade-relatedness':

- Framing the 'trade-related aspects' in conventional 'trade in goods' terms – essentially minimising ill-founded impediments to trade and discrimination in the impact of domestic regulation.
- Limiting positive IP disciplines within a multilateral trade context to suppressing trade in counterfeit goods, akin to unsuccessful earlier attempts under GATT to conclude a code on counterfeit trade.
- Remedying supposed distortions to trade, and denial of 'fair and equitable market access', by establishing positive standards for the grant, administration and enforcement of IP rights.

The 1989 midterm review of the negotiations settled the general 'trade-relatedness' question by accepting the goal of articulating 'adequate standards and principles concerning the availability, scope and use of trade-related intellectual property rights' and 'effective and appropriate means' for their enforcement.[47] In yoking the notion of trade-related IP rights to substantive standards for IP protection, this decision necessitated consideration of possible links between emerging TRIPS provisions and the established Paris and Berne texts, a question partly depending on whether a distinct agreement would address only trade in counterfeit and pirated goods or would frame a broader set of substantive standards.[48] Brazil argued that the Paris Convention's basic principles were sufficient for the international protection of IP and 'were not of a commercial nature, and thus should be discussed not in GATT, but in the competent international organisations'.[49] Some argued that attaining 'negotiating objectives would be enhanced by providing for an obligation for parties to a GATT agreement to adhere to and implement the Paris and Berne Conventions'.[50] Recognising border enforcement as a point of

---

of intellectual property rights' or that 'deny fair and equitable market access to United States persons that rely upon intellectual property protection'. It specifies that a 'foreign country denies adequate and effective protection of intellectual property rights if the foreign country denies adequate and effective means under the laws of the foreign country for persons who are not citizens or nationals of such foreign country to secure, exercise, and enforce rights relating to patents, process patents, registered trademarks, copyrights, trade secrets, and mask works'.

[47] Multilateral Trade Negotiations, Uruguay Round – Trade Negotiations Committee, Mid-Term Meeting, GATT Doc MTN.TNC/11 (21 April 1989) 4(b).
[48] Status of Work in the Negotiating Group, Chairman's Report to the GNG, GATT Doc MTN.GNG/NG11/W/76 (23 July 1990).
[49] Multilateral Trade Negotiations, Uruguay Round, Meeting of Negotiating Group, GATT Doc MTN.GNG/NG11/10 (17–21 October 1988) 4.
[50] Multilateral Trade Negotiations, Uruguay Round, Meeting of Negotiating Group, GATT Doc MTN.GNG/NG11/11 (14–15 November, 1988) 3.

intersection, one proposal was for countries to 'sign the Madrid Agreement for the Repression of False or Deceptive Indications of Source on Goods, administered by WIPO, as a preliminary to any further discussion of trade in counterfeit goods' and for this agreement to be extended also to registered trademarks, supposedly 'an easy task in the context of the Paris Union'.[51] The Swiss negotiator recalls that the incorporation of Paris and Berne, as 'a bold new step ... faced objections from some developing countries ... because of the possibility of making applicable the GATT dispute settlement system, or simply because they were not yet party to those Conventions. On the other hand, it would be impossible to take up each and every provision of the Conventions again.'[52] She recalls the 'great deal of time and energy' required to convince Brazil to incorporate the two conventions; incorporating Berne was less controversial for India, given its copyright content industry.[53]

Negotiators turned to considering specific modalities for referencing the existing conventions, such as requirements to 'comply with the substantive provisions' of these conventions;[54] to provide 'protection no less than the economic rights'[55] of Paris and Berne; 'as minimum substantive standards for the protection of Trademarks, Geographical Indications, Industrial Designs, and Patents, [to] provide protection under the substantive provisions of [Paris]' and a similar formulation for Berne;[56] and a coalition of developing countries advocated avoiding any binding reference.[57] The July 1990 composite chair text[58] included, as one option, an obligation to 'comply with the [substantive] provisions [on economic rights]' of Paris and Berne. By November that year, the

---

[51] Multilateral Trade Negotiations, Uruguay Round, Meeting of Negotiating Group, GATT Doc MTN.GNG/NG11/2 (10 June 1987).
[52] Thu-Lang Tran Wasescha, 'Negotiating for Switzerland' in Jayashree Watal and Antony Taubman (eds.), *The Making of TRIPS* (Geneva: World Trade Organization, 2015), pp. 168–9.
[53] A V Ganesan, 'Negotiating for India,' in Jayashree Watal and Antony Taubman (eds.), *The Making of TRIPS* (Geneva: World Trade Organization, 2015), pp. 211–38.
[54] European Communities Draft Agreement on Trade-Related Aspects of Intellectual Property Rights, GATT Doc MTN.GNG/NG11/W/68 (29 March 1990).
[55] Draft Agreement on Trade-Related Aspects of Intellectual Property Rights – Communication from the United States, GATT Doc MTN.GNG/NG11/W/70 (11 May 1990).
[56] Multilateral Trade Negotiations, Uruguay Round, Main Elements of a Legal Text for TRIPS – Communication from Japan, GATT Doc MTN.GNG/NG11/W/74 (15 May 1990).
[57] Multilateral Trade Negotiations, Uruguay Round, Communication from Argentina, Brazil, Chile, China, Colombia, Cuba, Egypt, India, Nigeria, Peru, Tanzania and Uruguay, GATT Doc MTN.GNG/NG11/W/71 (14 May 1990).
[58] Status of Work in the Negotiating Group, Chairman's Report to the GNG, GATT Doc MTN.GNG/NG11/W/76 (23 July 1990) [5A].

negotiators had settled on the formulae now present in TRIPS. Unlike in earlier drafts, Paris and Berne were dealt with separately, both structurally (Berne falling into one of the sections of substantive IP law in Part II, and Paris covered in Part I, under 'General Provisions and Basic Principles') and in their immediate context (compliance with provisions of Paris characterised as 'in respect of Parts II, III and IV', this formula later raising an interpretative issue, discussed later in the chapter). The negotiators' distinction between economic and other rights under those conventions was reduced to an exclusion of obligations concerning moral rights under Berne article 6*bis* (by contrast, TRIPS incorporates the right of inventors to be mentioned as such under Paris article 4*ter*).

The resultant framing of Paris and Berne as multilateral trade law was therefore contingent, an artefact of pragmatic negotiating decisions. Yet it is now integral to the architecture of the international law both of trade and of IP, largely taken for granted as a practical reality and a major influence on the evolution of domestic IP law and policy for WTO members and accession candidates. The implications are considerable: Provisions of Paris and Berne are now monitored, implemented, enforced and interpreted through a trade law prism, no longer only as discrete treaties but also as components of an annex to the WTO Agreement. Enforcement of WTO commitments in sectors other than IP has led to possible justifications for noncompliance with Paris and Berne.[59] Since GATT rules on non-discrimination have also been applied in IP dispute settlement, the Paris/Berne/TRIPS complex now incorporates three distinct conceptions of the bedrock principle of national treatment in the field of IP, and trade law jurisprudence guides its interpretation.[60] TRIPS is argued to have redefined the obligations to states parties to each other under Paris, notably concerning the scope of obligations on unfair competition.[61]

The implications of this complex linkage reach beyond the scope of multilateral law, since numerous bilateral and regional trade agreements concluded in the wake of TRIPS similarly incorporate Paris and Berne.[62]

[59] E.g., Decision by the Arbitrator, European Communities – Regime for the Importation, Sale and Distribution of Bananas – Recourse to Arbitration by the European Communities under Article 22.6 of the DSU, WTO Doc WT/DS27/ARB/ECU (24 March 2000).
[60] WTO, WTO Analytical Index: Guide to WTO Law and Practice – Annex 1C: Trade-Related Aspects of Intellectual Property Rights, article 3 (Jurisprudence), retrieved from www.wto.org/english/res_e/publications_e/ai17_e/trips_e.htm; see in particular US – Section 211 Appropriations Act, DS176.
[61] Carvalho, *The TRIPS Regime of Patents and Test Data*, 468.
[62] Raymundo Valdés and Maegan McCann, 'Intellectual property provisions in regional trade agreements: revision and update' in Rohini Acharya (ed.), *Regional Trade*

Individual countries may be bound by the same Paris and Berne provisions as parties to the original conventions, through their application via TRIPS, through separate bilateral undertakings giving effect to Paris and Berne and through bilateral undertakings to give effect to TRIPS itself (and thus the Paris and Berne provisions it incorporates). Each such formally distinct modality of application of what is, on its face, the same treaty language raises the possibility of distinct forums and interpretative contexts for dispute settlement. Similarly, since TRIPS binds WTO members to the latest versions of Paris and Berne, some countries are simultaneously bound by two separate revisions of the conventions[63] and are therefore bound by different obligations vis-à-vis other WTO members as such and other Paris and Berne Union members as such.

The ostensible mutual benefit of an objective legal standard that defines the rights of and obligations owed by countries to one another depends on the clarity and reasonable predictability of those standards. In clarifying the scope of complaints under TRIPS to the treaty text, the WTO Appellate Body has observed that the 'legitimate expectations of the parties to a treaty are reflected in the language of the treaty itself'.[64] Uncertainty or ambiguity in the relationship between Paris and Berne, on the one hand, and various avenues for settlement of trade disputes, on the other, could undermine these benefits. And the complex overlay of bilateral, regional and multilateral norms and standards, applying similar provisions through distinct avenues with distinct dispute settlement and interpretive contexts, creates a 'lasagna effect'[65] of overlapping standards, reducing the systemic benefits of a coherent and predictable system of law.

The question of coherence also arises even when interpreting Paris and Berne – and considering the status of their extensive *travaux* – as integral elements of the WTO Agreement. Incorporating Berne and Paris into TRIPS raised the prospect of two divergent streams of international IP law: a 'trade-related' stream and conventional interpretative readings grounded in the diplomatic history and the institutional framework of WIPO. Netanel distinguished 'Berne qua Berne' and 'Berne-in-TRIPS'

Agreements and the Multilateral Trading System (Cambridge: Cambridge University Press, 2016), p. 497.

[63] As pointed out in Carvalho, *The TRIPS Regime of Patents and Test Data*, 91–2.

[64] Appellate Body Report, India – Patent Protection for Pharmaceutical and Agricultural Chemical Products, WTO Doc WT/DS50/AB/R (19 December 1997) [45].

[65] Antony Taubman, 'The lasagna effect: What do layers of bilateral and regional norms mean for multilateral intellectual property law?' Lecture delivered at the Spangenberg Center for Law, Technology, and the Arts, Case Western Reserve University, Cleveland, OH, April 2016.

and argued for the primacy of state practice under Berne in interpreting Berne-in-TRIPS, guided also by state practice under TRIPS as well as by the treaty's object and purpose.[66] Since then, TRIPS dispute settlement panels have adopted a practice of ensuring jurisprudential coherence, including through close attention to the diplomatic history of Paris and Berne, as germane to their reading of TRIPS. Equally, the incorporation of Paris and Berne into the WTO legal architecture meant that mainstream trade law could provide greater depth of jurisprudence on broader principles of non-discrimination and national treatment.

10.6 In Respect of: Clarifying the Scope of Incorporation

The need for a stable and coherent reading of Paris and Berne as trade law inevitably led to close attention to how their immediate setting within TRIPS should be interpreted. If it is accepted that the diplomatic history of Berne can guide Berne-in-TRIPS, reading Berne as the source of the bulk of TRIPS standards on copyright is relatively straightforward (partly reflecting the relative maturity of its substantive provisions by contrast with Paris). Even so, differences arose in dispute settlement as to whether limitations and exceptions defined by TRIPS (in article 13) should apply only to those additional copyright standards defined by TRIPS and not drawn from Berne.[67]

The incorporation of Paris within TRIPS has provoked more uncertainty, despite a general assumption that the substantive provisions of Paris are integrated 'seamlessly'[68] into TRIPS and that TRIPS article 2.1 'has the effect of imposing the obligations contained in [articles 1 to 16, and 19 of Paris] to WTO Members not party to the Convention.'[69] The TRIPS requirement to comply with Paris provisions is preceded by the phrase '*in respect of* Parts II, III and IV':[70] the exact significance of this phrase proved to be surprisingly uncertain, even concerning the *categories* of industrial property forming the subject of TRIPS obligations. Carvalho considers that article 2.1 broadens the scope of TRIPS to include areas of IP that 'although not being the subject of Sections 1 through 7 of Part II, are nonetheless subject to mandatory protection under the Paris

---

[66] Neil Netanel, 'The next round: The impact of the WIPO copyright treaty on TRIPS dispute settlement' (1997) 37 *Virginia Journal of International Law* 441, 447.
[67] See United States – Section 110(5) of US Copyright Act dispute settlement proceedings.
[68] Ricketson, *The Paris Convention for the Protection of Industrial Property*.
[69] Daniel Gervais, *The TRIPS Agreement: Drafting History and Analysis*, 4th ed. (London: Sweet & Maxwell, 2012,), p. 187; see also Yusuf, 'TRIPS', 21.
[70] TRIPS Agreement, art. 2.1 (emphasis added).

Convention, namely trade names and repression of unfair competition',[71] yet other IP rights mentioned in Paris, but not 'subject to mandatory protection' therein (namely utility models and inventors' certificates) are not covered by TRIPS. Just what elements of IP are covered by this incorporation is critical not merely for the scope of positive obligations but also for the applicability of standards for non-discrimination and for enforcement.

The need for clarity came into sharp focus in the WTO dispute *US – Section 211 Omnibus Appropriations Act of 1998*. The panel concluded that TRIPS obligations did not cover trade names (the subject of article 8 of Paris but not expressly mentioned in TRIPS), since Paris obligations were incorporated in TRIPS only to the extent that they related to the forms of IP expressly provided for in the text of Parts II, III and IV of TRIPS: 'the words "in respect of" have the effect of "conditioning" Members' obligations' under TRIPS.[72] When, remarkably, both complainant and respondent appealed on the same point, the Appellate Body found instead[73] that TRIPS obliged protection of trade names (otherwise the reference in TRIPS to Paris article 8 would be otiose); it noted that the only debate over the scope of IP to be covered by TRIPS during its negotiations concerned trade secrets.[74] Kennedy observed, however, that the Appellate Body 'tellingly ... omitted to say what else that clause ["in respect of"] meant'.[75]

Clarifying the scope of industrial property protection incorporated from Paris becomes still more complex when it comes to the obligations under Paris articles 10*bis*(1) and 10*ter*(1) to suppress unfair competition and to apply effective legal remedies. In one dispute, the issue arose as to whether TRIPS extended this obligation to unfair competition 'in any guise', or again only in relation to areas of IP expressly mentioned.[76] The panel declined to take a 'view as to whether and in what respects Articles

---

[71] Nuno Pires de Carvalho, *The TRIPS Regime of Trademarks and Designs*, 4th ed (Alphen aan den Rijn, The Netherlands: Kluwer Law International, 2018), pp. 76–7.
[72] Panel Report, US – Section 211 Omnibus Appropriations Act of 1998, WTO Doc WT/DS176/ (6 August 2001) [8.34].
[73] Appellate Body Report, US – Section 211 Omnibus Appropriations Act of 1998, WTO Doc WT/DS176/AB/R (2 January 2002) [336]–[337], [341].
[74] Status of Work in the Negotiating Group, Chairman's Report to the GNG, GATT Doc MTN.GNG/NG11/W/76 (23 July 1990).
[75] Matthew Kennedy, 'Enforcing the WTO rulings on trade marks and trade names in Havana Club' (2015) 5 *Queen Mary Journal of Intellectual Property* 430, 438.
[76] Panel Report, European Communities – Trademarks and Geographical Indications for Agricultural Products and Foodstuffs (Australia), WTO Doc WT/DS290/R (15 March 2005) [7.725].

10*bis* and 10*ter* of the Paris Convention (1967) are incorporated by Article 2.1 of the TRIPS Agreement'.[77]

The scope of Paris obligations on unfair competition incorporated into TRIPS then arose in two parallel complaints against Australia's tobacco plain packaging measures.[78] Noting the Appellate Body's approach on trade names, the panel observed that TRIPS obligations in respect of unfair competition pursuant to Paris article 10*bis* 'should likewise not be assumed to be "conditioned" in such a manner that it would be limited in scope to those types of subject-matter expressly identified in Parts II, III or IV'.[79] Considering the ordinary meaning of the term *in respect of* within the grammatical structure of article 2.1, the panel understood it to require compliance with the identified provisions of the Paris Convention, with bearing 'not only on standards concerning the availability, scope and use of IP rights (Part II), but also on enforcement of IP rights (Part III), and the acquisition and maintenance of IP rights (Part IV)'.[80]

Whatever view is taken on these interpretative questions, it is striking that such a structural question as to the very range of IP subject matter covered by TRIPS obligations should be the subject of scholarly debate and even formal dispute settlement. The systemic implications extend to other jurisdictions giving effect to TRIPS jurisprudence,[81] notably the European Court of Justice on protection of trade names[82] and on the provisional measures to address unfair competition.[83]

10.7 Conclusion

Incorporating Paris and Berne into the framework of multilateral trade law was contentious from the point of view of its legitimacy and policy

---

[77] Ibid., [7.728] fn 629.
[78] Panel Reports, Australia – Certain Measures Concerning Trademarks, Geographical Indications and Other Plain Packaging Requirements Applicable to Tobacco Products and Packaging, WTO Docs WT/DS435/R, WT/DS441/R, WT/DS458/R, WT/DS467/R (28 June 2018).
[79] Ibid., [7.2628].
[80] Ibid., [7.2627] (footnotes omitted); at the time of writing the panel reports are subject to appeal by the Dominican Republic (WT/DS441/23) and Honduras (WT/DS435/23) but not concerning the panel's interpretation of article 2.1 (the reports in respect of the complaints by Cuba and Indonesia were not appealed).
[81] Gail Evans, 'Substantive trademark law harmonization by means of the WTO Appellate Body and the European Court of Justice: The case of trade name protection' (2007) 41 *Journal of World Trade* 1127.
[82] *Anheuser-Busch, Inc v. Budějovický Budvar, národní podnik* (C-245/02) [2004] ECR I-10989 [91].
[83] *Parfums Christian Dior SA v. Tuk Consultancy BV* (C-300/98, C-392/98), [2000] ECR I-11307.

impact. It gave rise to complex and challenging questions of treaty interpretation. Dispute settlement has grappled with the basic structural question of the scope of Paris standards enforceable under TRIPS, given differing views on interpreting the simple phrase *in respect of*. The growth, and greater diversity, of bilateral agreements directly and indirectly giving effect to Paris and Berne complicates the legal situation further still, and regional tribunals may be influenced further by 'trade' readings of IP norms. Yet it may not be tenable to maintain – empirically or theoretically – a firm disjunction between the international law of IP and that of trade relations. Even in the mid-nineteenth century, the notion that effective market access in foreign markets could pivot on workable access to IP protection had already begun to shape trade agreements. Even as the multilateral institutions dedicated, respectively, to IP and to trade diverged in the intervening period, significant thematic links between the two domains of law and regulation remained evident – to the extent that the precursor to the GATT was, in the 1920s, an active proponent of norms in the Paris system against unfair competition (ironically, that specific area of Paris being one that, by some readings, was partly excluded from TRIPS by virtue of that phrase *in respect of*). The practice of dispute settlement has, to date, operated to reinforce coherence between the two historic streams of multilateral law, although some efforts to apply a 'trade-related' reading to Paris and Berne have attracted critical responses.[84] Nonetheless, at a time of palpable contentiousness concerning IP in international trade relations, it remains vitally important to sustain coherence, clarity and legitimacy of the legal framework for settling the inevitable disputes. The integration of multilateral IP and trade law still potentially offers a foundation for working towards the mutual benefit and reduction of international tensions that formed the rationale of the TRIPS project.

---

[84] Notably the analysis by Kennedy, 'Enforcing the WTO rulings on trade marks and trade names in Havana Club'.

11 Intellectual Property, Innovation and New Space Technology

Melissa de Zwart

11.1 Introduction

The disruptions caused by technological innovation have now moved into the space industry, with the emergence of private, commercial operators ('New Space'). This chapter considers one of the unique challenges that the New Space industry encounters with its rapid development: the interaction of intellectual property with national security concerns, safety and financial risks, export controls and international law relating to cooperation in space.

Rapid technological change was the focus of Sam Ricketson's 1992 paper, 'New Wine into Old Bottles: Technological Change and Intellectual Property Rights'.[1] Ricketson's classic analysis considered 'what changes or revisions need to be made' to the contours of such rights to continue to serve the various goals of intellectual property (IP) rights protection.[2] Focussing on two examples of New Space operators – Rocket Lab[3] and SpaceX[4] – this chapter concludes that while IP protection has a unique role in the development of the nascent commercial space industry, government policy and legislative support will continue to be crucial to ensure the continued viability of the New Space sector for a number of years.

---

[1] Sam Ricketson, 'New wine into old bottles: Technological change and intellectual property rights' (1992) 10 *Prometheus* 53.
[2] Ibid., 53.
[3] In November 2018, New Zealand startup Rocket Lab successfully launched its innovative Electron rocket on its first commercial mission from the Mahia Peninsula in New Zealand: Jeff Foust, 'Rocket Lab performs first commercial launch', Space News, 10 November 2018, retrieved from https://spacenews.com/rocket-lab-performs-first-commercial-launch.
[4] In June 2018, Elon Musk's SpaceX successfully docked a Dragon capsule with the International Space Station (ISS): Curt Godwin, 'Swan song: Final SpaceX Block 4 Falcon 9 launches CRS-15 cargo mission', Spaceflight Insider, 29 June 2018, retrieved from https://bit.ly/2lyzkL4.

11.2 Space Technology and Commercialisation

Space exploration is expensive and risky and has long been the province of governments. However, changes in government policy, reduced costs of production and increased commercial uses of space have radically changed the approach to space innovation. Nevertheless, at least in the short term, governments remain the largest customers of space products and services.[5] They also continue to provide the bulk of funding for long-term research and development. However, commercial customers and private sources of funding for space research and services are increasing. It would seem to follow that further development of the commercial space sector would be promoted by greater certainty with respect to the application of IP laws to space objects and particularly inventions and creations made in space or on board a space object.[6] Certainty of IP rights facilitates licensing arrangements, collaboration, and security interests, as well as funding and investment.

The 2016 Organisation for Economic Co-Operation and Development (OECD) report, 'Space and Innovation', notes the specific and inherent tensions that lie at the heart of innovation in the space sector:

Since the beginning of the space age, space systems have been paradoxical technological beasts: they lead to the emergence of revolutionary technologies during their exploratory and development phases, but once they are operational, the focus often turns to reliability, durability and cost, stifling further innovations by risk averseness.[7]

The OECD report makes a number of recommendations to policy-makers for responses to stimulate space innovation. These include:

- *Reviewing national policy instruments that support space innovation:* presumably including a review of domestic space laws.
- *Participation in downstream space activities:* including identification and support of specialist or niche capabilities.
- *Capturing spin-offs and technology transfers*: recognising the value of new commercial products and services which have evolved from space-related research, including for example, medical, communication and mining technologies.[8]

---

[5] Organisation for Economic Co-Operation and Development (OECD), *Space and Innovation* (Paris: OECD Publishing, 2016), p. 10.
[6] International Bureau of the World Intellectual Property Organization (WIPO), 'Intellectual property and space activities', Issues Paper, 2004, 5.
[7] OECD, *Space and Innovation*, 15.   [8] Ibid., 11–12.

The specific issues with risk and reliability in the space sector and the lack of opportunities for diversification, create a particular need for continued government intervention or continued support in this sector.[9] However, new entrants to the space technology industry are creating challenges to the existing paradigm.

A number of challenges arise to the concept of IP, and its creation, enforcement and use, in the outer space context. First, do IP rights arise in outer space? If so, under which jurisdiction do such rights apply? Further, which aspects of IP rights may apply: copyright and patents in technology, trade secrets regarding payloads and experimental uses, trademarks in commercial branding and insignia? The absence of answers to these questions in international treaties leads to the question of treatment under domestic laws and the consequent matters of whether domestic jurisdiction may extend on board outer space objects registered to a state.

Second, there are real questions, given the huge expense and collaborative nature of space objects, regarding how third-party proprietary IP may be used on board outer space objects. A natural corollary to this is the overarching matter of determining jurisdiction and applicable domestic laws for the enforcement of breaches of IP rights in outer space.[10]

Third, the international treaty environment creates unique practical and policy issues for inventions and other IP rights made and used in outer space, due to the obligations created by the international space treaties with the principle that outer space is to be used for the benefit of all states. The treaties themselves barely contemplate that space will be used by private corporations rather than states.

11.3 The International Space Law Framework

International space law is created by the five major UN outer space treaties,[11] primarily the Treaty on Principles Governing the Activities

---

[9] Ibid., 17. See further, Nancy L Rose, 'The government's role in the commercialization of new technologies: Lessons for space policy', Working Paper No #1811-86, MIT Sloan School of Management, August 1986.

[10] For further discussion of the complexities of jurisdiction in outer space see Frans G von der Dunk, 'Effective exercise of "in-space jurisdiction": The US approach and the problems it is facing' (2015–2016) 40 *Journal of Space* 147.

[11] These treaties are the Agreement on the Rescue of Astronauts, the Return of Astronauts and the Return of Objects Launched into Outer Space, opened for signature 22 April 1968, 672 UNTS 119 (entered into force 3 December 1968); Convention on International Liability for Damage Caused by Space Objects, opened for signature 29 March 1972, 961 UNTS 187 (entered into force 1 September 1972) (cited as

of States in the Exploration and Use of Outer Space, including the Moon and Other Celestial Bodies ('Outer Space Treaty').[12] Of the UN Space Treaties, the Outer Space Treaty has the largest number of ratifying parties, standing currently at 107 ratifying parties and twenty-three signatories.[13] This high adoption rate supports the treaty's status at international law, with a number of the principles embodied in the Outer Space Treaty regarded as codifications of customary international law.[14] The Outer Space Treaty provides the overarching constitution for the use of outer space and adopts many of the principles articulated in the earlier resolutions of the UN General Assembly.[15]

Given the Cold War origins of the Outer Space Treaty and the fact that only nation states were regarded as being capable of undertaking space activities, the reach and scope of the Outer Space Treaty provides little guidance with respect to modern-day military, civilian and commercial uses of space. Its provisions were intended to maintain balance and transparency to ensure continued access to space by the Cold War superpowers – that is, the US and the Soviet Union. Later treaties reflect an interest by non-spacefaring and developing countries to be able to

Liability Convention); Convention on Registration of Objects Launched into Outer Space, opened for signature 14 January 1975, 1023 UNTS 15 (entered into force 15 September 1976) (cited as Registration Convention); Agreement Governing the Activities of States on the Moon and Other Celestial Bodies, opened for signature 18 December 1979, 1363 UNTS 3 (entered into force 11 July 1984) (cited as Moon Agreement) (collectively cited as the UN Space Treaties).

[12] Treaty on Principles Governing the Activities of States in the Exploration and Use of Outer Space, including the Moon and Other Celestial Bodies, opened for signature 27 January 1967, 610 UNTS 205 (entered into force 10 October 1967).

[13] Committee on the Peaceful Uses of Outer Space: Legal Subcommittee, Status of International Agreements Relating to Activities in Outer Space at 1 January 2018, 57th sess., Agenda Item 6, UN Doc A/AC.105/C.2/2018/CRP.3 (9 April 2018), 10.

[14] Quzhi He, 'The outer space treaty in perspective' (1997) 40 *Proceedings on the Law of Outer Space* 51, 53; but see Michael N. Schmitt, 'International law and military operations in space' in Armin von Bogdandy and Rudiger Wolfrum (eds.), *Max Planck Yearbook of United Nations Law*, vol. 10 (Leiden: Martinus Nijhoff, 2006), p. 89, who states that the accepted body of customary international law applicable to outer space extends only to 'the free use of space by all states, a prohibition on claims of sovereignty over space, free exploration of space' and, possibly, 'the obligation to rescue astronauts in distress' (at 99).

[15] See Regulation, Limitation and Balanced Reduction of All Armed Forces and All Armaments; Conclusion of an International Convention (Treaty) on the Reduction of Armaments and the Prohibition of Atomic Hydrogen and Other Weapons of Mass Destruction, GA Res 1148 (XII), UN GAOR, 12th sess., 716th plen. mtg., Agenda Item 24, Supp. No. 18, UN Doc A/RES/1148 (XII) (14 November 1957); Question of the Peaceful Use of Outer Space, GA Res 1348 (XIII), UN GAOR, 13th sess., 792nd plen. mtg., Agenda Item 60, Supp. No. 18, UN Doc A/RES/1348(XIII) (13 December 1958); and International Co-Operation in the Peaceful Uses of Outer Space, GA Res 1472 (XIV), UN GAOR, 14th sess., 856th plen. mtg., Agenda Item 25, Supp. No. 16, UN Doc A/RES/1472(XIV) (12 December 1959).

access the growing benefits of access to the space environment. Certainly, none of these treaties addresses the commercial uses of space, nor do the treaties deal specifically with matters of IP or how creations in space might be dealt with under international law. Therefore, much uncertainty now arises regarding the application of the Outer Space Treaty and the other UN Space Treaties to the modern uses of space.

In fact, it has been argued that the principles articulated in the UN Space Treaties mean that there can be no private property in space.[16] Article I of the Outer Space Treaty provides that: 'The exploration and use of outer space, including the Moon and other celestial bodies, shall be carried out for the benefit and in the interests of all countries, irrespective of their degree of economic or scientific development, and shall be the province of all mankind.' Further, it asserts 'freedom of scientific investigation in outer space, including the Moon and other celestial bodies, and States shall facilitate and encourage international cooperation in such investigation'. Article II states: 'Outer space, including the Moon and other celestial bodies, is not subject to national appropriation by claims of sovereignty, by means of use or occupation, or by any other means.' Other provisions deal with principles of openness and sharing of space technology and reciprocity of visiting and inspection rights to one another's space facilities on Earth and in space, for example, to 'observe the flight of space objects launched by those States' (article X), and the requirement that '[a]ll stations, installations, equipment and space vehicles on the Moon and other celestial bodies' be 'open to representatives of other States Parties to the Treaty on the basis of reciprocity' (article XII). These rights of inspection are clearly directed at the maintenance of peaceful uses of outer space but are anathema to protection of technological advantage and consequent IP rights.

Of course, the assertion that the Outer Space Treaty establishes outer space as an international commons has been identified as a potential hurdle to the application of IP rights as well as a disincentive to the commercialisation of outer space.[17] However, other provisions of the Outer Space Treaty provide some basis for the application of domestic

---

[16] See further, Lynn M Fountain, 'Creating momentum in space: Ending the paralysis produced by the common heritage of mankind doctrine' (2003) 35 *Connecticut Law Review* 1753; Christopher D Johnson, 'Reality and clarity in understanding the prohibition on national appropriation in Article II of the Outer Space Treaty', Paper presented at the 66th International Astronautical Congress, Jerusalem, Israel, 12 October 2015.

[17] See, for example, Leo B Malagar and Marlo Apalisok Magdoza-Malaga, 'International law of outer space and the protection of intellectual property rights' (1999) 17 *Boston University International Law Journal* 311.

IP laws in the space context. Article VI provides that states parties to the treaty 'bear international responsibility for national activities in outer space', whether such activities are conducted by government or non-government entities. The activities of non-government entities require 'authorisation and continuing supervision by' the appropriate state. Article VIII provides that states retain jurisdiction and control over space objects registered to the state and personnel on board that spacecraft. This article has been interpreted as meaning that the country of registry of the space object retains effective jurisdiction over all elements of the space object and any personnel on board. For example, when Canadian astronaut Chris Hadfield performed the David Bowie song 'Space Oddity' on board the International Space Station (ISS) in 2013, questions were raised regarding whether the performance of the song was subject to terrestrial copyright law and if so, which domestic law might apply. Hadfield performed the song in three elements of the ISS: the Destiny module (owned by NASA), the Cupola (formerly owned by the European Space Agency but transferred to NASA in 2005) and the Japanese Experiment Module (owned by the Japan Aerospace Exploration Agency).[18] The video was transmitted to Canada, where it was edited for release and a piano accompaniment added. As will be discussed further later in the chapter, the agreements regulating the ISS provide for the application of domestic laws in each element of the ISS, meaning had Hadfield not had permission of the copyright holder in each of those jurisdictions, liability for infringement may have arisen in Canada, the US and Japan, each of which retained effective domestic jurisdiction over its own elements.[19]

Further support for the application of domestic IP laws with respect to space objects is contained in statements made by the UN Committee on the Peaceful Uses of Outer Space (UNCOPUOS), including the annex to the Declaration on International Cooperation in the Exploration and Use of Outer Space (1996).[20] This document recognises IP as part of a state's 'legitimate rights and interests':[21]

---

[18] G F 'How does copyright work in space?' *The Economist*, 23 May 2013, retrieved from https://econ.st/2kqv3cr.
[19] See further, Tosaporn Leepuengtham, *The Protection of IP Rights in Outer Space Activities* (Northhampton, MA: Edward Elgar, 2017), pp. 42, 149–207.
[20] UN Declaration on International Cooperation in the Exploration and Use of Outer Space for the Benefit and in the Interest of All States, Taking into Particular Account the Needs of Developing Countries, GA Res 51/122, UN GAOR, 51st sess., 83rd plen. mtg., UN DOC A/RES/51/122 (13 December 1996).
[21] Ibid., annex 2.

States are free to determine all aspects of their participation in international cooperation in the exploration and use of outer space on an equitable and mutually acceptable basis. Contractual terms in such cooperative ventures should be fair and reasonable and they should be in full compliance with the legitimate rights and interests of the parties concerned as, for example, with intellectual property rights.

Such rights are explicitly recognised as fundamental to encouraging and rewarding greater involvement by many countries, and not just the traditional space faring nations, in space activities leading to innovation and technological advancement.

States can agree as between themselves on the operation of IP rights on jointly operated space objects. The best example of this is the Inter-Governmental Agreement (IGA) of 1998 relating to the ISS.[22] Article 5 of the IGA provides that 'each partner shall retain jurisdiction and control over the elements [of the Station] it registers and over personnel in or on the Space Station who are its nationals'. Article 19 requires the partners to exchange technical data and goods necessary for the safe operation of the ISS. Importantly, article 21(2) deems any activity in or on an element of the ISS to have occurred in the territory of the Partner State of that element's registry. Hence an invention made within or upon a module of the ISS will be deemed to have been made in the state to which that module belongs.[23] Thus the nexus for IP protection depends upon the Registration Convention,[24] a convention directed to state liability rather than any matters of commercial operation. The reliance upon the Registration Convention as providing a nexus for IP protection may lack sufficient flexibility for the growth in commercial space objects due to the inability to change the country of registration of a space object under that convention.[25]

---

[22] Agreement among the Government of the United States of America, Governments of Member States of the European Space Agency, the Government of Japan, and the Government of Canada on Cooperation in the Detailed Design, Development, Operation, and Utilization of the permanently Manned Civil Space Station, 29 September 1988 (entered into force 30 January 1992); and Agreement among the Government of Canada, Governments of Member States of the European Space Agency, the Government of Japan, the Government of the Russian Federation, and the Government of the United States of America concerning Cooperation on the Civil International Space Station, 29 January 1998 (entered into force 28 March 2001).

[23] With respect to the European Partner States, due to the delegation of registration authority to the European Space Agency, article 21(2) further provides that 'for the purposes of intellectual property law, any European Partner State may deem the activity to have occurred within its territory for ESA registered elements': WIPO, 'Intellectual property and space activities', 12 [48].

[24] See WIPO, 'Intellectual property and space activities'.

[25] Michael Chatzipanagiotis, 'Registration of space objects and transfer of ownership in orbit' (2007) 56 *Zeitschrift für Luft-und Weltraumrecht* 229, 230.

The 1999 Workshop on Intellectual Property Rights in Space, held in conjunction with the Third UN Conference on the Exploration and Peaceful Uses of Outer Space (UNISPACE III), identified a number of key recommendations relating to IP in the conference's report. These included:

- The need to pay greater attention to the protection of IP rights, given the growth in commercialisation and privatisation of space activities. However, the protection and enforcement of IP rights must be balanced against international legal principles such as non-appropriation.
- The consideration of the feasibility of harmonising key aspects of intellectual standards and practices, such as the applicability of domestic laws in space, ownership and use of IP rights created in space and contract and licensing laws.
- The need for states to provide appropriate protection of IP rights with respect to space technology, while still encouraging the 'free flow of basic science information'.[26]

After this meeting, further consideration was given by UNCOPUOS to whether IP matters should be included in the regular agenda of the Legal Subcommittee, but this was rejected.[27] It would appear timely that this position be revisited, given the recent expansion in New Space entrepreneurs and the increasing reliance by government space activities on commercial providers.

11.4 National Laws on Outer Space

11.4.1 United States

The US is one of the few countries to enact explicit provisions providing for quasi-territorial effect of patent laws on board space objects. It does this in 35 US Code Title §105, which provides:

(a) Any invention made, used, or sold in outer space on a space object or component thereof under the jurisdiction or control of the United States shall be considered to be made, used or sold within the United States for the purposes of this title, except with respect to any space object or component thereof that is specifically identified and otherwise provided for by an international agreement to which the United

---

[26] UN Office for Outer Space Affairs (UNOOSA), Report of the Third United Nations Conference on the Exploration and Peaceful Uses of Outer Space, Report No A/CONF.184/6 (1999).
[27] WIPO, 'Intellectual property and space activities', 9.

States is a party, or with respect to any space object or component thereof that is carried on the registry of a foreign state in accordance with the Convention on Registration of Objects Launched into Outer Space.

(b) Any invention made, used, or sold in outer space on a space object or component thereof that is carried on the registry of a foreign state in accordance with the Convention on Registration of Objects Launched into Outer Space, shall be considered to be made, used, or sold within the United States for the purposes of this title if specifically so agreed in an international agreement between the United States and the state of registry.

These provisions provide a model for other domestic space patent laws by explicitly clarifying what the jurisdictional arrangements will be with respect to inventions made, used or sold on a space object. As von der Dunk observes, as the interest and engagement of commercial operators with outer space continues to evolve at a rapid pace, the question of how the UN Space Treaties may be applied to these private operators becomes increasingly important.[28] As one of the few nations to address these issues in its domestic legislation, these 'legal tools' will be of great interest to the rest of the world, who will look to the US law as a model and, possibly, also to assess its application and usefulness.[29]

Of course, quite complicated IP arrangements exist with respect to contracts performed for the US government under government contracting and International Traffic in Arms Regulations (ITAR) rules.[30] There have been some efforts to relax these rules to encourage commercial investment in space technology. Further, there is some scepticism regarding whether companies such as SpaceX and Blue Origin, which supply the majority of their services to NASA, are truly 'commercial', given their limited customer base.[31] However, such doubts are readily overcome by the overwhelming and increasing demand for new commercial launches.

SpaceX, founded by Elon Musk in 2002, has succeeded in capturing the imagination of space enthusiasts. It has also been able to win lucrative government contracts for the resupply of the ISS. Musk's vision began with the concept of sending a settlement to Mars. Realising that NASA had no plans for a human mission to Mars, he started to investigate the

---

[28] von der Dunk, 'Effective exercise of "in-space jurisdiction"', 147.   [29] Ibid., 148.
[30] P J Blount, 'The ITAR Treaty and its implications for U.S. space exploration policy and the commercial space industry' (2008) 73 *Journal of Air Law & Commerce* 705.
[31] Eric Berger, 'Trump space adviser: Blue Origin and SpaceX rockets aren't really commercial', Ars Technica, 7 November 2017, retrieved from https://bit.ly/2lyBk62.

costs and logistics of a private enterprise. Musk encountered issues not only in terms of design and materials but also in breaking into the pool of contractors to the US government. Innovative processes of manufacture and materials, including reusable rockets, have drastically reduced the cost of launch, thus making SpaceX an attractive and competitive launch provider.[32]

But what of the IP issue? Musk has announced that there are no patents in SpaceX: 'Our primary long-term competition is in China – if we published patents, it would be farcical, because the Chinese would just use them as a recipe book.'[33] Thus the innovative cutting-edge technology of SpaceX continues to rely upon the trusted and most practical method of protecting IP rights in space technology: keeping it secret. The fact that launch vehicles are sent into space and recovered by the owner, makes it difficult (if not impossible) to inspect and copy such technology.

11.4.2 New Zealand

Similar concerns regarding protection by trade secret laws are reflected in the laws protecting New Zealand's space startup, Rocket Lab.[34] The Outer Space and High-Altitude Activities Act 2017 (NZ) was passed in July 2017 and came into force on 21 December 2017. That Act sets out a regime for the grant of various permits relating to commercial space operations, including launch, payload and facility permits. The US origins of the Rocket Lab technology have created particular issues for the company due to export control issues. This has necessitated specific provisions in the Outer Space and High-Altitude Activities Act to incorporate specific terms that derive from the bilateral Technology Safeguards Agreement (TSA) executed in 2016 between New Zealand and the US.[35] This agreement provides for the ability to export rocket technology

---

[32] Loren Grush, 'SpaceX's last Falcon 9 upgrade could finally make reusable rockets cost-effective', The Verge, 9 May 2018, retrieved from https://bit.ly/2ltniCS.
[33] Chris Anderson, 'Elon Musk's mission to Mars', Wired, 21 October 2012, retrieved from www.wired.com/2012/10/ff-elon-musk-qa/all.
[34] Founded by New Zealander Peter Beck in 2007, Rocket Lab is a US-based corporation, with a New Zealand subsidiary. Rocket Lab is focussed on the delivery of complete rocket systems for 'frequent and cost-effective launches': Baldwins Intellectual Property, 'Rocket Lab Ltd – Ready for launch', retrieved from https://bit.ly/2lAgUtp.
[35] Agreement on Technology Safeguards Associated with United States Participation in Space Launches from New Zealand, New Zealand-United States of America, signed 16 June 2016, TIAS 16-1212 (entered into force 12 December 2016); Steven Joyce and Murray McCully, 'NZ-US technology safeguards agreement reached', Media Release, 14 June 2016, retrieved from www.beehive.govt.nz/release/nz-us-technology-safeguards-agreement-reached.

which would otherwise be prohibited by the American Missile Technology Control Regime. Further, specific laws were enacted to protect potential debris sites and to prohibit the taking of photos within debris recovery areas, laws that were criticised in New Zealand as inconsistent with the Bill of Rights Act 1991 (NZ) regarding freedom of expression.[36] However, such laws were required under the TSA. Again, physical protection of space assets remains a key strategy in maintaining technological advantage.

11.4.3 Australia

The Review of Australia's Space Industry Capability, the report of the Expert Reference Group (ERG) published in March 2018, sets out 'an ambitious strategy to triple the size of Australia's nascent space industry to AU$10–$12 billion dollars per year by 2030'.[37] The recommendations of the ERG report to facilitate such growth include primarily the establishment of a dedicated Australian Space Agency (recommendation 2). Such an agency would be responsible for civil strategic policy direction and co-ordination of space policy. Most important, it could function as a single point of co-ordination for international collaboration with the Australian civil space sector. A further recommendation of the report is extending existing partnerships and treaty-level agreements (recommendation 5). As has been demonstrated by the New Zealand Rocket Lab example, an important boost to Australian space startups may be gained by strengthening international partnerships 'to allow greater technology transfer and technology development in Australia'.[38] This can be facilitated through relationships with key space agencies and commercial partners.[39] The ERG report further identifies that 'an important role of the Agency will be to co-ordinate national space regulation in a way that provides certainty for business; minimises regulatory burdens and bureaucratic red tape; and otherwise assists the growth of the space industry sector and maximises its ability to innovate'.[40] This of course includes a range of regulatory approvals and levers such as ITAR regulations, import/export controls and launch certificates.

---

[36] James Churchill, 'Regulating for disruption: A case study of the outer space law reform', Legal Research Paper No 63/2018, Victoria University of Wellington, 3 April 2018, p. 27.
[37] Expert Reference Group for the Review of Australia's Space Industry Capability, 'Review of Australia's space industry capability', March 2018, p. 5.
[38] Ibid., 13 (recommendation 5).   [39] Ibid., 47.   [40] Ibid., 53.

In response to the ERG report, the Australian federal government announced that it would be establishing an Australian Space Agency, with a $41 million initial investment, comprising $26 million operational funding and $15 million for an International Space Investment initiative from 2019 to 2022.[41] The Australian Space Agency officially commenced operation on 1 July 2018.

In order to further encourage commercial space activity, a revised statutory regime was introduced through amendments in 2018 to the Space Activities Act 1998 (Cth).[42] This revised statutory scheme adjusts the regulatory environment in an effort to make the regulatory scheme less onerous for Australian operators. Indeed, the objects of the Act now specifically state the need to ensure a balance between 'the removal of barriers to participation in space activities and the encouragement of innovation and entrepreneurship in the space industry' and the safety of space activities and risk of damage to persons or property.[43] The insurance limits for launch and return, which were a major impediment to small space operators, especially those contributing only a small part of a large payload, have been reduced. Interestingly, and possibly controversially, the new Act also includes a requirement for applications for a launch permit to include a strategy for debris mitigation.[44] This places Australia at the forefront of the global recognition of the need to minimise the risk of space debris, which poses a growing risk to access to vital earth orbits.

While there is a clear impetus to foster a strong domestic space industry in Australia, there is currently no contemplation of specific legislation to address the creation or use of IP in outer space. This may be because Australia perceives itself largely as a provider of ground services, such the Square Kilometre Array radio telescope project (in Western Australia and South Africa). On the other hand, it may simply be that at present, most countries lack the imagination to see that in the near future, vital technological developments may occur in space, on space objects or on the surface of an asteroid, planet or moon.

---

[41] Australian Government, 'Australian government response to the review of Australia's space industry capability', May 2018, p. 3.
[42] The Space Activities Amendment (Launches and Returns) Act 2018 (Cth) passed both Houses of Parliament on 23 August 2018 and received Royal Assent on 31 August 2018. At the time of writing the rules have yet to be released for comment. The new regime established by this Act will come into effect on 1 September 2019.
[43] Space Activities Amendment (Launches and Returns) Act 2018 (Cth) sch. 1 item 4.
[44] Space Activities Amendment (Launches and Returns) Act 2018 (Cth) sch. 1 item 34.

11.5 Conclusions

The questions raised by Ricketson in his 1992 article remain relevant for the space industry today. Ricketson's concerns at that time were with the challenges posed to IP rights by then new technologies of digital technology and the internet. In a characteristic and methodical fashion, Ricketson examined in turn the goals of IP, its current scope and duration, the challenges to the rights secured by that protection and national and international constraints upon change and future strategies for reform of existing regimes.[45] Noting that the inherent tensions within IP rights of public and private interests are constantly challenged by new technologies, Ricketson outlined a number of options for reform, including sui generis protection and altering the contours and scope of those rights with new limitations and exceptions.

Outer space technologies and the particularly demanding, expensive and risky nature of the space environment also seem to make new demands on the IP system. However, at present, despite the international treaties apparently demanding new levels of openness and sharing among nations, the IP system continues to function sufficiently effectively.[46] As noted earlier, very few nations have addressed the development and protection of IP in their domestic laws. Whether such laws will be effective in encouraging the development and commercialisation of space-based technology is an open question. As observed earlier, the lack of clear terrestrial jurisdiction and the expense and complexity of accessing space currently serves as a practical impediment to inspecting, copying or reverse engineering the inventions of other space operators. However, as with the internet, outer space will provide a challenge to terrestrially developed, jurisdictionally based laws.

It remains to be seen if space will cause the same disruptions to the intellectual dialogue around matters of open access, sharing and use as digital technologies have done. The rhetoric of 'common interest of mankind (sic)' and conducting 'exploration and use of outer space … for the benefits of all peoples'[47] suggests that there is scope in the UN Space Treaties to argue against the recognition of exclusive rights in inventions developed in outer space domains, providing the benefits of the 'exploration and use of outer space, including the Moon and other celestial bodies … for the benefit and in the interests of all countries,

---

[45] Ricketson, 'New wine into old bottles', 54.
[46] Mythili Sampathkuma, 'Woman sues NASA for right to own moon dust "given to her by Neil Armstrong"', *The Independent*, 12 June 2018, retrieved from https://bit.ly/2jW32cC.
[47] Outer Space Treaty, Preamble.

irrespective of their degree of economic or scientific development'.[48] There is no indication however, thus far, that any New Space entrepreneurs are deterred by the lack of sui generis space-related IP laws, but it seems fair to say at this moment that as Ricketson concluded in 1992, the old bottles are still serving us quite well.

---

[48] Outer Space Treaty, art. I.

12 Intellectual Property and Private International Law
Strangers in the Night?

Richard Garnett

12.1 Introduction

The relationship between intellectual property (IP) and private international law (PIL) has become fraught with tension. For many years the two fields barely intersected, as almost all IP disputes were wholly domestic in nature, concerning parties within a single national territory, rights conferred by the law of that territory and local infringements. The emergence of new forms of technology and greater mobility of goods and services have, however, substantially changed the picture. Now that the digital networked environment provides scope for simultaneous multi-territorial communication of works and trade symbols and consequent global infringements of rights in such material,[1] the problem of cross-border enforcement of IP rights cannot be ignored.

An exploration of the relationship between IP and PIL would therefore seem to be an excellent example of the theme of interconnectedness that permeates this volume. Sam Ricketson also addressed this issue in his scholarship.[2] As a background to considering the relationship between the disciplines, some key topics will first be explored: in the case of IP, harmonisation and territoriality and in the case of PIL, basic principles and rationale. The chapter will then examine the current practice and scholarship concerning the interaction of IP and PIL to determine whether they are, or should be, 'strangers in the night'.

---

[1] American Law Institute, *Intellectual Property: Principles Governing Jurisdiction, Choice of Law, and Judgments in Transnational Disputes* (Philadelphia: American Law Institute, 2008), p. 3 (cited as ALI Principles).

[2] See, for example, Sam Ricketson and Jane C Ginsburg, *International Copyright and Neighbouring Rights: The Berne Convention and Beyond*, 2nd ed. vol. II (Oxford: Oxford University Press, 2006), p. 1291.

12.2 Public International Law and Harmonisation of IP Rights

A key characteristic of IP compared to other areas of law is the influence of public international law – for example, treaties such as the Berne[3] and Paris[4] Conventions and the Agreement on Trade-Related Aspects of Intellectual Property Rights (TRIPS Agreement).[5] Such instruments provide minimum standards for protection and enforcement of rights and therefore some scope for global harmonisation of IP. However, the consensus among scholars is that while some harmonisation has been achieved in the field of copyright, the record in respect of patents and trademarks (at least outside the EU) is much more modest.[6] This position is not surprising. Not only are the standards in the cited treaties only 'minimum' in nature but the instruments grant member states considerable freedom to create rules that best suit their own social and economic conditions.[7] The varying level of development between countries and whether they are net importers or net exporters of IP creates a diversity of cultural and economic policies. Consequently, nation states, in creating IP protection, will draw the line between providing for competition in the public domain and encouraging innovation differently.[8]

Of course, if substantial global harmonisation of IP were to be accomplished then the problem of cross-border enforcement would in theory decrease since courts, wherever situated, would apply the same IP law to the same fact patterns. Yet in other contexts, such as international commercial arbitration,[9] experience has shown that achieving globally

---

[3] Berne Convention for the Protection of Literary and Artistic Works, opened for signature 9 September 1886, 828 UNTS 221 (entered into force 5 December 1887).
[4] Paris Convention for the Protection of Industrial Property, opened for signature 20 March 1883, 828 UNTS 305 (entered into force 7 July 1884).
[5] Marrakesh Agreement Establishing the World Trade Organization, opened for signature 15 April 1994, 1867 UNTS 3 (entered into force 1 January 1995) annex 1C (Agreement on Trade-Related Aspects of Intellectual Property Rights; cited as TRIPS Agreement).
[6] Rochelle Dreyfuss, 'Enforcing intellectual property claims globally when rights are defined territorially' in Daniel J Gervais and Susy Frankel (eds.), *The Internet and the Emerging Importance of New Forms of Intellectual Property* (Alphen aan den Rijn, The Netherlands: Kluwer, 2016), pp. 15, 21; Dário Moura Vicente, 'Intellectual property, applicable law' in Jürgen Basedow, Giesela Rühl, Franco Ferrari and Pedro de Miguel Asensio (eds.), *Encyclopedia of Private International Law* (Cheltenham, UK: Edward Elgar, 2017), pp. 961, 963–4; Mireille Van Eechoud, 'Bridging the gap: Private international law principles for intellectual property law' (2016) *Nederlands Internationaal Privaatrecht* 716, 723.
[7] Graeme Dinwoodie, 'International intellectual property litigation: A vehicle for resurgent comparativist thought' (2001) 49 *American Journal of Comparative Law* 429, 436.
[8] Ibid.
[9] George A Bermann, '"Domesticating" the New York Convention: The impact of the Federal Arbitration Act' (2011) 2 *Journal of International Dispute Settlement* 317.

consistent interpretations of uniform texts or standards can be difficult. Local policies and interests may often still intervene. Substantial global harmonisation of IP rights is, therefore, unlikely to occur soon.[10]

12.3 Territoriality and IP Rights

What particularly complicates the issue of cross-border regulation of IP is the deeply rooted notion of the 'territoriality' of IP rights. What this concept means is that IP protection is specific to a country (or a region in the case of the EU) in that while there may be a single work, invention or trade symbol, any rights in respect of such subject matter are confined to a single national territory and generally, may be infringed only in that territory. Consequently, for a rights holder to claim protection in multiple countries it must acquire separate rights under the IP law of each individual nation state.[11]

The territoriality of IP rights rests on the logical foundation that they are the product of uniquely domestic, cultural, social and economic policies, whereby states seek to balance the competing concerns of innovation and competition in granting a person exclusive rights to engage in a certain activity. A further key element underlying IP rights, therefore, is the public, sovereign interests of the state conferring protection.[12] Territoriality is also reflected in the well-accepted choice of law rule for IP infringement cases: the law of the country for which protection

---

[10] The ICANN Rules accompanying the Uniform Domain Name Dispute Resolution Policy (UDRP) for domain names are sometimes cited as an example of a transnational IP law (see Dinwoodie, 'International intellectual property litigation'). Under Rule 15(a), a dispute resolution panel may decide a complaint on the basis of the statements and documents submitted and in accordance with the policy, the rules and any rules and principles of law that it deems applicable. UDRP arbitration, however, is directed at only a narrow range of IP disputes – cybersquatting – and provides limited remedies.

[11] Methods have been adopted, such as in the European Patent Convention and the Patent Co-operation Treaty, to facilitate *acquisition* of multiple national IP rights, but the scope of protection remains confined to a specific national or regional territory.

[12] Richard Fentiman, 'Choice of law and intellectual property' in Josef Drexl and Annette Kur (eds.), *Intellectual Property and Private International Law – Heading for the Future* (Portland, OR: Hart Publishing, 2005), pp. 129, 131–3; Van Eechoud, 'Bridging the gap', 718; Benedetta Ubertazzi, 'Intellectual property, jurisdiction' in Jürgen Basedow, Giesela Rühl, Franco Ferrari and Pedro de Miguel Asensio (eds.), *Encyclopedia of Private International Law* (Cheltenham, UK: Edward Elgar, 2017), pp. 970, 972. IP protection has been said to be 'a matter of maximising social welfare': Jürgen Basedow, 'Foundations of private international law in intellectual property' in Jürgen Basedow, Toshiyuki Kono and Axel Metzger (eds.), *Intellectual Property in the Global Arena: Jurisdiction, Applicable Law, and the Recognition of Judgments in Europe, Japan and the US* (Tubingen, Germany: Mohr Siebeck, 2010), pp. 3, 6.

is claimed.[13] The effect of such a rule is that where a claimant sues in state A for infringement of an IP right conferred by the law of state A, that law must be applied.

The territoriality of IP rights therefore sharpens the mismatch between national IP laws and the increasingly global nature of production, exploitation and infringement and is at the heart of the relationship between PIL and IP.

12.4   The Nature and Rationale of PIL

To understand properly the relationship between IP and PIL a brief description of the nature and rationale of PIL may be helpful. Each national legal system has its own PIL rules which are designed to resolve cases with a foreign element. PIL rules fall into three groups: first, those that determine whether a court (the forum) has jurisdiction and will exercise jurisdiction in a matter; second, those that identify which law or laws are to be applied by the forum to resolve the merits of the dispute; and third, those that decide whether a judgment of a foreign country should be recognised and enforced in the forum.

Most systems of PIL are, at least in theory, cosmopolitan in nature in that they purport to treat local and foreign laws, judgments and claims to jurisdiction on an equal and non-discriminatory basis. Consequently, most systems strive to allocate jurisdiction to a court of a nation state that has a substantial connection to the dispute and the parties, and to apply a state's laws and enforce its judgments where the same condition is met. Such an analysis reflects the influence of the nineteenth-century writer Von Savigny, who asserted that every transaction has a 'centre of gravity' that should guide selection of the appropriate forum of adjudication and applicable law.[14] In EU law the centre of gravity principle is reflected in the neutral and balanced provisions of jurisdiction and applicable law in the Brussels I Regulation (recast) and Rome I and II Regulations, respectively. In common law countries, Savigny's influence can be seen in jurisdictional doctrines such as forum non conveniens and in the applicable law rules for tort, contract and property that emphasise close connection.

A key rationale for PIL is to avoid the injustice that would be caused to the parties and the defeat of their reasonable expectations if foreign laws,

---

[13] See, e.g., Regulation (EU) No 864/2007 of the European Parliament and Council on the Law Applicable to Non-Contractual Obligations OJ 2007 L199/40, art. 8.
[14] Friedrich Carl Von Savigny, *System des Heutigen Römischen Rechts*, vol. 8 (Berlin: Veit, 1849).

claims to adjudicate and court decisions were not respected.[15] The prevention of friction between nation states arising from exorbitant exercise of jurisdiction and application of local law is also an important goal. PIL rules also seek to make cross-border litigation efficient by limiting the scope for multiple proceedings in different countries in respect of similar subject matter.[16]

PIL does not however require total subservience to foreign laws and institutions: where, for example, giving effect to a foreign law or judgment would offend fundamental values of the forum state, then exceptionally it may not be recognised on public policy grounds. Note, however, that the mere fact that foreign law is 'different' to that of the forum is not sufficient to warrant its exclusion.

12.5 Is IP Compatible with PIL?

12.5.1 The Position in Principle

PIL rules aim to accommodate a range of interests: those of the forum state, the foreign state and the parties. The next question to determine is whether the distinctive character of IP should render it immune to the application of PIL rules. As its name suggests, PIL applies to all areas of private law – for example, torts, contracts, transfers and acquisition of rights in property, succession, corporations, trusts and restitution matters. Even areas of law with a more 'public' character based on important cultural and economic policies, such as family and insolvency law, are subject to regulation by PIL where matters cross borders. So, for example, a forum court may determine whether a foreign marriage or divorce is valid or whether a foreign liquidator or creditor is entitled to recover assets in the forum to satisfy claims in a foreign proceeding.

Where does IP fit into this picture? At the outset, it is important to note that the principal IP treaties do not contain PIL rules – namely, provisions allocating jurisdiction to a national court or identifying the law to be applied. A provision in the Berne Convention (article 5(1)) that addresses cross-border issues provides that rights holders must be given the same protection under the law of the country of IP protection,

---

[15] James J Fawcett and Janeen M Carruthers, *Cheshire, North and Fawcett Private International Law*, 14th ed. (Oxford: Oxford University Press, 2008), pp. 4–5; Lord Collins of Mapesbury and Jonathan Harris (gen. eds.), *Dicey Morris and Collins on the Conflict of Laws*, 15th ed. (London: Sweet & Maxwell, 2012), [1.005]; Christopher M V Clarkson and Jonathan Hill, *The Conflict of Laws*, 4th ed. (Oxford: Oxford University Press, 2011), pp. 9–10.

[16] Clarkson and Hill, *The Conflict of Laws*, 8.

regardless of nationality. This is a rule of 'national treatment'. Importantly also, no provision in the treaties precludes the application of *general* PIL rules to IP.

As noted earlier, IP has a strong public character, based as it is on a nation state's decision to confer exclusive protection for certain activity within its territory in accordance with the state's economic and cultural policies. Yet the public character and state interest in family and insolvency law do not prevent a foreign court from adjudicating such matters; PIL rules are not 'ousted'. In such cases, courts recognise that the 'private' interests of the parties in obtaining vindication of their rights are considered worthy of protection. Such persons would be expected to want prompt and efficient dispute resolution in a convenient forum. Indeed, there are public interests that *support* the application of PIL rules to IP, specifically the encouragement of international trade and commerce and the flow of information and cultural exchange that results from an enhanced transnational regime for enforcement of IP rights.[17]

Similarly, the territorial nature of IP should also not, in principle, be a bar to regulation by PIL rules. As noted, all that *territoriality* means is that the protection, use and infringement of an IP right is confined to a single national area. Such a principle says nothing about which national courts have jurisdiction to determine ownership, validity or infringement of an IP right, what law is to be applied to such issues or whether a judgment from a national court on an IP matter should be enforced in another country.[18]

12.5.2 *The Position in Practice*

Despite the observations discussed earlier, the legacy of state interests and territoriality in IP still informs many countries' jurisprudence in relation to adjudication of cross-border disputes. In Australia, for example, it remains the case that a court has no subject matter jurisdiction to resolve a

---

[17] Alexander Peukert, 'Preamble' in European Max Planck Group on Conflict of Laws in Intellectual Property, *Conflict of Laws in Intellectual Property: The CLIP Principles and Commentary* (Oxford: Oxford University Press, 2013), PRE C-23 (cited as CLIP Principles).

[18] For similar views see Graeme Dinwoodie, 'Developing a private intellectual property law: The demise of territoriality' (2009) 51 *William and Mary Law Review* 711; James J Fawcett and Paul Torremans (eds.), *Intellectual Property and Private International Law*, 2nd ed. (Oxford: Oxford University Press, 2011), p. 311; ALI Principles, ch. 3, ss. 221–3.

dispute for damages for infringement of a foreign statutory IP right such as trademark, patent, copyright or design.[19] The most commonly cited rationale for such a position is the act of state doctrine,[20] which provides that a court cannot pronounce upon the validity of a foreign state's acts within its own territory in deference to the sensibilities of that state. Such an approach is flawed, however, given that a pure infringement action involves no review of the validity of an act of a foreign state and in the case of copyright, whose rights arise upon creation of a work rather than state registration, there is no relevant 'act of state' at all. English courts as well as one Australian judge[21] referred to 'the *Moçambique* rule',[22] as a further justification for not adjudicating foreign IP rights. This rule prevents a court adjudicating upon questions of title or trespass to foreign land. However, not only is the analogy between land and IP rights dubious but the rule has been statutorily eroded in Australia and the UK.[23]

This approach arguably reflects a misplaced deference to foreign state interests and territoriality in IP cases. First, it is not at all clear why a forum court in not enforcing a foreign state's IP laws, at least in infringement cases, is being more respectful towards that state than if the forum adjudicated such matters. Why would foreign state officials not want their rights holders to obtain vindication in any possible tribunal? Also, would it not be 'the highest display of support for another sovereign to facilitate respect for and enforcement of its [IP] rights against a ... defendant [of the forum state]?'[24] Significantly, in no national IP legislation is exclusive jurisdiction conferred on the courts of the country under whose law the right arose. As argued, a finding of exclusive jurisdiction also does not follow from the principle of territoriality which speaks only of rights belonging to a territory, not of the adjudicative powers of courts of other states in respect of such rights.

The consequence of this restrictive approach is that where infringements under multiple national laws occur, the rights holder must pursue separate proceedings in each individual state where it enjoys protection, despite the allegations often involving the same conduct by the defendant in respect of similar subject matter. Such an outcome is obviously

---

[19] For a detailed discussion see Richard Garnett, 'Enhanced enforcement of IP rights in transnational cases in Australia' (2017) 27 *Australian Intellectual Property Journal* 114.
[20] *Potter* v. *Broken Hill Pty Co Ltd* (1906) 3 CLR 479.   [21] Ibid., 494 (Griffith CJ).
[22] *British South Africa Co* v. *Companhia de Moçambique* [1893] AC 602.
[23] The *Moçambique* rule has been abolished in New South Wales: Jurisdiction of Courts (Foreign Land) Act 1989 (NSW) and limited to cases where title to land is in issue in the UK: Civil Jurisdiction and Judgments Act 1982 (UK) s. 30(1).
[24] Dinwoodie, 'Developing a private intellectual property law', 758.

expensive and inefficient and is a deterrent to a claimant obtaining complete redress. Digital use of copyright works and trademarks has only intensified this problem.[25]

The anomaly of this analysis is also recognised when it is recalled that certain IP rights that are derived from the common law and not statute, such as passing off and protection of confidential information, are not the subject of exclusive jurisdiction. An Australian court, for example, has power or subject matter jurisdiction to adjudicate an action for foreign acts of passing off (a tort) or breach of confidence (equitable or contractual). The situation of passing off is particularly apposite in this context, given that the factual circumstances giving rise to this action are often similar to a claim for infringement of a registered trademark.[26]

A more balanced approach which recognises the reality and scope of international IP infringements has been adopted in the EU,[27] Commonwealth countries such as England[28] and New Zealand,[29] Japan[30] and most US courts.[31] According to this view, foreign state interests should bar adjudication only where the validity of a foreign registered IP right such as a patent or trademark is raised as a principal question for determination. In such a case the court would be reviewing the determination of a foreign government official on its own territory which may not only be sensitive, but any judgment given likely unenforceable.[32] This situation would arise, for example, where a claimant sought a declaration that a foreign registered right had been invalidly granted or the question of validity was raised as a counterclaim in an action for infringement.[33]

---

[25] Dinwoodie, 'International intellectual property litigation', 440–1.
[26] Sam Ricketson, 'Trade mark liability issues arising out of internet advertising' (2007) 12 *Media and Arts Law Review* 1, 20.
[27] Regulation (EU) No 1215/2012 of the European Parliament and Council of 12 December 2012 on Jurisdiction and the Recognition and Enforcement of Judgments in Civil and Commercial Matters (Recast) OJ 2012 L351/1 arts. 4, 24(4).
[28] *Lucasfilm Ltd* v. *Ainsworth* [2012] 1 AC 208; *Actavis Group HF* v. *Eli Lilly & Co* [2012] EWHC 3316 (Pat).
[29] *KK Sony Computer Entertainment* v. *Van Veen* (2006) 71 IPR 79; *Stewart* v. *Franmara Inc (No. 2)* (2012) 96 IPR 554.
[30] Toshiyuki Kono, 'Cross border enforcement of intellectual property: Japanese law and practice' in Paul Torremans (ed.), *Research Handbook on Cross Border Enforcement of Intellectual Property* (Northampton, MA: Edward Elgar, 2014), pp. 108, 120–1 citing the *Coral Sand* case (Tokyo District Court, 16 October 2003, 1847 *Hanrei Jiho* 23).
[31] *London Film Production Inc* v. *Intercontinental Communications*, 580 F Supp 47 (SDNY, 1984); *Armstrong* v. *Virgin Records Ltd*, 91 F Supp 2d 628, 637 (SDNY, 2000); *Ortoman* v. *Stanray Corp* 371 F 2d 154 (7th Cir, 1967).
[32] *Voda* v. *Cordis Corp*, 476 F 3d 887 (Fed Cir, 2007).
[33] *Lucasfilm Ltd* v. *Ainsworth* [2012] 1 AC 208 [103]; *Satyam Computer Services Ltd* v. *Unpaid Systems Ltd* [2008] EWHC 31 (Comm) [102]; *Anan Kasei* v. *Molycorp* [2016] EWHC 1722 (Pat); *Eli Lilly & Co* v. *Genentech Inc* [2017] EWHC 3104 (Pat).

Where, by contrast, validity arises only as a 'preliminary question' in an infringement action then a decision as to validity can be made by the forum court if it has only inter partes and not erga omnes effect.[34]

The advantages of such an approach are obvious. A claimant who faces multi-territorial infringements of its rights no longer is required to commence proceedings in every country where the rights are conferred (assuming it has the resources to do so) but may instead consolidate all infringements, local and foreign, in a single action in the forum. The benefits in terms of efficiency of litigation and in achieving full redress are clear. However, a forum court is not *required* to adjudicate a matter involving foreign IP rights. US and English courts have suggested that the forum should rely on discretionary principles of forum non conveniens in deciding whether to adjudicate such a claim,[35] which would allow the court to consider all the circumstances of the case. Hence, where a matter is strongly connected with the country of protection in terms of the location of evidence and the parties, for example, a decision to decline jurisdiction may be appropriate.

In practice, however, two limitations on claimant recovery may still exist even under this liberal approach. First, in many countries consolidation of claims involving multiple infringements can occur only when a court is exercising 'general' personal jurisdiction – that is, where the matter is being heard at the place of the defendant's habitual residence or domicile. If, by contrast, the foreign-based defendant is sued in the courts of the claimant's residence,[36] the claimant normally can obtain recovery only in respect of infringements that occurred in the forum under local law.[37] Claims for infringements under foreign law cannot be 'tacked on' in this situation. Since the defendant's habitual residence may be an undesirable forum in which to sue, other alternative forums for consolidation need to be considered.

In this regard, the ALI Principles would allow a court of a state to exercise jurisdiction where a defendant has substantially acted or taken

---

[34] This distinction is recognised in both the ALI Principles, ss. 211(2), 212(4) and 213(2) and the CLIP Principles, 2:401(2).

[35] *Lucasfilm Ltd* v. *Ainsworth* [2008] EWHC 1878 (Ch) [274]–[275]; *Actavis Group HF* v. *Eli Lilly & Co* [2012] EWHC 3316; *Boosey & Hawkes Music Publishers* v. *Walt Disney*, 145 F 3d 481 (2nd Cir, 1998).

[36] An exception may arise in common law countries where the defendant was served with process while transiently in the forum: this may also give rise to 'general' jurisdiction (although a controversial ground); see *Burnham* v. *Superior Court of California*, 495 US 604 (1990).

[37] Sophie Neumann, 'Ubiquitous and multistate cases' in Paul Torremans (ed.), *Research Handbook on Cross Border Enforcement of Intellectual Property* (Northampton, MA: Edward Elgar, 2014), pp. 497, 508.

substantial preparatory acts to initiate or further an infringement there. The court's jurisdiction extends to all damage arising out of such conduct, regardless of the place of injury.[38] The CLIP Principles provide that the court of the state where an infringement occurs shall have jurisdiction over ubiquitous infringements in the following circumstances. First, the infringer must have directed its activity at the forum state. Second, the activity must have no substantial effect in the state where the infringer is habitually resident. Third, substantial activities must have been carried out in the forum state or the harm caused by the infringement in the forum state must be substantial in relation to the infringement in its entirety.[39] The ALI provision perhaps has the advantage of simplicity, but the overall intent of both proposals is clear.

A second problem is that even if consolidation of infringements under multiple national laws is possible, there remains the logistical burden of having to plead, prove and apply all the relevant laws. Not only do the parties have to lead evidence of foreign law, which is normally through expert witness statements, but courts are required to apply all such laws. The result can be a protracted and expensive proceeding (assuming all laws are pleaded).

The problem has also been addressed in the ALI and CLIP Principles where application of a single law – the law with the closest connection to the dispute – is suggested as a solution in ubiquitous infringement cases – that is, where breaches are 'instantaneous and worldwide'.[40] The closest connection law will be determined by the court examining all the circumstances of the case, including the residence(s) of the parties[41] or of the infringer alone,[42] the place where substantial activities in furtherance of the infringement have been carried out or where substantial harm caused by the infringement has occurred[43] or the principal markets towards which the parties have directed their activities.[44] While some commentators have criticised the closest connection principle because of its breadth and uncertainty,[45] such an approach is common in other areas of PIL, such as the forum non conveniens doctrine and the applicable law rules for tort and contract, and is designed to balance multiple competing interests. Also, any uncertainty created is surely a worthy price to pay for

---

[38] ALI Principles, s. 204(1).   [39] CLIP Principles, art. 2:202, 203.
[40] Rita Matulionyte, *Law Applicable to Copyright: A Comparison of the ALI and CLIP Proposals* (Cheltenham, UK: Edward Elgar, 2011), p. 178.
[41] ALI Principles, s. 321.   [42] CLIP Principles, art. 3: 603.   [43] Ibid.
[44] ALI Principles, 321(1).
[45] Andrew Christie, 'Private international law principles for ubiquitous intellectual property infringement – A solution in search of a problem?' (2017) 13 *Journal of Private International Law* 152, 179.

avoiding the burden on the parties and the courts of having to plead and apply multiple laws in a ubiquitous infringement situation.

12.5.3 Extraterritorial Injunctions

Recently, a question has arisen concerning the capacity of PIL to regulate extraterritorial injunctive relief in IP cases involving the internet. In *Google Inc* v. *Equustek Solutions Inc*,[46] the Supreme Court of Canada issued an injunction requiring Google to de-index, on a worldwide basis, websites of a company that had been engaged in conduct in breach of the claimant's rights to confidential information under Canadian law. Similar extraterritorial relief was granted by the Supreme Court of New South Wales in *X* v. *Twitter*.[47] In response to the Canadian decree, a US judge then granted an order[48] that prevented enforcement of the Canadian injunction in the US to the extent that it prohibited Google from publishing search result information within the US.

While such extraterritorial injunctive relief carries the risk of retaliatory orders and conflicts of jurisdiction between national courts, more balanced approaches are possible. For example, issuing courts can exercise self-restraint in granting orders that may impact on persons in other countries, and courts in affected states can enforce such decrees, at least where their vital national interests are not threatened. Such suggestions are entirely consistent with a model of PIL that encourages the recognition of the interests of other states in decisions on jurisdiction and applicable law.

12.6 A Resurgence of State Interests and Territoriality?

12.6.1 The Hague Draft Convention

Very recently the US government, with the support of the Chinese delegation, has, in the current negotiations of the Draft Hague Convention on Recognition and Enforcement of Foreign Judgments (Draft Convention),[49] advocated an even wider operation for state interests and territoriality in IP matters. The Draft Convention currently contains

---

[46] [2017] 1 SCR 824.   [47] (2017) 95 NSWLR 301.
[48] *Google LLC* v. *Equustek Solutions Inc*, 2017 WL 5000834 (ND Cal, 2 November 2017).
[49] Special Commission on the Recognition and Enforcement of Foreign Judgments (24–29 May 2018), 2018 Draft Convention, retrieved from https://assets.hcch.net/docs/23b6dac3-7900-49f3-9a94-aa0ffbe0d0dd.pdf (cited as Draft Convention).

provisions (in square brackets) that would require a Contracting State to the Convention (the requested state) to recognise and enforce a judgment given by another Contracting State (the state of origin) where the judgment ruled on the infringement of a registered right such as a patent, trademark or design[50] or an unregistered right such as copyright[51] where such rights were conferred under the law of the state of origin. The obligation to enforce is subject to the traditional PIL defences of public policy (including lack of procedural fairness),[52] fraud,[53] res judicata[54] and insufficient notification of the defendant.[55]

The US government, however, wants the deletion of these provisions from the Draft Convention, a result that would leave IP rights entirely excluded. Yet the approach taken in the Draft Convention is wholly consistent with the territoriality of IP rights as described earlier: here the requested state is merely being asked to enforce a judgment of the state of origin that ruled on IP rights existing under the law of the latter state. Since the rights arose under the law of the state of origin, its courts are obviously the most appropriate forum to entertain an action for infringement or validity. Denying a claimant the opportunity to have any judgment recognised and enforced elsewhere leaves this person without an effective remedy where the defendant has no assets in the state of origin. Indeed, such provisions are entirely consistent with current national[56] and supranational laws on foreign judgments, where there is no bar to recognition and enforcement in country A of a judgment of country B that rules only on infringement of IP rights granted under the law of country B.

The US government argues that since IP rights are not globally harmonised, for a requested state to have to enforce an IP judgment from a state with differing protection standards would undermine and distort rights in respect of the same subject matter in the requested state. An example of this situation is where a requested state was asked to enforce a judgment for infringement of rights under the law of the state of origin, but such conduct would not have amounted to an infringement under the law of the requested state. In such a case, it is argued, enforcement of

---

[50] Ibid., art. 5(3)(a).   [51] Ibid., art. 5(3)(b).   [52] Ibid., art. 7(1)(c).
[53] Ibid., art. 7(1)(b).   [54] Ibid., art. 7(1)(e),(f).   [55] Ibid., art. 7(1)(a).
[56] See, e.g., in Australia, where section 7(3)(b) of the Foreign Judgments Act 1991 (Cth) provides that a judgment may be registered in Australia where it is given in an action of which the subject matter was immovable property situated in the country of the court of origin. Section 7(4)(a), however, prevents registration where the judgment concerned immovable property situated outside such country.

the foreign rights would weaken the local regime for IP protection in the requested state.

The first and most obvious response to this view is that any system of PIL accepts that laws differ between countries and that a nation state will often be required to enforce a law or a judgment that has no equivalent in the requested state. The public policy defence is there for the extreme cases of offence to local values, but otherwise foreign rights should be enforced. If such a process of recognition did not exist, then a national court would only ever apply its own laws in litigation and any judgment given could only ever be enforced within the same state's territory. Foreign infringers could therefore happily operate beyond the reach of justice, claimants would be left without redress and international co-operation and enforcement of rights across borders would cease to exist.

A second response is that, as discussed, any judgment of the state of origin concerns IP rights arising only under the law of that state. Rights under the law of the requested state are separate and distinct from those in the state of origin, even when applied to similar subject matter. A judgment of the court in the state of origin says nothing about a rights holder in the requested state's capacity to use a mark or exploit the work in that territory.[57] It is possible that enforcement of such a judgment may have a commercial effect on the exercise of parallel rights in the same subject matter in the requested state, but this result can occur whenever an entity trades in multiple countries and is not confined to the IP context.

Also, it is acknowledged that activity by a person based in the requested state, such as use of a mark, particularly taking place online, may 'spill over' and have effects in the state of origin. This problem can, however, be dealt with by the adoption of limiting devices such as are proposed by the EU in the Draft Convention that narrowly defines 'infringement' in the state of origin to require 'targeting' of and deliberate intent by a user to act in that state.[58]

12.6.2 The WIPO Study

Another recent rebuke to PIL has come in a report commissioned by the World Intellectual Property Organization (WIPO) on cross-border

---

[57] This is also the view of the chair of the Special Commission responsible for negotiating the Draft Convention: see D Goddard QC, 'The judgments convention: The current state of play', retrieved from https://bit.ly/2ktcF2P, 14.

[58] Draft Convention, art. 5(3)(a), (b).

online copyright infringement (WIPO Report).[59] In the report, Andrew Christie asserts by reference to national data collected for the report that:

> the plaintiff in most cross-border online IP infringement disputes appears not to require multistate claims and/or multistate enforcement of orders, apparently because in practice it can get most, if not all, of what it desires from a single action in a carefully chosen jurisdiction.[60]

Christie then goes on to suggest that rather than reforming rules of PIL relating to IP, a better strategy would be to undertake training activities and further research and to develop harmonised national law standards on the issue of what constitutes IP infringement.[61] The likely serious difficulties in achieving global harmonisation or establishing transnational IP 'norms' have already been mentioned. Furthermore, one commentator has recently said in response to the WIPO Report that the data sample used (particularly on US law) arguably underrepresents the position, since there are likely to be many cross-border disputes where parties failed to raise the PIL issues either through ignorance[62] or because of 'barriers' in national law that made it impractical (or impossible) to sue foreign defendants or bring claims based on foreign IP law.[63] This observation certainly rings true in Australia, where the bar on enforcement of foreign statutory IP rights has meant that claimants have had little option to consider cross-border vindication in IP cases. In other words, their path has been blocked by outdated national law restrictions rather than because they exercised a 'free choice'[64] not to pursue cross-border relief. PIL is still much needed by IP.

12.7 Conclusion

With the rise in cross-border exploitation and infringement of IP, the interaction of PIL and IP has become a focus of scholarly and practical concern. At first glance the strong influence of international treaties, state interests and territoriality on IP would suggest an aversion to regulation by PIL. Yet the need of rights holders to secure effective redress for both local and foreign infringements has led to a breaking down of the insulation of IP. In many countries as well as in 'soft law'

---

[59] Andrew Christie, *Private International Law Issues in Online Intellectual Property Infringement Disputes with Cross-Border Elements: An Analysis of National Approaches* (Geneva: World Intellectual Property Organization, 2015).
[60] Ibid., 29.   [61] Ibid., 29–30.
[62] Marketa Trimble, 'Undetected conflict-of-laws problems in cross border online copyright infringement cases' (2016) 18 *North Carolina Journal of Law and Technology* 119, 125–6.
[63] Ibid., 156–7.   [64] Ibid., 157.

proposals there is now a clear trend towards liberalising rules of jurisdiction, applicable law and recognition of judgments to facilitate enforcement of IP rights across borders. While a return to strict principles of territoriality has been suggested in the recent WIPO Report and by the US government in the Hague Convention negotiations, this appeal seems to run counter to a world of increasingly interconnected courts and legal systems, whose aim is to provide justice to parties. IP and PIL are strangers in the night no longer.[65]

---

[65] The Convention on the Recognition and Enforcement of Foreign Judgments in Civil or Commercial Matters was finally concluded at a Diplomatic Session in July 2019. The Convention excludes intellectual property from its scope in article 2(1)(m).

Part III

Across Disciplines

13 The Challenges of Intellectual Property Legal History Research

Isabella Alexander[*]

Having been allocated this title, I was presented with a challenge of my own; how to identify the challenges of intellectual property legal history research without discouraging students and scholars from undertaking it, and undertaking it well. But every type of law has its own challenges, and occasions upon which to reflect on them are far too rare. This chapter, therefore, provides a welcome opportunity in which to argue that doing intellectual property legal history is difficult, but rewarding, and to consider why this is so. I identify four broad challenges that it presents: first, challenges of identifying it; second, challenges arising in doing it, both as a process and as a methodology; third, challenges associated with interpreting findings; fourth, challenges relating to its purpose, relevance and audience.

Reflecting upon Sam Ricketson's contribution provides a fitting framework for this investigation. Legal history has been an integral part of Ricketson's work, whether in research, teaching or advocacy. His deep and nuanced appreciation of how laws have changed over time informs his approach to most topics with which he has engaged. But while his knowledge of history invariably forms the background to the matter at hand, legal history has also been the direct subject of his inquiry. This chapter takes as its starting point Ricketson's work directly concerned with the history of intellectual property law, and uses it to consider, more broadly, the challenges involved in intellectual property legal history research. A final objective is to address a further challenge: encouraging more students of both law and history to draw inspiration from Ricketson and other leaders in the field to consider how combining these two disciplines can enrich their own inquiries and analysis.

---

[*] I am grateful to Jill McKeough and David Lindsay for providing feedback on this chapter in draft, and to Kosta Hountalas for research assistance. Any errors are my own.

13.1 Intellectual Property History or History of Intellectual Property Law?

Perhaps the first distinction to make is between the history of intellectual property and the legal history of intellectual property (or history of intellectual property law, to put it another way). To some extent, this mirrors the distinction sometimes made between 'internal' and 'external' histories of law, where the former focusses primarily upon the history of legal doctrines or perhaps related matters like court jurisdiction, legal language or legal theories, while the latter is more concerned with the interaction between law, legal agencies or institutions, and the societies in which they operate.[1] Internal legal history, as Michael Lobban has noted, is largely carried out by lawyers, working in law faculties, and their concern is the history of the doctrines that they and their colleagues teach to students.[2] It looks at the passing of statutes, the decided cases and how doctrines and precedents emerged, were applied and were adapted. Its sources are largely legal but may encompass parliamentary debates, personal communications and other materials that cast light on the motivations or meanings of historical actors concerned.

This is the kind of history at which Sam Ricketson has excelled, in his work on the Berne Convention (at times co-authored with Jane Ginsburg, another skilled practitioner of the genre),[3] on originality in copyright law,[4] on the Australian Copyright Act of 1912,[5] on international copyright,[6] and on the *Union Label* case.[7] In these books and articles,

---

[1] For the distinction between internal and external histories, see Robert W Gordon, 'J Willard Hurst and the common law tradition in American legal historiography' (2012) 9 *Law & Society Review* 9, 11.

[2] Michael Lobban, 'The varieties of legal history' (2012) 5 *Clio@Thémis* 1, 3–4.

[3] Sam Ricketson and Jane C Ginsburg, *International Copyright and Neighbouring Rights: The Berne Convention and Beyond*, 2nd ed. (Oxford: Oxford University Press, 2006).

[4] Sam Ricketson, 'Common law approaches to the requirement of originality' in Catherine W Ng, Lionel Bently and Guiseppina D'Agostino (eds.), *The Common Law of Intellectual Property: Essays in Honour of Professor David Vaver* (Oxford: Hart Publishing, 2010), p. 221.

[5] Sam Ricketson, 'The Imperial Copyright Act 1911 in Australia' in Uma Suthersanen and Ysolde Gendreau (eds.), *A Shifting Empire: 100 Years of the Copyright Act 1911* (Cheltenham, UK: Edward Elgar, 2013), p. 52.

[6] Sam Ricketson, 'The public international law of copyright and related rights' in Isabella Alexander and H Tomás Gómez-Arostegui (eds.), *Research Handbook on the History of Copyright Law* (Cheltenham, UK: Edward Elgar, 2016), p. 288.

[7] *Attorney-General of New South Wales v. Brewery Employees Union of New South Wales* (1908) 6 CLR 469. Sam Ricketson, 'The *Union Label* case: An early Australian IP story' in Andrew T Kenyon, Megan Richardson and Sam Ricketson (eds.), *Landmarks in Australian Intellectual Property Law* (Cambridge: Cambridge University Press, 2009), p. 15.

Ricketson employs the legal records of the past – cases, statutes, debates, memoranda and other incidentally produced documents – to deepen our understanding of the law and its institutions as they operate today. This approach employs legal history as a technique of legal interpretation, and Ricketson's meticulous tracing of the official record of lawmaking offers new tools of interpretation through a fuller understanding of the past.

However, the field of intellectual property legal history is an ever-expanding one. Alongside the important role just described, it encompasses jurisprudential approaches to critiquing intellectual property's concepts and categories, and the work of scholars who look to history to explain the emergence of legal practices, approaches and assumptions.[8] Broken down into intellectual property's subcategories, copyright history continues to lead the field.[9] A considerable body of work addresses the question of whether copyright is a creature solely of statute, or whether there was a common law copyright which survived the passing of the Statute of Anne.[10] Key participants in this debate are Howard Abrams,[11] Mark Rose[12] and Ronan Deazley,[13] who have argued that the conventional view that copyright existed at common law is erroneous, and the House of Lords decision in *Donaldson v. Beckett*[14] concluded the opposite. This approach was countered by further meticulous research by Tomás Gómez-Arostegui, arguing that in fact the conventional view is correct.[15]

Notably, it is not just legal historians interested in this copyright debate. In the 1980s, bibliographer John Feather placed the history of copyright in the context of book trade history.[16] Literary scholar Mark Rose, mentioned earlier, along with others, took up the theoretical challenges of Foucault and Barthes in relation to authorship and applied

---

[8] A leading work in this field is Brad Sherman and Lionel Bently, *The Making of Modern Intellectual Property Law* (Cambridge: Cambridge University Press, 1999).
[9] A recent collection showcasing the variety and extent of the work in this field and with an extensive bibliography is Isabella Alexander and H Tomás Gómez-Arostegui (eds.), *Research Handbook on the History of Copyright Law* (Cheltenham, UK: Edward Elgar, 2016).
[10] Copyright Act 1710 (Imp) 8 Ann, c. 19.
[11] Howard Abrams, 'The historic foundation of American copyright law: Exploding the myth of common law copyright' (1983) 29 *Wayne Law Review* 1119.
[12] Mark Rose, 'The author as proprietor: *Donaldson v Becket* and the genealogy of modern authorship' (1988) 23 *Representations* 51.
[13] Ronan Deazley, *On the Origin of the Right to Copy* (Oxford: Hart Publishing, 2004).
[14] (1774) 98 ER 257.
[15] H Tomás Gómez-Arostegui, 'Copyright in common law in 1774' (2014) 47 *Connecticut Law Review* 1.
[16] John Feather, 'The book trade in politics: The making of the Copyright Act of 1710' (1980) 8 *Publishing History* 19 (and other works).

them to copyright history, providing new insights into the emergence of 'literary property' and the legal treatment of authorship.[17]

Alongside the ever-growing body of work on copyright history, patent history is also increasing in popularity with legal historians;[18] trade mark law languishes a little on the sidelines, although interest in it is slowly growing;[19] and very little has been done on the history of design rights.[20] For non-legal historians, histories of intellectual property are also proving a fertile field. It was also in the 1980s that historians of economics and science began to turn their attention to historical interactions between patenting and innovation, with debate focussing in particular on the role played by patents in the Industrial Revolution.[21] More recently, books written for a more generalist audience have begun to appear on topics such as 'the ownership of art and ideas' and the 'cultural commons'[22] or inventions like the steam engine.[23] Bridging the popular and the academic audiences is Adrian Johns's *Piracy*,[24] which seeks to turn traditional intellectual property scholarship on its head by starting on the other side of the coin, displacing inventors, authors and property owners from the centre of the story and replacing them with those who copy and counterfeit.

It is said that the historian is more interested in the *effects* of laws than the laws themselves, sometimes conveying the impression that the law is somehow fixed or external to society. However, this is not true of much

---

[17] Rose, 'The author as proprietor'; Peter Jaszi, 'Toward a theory of copyright: The metamorphoses of "authorship"' (1991) 40 *Duke Law Journal* 455(and other works); Martha Woodmansee, *The Author, Art and the Market: Rereading the History of Aesthetics* (Columbia: Columbia University Press, 1994) (and other works).

[18] For example, Sean Bottomley, *The British Patent System during the Industrial Revolution 1700–1852* (Cambridge: Cambridge University Press, 2014).

[19] For example, Amanda Scardamaglia, *Colonial Australian Trade Mark Law: Narratives in Lawmaking, People, Power & Place* (North Melbourne: Australian Scholarly Publishing, 2015); Lionel Bently, 'The first trade mark case at common law? The Story of *Singleton v Bolton*'(2014) *University of California Davis Law Review* 969.

[20] But see, for example, Lionel Bently and Brad Sherman, 'The UK's forgotten utility model: The Utility Designs Act 1843' (1997) 3 *Intellectual Property Quarterly* 267.

[21] See in particular, Harold Dutton, *The Patent System and Inventive Activity during the Industrial Revolution, 1750–1852* (Manchester, UK: Manchester University Press, 1984); Christine MacLeod, *Inventing the Industrial Revolution, the English Patent System, 1660–1800* (Cambridge: Cambridge University Press, 1988); Joel Mokyr, *The Lever of Riches: Technological Creativity and Economic Growth* (Oxford: Oxford University Press, 1990).

[22] Lewis Hyde, *Common As Air: Revolution, Art, and Ownership* (New York: Farrar, Straus & Giroux, 2010).

[23] William Rosen, *The Most Powerful Idea in the World: A Story of Steam, Industry and Invention* (Chicago: University of Chicago Press, 2010).

[24] Adrian Johns, *Piracy: The Intellectual Property Wars from Gutenberg to Gates* (Chicago: Chicago University Press, 2010).

of the research into intellectual property, where a growing number of scholars are attentive to the mutually constitutive interactions between society and law. The inter- and multi-disciplinary approach of sociolegal research involves combining approaches, methodologies and insights from other disciplines, such as sociology, politics, economics and the humanities. Such approaches in the field of intellectual property can offer new perspectives on the law, such as the roles played by individual actors, interest groups and ideologies in the creation and transformation of law and legal doctrine.[25] Others combine the internal focus on law with an external consideration of its effects. One area in which this approach flourishes is in the work of economic historians or historians of science and the law of patents. For example, Christine Macleod's work tells us about the emergence of the patent system as a legal institution,[26] and argues that its flaws meant that its role in fostering inventive activity was minimal, while a reassessment of the law and its application by Sean Bottomley reappraises this thesis.[27] Similarly, Stathis Arapostathis and Graeme Gooday are interested in the effect of patents and their litigation on the creation of inventor identity, but also make the more internal legal argument that the adversarial system of litigation in Britain in the late nineteenth century itself influenced the development of patent law.[28]

Cultural studies scholars, ethnographers and legal anthropologists have also engaged in productive interdisciplinary work and collaborations to open up new perspectives and areas of inquiry. Foundational work was carried out in the 1990s by Jane Gaines and Rosemary Coombes, considering the effects of intellectual property on cultural forms and aesthetics and the role of law in cultural production.[29] Similar approaches have been taken in collaborative work between legal scholars, literary scholars, art historians, and media scholars.[30] Developing and

---

[25] For example, Catherine Seville, *The Internationalisation of Copyright Law: Books, Buccaneers and the Black Flag in the Nineteenth Century* (Cambridge: Cambridge University Press, 2006).

[26] MacLeod, *Inventing the Industrial Revolution*.

[27] Bottomley, *The British Patent System during the Industrial Revolution*.

[28] Stathis Arapostathis and Graeme Gooday, *Patently Contestable: Electrical Technologies and Inventor Identities on Trial in Britain* (Boston: Massachusetts Institute of Technology, 2013).

[29] Jane M Gaines, *Contested Culture: The Image, the Voice and the Law* (Chapel Hill: University of North Carolina Press, 1991).

[30] For example, Katie Scott, 'Maps, views and ornament: Visualising property in art and law: The case of pre-modern France' in Ronan Deazley, Martin Kretschmer and Lionel Bently (eds.), *Privilege and Property: Essays on the History of Copyright* (Cambridge: OpenBook Publishers, 2010), p. 255; Megan Richardson and Julian Thomas, *Fashioning Intellectual Property: Exhibition, Advertising and the Press 1789–1918* (Cambridge: Cambridge University Press, 2012).

expanding the conversations between different disciplines allows our understanding of intellectual property to move beyond the interactions between law in the statutes and law in the cases, to appreciate the nuances of law's operation in everyday life, its role in shaping creative or innovative practices, and how it is understood by those who are affected by it.[31]

13.2 Challenges of Research and Methodology

Researching the history of intellectual property or intellectual property law throws up its own practical challenges, although they are challenges not unique to intellectual property history. Since access to the primary sources is absolutely essential, archives must be visited – this involves travel (particularly arduous and expensive for those who live far from their objects of study), forethought and planning, handling documents shrouded in the dirt of ages and the inevitable frustrations of unlocatable or missing materials. As noted in the preface to the 2006 edition of Ricketson and Ginsburg's *International Copyright*:

> When Sam began his research in 1984, access to many of the original documents meant trips to the WIPO library in Geneva or the Max Planck Institute in Munich. Holdings in London were dispersed and often difficult to track down; photocopying of original documents was often impossible because of conservation concerns and long hours of tedious transcription were often required.[32]

But the physical difficulties must be offset against the excitement gained by handling the same materials one's subject handled across the centuries and the ever-present lure of finding the smoking gun document that validates the hypothesis or changes the field entirely. With characteristic dry humour, Ricketson and Ginsburg continue:

> Since the mid-1990s, WIPO documentation has become available online and research into current developments in the international conventions can be done at the click of a mouse (with the necessary internet access). These developments have certainly made the writing of the second edition easier, but with some regrets for the rigours (and delights) of earlier times when dusty volumes and documents had to be tracked down and studied in places far from the normal comforts and conveniences of one's own desk and office (one should not

---

[31] For example, Laura J Murray, S Tina Piper and Kirsty Robertson, *Putting Intellectual Property in Its Place: Rights Discourses, Creative Labour and the Everyday* (Oxford: Oxford University Press, 2014).

[32] Ricketson and Ginsburg, *International Copyright and Neighbouring Rights*, vii–viii.

overstate here the difficulties involved in being 'required' to spend time in such places as Geneva and Munich in the pursuit of scholarship!).[33]

It is indeed true that many of the difficulties in locating and accessing sources are overcome by the exponential increase in material being placed on the World Wide Web. Notwithstanding the difficulties presented by copyright and privacy laws, memory institutions are digitising their collections apace. Scholars are also becoming more interested in using the internet to collate particular collections for more general access. In the context of intellectual property, the UK Arts and Humanities Research Council (AHRC)–funded Primary Sources of Copyright History project at www.copyrighthistory.org stands as an invaluable resource. It has opened up the key primary sources for copyright law of seven jurisdictions, as well as Jewish Law, providing both an entry point for new researchers and constant access to sources far away for experienced scholars. And it is not just primary source material that is increasingly accessible; many secondary sources are accessible almost instantaneously and free thanks to services like Google Books, HathiTrust, Wikipedia and Project Gutenberg or paid for higher up the academic food chain in the case of proprietary databases like JSTOR, Westlaw, Lexis and Gale-Cengage. At the same time, the emergence and constant improvement of optical character recognition (OCR) software enabling full-text searching of documents allows material to be searched by content as well as by indexes and metadata.

Digitisation has radically transformed the practice of history, including legal history, in myriad ways, many of which are still being explored. It allows historians to ask, and answer, new questions and to make connections that were previously invisible. In particular, it has allowed scholars to work more easily across jurisdictions, thus contributing to a flourishing of transnational histories.[34] The use of full-text searching can help expose more voices of 'ordinary people' – marginalised or secondary players who might not appear in traditional indexes or meta-data. Data mining of large datasets can also be used to test historical hypotheses empirically and display findings using data visualisation techniques. One such example is the exciting recent work of digital humanities programmer and literary scholar Douglas Duhaime. Duhaime mines the English Short Title Catalogue (ESTC) and Eighteenth-Century Collections Online (ECCO), to demonstrate, inter alia, that book prices did not fall following the decision in *Donaldson* v. *Becket* (contra the assertions of a

---

[33] Ibid., viii.
[34] Lara Putnam, 'The transnational and the text-searchable: Digitized sources and the shadows they cast' (2016) 121 *The American Historical Review* 377.

number of copyright history scholars) and to investigate how copyright rulings impacted the production of derivative publications in the eighteenth century.[35]

However, digitised collections offer their own challenges. In the 1940s, Marc Bloch, singing the praises of library and archive guides and their under-appreciated compilers, observed that '[d]espite what the beginners sometimes seem to imagine, documents do not suddenly materialize, in one place or another, as if by some mysterious decree of the gods'.[36] Yet this is what the internet has achieved for historians, beginners or otherwise. A potential problem this creates, as identified by Tim Hitchcock, is that of 'deracinated knowledge'.[37] Just because anyone can find an original source on the internet, does not mean that everyone is 'doing history'. Context is crucial for interpretation, whether that context is achieved through perceiving the physical place or location within a collection or perceiving its place within a discipline or field of knowledge.

It is important to remain aware that the infinite archive of the internet offers only the illusion of containing everything there is to know. As Lara Putnam points out, 'the new topography of information has systemic blind spots. It opens shortcuts that enable ignorance as well as knowledge.'[38] While new voices emerge, some are rendered invisible. Some sources become more prominent, such as eighteenth-century London-based newspapers, with the likely effect of obscuring the contribution and use of less accessible provincial papers.[39] Legal historians can easily supplement court or parliamentary records with newspaper records and debates, and those intellectuals, activists, victims and perpetrators appearing in their pages are brought into the light of historical inquiry. But we need to remember that we attribute causation to what we see and ignore the contribution of what we do not: we must 'remember not to mistake the window for the why'.[40] This is hardly a new problem of historical inquiry, but digitisation and the internet have perhaps cast a wider net to trap the unwary.

---

[35] Douglas Duhaime, 'Copyright and the early English book market: An algorithmic study', PhD dissertation (University of Notre Dame, Notre Dame, IN, 2019), retrieved from www.earlybookmarket.com.
[36] Marc Bloch, *The Historian's Craft* (Manchester, UK: Manchester University Press, 1954), p. 71.
[37] Tim Hitchcock, 'Confronting the digital' (2013) 10 *Cultural and Social History* 9.
[38] Putnam, 'The transnational and the text-searchable', 379.
[39] See Andrew Prescott, 'I'd rather be a librarian' (2014) 11 *Cultural and Social History* 335, 337.
[40] Putnam, 'The transnational and the text-searchable', 391.

13.3 Challenges of Interpretation and Methodology

Once the source materials have been located or acquired, further challenges arise over their treatment. A particular pressure placed on intellectual property history is its close relationship to technologies, whether they be enabling technologies such as the printing press, photographic camera or gramophone, or subject matter for protection, such as wireless technology or an incandescent light bulb (or both). Histories of technology are often histories of progress, of trial and error and steps of improvement towards a successful conclusion. But history itself cannot be such a story without falling prey to accusations of Whiggism[41] or making history the 'handmaid of dogma'.[42]

Another reason to be cautious, for lawyers engaging in legal history, is the training of common law methodology. One difference that is often noted between the approaches of lawyers and historians is in relation to causation. Both professions are interested in seeking out *why* things happened. However, where lawyers are often looking for a single actor to take legal responsibility, historians look for combinations of causes and for subtle distinctions: '[h]istory seeks for causal wave-trains and is not afraid, since life shows them to be so, to find them multiple'.[43] Another way of putting this is to say that while lawyers tend to be monists (looking for a single authoritative meaning from the past), historians are pluralists (seeking contested, ambiguous or multi-causal meanings).[44] Gordon uses this distinction to refer to lawyers' use of decided, past, cases as authority for a single proposition to guide a present dispute. However, this formulation could also refer to the way that lawyers, when resolving disputes, will seek to point to a (frequently single) proximate cause that can be used to attribute legal responsibility, while historians may be more interested in background social, economic or cultural causes. For example, in tort litigation, a lawyer might ask 'Whose act led this building

---

[41] *Whig history* takes its name from one of the two main political parties in eighteenth- and nineteenth-century Britain and its chief practitioner was the Whig writer Thomas Babington Macaulay. The term has come to be used to refer to historians who present the past as an inevitable progression towards improvement, in particular in relation to liberal democracy.

[42] Frederick Maitland, a leading legal historian of late nineteenth century Britain, wrote, '[i]f we try to make history the handmaid of dogma she will soon cease to be history': F W Maitland, *Why the History of English Law Is Not Written* (Cambridge: Cambridge University Press, 1888), p. 15.

[43] Bloch, *The Historian's Craft*, 194.

[44] Robert W Gordon, *Taming the Past: Essays on Law in History and History in Law* (Cambridge: Cambridge University Press, 2017), p. 3.

to collapse?' while an historian might ask 'What factors (personal, economic or societal) led this person to build a faulty structure?'

A second distinction is in the approach each profession takes to using the past as 'evidence'. As Frederick Maitland pointed out many years ago, historians want evidence, and the older the better, while lawyers want *authority*, and the newer the better.[45] Moreover, common lawyers are trained to look for cases from the past to support arguments they are making in the present. This is the very essence of the system of precedent and common law precedent. Because of this training, and also because lawyers researching legal development know what the doctrine, statute or institutions they are researching ended up becoming, there is a strong temptation to look for evidence of how that came to be, selecting examples and narratives accordingly.

It must be said that historians, too, are not immune from the temptation to select the evidence that suits their hypothesis formulated in the present. The present is the necessary starting point for all inquiries and historians have long grappled with the tension between seeking to tell the truth of the past while negotiating the pressures of the present, their own conscious and unconscious biases and influences, and the creative demands of a narrative and literary format. Some insist that historians must be objective and neutral; others insist that such a goal can never be achieved and should not even be strived for. Is it acceptable to make moral judgments of past actors or is it impossible not to? Is there a simple truth that can be located or is the past open to an infinite number of interpretations? There is a considerable body of sophisticated theoretical scholarship addressing and debating such questions. As Tom Griffiths has evocatively observed, historians

> scour their own societies for vestiges of past worlds, for cracks and fissures in the pavement of the present, and for the shimmers and hauntings of history in everyday action. They begin their inquiries in a deeply felt present. But as time travelers they have to forsake their own world for a period – and then, somehow, find their way back.[46]

To say that practitioners of both intellectual property history and intellectual property legal history must adopt the responsibilities and duties of an historian might seem to open a can of worms which would send an aspiring intellectual property historian down any number of rabbit holes (to mix angling and agrarian metaphors). But, while consciousness of these debates and the scholarly commitments they entail is necessary, an

---

[45] Maitland, *Why the History of English Law Is Not Written*, 14.
[46] Tom Griffiths, *The Art of Time Travel* (Carlton, VIC: Black Inc., 2016), pp. 2–3.

intimate knowledge or subscription to a particular version of them is probably less so. At a broad level, the responsibilities and duties of the historian are not so different to those of the lawyer: a commitment to investigating the past, to gathering and weighing evidence, to recognising and attributing sources and authorities and to making reasoned arguments supported by evidence, sources and authorities.

13.4 Challenges of Purpose

A final challenge facing the intellectual property historian or legal historian is the strength, even ferocity, of the debates over intellectual property policy in the twenty-first century. For example, as Gómez-Arostegui points out, one reason that the debates over common law copyright continue to attract interest is because commentators and interest groups refer to the evidence, or otherwise, of common law copyright to support their own arguments as to how broad or narrow copyright should be in the present.[47] Such debates rage so fiercely it is almost impossible to keep from being swept up in them and, indeed, if history is to be valued for more than its power to entertain, then it must be able to have some bearing upon the problems and politics of the present. It is not uncommon for books on intellectual property history or legal history to begin by situating their field in some current debate. But making connections is not necessarily determining outcomes, and these authors are not contending that their historical studies provide neat policy answers to current problems. Indeed, as Catherine Seville observes: '[v]iewed from a historical perspective, many of these "new" challenges may be seen as fresh presentations of familiar dilemmas which copyright law has attempted to address in the past'.[48]

If complete objectivity is impossible for the intellectual property historian, it is still important to avoid turning history into simple advocacy for whatever ideological viewpoint is being espoused.[49] But if so, what can intellectual property history and legal history offer, beyond a sense of déjà vu, and to whom do they offer it? The history of intellectual property law has long been of interest to lawyers seeking a fuller understanding of the nature of the rights involved. Such history also provides a vantage point for a critical perspective on the current formulations of these rights.

---

[47] Gómez-Arostegui, 'Copyright in common law in 1774' 6.
[48] Seville, *The Internationalisation of Copyright Law*, 2.
[49] See Barbara Lauriat, 'Copyright history in the advocate's arsenal' in Isabella Alexander and H Tomás Gómez-Arostegui (eds.), *Research Handbook on the History of Copyright Law* (Cheltenham, UK: Edward Elgar, 2016), pp. 17–26.

As Kathy Bowrey has noted, two important early works of copyright history, Lyman Ray Patterson's *Copyright in Historical Perspective* and Benjamin Kaplan's *An Unhurried View of Copyright*, sought to use history in ways that would allow readers to question copyright's legitimacy and undermine the sense of its inevitability.[50] More recently, Brad Sherman and Lionel Bently have similarly sought to 'disentangle the conditions of intellectual property law's history, to de-naturalise it and to show that what are often taken as givens or as constructs of nature are, in fact, the products of a complex and changing set of circumstances, practices and habits'.[51]

Such studies, moreover, can tell us not only how this particular area of law has changed but also how laws are made and changed more generally. Lobban observes that legal history is a valuable form of jurisprudence. Where legal theorists argue about legal reasoning or judicial behavior in abstract terms, legal history provides concrete examples of how they operate in practice.[52] Histories of intellectual property law can also make an important contribution to law reform. As David Ibbetson has written: '[i]f we are to make sense of today's law, we have to understand its history, and it is only when we make sense of it that we can confidently begin to reform it'.[53] The past offers a petri dish of finished, and unfinished, experiments. While conditions may have changed in innumerable ways, the past is still evidence of what has been tried before and what has or has not worked. In many cases, it may be the only evidence we have. While it might be naïvely optimistic to believe that knowledge of the past will prevent its repetition, it would be similarly foolish to give up hope that this might occur or that it might not be able to be repeated successfully with appropriate modifications.

The history of intellectual property itself covers the much broader terrain of things that are included in categories of 'intellectual property': inventions, books, artworks, brands, technologies and businesses. Such matters attract the attention of historians of science, technology, economics, material culture, art and literature, scholars of cultural studies

---

[50] Kathy Bowrey, 'Who's Writing Copyright's History?' (1996) 18 *European Intellectual Property Review* 322.
[51] Sherman and Bently, *The Making of Modern Intellectual Property Law*, p. 6.
[52] Lobban, 'The varieties of legal history', 25. An early example is the work of French Marxist theorist Bernard Edelman, *Ownership of the Image* (London: Routledge & Kegan Paul, 1979). More recent examples are Oren Bracha, *Owning Ideas: The Intellectual Origins of American Intellectual Property, 1790–1909* (Cambridge: Cambridge University Press, 2016)and Alain Pottage and Brad Sherman, *Figures of Invention: A History of Modern Patent Law* (Oxford: Oxford University Press, 2010).
[53] David Ibbetson, *An Historical Introduction to the Law of Obligations* (Oxford: Oxford University Press, 1999), p. vi.

and anthropologists. These scholars are interested in intellectual property for what it tells us about innovation and creativity and the conditions in which they flourish or fail. They may be interested in the interaction between legal regimes and economic development or cultural policy, the history of the book or the print trade or the visual arts.

While legal histories of intellectual property might find their key audience among other legal historians or intellectual property academics, they should also find a wider audience among historians. While it might appear insular or reductionist,[54] even boring or excessively technical, 'intellectual property law' is not a monolith, and even the more granular categories of 'copyright law', 'patent law', 'trade mark law' or 'trade secrets law' create complex sets of rights, interests and relationships. All of these have important legal, commercial and cultural effects and may implicate different incentives, causes, responsibilities and liabilities. A precise and nuanced appreciation of the shifting nature of the law as written and implemented is crucial. On the other hand, legal historians can also learn from historians less concerned by statutes and case reports that the law also takes place outside parliaments and court rooms, that it is enacted in day-to-day interactions and relationships, in unwritten customs and in choices made or eschewed.

13.5 Conclusion

Legal scholars and law students may find the challenges involved in straying outside their core discipline to be intimidating or the candle is not worth the game. However, the risks are more than compensated for by the potential rewards. Sam Ricketson has amply demonstrated throughout his career that legal history is an exceptionally effective technique for legal interpretation and therefore an integral part of the tool kit for any aspiring lawyer. Legal history can also offer alternative ways of thinking about contemporary problems. As Ricketson reminds us in his history of the public international law of copyright, 'while we may be familiar with the main roads, we often pass the side roads and laneways without looking down them' but these side roads may be of considerable utility to contemporary scholars and policymakers.[55] Studying the history of intellectual property law can also serve to highlight or develop broader historical themes – for example, Ricketson's historical analysis of

---

[54] See Richard Sher, who argues that an 'overemphasis' on the legal regime of copyright erroneously treats the history of copyright as synonymous with the history of authorship: *The Enlightenment and the Book* (Chicago: University of Chicago Press, 2006), p. 25.
[55] Ricketson, 'The public international law of copyright and related rights', 288.

the *Union Label* case is not just relevant to the development of trade mark law but also to the clash between labour and capital and the role of unions in Australia's history.[56] History allows us look beyond law on the books and think about how it works on the ground and how it impacts lives, cultures and nations. For scholars of all stripes, intellectual property history offers the matchless opportunity to deepen our understanding of both the law and the interactions among legal doctrine, institutions, technologies and society.

[56] Ricketson, 'The *Union Label* case', 35.

14 Connecting Intellectual Property and Human Rights in the Law School Syllabus

Graeme W Austin *

14.1 Introduction

The relationship between human rights and intellectual property provides a rich context for exploring this book's themes. Until recently, human rights and intellectual property kept mostly to their separate domains. For much of its modern history, the human rights movement has been focussed on articulating and developing legal norms and elaborating on the normative content of statements of rights and establishing monitoring mechanisms.[1] In contrast, the main focus of modern intellectual property law has been the expansion of subject matter and the strengthening of rights and, most significantly, the incorporation of intellectual property and international trade law through the adoption of the Agreement on Trade-Related Aspects of Intellectual Property Rights (TRIPS).[2]

Approximately two decades ago, however, this changed. Human rights law started to reach 'across intellectual property' in a number of respects. A key moment was the adoption in 2000 by the Sub-Commission on the Promotion and Protection of Human Rights of a resolution on 'Intellectual Property Rights and Human Rights'.[3] That document was highly critical of TRIPS, stating that 'actual or potential conflicts exist between the implementation of' TRIPS and 'the realization of economic, social and cultural rights'.[4] The sub-commission can be seen reaching 'across

---

* The chapter is dedicated to Professor Ricketson in appreciation for his gracious and generous mentoring over many years.
[1] Laurence R Helfer, 'Forum shopping for human rights' (1999) 148 *University of Pennsylvania Law Review* 285, 296–301.
[2] Marrakesh Agreement Establishing the World Trade Organization, opened for signature 15 April 1994, 1867 UNTS 3 (entered into force 1 January 1995) annex 1C (Agreement on Trade-Related Aspects of Intellectual Property Rights; cited as TRIPS Agreement).
[3] ESOSOC, Sub-Commission on Promotion and Protection of Human Rights, Intellectual Property Rights and Human Rights, Res. 200/7, UN Doc E/CN.4/Sub.2/RES/2000/7 (17 August 2000).
[4] Ibid., at Preamble, para. 11.

intellectual property' with its claim that human rights have 'primacy ... over economic policies and agreements'.[5] This resolution catalysed a number of other UN agencies responsible for human rights to respond, and reach further across intellectual property, in the form of resolutions, reports, comments and statements that, in broad outline, identified the many challenges to human rights represented by the expansion of intellectual property.[6]

It was shortly after this, in 2002, that Sam Ricketson produced one of the very early scholarly examinations of the relationship between the two bodies of law.[7] Since then, the topic has generated a significant volume of scholarship,[8] including some insightful critiques of the whole endeavour.[9] There is, however, relatively little in more recent debates that was not anticipated by Sam's 2002 paper. Among other topics, Ricketson's paper examined whether intellectual property might itself be regarded as a species of human rights in themselves; how intellectual property intersects with human rights, such a freedom of expression and the right to health; how conflicts between human rights and intellectual property should be mediated in the light of the expanding scope of intellectual property; and, perhaps most critically, how any resolution of conflicts between intellectual property and human rights should be based on a full understanding of the specific context in which the conflict arose.

In the light of the extensive work that has been done since the early 2000s on the relationship between these areas of law, this chapter approaches the topic from a different perspective: legal pedagogy and curricular design, drawing on my experience of developing law school courses on human rights and intellectual property.[10] The chapter first sets out the legal and political context from which the original course

---

[5] Ibid., at para. 3.
[6] The principal instruments are listed in Laurence R Helfer and Graeme W Austin, *Human Rights and Intellectual Property: Mapping the Global Interface* (New York: Cambridge University Press, 2011), pp. 53–4.
[7] Sam Ricketson, 'Intellectual property and human rights' in Stephen Bottomley and David Kinley (eds.), *Commercial Law and Human Rights* (Aldershot, UK: Ashgate Dartmouth, 2002), p. 187.
[8] Professor Helfer has recently provided a comprehensive overview of this scholarship in Laurence R Helfer, 'Intellectual property and human rights: Mapping an evolving and contested relationship' in Rochelle C Dreyfuss and Justine Pila (eds.), *The Oxford Handbook of Intellectual Property Law* (Oxford: Oxford University Press, 2018), p. 117.
[9] See, e.g., Ruth L Okediji, 'Intellectual property in the image of human rights: A critical review' in Rochelle Cooper Dreyfuss and Elizabeth Siew-Kuan Ng (eds.), *Framing Intellectual Property Law in the 21st Century: Integrating Incentives, Trade, Development, Culture and Human Rights* (Cambridge: Cambridge University Press, 2018), p. 234.
[10] An early version of the course was offered at the University of Arizona College of Law in the early 2000s, a course that informed a 2011 book co-authored with Professor Laurence Helfer. See Helfer and Austin, *Human Rights and Intellectual Property*.

sprang. It then discusses one of the key advantages of the course from a teaching perspective: connecting students with different backgrounds and interests. In terms of the themes of this book, a course on human rights and intellectual property has the potential to connect students 'across' different interests in substantive law: intellectual property, human rights, and the rights of indigenous peoples, to name just the obvious ones. The final sections discuss the various legal and policy contexts in which the interrelationship between human rights and intellectual property can be explored. The chapter concludes with some brief comments about the practical contexts in which the lessons from such a course might be deployed.

14.2 The Legal and Political Context

The original syllabus was designed during a period of increasing interest in intellectual property, tempered by intense concern about the expansion of intellectual property rights.[11] The finalisation of TRIPS, accompanied by its obligation to accord patent rights for inventions in all fields of technologies, including pharmaceutical and agricultural innovations, was a significant change in domestic and international intellectual property law.[12] The TRIPS obligations expanded through the adoption of the two World Intellectual Property Organization (WIPO) internet treaties, the WIPO Copyright Treaty[13] and the WIPO Performances and Phonograms Treaty.[14] Further expansions occurred through bilateral, plurilateral and regional trade arrangements.[15] At the same time, countries are under pressure to enhance protections even further.[16]

---

[11] See, e.g., Susan K Sell, *Private Power, Public Law: The Globalization of Intellectual Property Rights* (Cambridge: Cambridge University Press, 2003).
[12] See generally, Jean O Lanjouw, 'A new global patent regime for diseases: US and international legal issues' (2002) 16 *Harvard Journal of Law and Technology* 85, 90; Michael Kremer, 'Pharmaceuticals and the developing world' (2002) 16 *Journal of Economic Perspectives* 67, 74–5.
[13] World Intellectual Property Organization Copyright Treaty, opened for signature 20 December 1996, 2186 UNTS 121 (entered into force 6 March 2002).
[14] World Intellectual Property Organization Performances and Phonograms Treaty, opened for signature 20 December 1996, 2186 UNTS 203 (entered into force 20 May 2002).
[15] See Henning Grosse Ruse-Khan, 'The international law relation between TRIPS and subsequent TRIPS-plus free trade agreements: Towards safeguarding TRIPS flexibilities' (2011) 18 *Journal of Intellectual Property Law* 325. Rochelle Dreyfuss, 'In praise of an incentive-based theory of intellectual property protections' in Rochelle Cooper Dreyfuss and Elizabeth Siew-Kuan Ng (eds.), *Framing Intellectual Property Law in the 21st Century: Integrating Incentives, Trade, Development, Culture and Human Rights* (Cambridge: Cambridge University Press, 2018), pp. 1, 28.
[16] See, e.g., Amy Kapczynski, 'Harmonization and its discontents: A case study of TRIPS implementation in India's pharmaceutical sector' (2009) 97 *California Law Review* 1571.

These developments provoked a wave of claims that the expansion of intellectual property was profoundly unfair.[17] Some critiques were 'internal' to intellectual property rights, focussing on issues such as the dead-weight losses produced by over-protection[18] and the risks that the patenting of fundamental building blocks of science would leave insufficient raw materials in the public domain to provide the basis for subsequent innovation.[19] Others focussed on the potential for intellectual property rights to interfere with basic attributes of a good life, a concern that continues to be especially important for developing countries.[20]

Human rights offer a normatively powerful foundation for the claim that intellectual property rights should be constrained.[21] It is one thing, for example, to say that school textbooks are too expensive (and that copyrights are an input that is responsible for increasing the price). It is quite another to say that copyright's contribution to the costs of textbooks conflicts with human rights guarantees to an adequate education. Similar claims can of course be made in a range of areas, including, most obviously, in the context of impediments to the realisation of an adequate standard of health when life-saving patented medicines are unaffordable.

Grounding these limitations in human rights is complicated by the human rights guarantees for creators *to* the moral and material interests

---

[17] See, e.g., Donald P Harris, 'Carrying a good joke too far: TRIPS and treaties of adhesion' (2006) 27 *University of Pennsylvania Journal of International Economic Law* 681.

[18] See William M Landes and Richard A Posner, *The Economic Structure of Intellectual Property Law* (Cambridge, MA: Harvard University Press, 2003), pp. 16–21.

[19] For an illustration of the relevance of these concerns to patent doctrine, see *Association for Molecular Pathology* v. *Myriad Genetics*, 569 US 576, 589 (2013).

[20] See Madhavi Sunder, *From Goods to a Good Life: Intellectual Property and Global Justice* (New Haven, CT: Yale University Press, 2012).

[21] See, e.g., Lisa Forman, '"Rights" and wrongs: What utility for the right to health in reforming trade rules on medicines?' (2008) 10 *Health and Human Rights* 37; Lisa Forman and Gillian MacNaughton, 'Moving theory into practice: Human rights impact assessments of intellectual property rights in trade agreements' (2015) 7 *Journal of Human Rights Practice* 109; Henning Grosse Ruse-Khan, *The Protection of Intellectual Property in International Law* (Oxford: Oxford University Press, 2016), p. 261. The importance of an alternative normative and legal basis for constraining rights has become more urgent in the light of the shifting ground in international intellectual property relations. The strengthening of investor-state protections brings with it the potential to undermine the relevance of inbuilt flexibilities in the TRIPS Agreement to the realisation of public goals in areas such as health. *See* James Gathii and Cynthia Ho, 'Regime shifting of IP lawmaking and enforcement from the WTO to the international investment regimes' (2017) 18 *Minnesota Journal of Law, Science and Technology* 427, 430.

in their intellectual productions. From the beginnings of the post–World War II human rights movement, the rights of creators have been integrated into the human rights framework, with the Universal Declaration of Human Rights (UDHR) announcing that 'everyone has the right to the protection of the moral and material interests resulting from any scientific, literary or artistic production of which he is the author'.[22] A similarly worded guarantee eventually found its way into the International Covenant on Economic, Social, and Cultural Rights (ICESCR), as article 15(1)(c) of that instrument.[23] In this context, moral interests align with the familiar protections of authors' moral rights, or droit d'auteur, that finds expression in article 6*bis* of the Berne Convention.[24] Material interests capture the familiar economic rights attaching to intellectual property rights.

It is therefore not possible to claim simply that human rights claims require intellectual property to yield. At least some aspects of intellectual property are themselves fully embedded in core human rights commitments. At the same time, these commitments are accompanied by more explicitly public-regarding human rights guarantees. For example, immediately before the statement about authors' moral and material interests, the UDHR announces the right of everyone to 'freely ... participate in the cultural life of the community, to enjoy the arts and to share in scientific advancement and its benefits'.[25] And article 15(1)(b) of the ICESCR recognises 'the right of everyone ... to enjoy the benefits of scientific progress and its applications'.

---

[22] Universal Declaration of Human Rights, GA Res 217A (III), UN GAOR, 3rd sess., 183rd plen. mtg., UN Doc A/810 (10 December 1948) art. 27(2) (cited as UDHR).
[23] International Covenant on Economic, Social, and Cultural Rights, opened for signature 16 December 1966, 993 UNTS 3 (entered into force 3 November 1976) art. 15(1)(c) (cited as ICESCR).
[24] Berne Convention for the Protection of Literary and Artistic Works, opened for signature 9 September 1886, 828 UNTS 221 (entered into force 5 December 1887), as amended. The scope of article 15(1)(c) of the ICESCR has been the topic of a General Comment by the Committee on Economic, Social and Cultural Rights, General Comment No 17: 'The Right of Everyone to Benefit from the Protection of Moral and Material Interests Resulting from any Scientific, Literary or Artistic Production of Which He Is the Author' (article 15, paragraph 1 (c), of the Covenant), 35th sess., UN Doc E/C.12/GC/17 (12 January 2006). There have also been two reports by the Special Rapporteur on Cultural Rights, one focussing on patent rights and the other on copyright. See Farida Shaheed, 'Copyright policy and the right to science and culture: Report of the special rapporteur in the field of cultural rights', UN Doc A/HRC/28/57 (24 December 2014); Farida Shaheed, 'Report of the special rapporteur in the field of cultural rights', UN Doc A/70/279 (4 August 2015).
[25] UDHR, art. 27(1).

14.3 Connecting Students' Diverse Interests through Syllabus Design

Human rights and intellectual property intersect in key areas of life: patented pharmaceuticals and the right to health being the paradigm example. They also intersect through the recognition of the rights of creators in human rights instruments. Human rights and intellectual property are also brought together through the engagement of indigenous peoples with intellectual property issues. This intensified as a result of indigenous peoples' own fears that their knowledge and cultural productions would be misappropriated and commercialised.[26] At the same time, indigenous peoples' disquiet about intellectual property rights was accompanied by an increasing recognition of the importance of intellectual property protections to indigenous peoples. The latter is recognised in the UN Declaration on the Rights of Indigenous Peoples (UNDRIP). UNDRIP admonishes nations to protect indigenous intellectual property,[27] while recognising the right of indigenous peoples to 'maintain, control, protect, and develop' their 'intellectual property over such cultural heritage, traditional knowledge, and traditional cultural expressions'.[28]

The original course attracted three groups of students: those interested in intellectual property, those interested in human rights, and those interested in indigenous law and policy. A key aim was to help these students see connections across and between their various interests and across the cultural, intellectual, heuristic divides that had shaped their previous thinking about the issues.

The course design mirrored the conceptual and historical divide between intellectual property and human rights. The preoccupations of each area of law can seem quite different. In the Anglo-American utilitarian context, for example, the role of the state in intellectual property is understood as a kind of welfare economics referee, policing rules that ensure that the calibration of private rights optimises innovative activity. Within the human rights framework, however, the state is understood to have positive duties to protect the fundamental rights and freedoms of

---

[26] For an early discussion of these issues, see Rosemary J Coombe, 'Intellectual property, human rights and sovereignty: New dilemmas in international law posed by the recognition of indigenous knowledge and the conservation of biodiversity' (1998) 6 *Indiana Journal of Global Legal Studies* 59.

[27] UN Declaration on the Rights of Indigenous Peoples, GA Res 61/295, UN GAOR, 61st sess., 107th plen. mtg., Supp. No. 49, UN Doc. A/RES/61/295 (13 September 2007) art. 11.

[28] Ibid., art. 31.

individuals and to provide all members of the human family with the opportunity to flourish. Those tensions are amplified in the context of indigenous peoples' intellectual property. The indigenous human rights framework seeks to strengthen fundamental rights and freedoms, albeit in a manner that is enlivened by an emphasis on the group, rather than individuals – and yet this is increasingly accompanied by an urgent resurgence of indigenous peoples' interest in the role of private markets.[29]

The course also offered a context in which to question some of the ideas that conventionally structure intellectual property thinking. For example, the necessary emphasis in conventional intellectual property courses on the role of intellectual property rights in innovation policy[30] can assume away questions about their distributive consequences.[31] Human rights law puts distributive consequences front and centre. A course that introduces students to indigenous peoples' perspectives on intellectual property also provides an opportunity for students to explore some of the basic tenets of the field. What does *originality* mean in copyright law, for example, when the 'author' is drawing on traditional knowledge that has evolved over millennia? How do ideas about human authorship align with a worldview that knowledge is derived from an indigenous group's engagement with the natural environment? How do conventional intellectual property ownership structures map onto group-animated creativity, combined with deep networks of permissions for the use of the material?[32] Requiring students to engage with these issues also provides an opportunity to challenge tried-and-true ideas and to bring many of the assumptions that are at the heart of intellectual property law, and yet are often assumed away, to the surface of the discussion. The emphasis on indigenous peoples' rights also gave students an opportunity to consider the implications of the individualistic focus of much human rights thinking.[33]

---

[29] For an insightful exploration of these tensions, see Karen Engle, *The Elusive Promise of Indigenous Development: Rights, Culture, Strategy* (Durham, NC: Duke University Press, 2010).

[30] Okediji, 'Intellectual property in the image of human rights', 238, citing TRIPS Agreement, art. 7.

[31] For a recent exploration of distributive justice questions in the copyright context, see Justin Hughes and Robert P Merges, 'Copyright and distributive justice' (2016) 92 *Notre Dame Law Review* 513.

[32] Issues surrounding group-based creativity are not of course confined to the indigenous peoples' context. See, e.g., Anthony J Casey and Andres Sawicki, 'The problem of creative collaboration' (2017) 58 *William and Mary Law Review* 1793.

[33] Okediji, 'Intellectual property in the image of human rights', 235.

At the same time, a course on intellectual property and human rights offers opportunities for students immersed in human rights to challenge their own thinking and worldviews. An appreciation of the societal purposes of the incentive structures undergirding conventional intellectual property rights can add a useful perspective on demands grounded in human rights that are directed at constraining intellectual property. The analysis can be enriched by an appreciation of the undeniable positive externalities produced by conventional intellectual property. The benefits of, for example, pharmaceutical research are undeniable, even if they are unevenly distributed. The field is also complicated by the human rights guarantees for creators. Human rights thus do not operate in a straightforward oppositional relationship with intellectual property. Once again, many of the same issues arise in the context of indigenous peoples' rights.[34]

14.4 Human Rights and Intellectual Property in Context

The early version of the course was structured around various topics that engage both human rights and intellectual property in different contexts. As noted earlier, the connection between the human right to health and access to patented medicine is a paradigm case. Controversies over the pricing of pharmaceutical products in the light of the HIV/AIDS crisis provided a relevant context for engaging with these issues.[35] Patents over genetic material is another context in which interconnections between intellectual property and human rights are exposed. This topic also provides a perspective on how doctrinal levers *within* conventional

---

[34] In addition, the claim that indigenous peoples' rights can be understood through a human rights lens might be taken to imply that the former might be limited by that same human rights framework: James Anaya, 'International human rights and indigenous peoples: The move toward the multicultural state' (2004) 21 *Arizona Journal of International and Comparative Law* 12, 25.

[35] An important document in this context was a general comment by the Committee on Economic, Social, and Cultural Rights, which set out the relevant normative content of the right to health: 'General Comment No 14: The Right to the Highest Attainable Standard of Health' (Article 12), 22nd sess., UN Doc E/ C.12/ 2000/4 (11 August 2000). In the same year, the UN Sub-Commission on the Protection and Promotion of Human Rights issued a forceful resolution that was promulgated under the title 'Intellectual Property Rights and Human Rights', UN ESCOR, 52nd sess., 25th mtg., Agenda Item 4, UN Doc E/CN.4/Sub.2/RES/2000/7 (17 August 2000), which urged governments, inter-government organisations and non-government organisations (NGOs) to recognise the primacy of human rights over economic policies and agreements. See David Weissbrodt and Kell Schoff, 'A human rights approach to intellectual property protection: The genesis and application of Sub-Commission Resolution 2000/7' (2003) 5 *Minnesota Intellectual Property Review* 1.

intellectual property frameworks can limit the scope of intellectual property in the context of pharmaceutical innovations.[36] The relationship between the right to health and intellectual property also provides an opportunity to explore changes to international economic law to accommodate the urgent medical needs of many members of the human family,[37] as well as the scope to use the flexibilities in the TRIPS Agreement as a step toward the realisation of the human right to health.[38] Other topics contained in the original syllabus included indigenous peoples' intellectual property claims and the right to food and its relationship with intellectual property rights in biological materials and plant varieties.

Creators' rights provide a particularly rich context for exploring the themes of the course. In *Human Rights and Intellectual Property: Mapping the Global Interface*,[39] this topic is addressed early on, immediately following the right to health. The topic also has the advantage of complicating the assumption that the role of human rights in this context is *only* to provide a basis for constraining intellectual property.[40]

The connection between freedom of expression and intellectual property offers another helpful teaching context. Scope exists here for exploring the extent to which copyright limits expressive freedoms in the light of internal safety values, such as the idea/expression dichotomy and the array of copyright exceptions that exist under domestic legal systems. The topic also provides a framework for connecting domestic recognition of the right to freedom of expression (usually at the constitutional level)

---

[36] The work of the UN Secretary-General's High-Level Panel on Access to Medicines, which reported in 2016, offers a more recent context in which to explore this topic. See Secretary-General, 'Report of the United Nations Secretary-General's High-Level Panel on Access to Medicines: Promoting Innovation and Access to Medicine' (September 2016), retrieved from https://bit.ly/2kk1Gsy.

[37] See, e.g., Declaration on the TRIPS Agreement and Public Health, WTO Doc WT/MIN(01)/DEC/2 (20 November 2001, adopted 14 November 2001) (Ministerial Declaration). See Frederick M Abbott and Jerome H Reichman, 'The Doha Round's public health legacy: Strategies for the production and diffusion of patented medicines under the amended TRIPS provisions' (2007) 10 *Journal of International Economic Law* 921.

[38] See Paul Hunt, 'Report of the special rapporteur on the right of everyone to the enjoyment of the highest attainable standard of physical and mental health', UN Doc A/61/338 (13 September 2006), [47].

[39] Helfer and Austin, *Human Rights and Intellectual Property*.

[40] See Graeme W Austin, 'Authors' human rights in the intellectual property framework' in Rochelle Cooper Dreyfuss and Elizabeth Siew-Kuan Ng (eds.), *Framing Intellectual Property Law in the 21st Century: Integrating Incentives, Trade, Development, Culture and Human Rights* (Cambridge: Cambridge University Press, 2018), p. 210.

with international human rights guarantees,[41] including Article 19 of the International Covenant on Civil and Political Rights.[42]

The original course also explored the right to education, focussing on how this right can be realised when educational materials are usually protected by copyright. The connection between education rights and copyright distils an immediate conceptual puzzle: If, at least in the Anglo copyright system, copyright is meant to 'encourage learning',[43] why is the copyright system itself not a sufficient realisation of the human right to education? The course explored the difference between participation in private markets and the public, human rights obligation imposed on governments to provide educational materials.[44]

This topic is also a useful vehicle for introducing the 2013 Marrakesh Treaty to Facilitate Access to Published Works for Persons Who Are Blind, Visually Impaired or Otherwise Print Disabled (Marrakesh Treaty).[45] The Marrakesh Treaty also provides an important textual reminder of the increasing sites of interconnection between human rights and intellectual property. Its preamble begins: 'Recalling the principles of non-discrimination, equal opportunity, accessibility and full and effective participation and inclusion in society, proclaimed in the Universal Declaration of Human Rights and the United Nations Convention on the Rights of Persons with Disabilities'. A few paragraphs later, the preamble references 'the need to maintain a balance between the effective protection of the rights of authors and the larger public interest, particularly education, research and access to information, and that such a balance must facilitate effective and timely access to works for the benefit of persons with visual impairments or with other print disabilities'. The right to education offers a rich teaching and learning context in which to explore the implications of this new international instrument.

Teachers need to prepare for the likelihood that not all students will have a background in both intellectual property and human rights. This

---

[41] See Neil Weinstock Netanel, 'Asserting copyright's democratic principles in the global arena' (1998) 51 *Vanderbilt Law Review* 217.

[42] International Covenant on Civil and Political Rights, opened for signature 19 December 1966, 999 UNTS 171 (entered into force 23 March 1976) art. 19.

[43] Copyright Act 1710, 8 Ann, c. 19 ('An Act for the Encouragement of Learning').

[44] See, e.g., Fons Coomans, 'In search of the core content of the right to education' in Audrey Chapman and Sage Russell (eds.), *Core Obligations: Building a Framework for Economic, Social and Cultural Rights* (Antwerp; New York: Intersentia, 2002), pp. 217, 219. See also, Committee on Economic, Social and Cultural Rights, General Comment No. 13: The Right to Education, 21st sess., UN Doc E/C.12/1999/10 (8 December 1999).

[45] Marrakesh Treaty to Facilitate Access to Published Works for Persons Who Are Blind, Visually Impaired or Otherwise Print Disabled, opened for signature 27 June 2013, WIPO Doc VIP/DC/8 (entered into force 30 September 2016).

necessarily requires dealing with these topics separately – and leaves aside the more challenging task of bringing intellectual property and human rights together in the same conceptual framework.[46] Laurence Helfer and I addressed this in *Human Rights and Intellectual Property: Mapping the Global Interface* with an introductory chapter that provides an overview of both areas of law.[47]

Discussion of exactly how the two areas might be engaged was deliberately left until the final chapter of the book. The aim was for students to develop their own thinking on the topic independently of the instructor. Teachers of new courses in the area might consider it useful to engage directly with these contestations earlier on in the course, so as to provide students with a conceptual foundation from which to develop their thinking in the many areas in which human rights and intellectual property intersect.

14.5 Interconnections in Context

Along with the development in scholarly interest in the topic and the interest of international agencies, NGOs and civil society groups in invoking human rights as part of the normative discourse on intellectual property, new contexts are emerging that demonstrate the relevance of the topic. For example, the Charter of Fundamental Rights of the European Union[48] articulates a commitment to the protection of intellectual property as part of the right of property, while also giving expression to many of the more familiar categories of rights and freedoms, within an overarching commitment to human dignity.[49]

The Marrakesh Treaty explicitly brings human rights into the intellectual property framework in its provision for the human rights of members of the human family with print disabilities. It is likely to be at the domestic level that the level of commitment to human rights is tested, as the Marrakesh Treaty requirements are enacted into domestic law.

It appropriate to end with an Australian example. The Human Rights (Parliamentary Scrutiny) Act 2011 (Cth) requires the introduction of any Bill into the Australian Federal Parliament to be accompanied by a

---

[46] See Peter K Yu, 'The anatomy of the human rights framework for intellectual property' (2016) 69 *SMU Law Review* 37, 78–9 (exploring different ways of conceptualising the relationship between human rights and intellectual property).

[47] Professor Helfer's more recent study of the 'evolving and contested relationship' between the two areas is an especially valuable resource. See Helfer, 'Forum shopping for human rights'.

[48] Charter of Fundamental Rights of the European Union OJ 2000 No. C364/01, art. 41.

[49] Ibid. art. 17(2), which provides: 'Intellectual property shall be protected'.

statement of compatibility, which must assess whether the bill is 'compatible with human rights'.[50] This is a general enactment, not one that is limited to the intellectual property context. In theory, at least, this enactment should be especially important in Australia, which lacks any national human rights legislation or bill of rights. The 2011 Act provides a channel for domesticating human rights into the Australian parliamentary system.[51]

In the development of legislative policy, the intensity of the necessary engagement should be calibrated with reference to research suggesting that incumbent rights holders are often better equipped to participate in lobbying than user groups or small startups.[52] At the same time, given the powerful lobbying by firms whose fortunes are tied to limiting the scope of intellectual property rights,[53] sensitivity to the possibility that human rights issues may be co-opted by powerful economic interests will also be appropriate. A course on human rights and intellectual property could build the capacity of a generation of students to engage with questions such as these.

---

[50] Human Rights (Parliamentary Scrutiny) Act 2011 (Cth) s. 8(3).

[51] E.g., when the Copyright Amendment (Disability Access and Other Measures) Bill was introduced into the Australian Federal Parliament in 2017, in order to put into effect the new requirements of the Marrakesh Treaty, the bill was accompanied by a statement that assessed a variety of human rights issues. For recent discussion of the limitations of the 2011 legislation, see George Williams and Daniel Reynolds, 'The first four years of Australia's parliamentary scrutiny regime for human rights' (7 April 2016) *Australian Public Law*, retrieved from https://bit.ly/2m0ocqL.

[52] See, e.g., Cynthia Ho, 'Private power, public law: The globalization of intellectual property rights' (2004) 18 *Emory International Law Review* 117, 126.

[53] See Jonathan Taplin, *Move Fast and Break Things: How Facebook, Google, and Amazon Have Cornered Culture and What It Means for All of Us* (London: Macmillan, 2017). See also Abbey Stemier, 'The myth of the sharing economy and its implications for regulating innovation' (2017) 67 *Emory Law Journal* 197.

15 Copyright and Privacy
Pre-trial Discovery of User Identities

David Lindsay*

15.1 Introduction

The relationship between copyright and privacy is complex: copyright and privacy may be mutually reinforcing or may conflict.[1] This chapter explores the relationship between copyright and privacy in the context of discovery of identities of internet users allegedly committing copyright infringements by use of peer-to-peer (P2P), principally BitTorrent, networks.

The open internet facilitates mass copyright infringement and mass surveillance.[2] The prevalence of online infringement has seen the emergence of a copyright surveillance industry.[3] Monitoring P2P networks enables detection of Internet Protocol addresses (IP addresses), but not identities. An identity associated with an IP address can be ascertained only with assistance of an internet service provider (ISP), which maintains logs matching IP addresses to subscribers. To bring actions against alleged infringers, rights holders may need court orders requiring ISPs to disclose identities.

---

* Sam Ricketson introduced me to copyright in the LLM program at Melbourne Law School in the early 1990s and has been a mentor and colleague since. He was chief investigator on an Australian Research Council–funded project on data privacy law that I was fortunate to contribute to. Given Sam's formidable body of work in intellectual property law, readers may be less familiar with his contributions to privacy law and policy. For example, from 2001 to 2010 Sam was a commissioner of the Victorian Law Reform Commission (VLRC), where he had responsibility for its workplace privacy reference.

[1] David Lindsay and Sam Ricketson, 'Copyright, privacy and digital rights management (DRM)' in Andrew T Kenyon and Megan Richardson (eds.), *New Dimensions in Privacy Law* (Cambridge: Cambridge University Press, 2006), p. 121.

[2] Shoshana Zuboff, *The Age of Surveillance Capitalism* (London: Profile Books, 2019); Sonia K Katyal, 'The new surveillance' (2003) 54(2) *Case Western Reserve Law Review* 297; Sonia K Katyal, 'Privacy vs piracy' (2004) 7 *Yale Journal of Law & Technology* 222.

[3] Mike Zajco, 'The copyright surveillance industry' (2015) 3(2) *Media and Communication* 42; Ramon Lobato and Julian Thomas, 'The business of anti-piracy: New zones of enterprise in the copyright wars' (2012) 6 *International Journal of Communication* 606.

Common law jurisdictions have procedures for pre-trial identity discovery from non-parties.[4] Due to the risk of 'speculative invoicing' courts have imposed limits on the use of disclosed identities. Speculative invoicing involves collecting identities linked to IP addresses ostensibly for the purpose of litigation, then issuing letters of demand offering to settle for less than the costs of defending litigation but more than is recoverable in an infringement suit.[5] There is no intention to litigate, as the strategy is designed to create an incentive to settle to avoid litigation costs.[6] While courts acknowledge that, in this context, identity disclosure entails conflicts between copyright and privacy, preventing speculative invoicing has been the main express reason given for imposing limits on identity discovery.

This chapter examines the extent to which courts granting identity disclosure from ISPs satisfactorily address conflicts between copyright and privacy. The chapter is confined to discovery in the UK, Canada and Australia, as there are similarities in the law but also significant differences, especially in the recognition of rights. The chapter argues that the protection of rights in this context casts light on how common law courts take account of rights, and balance rights, in exercising judicial discretions.

15.2 Rights Balancing and Proportionality

Before the relationship between copyright and privacy is addressed, we must clarify one point: if there is a conflict, what is in conflict? This chapter assumes that copyright and privacy laws protect rights. 'Rights' terminology is used normatively, even in relation to Australian law (where there is no bill of rights), as it recognises the special weight or moral force of rights: regardless of the theoretical perspective, 'rights' are a distinctive form of moral or legal obligation, conventionally given greater weight than 'interests' which, unlike rights,

---

[4] Other jurisdictions have similar procedures: Frederica Giovanella, *Copyright and Information Privacy* (Cheltenham, UK: Edward Elgar, 2017), p. 29.
[5] David D'Amato, 'BitTorrent copyright trolls: A deficiency in the federal rules of civil procedure?' (2014) 40 *Rutgers Computer and Technology Law Journal* 190; Matthew Sag, 'Copyright trolling, an empirical study' (2015) 100 *Iowa Law Review* 1105.
[6] Patience Ren, 'The fate of BitTorrent John Does: A civil procedure analysis of copyright litigation' (2013) 64 *Hastings Law Journal* 1343.

are subject to utilitarian trade-offs.[7] Internationally, 'rights balancing' is the preferred means for addressing conflicts between copyright and privacy.[8]

There are many ways to analyse rights conflicts.[9] For example, some rights, such as the right not to be tortured, may be given 'lexical priority'[10] over other rights, such as freedom of expression.[11] In a book-length analysis of the balance between copyright and privacy in identity disclosure orders, Giovanella has argued that courts faced with rights conflicts apply 'conceptual balancing', giving priority to the right 'to which the legal system as a whole attaches more importance'.[12] But, while courts often seem influenced by some form of rights ordering, judicial reasoning is not as systematic as Giovanella suggests, commonly being no more than an implicit ranking. Moreover, in practice, as the UK Supreme Court has observed, applying balancing (in the form of proportionality analysis) 'depends to a significant extent upon the context'.[13] Therefore, this chapter does not pursue comparative ranking of copyright and privacy – such as might arise from conceiving copyright as protecting 'economic rights' and privacy as protecting 'personality rights' – but assumes that, in general, the rights should be given equal weight, with outcomes depending on context.

What, then, does the context of applications for identity disclosure from ISPs tell us about the relationship between copyright and privacy rights? On the one hand, as a right entails its vindication, a copyright holder should have a right to discover the identity of alleged infringers, as a prerequisite to vindicating its rights. On the other hand, the right to (data) privacy generally prohibits disclosure of personal information held by a third party, unless justified.[14] The issue facing courts is therefore not

---

[7] Ronald Dworkin, *Taking Rights Seriously* (London: Duckworth, 1977); Jeremy Waldron, 'Rights in conflict' (1989) 99 *Ethics* 503.
[8] We do not, however, have to go so far as Giovanella, who claims that resolving rights conflicts is the 'predominant task' of courts: Giovanella, *Copyright and Information Privacy*, 6.
[9] Frances Myrna Kamm, 'Conflicts of rights: Typology, methodology, and nonconsequentialism' (2001) 7 *Legal Theory* 239.
[10] On 'lexical ordering' see John Rawls, *A Theory of Justice* (Oxford: Oxford University Press, 1971), pp. 42–4.
[11] Waldron, 'Rights in conflict', 513–15.
[12] Giovanella, *Copyright and Information Privacy*, 42.
[13] *R (Lumsden)* v. *Legal Services Board* [2016] AC 697, 717.
[14] Reflected in the purpose limitation principle of data privacy law, which prohibits use or disclosure of personal information otherwise than for the purpose for which it was collected unless it is justified: Lee Andrew Bygrave, *Data Privacy Law: An International Perspective* (Oxford: Oxford University Press, 2014), pp. 153–7.

which of the two rights is weightier in the abstract, but whether, *in this context*, identity disclosure is justified (and, if so, to what extent)?

In dealing with conflicts between rights (or between rights and interests), the proportionality principle is the dominant international standard for justifying rights infringements.[15] Proportionality is, nevertheless, highly contested,[16] and subject to different formulations.[17] It is neither possible nor desirable to enter into these controversies here, except for two brief points. First, while proportionality and balancing are sometimes equated,[18] proportionality is but one form of balancing, for which special advantages are claimed.[19] Second, the claimed advantages include that, as a constrained form of legal reasoning, proportionality escapes allegations of subjectivity and arbitrariness;[20] it directs attention to considerations that may be overlooked;[21] and it recognises rights are weightier than interests.[22]

15.3 Conditions for Identity Discovery

This section identifies the conditions that must be satisfied for courts to grant identity discovery against non-parties in the three jurisdictions.

---

[15] Alec Stone Sweet and Jud Mathews, 'Proportionality, balancing and global constitutionalism' (2008–9) 47 *Columbia Journal of Transnational Law* 72; Aharon Barak, *Proportionality: Constitutional Rights and Their Limitations* (Oxford: Oxford University Press, 2012).
[16] See the collection of essays in Grant Huscroft, Bradley W Miller and Grégoire Webber (eds.), *Proportionality and the Rule of Law: Rights, Justification, Reasoning* (Cambridge: Cambridge University Press, 2014).
[17] Martin Luterán, 'The lost meaning of proportionality' in Grant Huscroft, Bradley W Miller and Grégoire Webber (eds.), *Proportionality and the Rule of Law: Rights, Justification, Reasoning* (Cambridge: Cambridge University Press, 2014), p. 21; Bradley W Miller, 'Proportionality's blind spot: "Neutrality" and political justification' in Grant Huscroft, Bradley W Miller and Grégoire Webber (eds.), *Proportionality and the Rule of Law: Rights, Justification, Reasoning* (Cambridge: Cambridge University Press, 2014), p. 370.
[18] Charles-Maxime Panaccio, 'In defence of two-step balancing and proportionality in rights adjudication' (2011) 24 *Canadian Journal of Law and Jurisprudence* 109.
[19] Luterán, 'The lost meaning of proportionality', 23–5.
[20] Robert Alexy, 'On balancing and subsumption. A structural comparison' (2003) 16(4) *Ratio Juris* 433; Aharon Barak, 'Proportionality and principled balancing' (2010) 4 *Law & Ethics of Human Rights* 1.
[21] Miller, 'Proportionality's blind spot'.
[22] Frederick Schauer, 'Proportionality and the question of weight' in Grant Huscroft, Bradley W Miller and Grégoire Webber (eds.), *Proportionality and the Rule of Law: Rights, Justification, Reasoning* (Cambridge: Cambridge University Press, 2014), pp. 173, 177.

In the UK, the availability of identity discovery from a non-party was for long unclear[23] and only conclusively resolved in *Norwich Pharmacal*.[24] Despite variations in how courts have expressed the conditions for making an order, it is accepted that the following must be satisfied:

1. A wrong must have been arguably carried out.
2. The person against whom the order is sought must be mixed up in the wrongdoing so as to have facilitated it, and is likely able to provide the necessary information.
3. The applicant must be intending to seek redress (by court proceedings or otherwise, such as by disciplinary action or dismissal of an employee) for the alleged wrongs.
4. Disclosure of the information must be necessary to pursue the redress.[25]

While the UK Civil Procedure Rules provide for disclosure against non-parties, the court's power to make a *Norwich* order is expressly preserved.[26]

In both Canada and Australia, pre-trial identity discovery is provided for by court rules (although *Norwich* orders remain available), but the relationship between the rules and *Norwich* orders differs between the two countries.

In Canada, identity discovery is relevantly[27] governed by rule 238 of the Federal Court Rules.[28] In *BMG Canada Inc v. Doe*,[29] however, the Federal Court of Appeal held that the principles for making an order under rule 238 were the same as those for making *Norwich* orders.[30] While UK courts have held that the applicant for a *Norwich* order must establish there is an arguable wrong, the threshold is imprecise.[31]

---

[23] While Bray suggested that an exception allowed a bill of discovery to be filed against a non-party to discover the name of a potential defendant, authority was scant: Edward Bray, *The Principles and Practice of Discovery* (London: Reeves and Turner, 1885), p. 40.
[24] *Norwich Pharmacal Co v. Customs and Excise Commissioners* [1974] AC 133 (cited as *Norwich Pharmacal*). In *Cartier International AG v. British Sky Broadcasting* [2018] 1 WLR 3259, the UK Supreme Court held that *Norwich* orders were part of a more general duty imposed on a non-party that is 'mixed up' in a wrongdoing not to assist in that conduct, which may consist in providing information to a rights holder, but is not confined to that.
[25] *The Rugby Football Union v. Viagogo Ltd* [2011] EWCA Civ 1585 (Court of Appeal); *Koo Golden East Mongolia v. Bank of Nova Scotia* [2008] 2 WLR 1160.
[26] Civil Procedure Rules 1998 (UK) SI 1998/3132, r. 31.18.
[27] In the context of discovery for copyright infringements.
[28] Federal Court Rules, SOR/98-106, r. 238.   [29] [2005] 4 FCR 81 (cited as *BMG*).
[30] Ibid., [30]-[31].
[31] *United Company Rusal Plc v. HSBC Bank Plc* [2011] EWHC 404, [50]-[52].

In *BMG*, however, the court rejected the suggestion that the applicant must demonstrate a prima facie case, concluding it was sufficient to establish the lesser threshold of a bona fide claim.[32] In addition to a bona fide claim, the *BMG* court held that an applicant must show evidence that the information cannot be obtained from another source and does not cause undue costs to the non-party.[33]

In Australia, the relevant provision is rule 7.22 of the Federal Court Rules,[34] which provides that an applicant must satisfy the court of multiple factors, including that there may be a right to obtain relief against a prospective respondent and that the applicant is unable to ascertain the description of the prospective respondent. Unlike *Norwich* orders, the non-party need not be 'mixed up' in the wrongdoing.[35] Moreover, in Australia, while an order will not be granted in aid of 'merely speculative proceedings',[36] the applicant need not establish a prima facie case.[37] The Australian rules therefore set a lower threshold than *Norwich* orders.[38]

15.4 Discretion to Grant Identity Disclosure

Identity disclosure orders are discretionary. As the conditions for making an order may be readily satisfied,[39] orders for discovering identities from ISPs have, in practice, depended upon the exercise of the court's discretion. Courts in the three jurisdictions dealt with in this chapter have reached similar conclusions in assessing identity discovery applications: granting discovery subject to conditions safeguarding against speculative invoicing. But, while conflicts between copyright and privacy have been addressed by the courts, the reasoning on the balance between the rights has differed in the three jurisdictions. This section identifies the differences.

---

[32] *BMG* [2005] 4 FCR 81, [34].   [33] Ibid., [35].
[34] Federal Court Rules 2011 (Cth) r. 7.22.
[35] See *Ashworth Hospital Authority* v. *MGN Ltd* [2002] 1 WLR 515, [35].
[36] *Levis* v. *McDonald* (1997) 75 FCR 36, 44.
[37] *Hooper* v. *Kirella Pty Ltd* (1999) 167 ALR 358, 366.
[38] Nicolas Suzor, 'Privacy v intellectual property litigation: Preliminary third party discovery on the internet' (2004) 25 *Australian Bar Review* 227, 248.
[39] Alexandra Sims, 'Court assisted means of revealing identity on the internet' in Chris Nicoll, J E J Prins and Miriam J M van Dellen (eds.), *Digital Anonymity and the Law: Tensions and Dimensions* (The Hague: TMC Asser Press, 2003), pp. 271, 274.

15.4.1 The UK

In the UK, prior to the Human Rights Act 1998 (UK), the discretion to grant a *Norwich* order involved courts balancing public interest considerations.[40] Since then, however, exercising the discretion has required courts to determine whether an order is proportionate, applying European jurisprudence.[41] More recently, this has entailed reference to the right to data privacy under Article 8 of the Charter of Fundamental Rights of the European Union (EU Charter).[42]

In the principal authority on *Norwich* orders, *Viagogo*,[43] the Supreme Court drew from prior case law to identify ten factors relevant to exercising the discretion, noting that many are 'self-evidently relevant to the question of whether the issue of a *Norwich* order is proportionate'.[44] The factors most relevant to proportionality included (2) the strong public interest in allowing an applicant to vindicate his or her legal rights, (7) the degree of confidentiality of the information sought, (8) the privacy rights under Article 8 of the European Convention of Human Rights (ECHR) of the individuals whose identity is to be disclosed, and (9) the rights and freedoms under EU data protection law of the individuals whose identity is to be disclosed.[45]

The main UK authority on identity discovery from an ISP, *Golden Eye*,[46] was an application by rights holders in pornographic films, either as exclusive licensees or on behalf of others. Holding that the court's discretion was reducible to proportionality analysis based on a balance between rights of copyright holders and privacy rights of subscribers, Arnold J identified the 'correct approach' as follows:

(i) neither [right] as such has precedence over the other; (ii) where the values under the two [rights] are in conflict, an intense focus on the comparative importance of the specific rights being claimed in the individual case is necessary; (iii) the justifications for interfering with or restricting each right must be taken into account; (iv) finally, the proportionality test – or 'ultimate balancing test' – must be applied to each.[47]

---

[40] *Norwich Pharmacal Co* v. *Customs and Excise Commissioners* [1974] AC 133, 182 (per Morris LJ); *British Steel Corp* v. *Granada Television Ltd* [1981] AC 1096.
[41] *Ashworth Hospital Authority* v. *MGN Ltd* [2002] 1 WLR 515, [36], [57]; *R (Mohamed)* v. *Secretary of State for Foreign and Commonwealth Affairs (No 1)* [2009] 1 WLR 2579, [94].
[42] [2010] Official Journal of the European Union C 83/389, art. 8.
[43] *Rugby Football Union* v. *Consolidated Information Ltd* [2012] 1 WLR 3333 (cited as *Viagogo*).
[44] Ibid., 3339.   [45] Ibid.
[46] *Golden Eye (International) Ltd* v. *Telefonica UK Ltd* [2012] EWHC 723 (Ch); *Golden Eye (International) Ltd* v. *Telefonica UK Ltd* [2012] EWCA Civ 1740 (cited as *Golden Eye*).
[47] *Golden Eye* [2012] EWHC 723 (Ch), [117], applying *Re S* [2005] 1 AC 593.

Arnold J held that, in this case, an order was proportionate in that the claimant's interest in enforcing their copyrights outweighed the prospective defendants' interest in protecting their privacy, *provided* the order incorporated safeguards to prevent speculative invoicing. In relation to the application made for other owners, however, Arnold J held that an order would be disproportionate as it would involve sale of the defendants' privacy to the highest bidder (namely, the applicants). Subsequently, the Court of Appeal overturned Arnold J on this point, concluding that there was no relevant distinction between Golden Eye's claims and those made on behalf of others.[48]

In *Viagogo*, the Supreme Court approved Arnold J's approach to proportionality. In doing so, however, the court rejected an argument that it would 'generally be proportionate' to make an order once it was established there was an arguable wrong and no other realistic way of discovering the identity of the alleged wrongdoer, with Lord Kerr observing that the privacy rights of an individual could:

in some limited instances, displace the interests of the applicant for the disclosure of the information even where there is no immediately feasible alternative way in which the necessary information can be obtained.[49]

15.4.2 Canada

In Canada, the Federal Court of Appeal in *BMG* held that the exercise of the court's discretion required determining whether the public interest in disclosure outweighed 'legitimate privacy concerns',[50] as protected under the federal data privacy law, PIPEDA.[51] In addressing the conflict between copyright and privacy, however, Sexton JA concluded that:

Although privacy concerns must also be considered, it seems to me that they must yield to public concerns for the protection of intellectual property rights in situations where infringement threatens to erode those rights.[52]

Although the appeals court affirmed the first instance ruling denying discovery, this was on the basis of inadequacies with the evidence. Giovanella, accordingly, seems to over-state the significance of the case when she regards it as supporting her conclusion that, applying

---

[48] *Golden Eye* [2012] EWCA Civ 1740, [28].
[49] *Viagogo* [2012] 1 WLR 3333, 3347 [28].
[50] *BMG* (2005) FCA 193, [15].
[51] Personal Information Protection and Electronic Documents Act, SC 2000, c. 5.
[52] *BMG* (2005) FCA 193, [41].

'conceptual balancing', Canadian courts give more weight to privacy than to copyright (at least relative to other jurisdictions).[53]

In the main case applying *BMG* to disclosure of subscriber names associated with downloading torrent files, *Voltage Pictures*,[54] the Federal Court granted the order, concluding that the rights of the copyright holder outweighed the privacy rights of internet users,[55] largely on the basis that '(p)rivacy considerations should not be a shield to wrongdoing'.[56] The court went on, however, to point out that the order must ensure that 'privacy rights are invaded in the most minimal way possible'.[57] While the court considered that users of BitTorrent networks had no 'reasonable expectation of privacy',[58] it held that safeguards were required to protect users against speculative invoicing.[59] The safeguards included ensuring that the information released remains confidential and is used only in connection with the proposed action.[60]

15.4.3 *Australia*

In the principal Australian case dealing with identity discovery from ISPs, *Dallas Buyers Club*,[61] Perram J held that the conditions for discovery were satisfied, before turning to the court's discretion. Accepting the relevance of privacy concerns, the judgment referred to the privacy obligations of ISPs imposed under two relevant data privacy laws.[62] In both cases, however, disclosure is permitted when required or authorised by law, such as by a disclosure order.[63] While Perram J acknowledged a conflict between copyright and privacy – and the need for courts to 'try and accommodate both rights as best they can'[64] – like the UK and Canadian courts, he held this could be achieved by imposing safeguards on disclosure. The safeguards imposed included that email addresses not be disclosed and that disclosed identities be used solely for the purpose of legal proceedings.

Concerned at the potential for speculative invoicing, Perram J stayed the order to permit scrutiny of the applicant's letter of demand. In a subsequent application to lift the stay, however, Perram J held that

---

[53] Giovanella, *Copyright and Information Privacy*, 310–12.
[54] *Voltage Pictures LLC* v. *Doe* (2014) FC 161 (cited as *Voltage Pictures*). [55] Ibid., [57].
[56] Ibid., [54]. [57] Ibid., [57]. [58] Ibid., [59]. [59] Ibid., [60]. [60] Ibid., [134].
[61] *Dallas Buyers Club LLC* v. *iiNet Limited* (2015) 245 FCR 129 (cited as *Dallas Buyers Club*').
[62] These are the Telecommunications Act 1997 (Cth) and the Privacy Act 1988 (Cth).
[63] See Telecommunications Act 1997 (Cth) s 280; Privacy Act 1988 (Cth) sch 1, Australian Privacy Principle 6.2(b).
[64] *Dallas Buyers Club* (2015) 245 FCR 129, 149 [86].

supervision of correspondence with subscribers undertaken by the courts in *Golden Eye* and *Voltage Pictures* was based on:

> the fact that in both the United Kingdom and Canada there are human rights instruments which guarantee privacy, the application of which requires the Courts in those countries to engage in a proportionality analysis foreign to Australian law.[65]

While Perram J concluded that Australian courts could not exercise such overarching supervision, he held that a degree of supervision was authorised to ensure the disclosed information was used for obtaining relief and not for any ulterior purpose.[66] The applicant rights holder subsequently announced it would not challenge termination of proceedings.

15.5 Copyright and Privacy: Rights-Based Analysis

Taking rights seriously involves establishing a principled means for determining limits on rights, including limits arising from rights balancing. When evaluating rights conflicts, however, there are dangers in courts being influenced by unexpressed values, leading to arbitrariness. Structured legal analyses are a means for defending against arbitrariness and subjectivity.

In contrast to traditional common law reasoning, rights-based reasoning is top-down, entailing application of high level principles to facts. A difficulty is that, while it is comparatively easy to formulate abstract tests, applying such tests to facts risks introducing subjectivity and arbitrariness. And yet, the application of rights-based analysis (such as proportionality) is, as courts acknowledge, highly context dependent.[67] In application, rights-based analysis can degenerate into the pro forma,[68] with courts paying lip service to rights but with outcomes hinging on unstructured, multi-factor tests. The reasoning of common law courts determining applications for identity discovery therefore illustrates broader problems. In the context of the discretion to award identity discovery orders, the analysis of the relationship between copyright and

---

[65] *Dallas Buyers Club LLC v. iiNet Limited (No 4)* (2015) 327 ALR 702.   [66] Ibid., [8].
[67] The distinction between balancing of abstract rights and balancing of rights as applied to specific cases is also known as the distinction between 'definitional balancing' and 'ad hoc balancing': Melville B Nimmer, 'The right to speak from times to time: First Amendment theory applied to libel and misapplied to privacy' (1968) 56 *California Law Review* 935; Giovanella, *Copyright and Information Privacy*, 12–14.
[68] As Aleinikoff puts it, balancing can degenerate into 'mechanical jurisprudence': T Alexander Aleinikoff, 'Constitutional law in the age of balancing' (1987) 96 *Yale Law Journal* 943.

privacy has, even in the UK (where courts are required to apply 'proportionality'), been unduly unstructured and, therefore, unsatisfactory.[69]

Is there a way for the analysis to be improved, so rights conflicts are more clearly acknowledged and resolved? To begin, recall how rights-based analysis differs from other legal 'balancing'. Common law balancing, such as traditionally occurred in the exercise of the discretion to award discovery, entails weighing 'public interest' factors in what has been termed 'a broad brush, and sometimes opaque, analysis aimed at a resolution of the rights and interests involved'.[70] Compared with rights-based approaches, such as proportionality, common law balancing fails to expressly give special weight to rights, is less structured and is more likely arbitrary.

But top-down, rights-based analyses are difficult for courts to apply.[71] Take, for example, the reasoning of the UK courts in *Golden Eye* and *Viagogo*. In *Golden Eye*, Arnold J set out an abstract framework (the 'correct approach') for determining whether an interference with privacy rights is proportionate.[72] While, in *Viagogo*, the Supreme Court approved this framework, it also held that the 'essential purpose' of a *Norwich* order is 'to do justice', which involves 'the exercise of discretion by a careful and fair weighting of *all* relevant factors'.[73] The court then identified ten factors, only some of which are relevant to rights-based proportionality.[74]

What does this tell us about common law courts applying rights-based analyses? First, consider the paradox of how rights-based analysis aims to avoid reducing rights to utilitarian balancing, yet rights conflicts involve trade-offs. The absence of an accepted form of weighing arguably qualitatively equivalent rights, such as copyright and privacy, appears to result in courts gravitating to unstructured, multi-factorism. What seems to be needed is the development of second-order rules – what Schauer refers to as 'rules of weight'[75] and Luizzi as 'specific guides'[76] – so as to better

---

[69] As Giovanella points out in relation to identity discovery jurisprudence in the US, Canada and Italy, judges 'have found themselves struggling to understand which right should prevail': Giovanella, *Copyright and Information Privacy*, 36.
[70] Benjamin J Goold, Liora Lazarus and Gabriel Swiney, 'Public protection, proportionality, and the search for balance' (Research Paper No. 10/07), UK Ministry of Justice, 2007, i.
[71] For a controversial attempt at integrating rights-based analysis with common law reasoning see Trevor R S Allan, *Constitutional Justice, A Liberal Theory of Law* (Oxford: Oxford University Press, 2001).
[72] *Golden Eye* [2012] EWHC 723 (Ch), [117].
[73] *Viagogo* [2012] 1 WLR 3333, 3338 (emphasis added).   [74] Ibid., 3339.
[75] Schauer, 'Proportionality and the question of weight', 178.
[76] Vincent Luizzi, 'Balancing of interests in courts' (1980) *Jurimetrics* 373, 394.

bridge the gap between high-level principles and factual context. While it seems that the factors identified by the Supreme Court in *Viagogo* were intended to serve this purpose, they are too general and diffuse and insufficiently tailored to resolving rights conflicts.

Second, and more controversial, establishing 'rules of weight' or 'specific guides' should, as potentially hinted by Arnold J in *Golden Eye*, involve some substantive analysis of the values and interests underpinning the respective rights.[77] For example, as pointed out by the court in *Voltage Pictures*, the right to privacy is not intended to shield wrongdoers. On the other hand, in that case, the court apparently held that, apart from the risk of 'speculative invoicing', users of P2P networks have no 'reasonable expectation of privacy', as they necessarily reveal an IP address.[78] This would seem, in some way, to reduce privacy to a right not to be subject to 'speculative invoicing', when the two (privacy and speculative invoicing) are distinct.

In short, in the exercise of the court's discretion, privacy has been paid lip service, with the value and importance of online anonymity not being referred to[79] and systemic threats of surveillance ignored. A potential benefit of rights-based reasoning, however, is the ability for courts to take account of system-wide effects, such as surveillance practices, extending beyond the individual case.[80] Moreover, the reluctance of common law courts to engage in substantive analysis of the relationship between rights may potentially explain how, in the relevant cases, the relationship between copyright and privacy has been subsumed by concerns about speculative invoicing. This is not to say that avoiding the potential for speculative invoicing is unimportant. The underlying issue, however, is the extent to which reasoning in the exercise of judicial discretion is properly structured. If rights are to be prioritised, then analysis of interference with privacy should not be conflated with the potential economic harms of speculative invoicing.

It may be helpful, at this point, to illustrate weaknesses in the reasoning of the courts by providing a sketch of what a rights-based approach to

---

[77] This conclusion may be similar, but is certainly not identical, to Giovanella's 'conceptual balancing': Giovanella, *Copyright and Information Privacy*. For example, I do not agree that 'concepts' of rights are necessarily jurisdiction specific.
[78] *Voltage Pictures* (2014) FC 161, [59]-[60].
[79] See, for example, Julie E Cohen, 'A right to read anonymously: A closer look at "copyright management" in cyberspace' (1996) 28 *Connecticut Law Review* 981.
[80] McFadden points out that 'sophisticated', as opposed to 'elementary', balancing takes into account societal interests beyond the facts of the particular dispute: Patrick M McFadden, 'The balancing test' (1988) *Boston College Law Review* 585, 586.

the exercise of the discretion to award identity discovery might look like. The privacy rights of internet users, consisting of a right not to have personal data disclosed for a purpose other than the purpose of collection, will be breached unless disclosure is justified. Disclosure may be justified where it is necessary to protect other rights, such as the right of copyright owners to vindicate their rights. But disclosure should be restricted to what is strictly necessary to vindicate the relevant rights. Therefore, it must be limited to where there is a genuine intention to vindicate rights, by bringing an infringement action or good faith settlement negotiations, but not for other purposes, such as speculative invoicing. The problem with speculative invoicing is therefore not that it is an infringement of privacy, but that identity disclosure for that purpose would be a disproportionate infringement of the right to privacy (whereas disclosure for the purpose of legitimate litigation is generally not). Similarly, the litigation agreement in *Golden Eye*, which provided for the applicant to bring actions on behalf of other owners, was problematic not because it involved trading privacy rights (as suggested by Arnold J), but because it risked privacy being infringed for an illegitimate purpose (that is, a purpose apart from vindicating rights).

So far, in this section, we have not distinguished rights-based analyses in general from proportionality analysis. Proportionality, as a constrained form of rights-based reasoning, promises much, including safeguarding against subjective and arbitrary reasoning. Like any form of high-level reasoning, however, it is not a panacea. That is why this chapter suggests that the critical proportionality sub-test – proportionality stricto sensu (that a limitation on a right must not impose excessive burdens on other rights or interests)[81] – needs to be supplemented by 'rules of weight' or 'specific guides'.

In the cases dealt with in this chapter, which reach similar conclusions but by different routes, it is hard to criticise the outcomes, with the safeguards imposed by the courts reflecting concerns at the pre-trial stage to protect rights and interests of users, especially potentially innocent users. It is, however, also hard not to be critical of the reasoning of the courts in balancing rights and interests, which seems insufficiently structured. What might this mean for a jurisdiction such as Australia where, for example, Perram J in *Dallas Buyers Club* concluded that, absent a rights-based framework, courts may be prevented from applying proportionality analysis? While the argument

---

[81] Barak, *Proportionality*, 3.

cannot be made in full here, this should properly be regarded as part of broader questions of whether common law courts should incorporate rights into their reasoning and, if so, how.[82] For this chapter, it is sufficient to observe that in exercising judicial discretion common law courts, even Australian courts, commonly loosely refer to 'rights', including the right to privacy, but without attempting to pursue the implications of using this terminology. The flexibility of traditional common law balancing, however, is such that there may be no insurmountable obstacle to courts in exercising broad discretions adopting a more highly structured approach to identifying and resolving rights conflicts.

15.6 Conclusion

The ease with which content may be downloaded and disseminated, and the proliferation of metadata (such as IP addresses) that may be linked to users, mean that conflicts between copyright and privacy are more intense online than offline.[83] This chapter has suggested that if we are to take rights seriously, conflicts between copyright and privacy should be resolved through rights-based reasoning. Adopting a structured, rights-based framework for analysing conflicts between copyright and privacy promises more precise, and less subjective and arbitrary, decision making than multi-factor analyses. But the demands and discipline of rights-based analyses can be formidable.

Given that courts applying rights-based proportionality and multi-factor balancing may reach the same conclusions, is there any point in burdening common law courts with the demands of top-down, rights-based reasoning? The answer depends upon, first, the extent to which it is considered important to integrate rights into discretionary judicial decision making and, second, whether there is a concern to improve the precision and quality of such decision making. This chapter has suggested some ways in which judicial analysis of conflicts between copyright and privacy might be improved, principally by developing rules of weight or specific guides. Overarching these suggestions, however, is the prospect that a focus on the substantive relationship between potentially conflicting rights in judicial reasoning may assist in greater

---

[82] See, for example, Michael D Kirby, 'The role of the judge in advancing human rights by reference to international human rights norms' (1988) 62 *Australian Law Journal* 514.
[83] Orit Fischman Afori, 'Proportionality – A new mega standard in European copyright law' (2014) 46 *International Review of Intellectual Property and Competition Law* 889.

understanding of those rights, and of the evolving nature of rights online. In this sense, as acknowledged in Giovanella's book,[84] pre-trial identity discovery raises broader issues about the nature of judicial reasoning than those involved in resolving conflicts between copyright and privacy in this specific context.

[84] Giovanella, *Copyright and Information Privacy*.

16 Resisting Labels
Trade Marks and Personal Identity

Megan Richardson *

In a typically thoughtful and illuminating early article,[1] Sam Ricketson asks what value is to be found in according individual rights against unauthorised exploitation of a personal name or likeness in trade and advertising.[2] In various writings since then I have tried to answer this question by arguing that creative self-fashioning provides at least a minimal reason – whether the policy is understood in liberal-utilitarian terms of human flourishing or in dignitarian terms as an acknowledgement of the importance of the individual (or both, as I am inclined to think).[3] Even so, I doubt that my answer is all that different from one suggested tentatively by Sam Ricketson when he observes, drawing an analogy with moral rights of authors, that 'for reasons of both personal integrity and economic good sense' people 'will wish to limit and control carefully the uses that are made of their names and images', treating this as a possible

---

* I am grateful to David Lindsay, Janice Luck and especially Sam Ricketson for insightful comments and suggestions on this chapter (as on many other things).
[1] Sam Ricketson, 'Character merchandising in Australia: Its benefits and burdens' (1990) 1 *Australian Intellectual Property Journal* 191.
[2] Ibid., 204.
[3] See, e.g., Megan Richardson, 'Larger than life in the Australian cinema: *Pacific Dunlop v Hogan*' in Andrew T Kenyon, Megan Richardson and Sam Ricketson (eds.), *Landmarks in Australian Intellectual Property Law* (Cambridge: Cambridge University Press, 2009), pp. 160–70; Megan Richardson and Andrew T Kenyon, 'Fashioning personality rights in Australia' in Andrew T Kenyon, Ng-Loy Wee Loon and Megan Richardson (eds.), *The Law of Reputation and Brands in the Asia Pacific* (Cambridge: Cambridge University Press, 2012), pp. 86–98; Megan Richardson, *The Right to Privacy: Origins and Influence of a Nineteenth-Century Idea* (Cambridge: Cambridge University Press, 2017), ch. 3; Graeme Dinwoodie and Megan Richardson, 'Publicity rights, personality rights or just confusion?' in Megan Richardson and Sam Ricketson (eds.), *Research Handbook on Intellectual Property in Media and Entertainment* (Cheltenham, UK: Edward Elgar, 2017), pp. 425–45; Megan Richardson and Julian Thomas, 'Image rights and other unorthodox forms of intellectual property' in Rochelle Cooper Dreyfuss and Elizabeth Siew-Kuan Ng (eds.), *Framing Intellectual Property Law in the 21st Century: Integrating Incentives, Trade, Development, Culture and Human Rights* (Cambridge: Cambridge University Press, 2018), pp. 154–70.

basis for legal rights – and adding that fostering 'truth in advertising' could also work for the benefit of consumers.[4]

Like Ricketson and others writing on character merchandising in Australia and the UK, or the right of publicity as it is known in the US, I have mostly been considering the operation of the common law, backed up by statutory provisions proscribing unfair or deceptive conduct or what may generally be termed 'unfair competition', as well as statutory rights of publicity.[5] But in this chapter, I turn my focus to the parallel development and functioning of the registered trade mark system in these jurisdictions – a system established towards the end of the nineteenth century and already taking on many of its modern characteristics in the period up to World War I. As such, it was shaped to an extent by a modern idea of the individual's power and desire to establish, maintain and manifest a personal identity, drawing on the world of signs.[6] In part, this can be seen in the liberty allowed for registration of personalised signs that traders might wish to adopt and use to express themselves. But, in part also, it offered a response to what German sociologist Georg Simmel at the beginning of the twentieth century termed 'the deepest problems of modern life' flowing from 'the attempt of the individual to maintain the independence and individuality of his existence against the sovereign powers of society, against the weight of the historical heritage and the external culture and technique of life'.[7] It is the latter aspect, focussed on the domain of resistance to labels, that especially interests me in my contribution to this volume.

Of course, the focus on *trade* marks means that the system's compass is necessarily limited. But being premised on an idea of individual

---

[4] Ricketson, 'Character merchandising in Australia', 206. Cf. Dinwoodie and Richardson, 'Publicity rights, personality rights' and (for an extended discussion) David Tan, *The Commercial Appropriation of Fame: A Cultural Analysis of the Right of Publicity and Passing Off* (Cambridge: Cambridge University Press, 2017).

[5] For instance, on misleading or deceptive conduct in Australia (currently Competition and Consumer Act 2010 (Cth) sch. 2 (Australian Consumer Law), s. 18), on false descriptions and dilution under the US Trademark Act of 1946, Pub L No 79-489, 60 Stat. 427, as amended (Lanham Act) § 43, on 'unfair competition' in states such as California, and on the right to privacy or publicity variously in states such as New York and California: see Dinwoodie and Richardson, 'Publicity rights, personality rights'.

[6] In other words, employing names, images and other signs to convey specific meanings attached to those signs, operating in association with them, and which come to be understood through social conventions and practices (or 'language games' as Ludwig Wittgenstein called them): see Roy Harris, *Language, Saussure, and Wittgenstein: How to Play Games with Words* (London: Routledge, 1988), pp. ix–xi.

[7] Georg Simmel, 'The metropolis and mental life' (Edward A Shils, trans.) in Donald L Levine (ed.), *On Individuality and Social Forms: Selected Writings* (Chicago: University of Chicago Press, 1971), p. 324 ['Die Grosstadt und das Geistesleben' in *Die Grosstadt Jahrbuch der Gehe-Stiftung* (first published 1903)].

autonomy and to an extent, I would argue, dignity, it can potentially extend quite broadly within the boundaries of that constraint. The challenge from the beginning was to take a system established with the idea that a trader's personal name could function as 'the archetypal trade mark' when applied to the trader's goods[8] and develop that to allow a measure of protection for signs of personal identity more generally. While quite significant protection is now available for celebrities and others directly engaged in trade, I suggest that the system still has a way to go in offering protection to ordinary people who might have personal interests in controlling the exploitation of their identities as trade marks.

16.1 Celebrities

Celebrities were among the first to push for an expansive reading of the nascent trade mark system. Being directly interested in capitalising on their fame in the Gilded Age, they logically turned to a system already geared to protecting signs of trade identity, arguing that they equally were in the business of 'selling fame'.[9] Samuel Clemens was prophetic in his bold attempt in *Clemens* v. *Belford* in 1883 to have his literary pen name recognised as not just a sign of authorship, but as a commodity of value both to himself in his reputation and to the book-purchasing public.[10] The court's response to the argument that 'Mark Twain' was 'a commercial designation of authorship' having the character of 'property'[11] was that an author's name should be treated as different from a trade mark constituting 'the means by which the manufacturers of vendible merchandise designate or state to the public the quality of such goods, and

---

[8] See Lionel Bently, 'The making of modern trade mark law' in Lionel Bently, Jennifer Davis and Jane C Ginsburg (eds.), *Trade Marks and Brands: An Interdisciplinary Critique* (Cambridge: Cambridge University Press, 2008), pp. 1, 20–2 (although noting that this was only in a restricted fashion in s. 10 of the Trade Marks Registration Act 1875, 38 & 39 Vict, c. 91, limited (in respect of new trade marks) to 'a name of an individual or firm printed, impressed or woven in some particular and distinctive manner' or 'a written signature or copy of a written signature of an individual or firm'. This restriction was maintained in s 64 of the Patents, Designs and Trade Marks Act 1883, 46 & 47 Vict, c. 57, and in s. 9 of the Trade Marks Act 1905 Act (UK). Cf. Trade Marks Act 1905 (Cth) s. 16, and US Trademark Act of 1905, § 5 proviso. Contrast the broader terms of the Trade Marks Act 1994 (UK) s. 1(1); Trade Marks Act 1995 (Cth) s. 41; Lanham Act, § 2 (15 USC § 1052).
[9] See Stuart Banner, *American Property: A History of How, Why, and What We Own* (Cambridge, MA: Harvard University Press, 2011), ch. 7.
[10] *Clemens* v. *Belford, Clark & Co*, 14 F 728 (CC ND Ill, 1883). [11] Ibid., 730.

the fact that they are the manufacturers of them'.[12] But as Loren Glass notes, the line between a professional author's designation of qualities of the works aligned to their source and a commercial trade mark was a fine one,[13] and 'the idea of an authorial name as a trademark did gain *cultural* ascendancy at this time', despite the legal decision.[14]

In fact, Clemens and subsequently his estate continued to use his 'authenticating' name, portrait and signature as markers of his books and other products such as whiskey and tobacco long after the decision.[15] And, to an extent, the law supported him in the exercise of this right, not only permitting the registration of his nom de plume as a trade mark (for whiskey and tobacco) in 1907.[16] By 1905, five years before his death, Clemens had the right to object not only to the unauthorised use of his name or likeness in advertising, relying on the 'right to privacy' in the New York Civil Rights Law of 1903, and a similar provision by common law or statute in a number of other states,[17] precursors of the right of publicity recognised in 1953 in *Haelan Laboratories, Inc* v. *Topps Chewing Gum, Inc*.[18] He could also likewise object to the registration of his 'portrait' as a trade mark under the federal Trademark Act of 1905, later extended to a 'name, portrait or signature identifying a particular individual' in the equivalent provision of the Lanham Act in 1946.[19] Such

---

[12] Ibid., 731–2 (Blodgett DJ) (although going on to suggest that the reason lay more in policy than logic: specifically, 'that the publication of literary matter without protection by copyright has dedicated such matter to the public, and the public are entitled to use it in such form as they may thereafter choose, and to quote, compile, or publish it as the writing of its author', giving the name of the author 'either upon the title-page, or otherwise as best suits the interest or taste of the person so republishing').

[13] Loren Glass, *Authors Inc: Literary Celebrity in the Modern United States, 1880–1980* (New York: New York University Press, 2004), ch 2.

[14] Ibid., 80.   [15] Ibid., 79–80.

[16] Glass states that the first registrations were made in 1907 by Clemens's business adviser, Ralph Ashcroft. These do not show up in TESS, the US Patent and Trademark Office's online database, but for reproductions of the registrations (granted in 1908), see Judith Yaross Lee, 'Samuel Clemens, trademarks and the Mark Twain enterprise' in Henry B Wonham and Lawrence Howe (eds.), *Mark Twain and Money: Language, Capital, and Culture* (Tuscaloosa: University of Alabama Press, 2017), pp. 39, 56–7.

[17] NY Civil Rights Law § 51 (1903). The same was achieved by common law and/or statute in a number of other states: see Samantha Barbas, *Laws of Image: Privacy and Publicity in America* (Stanford, CA: Stanford Law Books, 2015); (for the role of women in promoting the change) Jessica Lake, *The Face That Launched a Thousand Lawsuits: The American Women Who Forged a Right to Privacy* (New Haven, CT: Yale University Press, 2016).

[18] 202 F2d 866 (2nd Cir, 1953).

[19] Trademark Act, 1905, § 5 proviso, specifying that consent must be in writing (as also required under the New York Civil Rights Law); Lanham Act, § 2(c). Consent conferred by a bare licence might also be withdrawn: see *Mary Garden* v. *Parfumerie Rigaud, Inc*, 151 Misc 692 (NYSC 1933) – although for the possibility of an estoppel operating, see *Rick* v. *Buchansky*, 609 F Supp. 1522, 1539 (SDNY, 1985).

indirect measures reinforced Clemens's ability to exert a measure of control over the signs of his identity even without the need for registration, paving the way for a new generation of film stars, fashion designers and other celebrities of the early twentieth century to lend their names, signatures and faces to literary products, portraits, films, fashion, perfume and 'what not' across the country.[20] And if they still complained about pirating practices, this may have had more to do with the limited enforcement of law in the US than with law itself at the fin de siècle.

Now the distinctive names, signatures, portraits and other signs identified with celebrities are quite commonly registered as trade marks, and not just in the US but also in the UK and Australia, whose initial strictures against 'trafficking' in trade marks have been eroded in favour of freer licensing and assignment.[21] So we seem to have moved past the position identified by Dixon J in *Radio Corporation* v. *Disney*, in 1937,[22] that some mere 'intangible advantage arising from public celebrity, widespread fame and interest' did not give a right to register a sign as a trade mark for heterogeneous goods,[23] even if it could provide a right to object to registration by another party on the basis that the public would likely be deceived into thinking their use was authorised, as in that case where the defendant sought to register 'Mickey Mouse' and 'Minnie Mouse' for radios.[24] Thus the law in these jurisdictions now seems to run a little more in sync with the realities of celebrities and their publics

---

[20] The language comes from *Wood* v. *Lucy, Lady Duff-Gordon*, 222 NY 88, 90 (1917) (Cardozo J). The case involving fashion designer Lady Duff-Gordon's efforts to exploit and control the use of her 'Lucile' label for a variety of products, was cited as authority for the right of publicity in *Haelan Laboratories*, cited earlier.

[21] The anti-trafficking provisions in the Trade Marks Act 1938 (UK) and the Trade Marks Act 1955 (Cth) (construed in the *Holly Hobbie* case: *American Greetings Corp's Application* [1984] RPC 329 to prohibit trade mark registration for a wide variety of unrelated goods) was noted by Ricketson as an impediment to reliance on trade marks for the protection of character merchandising interests: Ricketson, 'Character merchandising in Australia', 198–200. The provisions were substituted by more liberal provisions on licensing and assignment in the Trade Marks Act 1994 (UK) ss. 24 and 28; and Trade Marks Act 1995 (Cth) s. 8 and Pt. 10. There may be other hurdles to registration, as where celebrity signs have been used ubiquitously rendering them non-distinctive (or generic): see *Re Elvis Presley Trade Marks* [1999] RPC 567 (cited as Elvis Presley); although contrast in Australia *McCorquodale* v. *Masterton* (2005) 63 IPR 582, 598 (Kenny J) ('Diana's Legacy in Roses' would 'bespeak an association with the [Princess of Wales Memorial] fund and the estate of the late Princess').

[22] *Radio Corporation Pty Ltd* v. *Disney* (1937) 57 CLR 448.   [23] Ibid., 455–9.

[24] Ibid. And see Latham CJ at 453: '[t]he names and figures are so closely associated in the public mind ... with Walter E Disney and his activities, that the use of either of the names or figures in connection with any goods at once suggests that the goods are "in some way or other connected" with Walter E Disney'.

constructing relationships of public performance and allegiance,[25] which may not be all that different from successful brands which develop 'identities' of their own and provide badges of 'allegiance' and 'status' to their consuming publics.[26] Nevertheless, the practically more useful provision of the US Lanham Act, giving a 'living individual' the right to object to the registration of his or her identifying name, signature or portrait as another party's trade mark without consent,[27] has no equivalent in the UK Act. And although earlier Australian Acts included a version (beginning with the 1905 Act passed a few months after the US Act), it was little noticed,[28] and was omitted in the latest Act. Thus celebrities in these jurisdictions are left to fall back on a provision framed in terms of likely deception, even if this may readily be found from the use of their familiar features[29] – in the same way that the common law action for passing off may arguably approach a de facto right of publicity.[30]

16.2 Non-Celebrities

Is there such a thing as a non-celebrity these days? This is something I come back to later in the chapter. But in the past, a clear distinction

---

[25] See Joseph A Boone and Nancy J Vickers, 'Introduction – Celebrity rites' (2011) 126(4) *PMLA* 900.
[26] Geoffrey Jones, 'Brands and marketing' in Geoffrey Jones and Nicholas Morgan (eds.), *Adding Value: Brands and Marketing in Food and Drink* (London: Routledge, 1994), pp. 1, 3. And see also Jason Bosland, 'The culture of trade marks: An alternative cultural theory perspective' (2005) 10 *Media & Arts Law Review* 99; David Tan, 'The semiotics of alpha brands: Encoding/decoding/recoding/transcoding of Louis Vuitton and implications for trademark laws' (2013) 32 *Cardozo Arts & Entertainment Law Journal* 225.
[27] A ground of objection available especially to celebrities (and trade mark examiners deciding on registration): see J Thomas McCarthy, *McCarthy on Trademarks and Unfair Competition*, 5th ed (Eagan, MN: Thomson Reuters, 2017), §13.37, giving examples of 'Obama Pajama' rejected for pyjamas in *Richard M. Hoefflin*, 97 USPQ 2d 1174 (TTAB 2010) and 'Princess Kate' for fashion products in *In Re Nieves & Nieves LLC* 113 USPQ 2d 1629 (TTAB 2015).
[28] The provisions were Trademark Act 1905 (Cth) s. 26 (Registrar may require consent to name or representation of a living person) and Trade Marks Act 1955 (Cth) s. 30 (in similar terms). And for one application of the latter, see *In re Application by Belle Jardiniere* (1989) 14 IPR 159 (consent required to signature of the well-known French fashion designer Ted Lapidus in applicant's trade mark for glasses).
[29] As, for example, *Worcester Corset Co's Appn* [1909] 1 Ch 459 ('Royal' suggesting patronage of corsets); *McCorquodale v. Masterton* (2005) 63 IPR 582 ('Diana's Legacy in Roses' suggesting association with the fund). In fact, now royal emblems have their own provision under the UK Act: see Trade Marks 1994 (UK) s. 4. Cf. previously in Australia, Trade Marks Act 1905 (Cth) ss. 18(b), 19(a)-(b); Trade Marks Act 1955 (Cth) s. 29(1)(b)-(d).
[30] And see Ricketson, 'Character merchandising in Australia', 196 (re the Australian cases); Dinwoodie and Richardson, 'Publicity rights, personality rights'.

could be made, and was made as a matter of law, between celebrities and non-celebrities, whose protection against unauthorised use of their name, signature or likeness was less assured – mirroring the cultural distinction that existed between celebrities and others at the fin de siecle.[31] Moreover, even within the latter category, distinctions were made that reinforced the lowly status of non-celebrities, who were considered simply as individuals. For instance, some privilege was accorded to those whose names, signatures and likenesses were employed in trade and advertising on account of their professional status and expertise, for instance, company founders, business and professional types testifying to the qualities of a company's products, and medical experts testifying to the medicinal attributes of tea, coffee, soaps, digestive powders and other elixirs of life.[32] They at least could conceivably object to the unauthorised use of their name, signature or likeness (or other personal features) on the basis that the relevant public would likely assume they had endorsed or approved the goods,[33] and similarly after the US portrait-consent provision in the Trademark Act, 1905, later expanded to names, portraits and signatures in the Lanham Act, they might have rights directly under that provision.[34] They might also, if they were union members, object to the false use of labels affixed to goods indicating that these were made by 'union labour' – provided the label was property registered under the statute, as provided for in various US states from New York to California, and briefly also in Australia until the provisions authorising registration of union labels were declared unconstitutional by the High Court in

---

[31] Even if there was a democratisation of the process by which one might become a celebrity (especially in the US) with the benefit of modern media and especially proliferating newspapers and magazines: see Leo Braudy, *The Frenzy of Renown: Fame and Its History* (New York: Oxford University Press, 1986), pp. 506-14.

[32] See generally, for advertising practices extending not just to celebrities, Richardson, *The Right to Privacy*, ch. 3.

[33] Would the case of *Dockrell* v. *Dougall* (1898) 78 LTR 840 present a barrier to such an objection? In that case, a doctor was held unable to object to the use of his endorsement on the basis that he was not entitled to sell medicines, thus there was no relevant damage flowing from any likely public deception (although for a different result in the US, see *Mackenzie* v. *Soden Mineral Springs Co*, 18 NYS 240 (NYSC 1891). In any event, the common law has become more liberal in its recognition of damage to reputation: see Dinwoodie and Richardson, 'Publicity rights, personality rights'.

[34] And see, for an instance where an objection succeeded on the basis of professional reputation, *Krause* v. *Krause Publications, Inc*, 76 USPOQ 2d 1904, 1909-1910 (TTAB, 2005). Cf. also in Australia under the equivalent provision in the Trade Marks Act 1955 (Cth), *Belle Jardiniere* (1989) 14 IPR 159. But see also for instances where objections failed on the basis that the requisite business reputation had not been established, *Martin* v. *Carter Hawley Hale Stores, Inc*, 206 USPQ 931, 933 (TTAB 1979); *Rick* v. *Buchansky*, 609 F Supp. 1522, 1539 (SDNY, 1985); *Zuppardi's Apizza, Inc* v. *Tony Zuppardi's Apizza*, 2014 US Dist LEXIS 136763 (D Conn 2014) and further discussion later in the chapter.

1908.[35] Thus these labels provided members with a way to claim their identity as a 'union man' (or woman) – as well as 'some guarantee that the articles [were] what they are represented to be: made under fair [i.e. union] conditions'.[36] But harder to deal with was the situation of amorphous individuals whose names, signatures and likenesses were employed in advertising and trade simply on account of their ordinariness, serving as exemplars of informed public opinion.[37] As anonymous individuals without a public reputation, their position in objecting to the use of their names, signatures or portraits (or other identifying features) was deeply ambiguous – making it difficult for them to argue that when it came to registration of a trade mark, the public would likely be deceived into thinking that they had authorised the deployment of these same features in the trade mark.[38]

Nominally, from 1905 the US portrait-consent provision should have been available to those who fell within the Trademark Act's remit. And coming two years after the comparable right to privacy in the New York Civil Rights Law, one can imagine that the case of Abigail Roberson, whose portrait became widely associated with Franklin Mills flour and appeared below the slogan 'Flour of the Family' and above the company's name and logo on its advertising posters, was fresh in the mind of the legislator. Certainly, when Roberson brought her case in New York, framing her claim in terms of breach of privacy and citing Samuel Warren and Louis Brandeis's article on 'The Right to Privacy' in the *Harvard Law Review* of 1890,[39] the trial judge seemed to conceive the nature of her interest as being as much in the nature of a trade mark interest as a privacy interest. The trial judge stated that '[i]f [Roberson's] image, owing to its beauty, is of great value as a trade-mark or an advertising medium, it is a property right which belongs to her'.[40] And

---

[35] *Attorney-General for New South Wales* v. *Brewery Employees Union of New South Wales* (1908) 6 CLR 469. See Sam Ricketson, 'The *Union Label* case: An early Australian IP story' in Andrew T Kenyon, Megan Richardson and Sam Ricketson (eds.), *Landmarks in Australian Intellectual Property Law* (Cambridge: Cambridge University Press, 2009), pp. 15 (adding that such labels might be characterised as certification trade marks under the Trade Marks Act 1995 (Cth): at 21).
[36] M E J Kelley, 'The *Union Label*' (1897) 165 *North American Review* 26, 34.
[37] See Richardson, *The Right to Privacy*, ch. 3.
[38] Note, for instance, the reasoning in *Radio Corporation* v. *Disney* (1937) 57 CLR 448 (discussed earlier) was premised on a celebrity's reputation giving rise to likely deception.
[39] Samuel D Warren and Louis D Brandeis, 'The right to privacy' (1890) 4 *Harvard Law Review* 193 (inter alia citing concerns about the circulation of portraits as a reason for more explicit and effective protection of the right to privacy as a matter of law).
[40] *Roberson* v. *The Rochester Folding Box Co*, 32 Misc 344, 349 (NYSC, 1900) (Davy J).

although the appeal court rejected the claim,[41] the decision led to the enactment of the Civil Rights Law's 'right to privacy' extending to unauthorised use in trade or advertising of a person's name or likeness, followed up shortly by the prohibition on registration in the Trademark Act, and later broadened to encompass not only the use of a portrait but also a name and signature in the Lanham Act.[42] Unfortunately, the Trademark Trial and Appeal Board fairly early on took the position that the Trademark Act provision 'was not designed to protect every person from having a name which is similar or identical to his or her name registered as a trademark', and that the requisite 'damage' will not be found 'in the absence of other factors from which it may be determined that the particular individual bearing the name in question will be associated with the mark as used on the goods, either because that person is so well known that the public would reasonably assume the connection or because the individual is publicly connected with the business in which the mark is used'.[43] This position has been endorsed by the courts.[44] Thus although it is said that what is involved here is 'the right to control the use of one's identity',[45] that is not a right which necessarily or fully extends to the identities of ordinary private individuals. In short, a *Roberson* scenario seems to be excluded – certainly as far as names are concerned (although the protection of portraits, the earliest form of statutory protection and also the most capable of operating as a unique identifier, might be treated as relatively more absolute).[46]

Now, non-celebrities can more easily become celebrities of a sort with the benefit of ubiquitous social media, enjoying their fifteen minutes of fame.[47] Moreover, they may achieve a quasi-expert status in commenting

---

[41] See *Roberson v. Rochester Folding Box Co*, 64 NE 442 (1902) and Lake, *The Face That Launched a Thousand Lawsuits*, ch. 2.
[42] See notes 17 and 19.
[43] *Martin v. Carter Hawley Hale Stores, Inc*, 206 USPQ 931, 933 (TTAB 1979).
[44] See, e.g., *Rick v. Buchansky* 609 F Supp. 1522, 1539 (SDNY, 1985) (Ward DJ); *Zuppardi's Apizza v. Tony Zuppardi's Apizza*, 2014 US Dist LEXIS 136763 (D Conn 2014) [16]-[18] (Chatigny DJ) (adding this must be a national reputation within the field).
[45] *The University of Notre Dame du Lac v. JC Gourmet Food Imports Co, Inc* 703 F 2d 1372, 1376, fn. 8 (USCA 1983) (Nies CJ).
[46] See *In re McKee Baking Co* 218 USPQ 287 (TTAB 1983) (trade mark for cakes, cookies and pies consisting of 'Little Debbie' coupled with a portrait of the daughter of the company's president held to be subject to consent).
[47] See Andrea L Press and Bruce A Williams, 'Fame and everyday life: The "lotteries celebrities" of reality TV' in Mark D Jacobs and Nancy Weiss Hanrahan (eds.), *The Blackwell Companion to the Sociology of Culture* (Chichester, UK: Blackwell, 2013), pp. 176, 177, quoting Andy Warhol's possibly apocryphal statement from 1968, adding that in the age of reality television the problem may be less one of obtaining celebrity as, aided and hindered by technology, maintaining this through a 'second act'

on the qualities of goods and services online. Such ways of reasoning can be seen in the recent case of *Fraley v. Facebook, Inc*,[48] where right of publicity and unfair competition claims were allowed to proceed against Facebook's use of users' 'likes' of particular products coupled with their names and portraits in advertising for the products, exploiting their 'local celebrity' and the selling power of a 'friend's' endorsement (and the case was later settled).[49] But overlooked in the discussion was the more general problem that individuals, rather in the way of Abigail Roberson, may wish to object to the unauthorised use of their name, signature or likeness or other identifying features,[50] not on the basis that they might wish to exploit their publicity potential on their own account but rather because they prefer not to be public – whether or not they frame this in terms of 'privacy' or in terms of 'the right to control the use of one's identity' more broadly. For these individuals, the 'name, portrait or signature' consent provision in the Lanham Act, on current reading premised on celebrity or trade connection, seems inadequate – although query whether in the UK and Australia more general protections premised on likely deception are any better.[51]

16.3 Final Reflections

There is a certain irony in the fact that the trade mark system was slow to accept the arguments of celebrities that their names, signatures and portraits could be registered trade marks applied to heterogeneous goods yet allowed them the right to object to other traders' registrations, whether under a specific statutory provision (as in the US and for a while Australia) or on the general principle that a trade mark should not be registered if it would be likely to deceive the public that the use was authorised (as in the UK and now Australia). In both respects, non-celebrities, and especially those without a recognised professional status,

---

(requiring a different kind of control over public identity). Of course, the point applies even more strikingly in the age of social media and the internet.

[48] *Fraley v. Facebook, Inc*, 830 F Supp. 2d 785 (ND Cal 2011).
[49] See ibid., 799 and 804–5; Dinwoodie and Richardson, 'Publicity rights, personality rights', 438–9.
[50] Features that may be used to identify them specifically far more freely than in the past, with the benefit of modern media and other technologies (including data-matching and facial recognition technologies).
[51] Indeed, the current UK statutory provision contemplates the ability to claim passing off (founded on reputation) as the basis for an objection to registration: see Trade Marks Act 1994 (UK) s 5(4)(a); although the Australian Act may be more open, referring to likely deception or confusion arising out of a trade mark or sign's 'connotation': Trade Marks Act 1995 (Cth) s. 43.

fared worse in a system which allowed their identifying features to be exploited in others' trade marks and made it hard for them to object without an actual or prospective trading base of their own. The result has been that a trade mark system which for celebrities and traders may function as an identity-protection system has been only marginally involved in supporting ordinary individuals who seek to maintain a right to personal identity. And although things may change as we approach a future when anyone may be a celebrity, capitalising on fifteen minutes of fame, we may wonder why we have to present ourselves in this way to enjoy such a basic right.

17 Trade Marks and Cultural Identity

Rochelle Cooper Dreyfuss and Susy Frankel

Trade mark law provides exclusive rights over distinctive signs. A fundamental reason for requiring distinctiveness is that it supports the role of identifying one trader's goods from those of other traders, thereby preventing consumer confusion. The two concepts – distinctiveness and preventing consumer confusion – are interwoven. However, sometimes distinctive trade marks can have other effects, such as racial disparagement, which can, in turn, be associated with an erosion of cultural identity.

International trade mark law generally requires nations to protect distinctive marks.[1] However, it also recognises and allows for the possibility that nations will seek to exclude distinctive signs from registration on grounds other than their likelihood of confusing consumers. Thus the Paris Convention provides that trade marks may be denied registration or revoked[2]

when they are contrary to morality or public order and, in particular, of such a nature as to deceive the public. It is understood that a mark may not be considered contrary to public order for the sole reason that it does not conform to a provision of the legislation on marks, except if such provision itself relates to public order.

As Sam Ricketson explained, this article 'seeks to ensure that any local restriction or prohibition on marks is confined to "public order" matters'.[3] He also noted that the second sentence, a proviso to the first, 'still allows individual [Paris Convention] members considerable

---

[1] See, e.g., Marrakesh Agreement Establishing the World Trade Organization, opened for signature 15 April 1994, 1867 UNTS 3 (entered into force 1 January 1995) annex 1C ('Agreement on Trade-Related Aspects of Intellectual Property Rights') art. 16.
[2] Paris Convention for the Protection of Industrial Property, opened for signature 20 March 1883, 828 UNTS 305 (entered into force 7 July 1884) art. 6 quinquies (B) (iii).
[3] Sam Ricketson, *The Paris Convention for the Protection of Industrial Property: A Commentary* (Oxford, Oxford University Press, 2015), [12.24]–[12.25].

flexibility in determining for themselves what is "contrary to public order".[4] In some jurisdictions, such as New Zealand, trade mark law includes grounds for refusing registration in order to reflect the underlying public policy of not denigrating minorities or indigenous peoples. In other jurisdictions, concerns such as free speech are given greater weight.

A 2017 decision of the US Supreme Court provides us with an opportunity to consider whether, consistent with a nation's commitment to the right of free expression, a government can have a role in determining when trade marks are culturally offensive and refuse them registration. In this contribution, we examine the decision in *Matal* v. *Tam*,[5] which invalidated, based on constitutional principles, a statutory bar on disparaging marks and thus facilitated their use in commerce. We question that result because we are concerned that the subjects of that disparagement, as well as many others, will equate registration with government approval of disparagement. Furthermore, we see the hands-off approach as privileging speech over other, equally important, societal interests. While we acknowledge that any interference with speech can have disturbing overtones for censorship, we also note that there are many jurisdictions that value free speech, yet take a proportionality approach to competing values and do limit speech in appropriate circumstances.[6] We suggest that even in the United States there are substantive and procedural approaches that can be used to identify and refuse the registration of marks that are particularly prone to promote racial divisiveness. We offer a vision drawn from New Zealand trade mark practice and jurisprudence that we believe better accommodates the commitment to free speech with the obligation to respect cultural identity and

---

[4] Ibid. [5] 137 S. Ct. 1744 (2017) (cited as *Tam*).
[6] See Vicki C Jackson and Mark Tushnet (eds.), *Proportionality: New Frontiers, New Challenges* (Cambridge: Cambridge University Press, 2017). See also Lisa P Ramsey, 'Trademark rights and free expression locally and globally' in Daniel J Gervais (ed.), *International Intellectual Property: A Handbook of Contemporary Research* (Cheltenham, UK: Edward Elgar, 2015), p. 341. Despite its increasing recognition of the application of fundamental rights to trade marks, the EU continues to reject marks that are salacious, see, e.g. *Federico Cortés del Valle López* v. *Office for Harmonisation in the Internal Market (Trade Marks and Designs)* (General Court (First Chamber), T-417/10, 9 March 2012) (upholding, against a challenge brought on free expression grounds, the rejection of the registration of the mark *Hijoputa* (a highly derogatory term in Spanish) for *eaux de vie*, on the ground that it violates public morals within the Spanish-speaking segment of the EU); *La Mafia Franchises, SL* v. *European Union Intellectual Property Office* (General Court (Ninth Chamber), T-1/17, 15 March 2018) (rejecting registration of La Mafia for footwear, business management, and food services on the ground it brought to mind a criminal organisation responsible for a series of breaches of public policy). See Jens Schovsbo, '"Mark my words" – Trademarks and fundamental rights in the EU' (2018) 8 *UC Irvine Law Review* 555.

which could, perhaps with some modification, be implemented in the United States.[7]

17.1 The Case

Matal v. Tam began with a decision by Simon Tam, the front man of an Asian rock band, to reclaim racial slurs targeted at Asians. To renormalise these terms, he adopted The Slants as his band's name, titled the band's albums and used lyrics in its songs that include Asian references (Slanted Eyes, Slanted Hearts and The Yellow Album), and developed a logo suggestive of the stereotypical Asian dragon. Tam also attempted to register The Slants as a federal trade mark. However, he fell afoul of a legislative bar on registering marks that 'may disparage ... persons, living or dead ... or bring them into contempt, or disrepute'.[8] Applying the statute, the trade mark examiner determined that the mark referred to Asians, that a substantial composite of the Asian community would regard the term as disparaging, and that Tam – who adopted the mark *because* it disparaged Asians – had failed to rebut the prima facie case that registration of the term would violate the statute.

Rather than change the mark, Tam appealed, arguing that the measure violated the First Amendment to the US Constitution, which provides that 'Congress shall make no law ... abridging the freedom of speech'.[9] The Supreme Court agreed. Writing for the Court, Justice Alito held that because registration confers important legal rights (such as constructive notice of a claim and evidence of validity), refusing to register constitutes a burden on speech. And since the statute was aimed at content – at 'preventing speech expressing ideas that offend' – and was not viewpoint neutral, the measure 'str[uck] at the heart of the First Amendment'.[10] Even if the provision were regarded as regulating commercial speech (which is entitled to less protection), four justices found it could not stand because it did not serve a 'substantial interest'. It was, in their view, merely a 'happy-talk clause'. Nor was the provision 'narrowly drawn'.[11]

---

[7] For a comparison between the United States and New Zealand approaches to culturally offensive trade marks, see Susy Frankel, 'Trade marks and traditional knowledge and cultural intellectual property rights' in Graeme B Dinwoodie and Mark D Janis (eds.), *Trademark Law and Theory: A Handbook of Contemporary Research* (Cheltenham, UK: Edward Elgar, 2008), p. 433.

[8] 15 U.S.C. § 1052(a), which reads in relevant part that no trademark shall be refused registration unless it '(a) Consists of or comprises immoral, deceptive, or scandalous matter; or matter which may disparage or falsely suggest a connection with persons, living or dead, institutions, beliefs, or national symbols, or bring them into contempt, or disrepute'.

[9] US Constitution amend I.   [10] *Tam*, 137 S. Ct. 1744 (2017).   [11] Ibid., 1764–5.

In the process of concluding that The Slants could be registered for an Asian rock band, the Court also rejected the notion that trade mark registration is government speech, which is not subject to a requirement of viewpoint neutrality. Noting that the government does not dream up marks or curate the register, Justice Alito argued that if registered marks were government speech, then 'the Federal Government is babbling prodigiously and incoherently'.[12]

17.2 Analysis

It is difficult to argue with the US Supreme Court's core concern about censorship or the notion that the government may not remove certain ideas or perspectives from a broader debate.[13] Free speech is, after all, unambiguously essential to democratic discourse.[14] Still, there are several points in the decision that demand critical examination. First, it is hard to see how denying registration burdens speech in a constitutionally significant way. The United States recognises common law marks and the states have their own registration systems. Thus, even without federal registration, Tam can still call his band The Slants and enforce the mark under state law against uses that are likely to cause confusion. Indeed, he may even be able to bring a federal claim.[15] Furthermore, some of the benefits that accompany federal registration can be duplicated under state law; others are not very important. For example, validity is rarely an issue in trade mark litigation so the presumption of validity that attaches to registration does not do much work. (Aside from the disparagement problem, the term *Slants* could clearly be used to signify a rock band.)

Second, it is difficult to credit the notion that trade marks do not carry a government imprimatur. Were observers to read the *Trademark Register*, they might view the government as 'babbling prodigiously'. But few

---

[12] Ibid., 1759.
[13] Ibid., 1767 (Kennedy J, concurring). We note of course that many democratic countries have a different view of free speech and allow censorship in order to protect other fundamental interests such as freedom from racial discrimination.
[14] E.g., Robert Post, 'Participatory democracy and free speech' (2011) 97 *Virginia Law Review* 477.
[15] 15 U.S.C. § 1125(a). The availability of an action under this provision for marks deemed unregistrable federally is, however, in doubt: see *Tam*, 137 S, Ct, 1744, 1752 n. 1 (2017). However, in a subsequent case on the constitutionality of an exclusion of immoral and scandalous marks from registration under15 U.S.C. § 1052(a), Chief Justice Roberts, in a partial dissent, noted that '[w]hether … marks can be registered does not affect the extent to which their owners may use them in commerce to identify goods. No speech is being restricted; no one is being punished'. *Iancu* v. *Brunetti*, 139 S. Ct. 2294, 2303 (2019).

observers read the *Register*. Rather, their exposure is to individual marks, used in connection with specific goods. In those contexts, registration could easily be seen as government approval. Tellingly, patent medicines got their bad name because the public understood a patent as the government's endorsement of a potion's efficacy;[16] even now, firms advertise their patents to suggest their goods are superior.[17] As Rebecca Tushnet has observed, registration of a mark can be understood similarly, as the government 'endorsing the boundaries of appropriate public discourse'.[18]

More disturbing, however, is the rationale underlying the unmitigated enthusiasm with which the First Amendment is currently enforced. In his opinion, Justice Alito boasted that the nation protects the freedom to express hated thoughts. Why? As Justice Kennedy explained in his concurring opinion, '[a]n initial reaction may prompt further reflection, leading to a more reasoned, more tolerant position'.[19] Or as he stated in *United States* v. *Alvarez*,[20] which invalidated a statute that criminalised false claims about receiving a military medal of honour,[21] '[t]he remedy for speech that is false is speech that is true. ... The response to the unreasoned is the rational; to the uninformed, the enlightened; to the straightout lie, the simple truth'.[22]

But is it the case that good speech drives out bad speech? Recent events suggest otherwise. In his campaign for president, Donald Trump made surprisingly effective use of demeaning sobriquets – 'Little Marco', 'Lyin' Ted', 'Crooked Hillary' – suggesting just how easily soundbites can substitute for critical thinking and how difficult it is to rebut their implications.[23] Not surprisingly, in his campaign for re-election, he has already tarred one of the candidates by repeatedly referring to her as 'Pocahontas'. As the epistemologist Jeremy Sherman notes, 'nounism' quickly identifies winners and losers and describes people in an absolutist

---

[16] Colorants Industry History, 'Patent medicines', ColorantsHistory.org, 2009, retrieved from www.colorantshistory.org/PatentMedicines.html; James Harvey Young, *The Toadstool Millionaires: A Social History of Patent Medicines in America before Federal Regulation* (Princeton, NJ: Princeton University Press, 1961).

[17] See, e.g., '2013 Mercedes-Benz E 350 TV commercial, *Patents*', iSpot.tv, retrieved from www.ispot.tv/ad/7dVm/2013-mercedes-benz-e-350-patents.

[18] Rebecca Tushnet, 'The First Amendment walks into a bar: Trademark registration and free Speech' (2016) 92 *Notre Dame Law Review* 381, 392. See also *Brunetti*, 139 S. Ct. at 2307 (2019) (Breyer J, dissenting in part, noting that 'when the Government registers a mark, it is necessarily "involv[ed] in promoting" that mark'. (internal citation omitted).

[19] *Tam*, 137 S. Ct. 1744, 1767 (2017).   [20] 567 US 709 (2012).   [21] 18 U.S.C. §704.

[22] *United States* v. *Alvarez*, 132 S. Ct. 2537, 2550 (2012) (cited as *Alvarez*).

[23] Rochelle Cooper Dreyfuss, 'Expressive genericity: Trademarks as language in the Pepsi generation' (1990) 65 *Notre Dame Law Review* 397, 415.

way that defies reason.[24] Furthermore, use by some can unleash others – witness the increasing use of Dixie and Nazi flags; the chants of 'our blood, our soil' and 'Jews will not replace us';[25] or the reference to the (mostly black) members of a professional football team as prison inmates.[26] Racism, nativism, and xenophobia and like forms of 'othering' have deep social roots[27] and there is little reason to think they can be driven out by the rational, the enlightened or the simple truth.

The seeming government endorsements of racial slurs can do a great deal of damage. Thus one of the most worrisome impacts of *Tam* is the possibility that trade mark holders will seek to reinstate marks previously cancelled on disparagement grounds.[28] For example, Redskins, the mark of a football team in Washington DC, was to be cancelled, but under the Supreme Court's ruling in *Tam*, its continued registration is ensured.[29] Yet, as one commentator noted, 'Washington's football team promotes, markets and profits from the use of a word that is not merely offensive – it is a dictionary-defined racial slur designed from the beginning to promote hatred and bigotry against Native Americans'.[30] *Redskins* is not a term that Native Americans now use to describe themselves. Nor has any

---

[24] Quoted in Colby Itkowitz, '"Little Marco," "Lyin' Ted," "Crooked Hillary": How Donald Trump makes name calling stick', *Washington Post*, 20 April 2016, retrieved from https://wapo.st/2lUftpU. See also Matthew Choi, 'Trump vows to revive "Pocahontas" attack against Warren', Politico, 15 August 2019, retrieved from https://politi.co/2n2QSQf.

[25] Joe Heim, 'Recounting a day of rage, hate, violence and death', *Washington Post*, 14 August 2017, retrieved from https://wapo.st/2kv6qLS.

[26] Ken Belson, 'Texans owner Bob McNair apologizes for "inmates" remark', *New York Times*, 27 October 2017, retrieved from www.nytimes.com/2017/10/27/sports/football/bob-mcnair-texans.html.

[27] Lajos Brons, 'Othering, an analysis' (2015) 6 *Transcience* 69. As Susy Frankel and Peter Drahos have noted, indigenous peoples, and particularly New Zealand Māori, have been able to pursue claims relating explicitly to cultures and identity more effectively when they also have land rights. In other words, the ownership of land gives rise to the possibility of legal claims to traditional knowledge and culture more generally in the same way that identity is connected to place, or as Aboriginal Australians would say 'country'. See Peter Drahos and Susy Frankel, 'Indigenous peoples' innovation and intellectual property: The issues' in Peter Drahos and Susy Frankel (eds.), *Indigenous Peoples Innovation: Intellectual Property Pathways to Development* (Canberra: ANU Press, 2012).

[28] Indeed, in *Iancu v. Brunetti*, 139 S. Ct. 2294 (2019), the Supreme Court of the United States similarly held that marks cannot be barred on the ground that they are immoral or scandalous. The case concerned the mark FUCT (which can be pronounced *fucked*) for clothing.

[29] *Pro-Football, Inc v. Blackhorse*, 709 F App'x 182, 183 (4th Cir, 2018) (remanding the decision to cancel the mark for reconsideration in light of *Matal v. Tam*).

[30] Chuck Schilken, 'Redskins are "thrilled" by Supreme Court decision striking down law banning offensive trademarks', *Los Angeles Times* (online), 19 June 2017, retrieved from https://lat.ms/2sI8tOx (quoting the 'Change the Mascot' campaign).

group chosen to reclaim it in the manner that Simon Tam has declared as his motive in using 'The Slants'. Thus the use of Redskins is different from use of The Slants, but under the Supreme Court's approach, the law is blind to the difference: *Tam* leaves no room for fine distinctions. We suggest that those nuances are important and can be recognised, as the next section shows occurs in the New Zealand system.

17.3 The New Zealand Approach

When New Zealand amended its trade mark legislation in 2002, the legislature decided to directly address whether to allow registration of trade marks that are offensive and particularly if they are offensive to Māori (the indigenous people of New Zealand). Prior measures, which had followed the tradition of English laws across countries that were former colonies of the UK, including New Zealand, Australia, Canada, and even the United States, included the possibility of the Commissioner raising an objection to an application to register a trade mark when it was contrary to morality.[31] However, none of these laws was explicit about the rights of indigenous peoples. In New Zealand, some registrations which were offensive to Māori were removed from the register under the morality provision, but this was occasional.[32]

In its review of existing legislation, the government found that the morality provision was ineffective to prevent offensive use Māori symbols. Accordingly, the question was presented whether Māori words, symbols, sounds and even smells ought to be registered at all.[33] The government concluded that non-offensive registration of such trade marks assisted recognition of Māori culture and potentially Māori economic development, and that the registration process could offer a greater opportunity for addressing cultural inappropriateness.[34] But the review also determined that the definition of 'offensive' should apply to

---

[31] Trade Marks Act 1953 (NZ) s. 16(1) (repealed by Trade Marks Act 2002 (NZ) s. 202 (1)). In some jurisdictions the morality provision can be invoked only by the commissioners (registrar or equivalent), and in others it can be invoked as a third-party objection.

[32] See the examples at, New Zealand Intellectual Property Office, 'Māori advisory committee and Māori trade marks' (Practice Guidelines), ch. 3.2 ('Identification of Maori imagery'), retrieved from https://bit.ly/2Frq1ol.

[33] Maori Trade Marks Focus Group, *Māori and Trade Marks: A Discussion Paper* (Wellington: Ministry of Commerce, 1997).

[34] Ibid., [19].

trade marks that are both culturally offensive and culturally inappropriate.[35]

The 2002 law placed responsibility on the organs of the state to ensure that a trade mark would not be registered if it is 'offensive to a significant section of the community, including Māori'.[36] This section is operationalised by the Māori Trade Mark Advisory Committee which provides advice to the Commissioner about whether the trade mark applied for 'is, or appears to be, derivative of a Māori sign, including text and imagery, is, or is likely to be, offensive to Māori'.[37] The system has since developed guidelines about trademarks with a Māori element.[38] Also importantly, those who sit on the Committee must have an understanding of 'te ao Māori (Māori worldview) and tikanga Māori (Māori protocol and culture)'.[39]

New Zealand's provision is somewhat unique in both its scope and the manner in which it operates in relation to Māori language and symbols. Internal committees in trade mark and patent offices are not unknown, but we are unaware of others that exist for the same purpose as the Māori Trade Mark Advisory Committee. Under the Trade Marks Act 2002 (NZ), the Committee is, as its name suggests, advisory to the Commissioner. It is not the decision maker, as the Commissioner has ultimate responsibility for all registrations and related decisions made under the Act. To date, however, the Commissioner has always followed the committee's advice. Furthermore, the Committee is not passive. In addition to giving specific advice on applications, it also gives general guideline advice. This general guidance has, for example, included advice on the word *Kiwi* and whether it is offensive. (That word was found not to be offensive and to be acceptable for general use.[40]) According to the guidelines, the Committee will examine a trade mark application for offensiveness in the following circumstances:[41]

- Anything that could be considered offensive or ambiguous in relation to the particular goods and services the trade mark represents.
- An atua or tupuna (ancestors) name/image.

---

[35] Ibid., [19]–[24]. See also discussion of the law reform process in Susy Frankel, *Intellectual Property in New Zealand*, 2nd ed. (Wellington: Lexis Nexis, 2011).
[36] Trade Marks Act 2002 (NZ) s. 17(1)(c). [37] Ibid., s. 178.
[38] See New Zealand Intellectual Property Office, 'Protecting intellectual property with a Maori cultural element: User guide', June 2016, retrieved from https://bit.ly/2k1XIEB.
[39] Trade Marks Act 2002 (NZ) s. 179(2).
[40] New Zealand Intellectual Property Office, 'Māori words and designs', retrieved from www.iponz.govt.nz/about-ip/maori-ip/words-designs.
[41] Ibid.

- An association with wahi tapu – a place sacred to Māori in the traditional, spiritual or religious, ritual or mythological sense.
- A word that may be regarded by whānau/hāpu/iwi as having mana (high importance).

Even with this system, an offensive mark might still be used. However, it will not be given registration, which, as discussed above, can be interpreted as a seal of approval. The burden is on the government (specifically the Commissioner of Trade Marks) not to register trade marks that are offensive to Māori. This is significant not only because it recognises the responsibility of the state in relation to the rights of the Māori, in particular under the Treaty of Waitangi,[42] but also because it makes the system much more effective than if the burden were placed only on others to oppose the mark. After all, there is a distinct possibility that potential opposers, such as indigenous minorities, may not enjoy equal access to justice.[43]

The unique strength of New Zealand's approach lies not only in the mechanism the state uses to fulfil its burden to protect consumers and the subjects of disparagement but also in the palpable difference in the standard used to determine what cannot be registered. As interpreted by the US Patent and Trademark Office (USPTO), the Lanham Act[44] required that the mark appear 'disparaging to a substantial composite of the referenced group'.[45] Because the terms *disparaging* and *substantial* are susceptible to multiple interpretations, there could easily be significant inter-examiner variation and a degree of uncertainty that is hard to square with free speech values. Further, this results in little ability to

---

[42] The Treaty of Waitangi (Te Tiriti o Waitangi) is a founding document of New Zealand. See Claudia Orange, *The Treaty of Waitangi* (Wellington: Bridget Williams Books, 1992). In essence, the treaty sets out the agreement between Māori and the Crown over the governance of New Zealand and is consequently of constitutional significance. The Treaty of Waitangi is in both Māori and English and both versions are official versions. They are not direct translations of each other. The Second Article, Ko te Tuarua, and in particular its reference to taonga, is of direct relevance to mātauranga Māori and its relationship with intellectual property: Waitangi Tribunal, *Ko Aotearoa Tēnei: A Report into Claims Concerning New Zealand Law and Policy Affecting Māori Culture and Identity* (Wellington: Legislation Direct, 2011), ch. 1 ('Taonga works and intellectual property') (cited as Waitangi Tribunal).
[43] See Expert Mechanism on the Rights of Indigenous Peoples, 'Access to justice in the promotion and protection of the rights of indigenous peoples,' UN GAOR, Human Right Council, 24th sess., Agenda Item 5, UN Doc A/HRC/24/50 (30 July 2013), retrieved from http://undocs.org/A/HRC/24/50.
[44] Trademark Act of 1946, Pub L No 79-489, 60 Stat. 427, as amended.
[45] *Tam*, 137 S. Ct. 1744, 1753–54 (2017). See also *Brunetti*, 139 S. Ct. at 2300–1 (2019) (noting inter-examiner variation in the application of the bars on scandalous and immoral matter).

distinguish between different trade marks, such the Redskins and The Slants or, more broadly, among racially disparaging marks and those that are disparaging for other reasons. In contrast, the New Zealand standard is quite precise. While the term *likely to offend* recognises the views of those offended and the statute names Māori as a potentially affected group, the other parts of the test recognise that offensiveness should not be measured too subjectively. In practice, the involvement of the Advisory Committee and the detailed information and referencing to Māori words, symbols and culture that are part of the procedures of the Intellectual Property Office mean that the process does not simply engage with an analysis of the affected group as a contestant against the applicant. Rather, the affected group's identity is always a consideration of the process. This creates a real understanding within the Intellectual Property Office of the affected group and makes the Office more than simply an arbiter between two competing viewpoints.

The statutory standard and the mechanism of application combine with two other significant aspects of the New Zealand system. First, because of its history with the Māori, there may be greater awareness of the disparagement problem in the New Zealand population than among people in the United States (although, of course, attitudes in neither country are uniform). Accordingly, even if it is possible to use, as opposed to register, offensive marks, many traders will not do so because there is a significant percentage of the New Zealand population (including both Māori and non-Māori) who would not be attracted to such products. The second aspect has been the recommendation of even further reforms to prevent culturally offensive use of trade indicia and names. In 2011 the Waitangi Tribunal[46] recommended that the Advisory Committee receive more extensive power and that its remit be expanded beyond trade mark law.[47] The tribunal also recommended that the Committee drop its advisory status and act as an equal decision maker with the Commissioner of trade marks over registration matters. This was in part in recognition of the partnership between Māori and the government of New Zealand (the Crown) as recognised under the Treaty of Waitangi.[48] To date, however, the government has not implemented this recommendation to further reform the system. Even so, the proposal

---

[46] The Waitangi Tribunal is a tribunal of inquiry established by statute to investigate claims of breach of promises made in the Treaty of Waitangi and to make recommendations to government regarding those claims: Treaty of Waitangi Tribunal Act 1975 (NZ) s. 5.
[47] Waitangi Tribunal, 99–100.
[48] Ibid., 99 stating, 'We recommend a commission be established. It should have multi-disciplinary expertise ... It would replace the Trade Marks Advisory Committee currently operating in the Intellectual Property Office'. The passage then elaborates on

has had the effect of drawing considerable attention to the issue and its appropriate implementation.[49]

17.4 Implications for the United States

Could the United States adopt a similar approach? We are hardly the first to urge that the absolutist view of the First Amendment should be reconsidered. As Rebecca Tushnet has suggested, valorising unfettered expression strips the government of authority to regulate in almost any area that touches on speech.[50] And in advocating for space for government regulation, Tim Wu has observed that speech has become increasingly 'weaponized' through, among other things, the propagation of 'fake news'.[51]

One person's fake news is, however, another's factual reportage. Accordingly, regulating speech must be approached gingerly. In this connection, New Zealand's practice is important in several ways. Most significantly, it is worth noting that government views can evolve. New Zealand changed its position on the impact of offensive words and symbols and acknowledged their role in distorting how the public perceives the targeted group and in influencing how the public treats those who are disparaged. The government accordingly shifted its practice and put a greater burden on the state to prevent these effects from occurring. Given the racial tensions of the Trump era,[52] there is an important lesson for the United States in New Zealand's decision to put more emphasis on cultural integrity.

Second, the factors New Zealand uses – distortion (a form of deception) and harm – support the constitutionality of bars on speech,[53] including, in trademark law, bans on deceptive and mis-descriptive marks, such as marks that characterise cultures in misleading ways.[54]

---

the adjudicative, facilitative and administrative functions of the recommended commission.

[49] Indeed, the several partial dissents in *Iancu v. Brunetti*, 139 S. Ct. 2294 (2019), the Supreme Court's decision invalidating bars on immoral and scandalous marks, suggest that the US approach is already changing. See especially ibid., 2308–2318 (Sotomayor J, dissenting in part).
[50] Tushnet, 'The First Amendment walks into a bar', 424.
[51] Tim Wu, 'Is the First Amendment obsolete?', Knight First Amendment Institute, Columbia University, September 2017, retrieved from https://knightcolumbia.org/content/tim-wu-first-amendment-obsolete.
[52] 'Most Americans say Trumps election has led to worse race relations in the US', Pew Research Center, 19 December 2017, retrieved from https://pewrsr.ch/2z4hxMT.
[53] *Alvarez*, 132 S. Ct. 2537, 2539 (2012); 15 U.S.C. §§ 1052 (a), (d), (e), (f).
[54] Lisa P Ramsey, 'A free speech right to trademark protection?' (2016) 106 *Trademark Reporter* 797, 835–6.

Third, the New Zealand approach emphasises the perspective of the targeted group: disparaging marks injure group members' sense of personhood and undermine their dignity. Since it is not the *speaker's* perception that counts in the assessment, the measure is not, as the US Supreme Court thought, discrimination based on the views expressed.[55] Furthermore, focussing on the deleterious impact of the mark on the target makes it evident why a law regulating disparaging marks is not a 'happy talk' clause (whatever that might mean). Fourth, New Zealand's tougher standards (for both choosing marks to examine and determining that they are unregistrable), coupled with the mechanism of referring questions to the Māori Trade Mark Advisory Committee, assuage concerns over the chilling effect of vagueness, a problem that lurked beneath both the Supreme Court's decision and that of the Court of Appeals whose decision was affirmed.[56]

To be sure, these provisions of New Zealand law cater mainly to a single minority population with a unique relationship to the government; the United States includes many more minority groups and there is nothing comparable to the Treaty of Waitangi to guarantee a positive commitment from the state to their unique interests. Accordingly, implementing this approach would not be easy.[57] However, mechanisms exist that could go a long way towards adopting the New Zealand system. For example, the USPTO regularly convenes expert panels on new questions of patent law.[58] It could adapt that practice in order to promulgate narrowly tailored and concrete guidance on marks that are disparaging. Moreover, the pre-grant opposition system used in connection with marks likely to cause dilution,[59] or the post-grant opposition procedure used in connection with patents,[60] could be adapted to enlist private parties in making the state aware of problematic marks. The adaptation would not be complete because, under existing law, the burden is placed on the opposer to demonstrate why the mark or patent should not be registered. To enjoy the same advantages experienced in New Zealand, the private burden should only be one of production; ultimate

---

[55] See Tushnet, 'The First Amendment walks into a bar', 419.
[56] *Tam*, 137 S. Ct. 1744, 1755–56 (2017).
[57] Note, however, that the same problem confronts the EU, which is composed of multiple groups. Nonetheless, it maintains a system that weeds out marks to promote other societal interests. See note 6.
[58] See, e.g., 'USPTO announces new Patent and Trademark Advisory Committee members' (Press Release 17-01), US Patent and Trademark Office, 9 January 2017, retrieved from https://bit.ly/2k1YX6; 'Public Advisory Committees', US Patent and Trademark Office, retrieved from www.uspto.gov/about-us/organizational-offices/public-advisory-committees.
[59] 15 U.S.C. § 1052(f). [60] 35 U.S.C. §§ 311, 321.

responsibility to refuse registration to disparaging marks should remain with the state.

As in all things IP-related, Sam Ricketson's insights are of enduring relevance. In a commentary he wrote on Australia's *Union Label* case,[61] he noted the importance of considering 'political context', of learning from 'the legislative models to be found in other common law jurisdictions', and of 'liberating' the regulatory power of government from an earlier generation's shackles.[62] Although that case concerned the power of government to *register* marks (in that case, workers' marks), his observations are equally relevant to questions that arise in a world in which speech – including hateful speech – has become ubiquitous. In our view, New Zealand provides a model that others, including the United States, could use to protect cultural identity from disparagement.

---

[61] *Attorney-General of New South Wales* v. *Brewery Employees Union of New South Wales* (1908) 6 CLR 469.

[62] Sam Ricketson, 'The *Union Label* case: An early Australian IP story' in Andrew T Kenyon, Megan Richardson and Sam Ricketson (eds.), *Landmarks in Australian Intellectual Property Law* (Cambridge: Cambridge University Press, 2009), pp. 15, 34–5.

18 Intellectual Property Law and Empirical Research

Emily Hudson and Andrew T Kenyon

18.1 Introduction

Over the last few decades, intellectual property (IP) law scholarship has taken an empirical turn, a turn that has led to a significant change in the methodologies used by academic researchers and hence the range of work being produced in the IP field. This empirical analysis has taken numerous forms. Some scholars have reconsidered traditional doctrinal work by undertaking a systematic examination of case law,[1] while others have used data from IP registers and other sources to understand trends in registration, use and enforcement.[2] The decision making of creators, consumers and other IP stakeholders has been interrogated through interviews and surveys.[3] There have even been efforts to test various IP principles through experiments.[4] The potential benefits of empirical work are clear. Use of such techniques can develop understandings of legal practices that academic work otherwise might lack and can reveal subtleties and ambiguities of law as it is practised. Done well, empirical work might help temper some of the doctrinaire positions that can be offered in IP law reform debates. It might also assist with scholarly reimagination of the subject of analysis. We have attempted previously to contribute to this trend, having undertaken extensive interview-based

---

[1] E.g., Kimberlee G Weatherall and Paul H Jensen, 'An empirical investigation into patent enforcement in Australian courts' (2005) 33 *Federal Law Review* 239; Barton Beebe, 'An empirical study of US copyright fair use opinions' (2008) 156 *University of Pennsylvania Law Review* 549.
[2] E.g., Barton Beebe and Jeanne C Fromer, 'Are we running out of trademarks? An empirical study of trademark depletion and congestion' (2018) 131 *Harvard Law Review* 945.
[3] E.g., Marta Iljadica, *Copyright beyond Law: Regulating Creativity in the Graffiti Subculture* (Oxford: Hart, 2016).
[4] E.g., Michael S Humphreys, Kimberley A McFarlane, Jennifer S Burt, Sarah J Kelly, Kimberlee G Weatherall and Robert G Burrell, 'How important is the name in predicting false recognition for lookalike brands?' (2017) 23 *Psychology, Public Policy, and Law* 381.

work as part of our own research into copyright and other laws.[5] The empirical turn in IP research in some ways builds on the pioneering work of Sam Ricketson, whose archival research added greatly to the scholarship's historical sensitivity. Through such work, archives can help illuminate questions of IP law just as, for example, interviews or court files can do.

Various factors have driven the increased use of empirical methods in IP research. Many of these are not specific to IP. They include the number of law and economics graduates entering the US academy and wishing to apply insights from that discipline to their legal analysis; the number of legal academics with degrees in disciplines other than law; the growth in industry driven or funded research projects; pressures for university research to have external 'impact'; and apparent government interest in evidence-based legislative reform. More generally, longstanding scholarly interest in how law in action compares with the law in books has moved into IP law. Academics in the field have long been aware of the limits of doctrinal work and the possible disjuncture between the understandings of IP experts and non-experts.[6] But more recently this has resulted in efforts to find more methodologically sophisticated ways of understanding that difference than anecdotal and impressionistic reflections on law's life beyond doctrine.

Our aim in this chapter, as researchers with experience in some empirical approaches, is to turn a critical eye towards empirically informed research. We start from the premise that empirical work provides its own justification, that it has the capacity to reveal matters that go beyond those answered by a solely black letter analysis. Indeed, the meaning of legal language, including differences in the interpretations of similar terms in different jurisdictions, may become clear only through empirical research.[7] But just as scholars have critiqued the role of doctrinal analysis in legal scholarship and have asked whether such analysis suffers from

---

[5] See, e.g., Emily Hudson and Andrew T Kenyon, 'Digital access: The impact of copyright on digitisation practices in Australian museums, galleries, libraries and archives' (2007) 30 *University of New South Wales Law Journal* 12; Andrew T Kenyon and Robin Wright, 'Whose conflict? Copyright, creators and cultural institutions' (2010) 33 *University of New South Wales Law Journal* 286; Emily Hudson, 'Implementing fair use in copyright law: Lessons from Australia' (2013) 25 *Intellectual Property Journal* 201. See also Andrew T Kenyon, *Defamation: Comparative Law and Practice* (London: UCL Press, 2006), appendix, for an example of relative transparency about the approach taken in empirically informed research involving court files and interviews as well as a discussion of wider issues that arise in this style of social research.

[6] E.g., Jessica Litman, 'Copyright as myth' (1991) 53 *University of Pittsburgh Law Review* 235.

[7] E.g., Kenyon, *Defamation*.

'legal centralism',[8] empirical work should also be examined to consider the robustness of its techniques and what insights the research provides. As relatively late starters in the use of empirical methodologies, can IP scholars learn from the challenges faced by other disciplines? Many will have heard of the so-called replicability crisis in medicine and psychology, in which the results of experiments cannot be consistently repeated in later studies.[9] But this is just one of the concerns about the reliability and validity of research in those fields.[10] In this chapter, we start in Section 18.2 by identifying some framing questions that IP scholars may wish to ask when conducting empirical research. We then consider problems that have been observed in empirical analysis of IP law in Section 18.3, and examine some lessons from other disciplines in Section 18.4. It is not our intention to provide solutions to all the issues we canvas. The more interesting issues may well not be 'solvable' in any simple sense; rather, they are prompts to conducting, understanding and using empirical research more carefully.

18.2 Questions about Empirical Research

We start by setting out three inter-related questions researchers might ask when conducting empirically informed projects.

The first is what makes for a good empirical study, in terms of being valuable due to its methodology, sample choice and size, execution, reporting and so forth. Based on these matters, which studies might be assessed as containing a powerful set of data that make a real contribution to understandings in the field?

The second question relates to the limits of empirical research, for instance whether the work is seeking to address imponderable or immeasurable questions, or whether the researchers have realistically estimated the time and resources needed to conduct their studies. In relation to this aspect, one might think of Sir Robin Jacob's contribution to a collection edited by fellow authors in this volume, Rochelle Cooper Dreyfuss and Jane Ginsburg.[11] Part of Jacob's chapter discussed the

---

[8] Robert Ellickson, *Order without Law: How Neighbors Settle Disputes* (Cambridge: Harvard University Press, 1991).
[9] E.g., Open Science Collaboration, 'Estimating the reproducibility of psychological science' (2015) 349(6251) *Science* aac4716.
[10] See generally John P A Ioannidis, 'Why science is not necessarily self-correcting' (2012) 7 *Perspectives on Psychological Science* 645.
[11] Sir Robin Jacob, 'Parody and IP claims: A defence? – A right to parody?' in Rochelle Cooper Dreyfuss and Jane C Ginsburg (eds.), *Intellectual Property at the Edge: The Contested Contours of IP* (Cambridge: Cambridge University Press, 2014).

public consultation run by the UK government following the Hargreaves Review, and in particular its recommendation that the UK introduce a parody exception into the Copyright, Designs and Patents Act 1988.[12] In his characteristic no-holds-barred language, Jacob left readers in no doubt as to what he really thought:

> Hargreaves said decisions on IP policy should be 'evidence based'. I do not know what he had in mind as to what constitutes 'evidence'. I do not suppose the UK Government knows either but it says it agrees. I rather think 'evidence' is, and can only be, either material put forward by various lobbying groups, or so-called 'economic' evidence based on tenuous or speculative data. The Consultation has four and a half pages on the subject. It consists mainly of statements of the blindingly obvious or questions which cannot possibly be answered either at all or quantitatively.[13]

Jacob gave a number of examples to support his complaints. For instance, he criticised the call for evidence on whether a parody exception might lead to 'lost sales due to confusion between a parody and an original work'. He found this a 'rather ridiculous' question, first because a parody that is liable to be mistaken for the original is a failed parody, and second because works that might be deceptive already generate a remedy in passing off.[14] He wrote: '[n]o one suggests that a parody which deceives should be allowed. You do not have to consult about such a self-evident matter.'[15] In contrast, other questions were 'obviously unanswerable' or 'not usefully answerable', such as '[d]o you agree that a parody exception could create new opportunities for economic growth' and '[w]hat is the value of the market for parody works in the UK and globally?'[16] He was of the view that no reasonable person could expect 'concrete reliable answers' to be given to such questions.[17] Jacob's observations reflect a broader issue for IP law: that many justifications based on incentives and economic free riding sound like they are empirical and can be measured, but that (1) it can be very difficult, if not impossible, to quantify the effects of IP on stakeholder behaviour and (2) care must be taken so that empirical evidence is not used in a way that masks the existence of underlying normative or policy goals.[18] As one of

---

[12] Ian Hargreaves, 'Digital opportunity: A review of intellectual property and growth' (independent report), May 2011; 'The government response to the Hargreaves review of intellectual property and growth' (Newport, UK: Intellectual Property Office, August 2011).
[13] Jacob, 'Parody and IP claims', 433.   [14] Ibid., 433–4.   [15] Ibid., 434.   [16] Ibid.
[17] Ibid., 435.
[18] E.g., Emily Hudson, 'The *Georgia State* litigation: Literal copying in education' (2019) 82 *Modern Law Review* 508.

us has previously commented, all empirical methods 'can be used without appropriate awareness of their presuppositions and weaknesses':[19]

For example, the apparently objective statistics arrived at in some quantitative research can be questioned in various ways, such as the initial choice of categories and the allocation of material to them. Interpreting quantitative material can be seen to involve 'measurement by fiat'; that is, explaining correlations between variables may be based on researchers' values more than on empirical data.[20]

The questions pursued and categories chosen in designing and interpreting such projects 'are not value-free' and empirical research 'cannot escape questions that flow from its own interpretive power'.[21] Concerns sometimes raised about the role of interpretation in qualitative research can also be relevant to quantitative approaches. We return to some aspects of this issue in Section 18.3.

Third, one might ask what wider conclusions or lessons can reasonably be drawn from the research. Given its resource intensiveness, empirical research is often focussed narrowly and can therefore be local, disjointed and incomplete. It is not that single case studies are without explanatory power, but they need to be conducted with skill and methodological awareness.[22]

For existing IP empirical projects, there have at times been issues of scalability, both across stakeholders and across the law. To illustrate, consider a research project examining authorship in the theatre community.[23] Given the target cohort, to what extent can the results of this study inform our legal conception of authorship? Imagine there are other studies of authorship in other communities, such as chefs and magicians.[24] Will there be synergy between a series of projects that take a different focus on the same basic questions? Let's say that our studies

---

[19] Kenyon, *Defamation*, 398.
[20] Ibid, internal notes removed. The measurement by fiat quote is from Clive Seale, *The Quality of Qualitative Research* (London: Sage, 1999), p. 120, drawing on Aaron V Cicourel, *Method and Measurement in Sociology* (New York: Free Press 1964).
[21] Ibid.
[22] E.g., Bent Flyvbjerg, *Rationality and Power: Democracy in Practice* (trans. Steven Sampson) (Chicago: University of Chicago Press 1998), a study of town planning in a single city across more than a decade, which as the title suggests offers wider lessons for the operation of democracy and underpins some of Flyvbjerg's later writing on social research.
[23] For a case to consider these issues, see *Brighton v. Jones* [2004] EWHC 1157 (Ch), [2004] EMLR 26.
[24] E.g., Christopher J Buccafusco, 'On the legal consequences of sauces: Should Thomas Keller's recipes be per se copyrightable' (2007) 24 *Cardozo Arts & Entertainment Law Journal* 1121; Jared R Sherlock, 'The effects of exposure on the ecology of the magic industry: Preserving magic in the absence of law' (2015) 6 *Cybaris: An Intellectual Property Law Review* 1.

suggest some disjunction between authorship as a legal concept and authorship as understood in different communities.[25] How do we draw lessons in a complex system in which our recommendations on one aspect can create significant upstream and downstream consequences. For instance, any recalibration of the legal test for authorship might have flow-on effects for ownership, exploitation, moral rights and so forth. Recommendations that might improve experiences and outcomes for one community might do the opposite for others.

In sum, as the IP community generates more empirically grounded research, there can be value in asking: Are the studies robust and well executed, do they reveal information or viewpoints previously not recognised, and do they produce work from which useful legal or scholarly lessons can be drawn?

18.3 Challenges for Empirical Research in IP Law

In some respects, the first challenge – what we will call robustness here, by way of shorthand – is easier to deal with, as IP scholars can draw from the existing literature on designing and executing empirical work, as informed by numerous disciplines (medicine, psychology, socio-legal studies, etc.). In deploying qualitative and quantitative methods, we are not, therefore, starting from scratch.[26] From our observation, one challenge is to ensure that IP academics acquire this knowledge. Certain methodologies, especially some qualitative ones, can give the appearance of being straightforward and ripe for dabbling. For instance, we have come across academic papers that include interview data without sufficient discussion of the methodology or the strength of conclusions that can be drawn from the work. There are also limits to what empirical research can attempt, given ethical matters, financial constraints, and the very nature of the question to be addressed. For instance, some empirical questions permit randomized controlled studies; others can only be carried out using observational methodologies.[27] But bearing in mind those factors, we can still think critically about the appropriateness of various empirical techniques and what a good empirically informed study might look like.

---

[25] E.g., Daniela Simone, *Copyright and Collective Authorship: Locating the Authors of Collaborative Work* (Cambridge: Cambridge University Press, 2019).
[26] For useful overviews aimed at social researchers, see Clive Seale (ed.), *Social Research Methods: A Reader* (London: Routledge 2004); Clive Seal (ed.), *Researching Society and Culture*, 3rd ed. (London: Sage 2012).
[27] E.g., Michael R Powers, *Acts of God and Man* (New York: Columbia University Press, 2012), p. 224.

Questions about limits and scalability seem to be more difficult, and our aim at this point is to elaborate on four challenges in empirical study of IP, rather than providing a list of solutions. First, as noted earlier, one problem for those undertaking empirical research is the difficulty in applying a comprehensive or sufficiently encompassing view, both at (1) the methodological level (i.e., will the research produce meaningful data that are reported and used with relative transparency and which could, in appropriate instances, be the subject of some form of meta-analysis) and (2) the IP system level (i.e., being aware of broader consequences of the conclusions on other aspects of the relevant law). Although not curing all such ills, there are steps that can help bolster the ability to analyse and integrate data from different studies, for instance by ensuring outputs contain adequate detail about a study's methodology and results, by applying appropriate transparency in explaining the results and by giving thought to existing studies when designing new projects.

A second problem relates to researchers analysing data using undisclosed or poorly articulated normative values. This is not peculiar to the empirical limb of IP research. Consider Jessica Litman's comments on what she describes as the politics of copyright scholarship.[28] She has described reading,

a lot of pieces for which it was absolutely clear that the author had settled on the answer before coming up with the question. I ran into economic models that had been designed to deliver particular results. In most of those pieces, there was more than one moment where an inconvenient discrepancy or undesirable inference threatened to lead somewhere interesting and unexpected, and, wouldn't you know it, those moments were glossed over or ignored.[29]

Litman identifies various reasons for these phenomena, including the pressure to publish (such that it is quicker and easier to write on topics for which the author is already confident in their conclusion) and the polarisation of copyright debates, which Litman speculates might make it more attractive to make grand statements rather than adopting more nuanced positions.

The influence of the researcher's normative framework can be seen in one experimental study in relation to attribution rights.[30] The authors, all

---

[28] Jessica Litman, 'The Politics of intellectual property' (2009) 27 *Cardozo Arts & Entertainment Law Journal* 313.
[29] Ibid., 317.
[30] Christopher Jon Sprigman, Christopher Buccafusco and Zachary Burns, 'What's a name worth: Experimental tests of the value of attribution in intellectual property' (2013) 83 *Boston University Law Review* 1389.

US-based, were interested in the difference in the scope of rights afforded in European law (more extensive) and US law (less extensive). They devised a series of experiments modelling photographic contests. These experiments suggested that creators value attribution rights very highly, which led the authors to conclude that it was best if US law did *not* grant such rights to those individuals. This conclusion rested on the view that creators have a tendency to greatly over-value their works – i.e., that for authors of creative works, the endowment effect is turbo-charged.[31] This led to the concern that in a world with strong attribution rights for authors, desirable transactions would not take place.

There are various comments that can be made about the design of these experiments, but our focus is on the leap from the quantitative data to the conclusion that broader attribution rights would not be a desirable addition to US law. The authors reached this conclusion on the basis that it would lead to greater efficiency. But should efficiency be the driving concern, and what does *efficiency* mean in this context? One might also question whether, in a world where creators are often beholden to publishers, commercial galleries, record companies and the like, and routinely do poorly on measures of annual income, these experimental conditions really translate to practice. Our aim here is not to suggest that the authors were wrong to choose efficiency as their normative standard, as it is clearly one prism through which to analyse such data. Rather, this example illustrates that the data did not inherently demand the conclusion reached by the authors, and that other authors may have made different recommendations about US law had they assessed the data via other yardsticks.

The variety of conclusions that might be drawn from this experiment shows a third challenge for empirical research in IP: the lack of a clear, agreed set of normative values that underpin the law. That is not surprising; it is an inevitable aspect of many areas of law. But it does create a challenge for researchers in clarifying their own position within the variety of rationales commonly referenced in many areas of IP and situating their work for readers – that is, a challenge of reflexivity.

The issue of values within IP law was raised by George Priest in his 1986 paper on what economists can tell lawyers about intellectual property.[32] His point was that while some areas of law may have relatively clear goals – for instance, that in criminal law, crime should be reduced

---

[31] See also, Christopher Buccafusco and Christopher Jon Sprigman, 'The creativity effect' (2011) 78 *University of Chicago Law Review* 31.
[32] George Priest, 'What economists can tell lawyers about intellectual property' (1986) 8 *Research in Law and Economics* 19.

rather than increased – no such clarity exists in intellectual property law. To illustrate, let us return to parody, a topic mentioned earlier in this chapter. It has been said that copyright law should provide accommodations for parody on the basis that (1) parody is socially desirable due to its cultural and artistic contributions; (2) as an act of speech, parody implicates the expressive freedom of the parodist but (3) we cannot leave parody to voluntary licensing, because the subversive and at times critical nature of the genre leaves such negotiations susceptible to holdout by copyright owners.[33] In many countries, the answer has been found in unremunerated exceptions.[34] But precisely what normative vision is being furthered? Without wishing to be too cynical, one might question whether human experience has *really* been improved by the proliferation of parody videos on YouTube or song lyrics that read as simply misogynistic.[35] Even for parody – in our view, one of the least controversial targets of free exceptions in copyright law – it cannot be said that *all* or even *most* parodies are socially desirable or that there are not opportunity costs from encouraging authors to engage in parody – for instance, due to creative labour being directed towards predictable and banal send-ups rather than more innovative work.

Given disagreement about the policy considerations that should underpin IP law, researchers need to consider how their work fits within the prevailing normative environment. Does the research focus on a matter for which there is relatively general consensus on policy goals (e.g., that unused marks on the trade mark register are undesirable)[36] or relate to a matter where there is contingent agreement on policy but questions about the law's impact or consequences (e.g., that mechanisms are needed to deal with orphaned works in copyright law)[37] or pertain to a question with irreconcilable policy positions (e.g., that patent law should provide stronger protections for inventions that deal with 'wicked'

---

[33] E.g., Ronan Deazley, 'Copyright and parody: Taking backward the gowers review?' (2010) 73 *Modern Law Review* 785

[34] E.g., Copyright, Designs and Patents Act 1988, s. 30A (fair dealing exception for caricature, parody and pastiche); US Copyright Act of 1976, s. 107 (fair use).

[35] An obvious example in terms of copyright law, is the reworked 'Pretty Woman' by 2 Live Crew, the so-called parody the subject of *Campbell* v. *Acuff-Rose Music, Inc*, 510 US 569 (1994). Its lyrics included: 'Big hairy woman you need to shave that stuff / Big hairy woman you know I bet it's tough / Big hairy woman all that hair it ain't legit / 'Cause you look like "Cousin It"'. The Supreme Court did not actually conclude that the song was a parody protected by fair use but remanded the case for rehearing consistent with its opinion.

[36] E.g., Georg von Graevenitz, Richard Ashmead and Christine Greenhalgh, *Cluttering and Non-use of Trade Marks in Europe* (Newport, UK: Intellectual Property Office, 2015).

[37] E.g., United States Copyright Office, *Orphan Works and Mass Digitization: A Report of the Register of Copyrights* (Washington, DC: US Copyright Office, June 2015).

problems such as climate change and antimicrobial resistance; or that such inventions ought not to be protected at all)?[38] At the very least, clarity is needed about the role of normative dimensions, including the researchers' backgrounds and views, and the framing questions for study. None of that is to suggest empirically informed research should be aimed only at questions of reform. It is equally possible to imagine research that changes academic understanding of the issues being considered without a policy position flowing from the research.

The fourth and final challenge relates to the use of empirical evidence in IP litigation. Some of these challenges correspond with issues that arise for empirical work in scholarly outputs, commissioned reports and so forth, going to matters of robustness and relevance. One issue already mentioned is whether some IP concepts are not as empirical as they first appear. Consider the debate about the use of survey evidence in trademark cases. It may seem that, so long as it is methodologically sound, this sort of evidence is probative and should be admissible to help demonstrate consumer knowledge or confusion. But courts have been reluctant to allow such evidence,[39] a position for which there is scholarly support.[40] There are a number of reasons for this stance, but one is that trade mark law's hypothetical consumer is a legal construct and is imbued with much normative content.[41] Indeed, it has been said that given the multi-faceted goals of trademark law, which include pro-competition aspects focussing on the needs of other traders, care must be taken in how the hypothetical consumer is deployed.[42]

Other issues are more peculiar to litigation and include whether judges have the training to understand and weigh empirical evidence and whether certain questions pertain to such far-reaching policy matters and/or require such extensive evidence that it is not realistic or desirable for those matters to be decided in court proceedings. An illustration can

---

[38] E.g., Peter Drahos, 'Six minutes to midnight – Can intellectual property save the world?' in Kathy Bowrey, Michael Handler and Dianne Nicol (eds.), *Emerging Issues in Intellectual Property* (South Melbourne: Oxford University Press, 2011).

[39] E.g., *Arnotts Ltd* v. *Trade Practices Commission* [1990] FCA 473; *Interflora Inc* v. *Marks & Spencer Plc* [2012] EWCA Civ 1501.

[40] Especially Robert Burrell and Kimberlee Weatherall, 'Towards a new relationship between trade mark law and psychology' (2018) 71 *Current Legal Problems* 87.

[41] E.g., Graeme Dinwoodie and Dev Gangjee, 'The image of the consumer in European trade mark law' in Dorota Leczykiewicz and Stephen Weatherill (eds.), *The Image(s) of the Consumer in EU Law: Legislation, Free Movement and Competition* (Oxford: Hart, 2015). This is not dissimilar to the ordinary recipient of a publication in defamation law, where it is well accepted that the way in which law deals with questions of defamatory meaning is highly artificial: e.g., Kenyon, *Defamation*.

[42] Burrell and Weatherall, 'Towards a new relationship between trade mark law and psychology'.

be found in the recent challenge to the legality of UK regulations implementing standardised packaging for tobacco products. That litigation involved the production of an enormous quantity of expert evidence and highlights the risk of judges being overwhelmed by the volume and content of the evidence, especially where litigants have almost unlimited resources to spend on expert reports. In the trial judgment, Green J even discussed the limits of judicial decision making and devised a list of measures that might help courts cope with the sort of complex, technical evidence that characterized much of the material before him.[43] This process included the early mutual engagement of experts, identification of (material) areas in dispute, and so forth. Green J stated:

> In the present case, no process … was conducted and I was left to read and absorb with scant assistance a vast amount of material on a wide range of expert issues including qualitative evidence of a psychological and medical nature; quantitative regression analyses; methodological critiques; economic commentary and opinion evidence on the mechanics of downtrading and price competition in the tobacco market; opinion evidence on the purpose and economics of trade marks; and expert evidence on the valuation of the Claimants' property rights, etc. Having read it in detail I came to the conclusion that much of it was immaterial to the true issues in dispute in the case.[44]

In the Court of Appeal, the process suggested by Green J was criticized on the basis that it sought to 'apply to judicial review … the kind of procedure that would be appropriate for the resolution of expert disputes in the context of commercial litigation.'[45] On the other hand, it seems that the Court of Appeal also questioned the relevance of much of the evidence before the trial judge, describing the resulting 1,000 paragraph judgment as a *'tour de force'* but 'much longer than was necessary or desirable.'[46] Although an extreme example and involving judicial review rather than private litigation, this case demonstrates many of the challenges for the use of empirical work in litigation.

18.4 Other Lessons

We conclude by mentioning some of the empirical challenges recognised in other disciplines, as these might provide lessons and insights for the IP

---

[43] *British American Tobacco (UK) Ltd* v. *Secretary of State for Health* [2016] EWHC 1169 (Admin), at paras. 633–648.
[44] Ibid., at para. 646
[45] *British American Tobacco UK Ltd* v. *Secretary of State for Health* [2016] EWCA Civ 1182, at para. 252.
[46] Ibid., at para. 2. The Court of Appeal also supplied citations for the trial judgment, 'for those with the stamina' to read it.

community. We start with the replicability crisis, mentioned in the introduction, which has been explained on the basis that certain research is far more likely to be funded and published, such as studies that break new ground or whose results are positive or 'interesting'.[47] Applying this to replication experiments, not only are such projects less likely to be conducted but, if conducted, are less likely to be published, especially if they yield null results.[48] Publication bias – defined as 'the tendency on the parts of investigators, reviewers, and editors to submit or accept manuscripts for publication based on the direction or strength of the study findings'[49] – has been described as 'an 800-lb gorilla in psychology's living room',[50] resulting in certain theories being 'virtually unkillable' because the absence of 'a true process of replication' makes them difficult to falsify.[51] Importantly, issues with publication bias result in studies not only not being submitted for publication (the 'file drawer' problem) but never being written up in the first place.[52]

Issues with publication bias are not unique to the social sciences, with medicine also facing claims about publication bias and the active suppression of results. Ben Goldacre has written extensively about such problems in the context of the pharmaceutical industry, identifying a litany of problems in the way that drug trials are constructed, conducted and reported, including that great swathes of data never see the light of day.[53] Importantly, studies that are never publicly disseminated tend to be those which do not show any benefit from a new drug or protocol, and Goldacre argues that this is not merely about publication bias but a system that allows data to be massaged and cherry-picked, thus giving the impression to doctors, scientists, patients, etc., that new drugs are more effective and less prone to side effects than is in fact the case. For instance, Goldacre notes that it is common for sponsors of drug trials to retain the right to terminate the trial at any stage, for any reason, and to decide whether trial results will be published.

---

[47] E.g., Powers, *Acts of God and Man*, 225.
[48] E.g., Christopher J Ferguson and Moritz Heene, 'A vast graveyard of undead theories: Publication bias and psychological science's aversion to the null' (2012) 7 *Perspectives on Psychological Science* 555
[49] Kay Dickersin, 'The existence of publication bias and risk factors for its occurrence' (1990) 263(10) *JAMA* 1385.
[50] Ferguson and Heene, 'A vast graveyard of undead theories', 556.   [51] Ibid., 559.
[52] Annie Franco, Neil Malhotra and Gabor Simonovits, 'Publication bias in the social sciences: Unlocking the file drawer' (2014) 345(6203) *Science* 1502.
[53] Ben Goldacre, *Bad Pharma: How Medicine Is Broken, and How We Can Fix It* (London: Fourth Estate, 2013), ch. 1.

In addition to withholding data, Goldacre also discusses issues in trial design and how decisions about how a study is conducted can increase the likelihood of – or be manipulated to encourage – positive results.[54] For instance, many studies use young, healthy participants who are more likely to respond positively to a drug and who do not necessarily share the characteristics of patients likely to be prescribed the medication. Furthermore, the take-home message from a study will be influenced by what outcomes the researchers choose to measure and how they interpret results. Goldacre uses the example of a study that shows a 10 per cent improvement in symptoms. If that still leaves patients profoundly disabled, it is open to question whether that arbitrary figure really represents 'success'.[55]

IP scholars can learn from these experiences in various ways. For instance, we might consider whether solutions identified for other disciplines might help improve the quality of empirical work in IP law, such as maintaining a register of empirical studies or allowing studies to be peer reviewed early, in relation to their methodology, with a commitment to publish irrespective of the results. But to our minds the broader lesson is the need to be aware of the weaknesses and fallibilities of empirical analysis. At their worst these include such things as the suppression and manipulation of results and poor study design. But also needing recognition are the much milder, and we would suggest, more common problems, such as the relative lack of transparency in a project's published version around how the study was developed, conducted and analysed, or the criticism of empirical work that is said to merely confirm 'common sense' rather than yielding surprising results. In the introduction we said that this chapter was written on the basis that empirical work provides its own self-justification, but that statement needs some qualification. While robust, well-conducted studies may provide insights that improve the quality of IP policy and decision making and may develop new insights or viewpoints on long-standing academic debates, weak studies may yield results that are of more limited value, and even weaker studies produce results that are positively harmful. It is therefore crucial that we are not complacent about empirical analysis but are open to rigorous questioning, both individually and collectively, about our practices.

---

[54] Ibid., ch. 4. [55] Ibid., 197–8.

Part IV

Across Professions

19 Intellectual Property Scholars and University Intellectual Property Policies

Ann Monotti[*]

19.1 Setting the Scene

Intellectual property (IP) scholars have a multi-faceted relationship with their university. They contribute in the daily performance of employment duties that include teaching, research and engagement. They publish scholarly work, apply for research grants, teach across a range of areas including IP, mentor junior colleagues and train the next wave of IP scholars through higher degree supervisions. While central to their employment contracts, these aspects of the employee–employer relationship are unremarkable as they mirror the roles performed by all academic scholars in their own subject disciplines.

However, a considerable body of IP scholarship enhances understanding of many IP issues that universities face and explores solutions that might benefit all affected parties. The scholarship traverses a range of issues, including critiques of the balance of rights in IP created within universities, the role of universities in protecting and commercially exploiting IP, evaluation of attempts to preserve rights in scholarly publications for open access availability, and the legal principles that should apply to IP created in employment.[1] IP scholars have tended to dominate the published scholarship that focusses on ownership and exploitation of IP rights as opposed to issues that concern the employment contract. Employment law scholarship dominates in areas such as enforceability of employment contracts, mobility of the workforce and trade secrecy, but

---

[*] Sam Ricketson is a giant and gentleman among international IP scholars. He inspired my interest in IP law and in academia when I returned to study an LLM at the University of Melbourne. Our paths crossed a year or so later when we both joined the Law Faculty at Monash University, he as a professor, me as a tutor. From that time on and throughout my academic career, Sam has provided an outstanding role model for aspiring law professors. His mentorship has been generous, kind and always encouraging. Thank you, Sam – I am honoured to be included as an author of a chapter in this Festschrift.

[1] Much of the earlier commentary appears in the bibliography of Ann Louise Monotti with Sam Ricketson, *Universities and Intellectual Property: Ownership and Exploitation* (Oxford: Oxford University Press, 2003).

the application to the university context remains relatively limited. Copyright issues commonly enter the domain of librarians who must often manage the university's compliance with access to third-party copyright subject matter and licensing arrangements.

Apart from these significant contributions to scholarship, the special expertise that IP scholars possess provides an invaluable resource for those charged with formulating university IP and associated policies. This became evident in the late twentieth and early twenty-first centuries when governments and public research funding organisations intensified their expectations that universities maximise any unrealised value from public investment in research. Universities found themselves under pressure to develop and review IP policies to align their terms with these external conditions and expectations.

What role did IP scholars perform in this policy development? The evidence from the three universities surveyed in this chapter – the University of Cambridge, Columbia University and Monash University in Australia – discloses individuals participating at national and institutional levels in the design of policies that aim to balance competing rights effectively and with minimal controversy. The early focus was to clarify ownership and division of rights in inventions as well as procedures for implementing government expectations for their licensing to the private sector for development into commercial products and processes. However, policies were also necessary to clarify rights and responsibilities in relation to all forms of IP created within universities by a range of actors. The US approach tended to produce independent policies for each form of IP whereas the general approach in Australia and the UK, for instance, was to combine all forms of IP in a single policy.

Over the years, the policy debates ebbed and morphed as external pressures intensified for universities to maximise revenue from all sources of IP. For instance, recent debates concern the management of rights in course materials, multimedia products and other copyright subject matter as universities become aware of the commercial potential of these products.

This chapter approaches the subject of IP scholars and universities in the following way. First, it considers the historical contributions of IP scholars to overarching IP policy design with reference to examples drawn from experience in the UK, Australia and the US, and focussed especially on the experience at the University of Cambridge, Columbia University and Monash University.

Second, while recognising the substantial contributions made by many IP scholars, it explores a small number of prominent examples that demonstrate involvement of IP scholars in their own institutions. One of these, a key actor at Monash and Melbourne universities, was Professor Sam Ricketson, in whose honour this book is dedicated.

Finally, the chapter considers some speculative explanations for what appears to be a diminished role for IP scholars in more recent IP management and policy reviews, focussing here on the experience at Monash University. While IP scholars continue to contribute actively to the policy and legal debates through scholarship and representation on expert groups formed to investigate specific topical issues for the academy, anecdotal evidence also suggests a decline in other institutions embracing the knowledge of IP scholars to add to significant changes in policy.

19.2 Involvement of IP Scholars at the National Level

The early 1990s was a period in which the need escalated for universities in receipt of public research funds to have policies for managing IP that arose from the funded research. However, demands for clear patent policies had been escalating for some time, especially following the enactment in the US of the Bayh-Dole Act of 1980, provisions which enabled universities for the first time to elect to pursue ownership and commercial exploitation of inventions arising from federally funded research.[2] Governments became increasingly aware of the social and economic value that might result from effective transfer of knowledge from universities to the marketplace. Pressure was rising for increased collaboration between the academy and industry on issues of national significance and benefit to the public. It was not long before *entrepreneurial* behaviour and *technology transfer* entered the vocabulary of universities and publicly funded research organisations. Commercial exploitation of IP generated within the university became an express goal of many universities, alongside the traditional roles of education, research and engagement.

While patent policies were relatively common at research-intensive universities long before the 1990s, they were inadequate to meet the demands and challenges of the late twentieth century. Expansion of collaborative research along with government exhortations for maximising the benefits of research raised new and difficult issues concerning ownership and management of IP generated in universities. There was wide recognition that universities are in some ways distinctive: that the laws that determine ownership and rights in IP that are created in

---

[2] Public Law No 96-517, 94 Stat. 3015-28.

employment 'do not apply with complete clarity to academic situations'[3] and should not apply without some adjustment. As the National Academies Policy Advisory Group (NAPAG) in the UK observed in 1995, critical questions required answers. 'Which ideas should be protected and when? Who should exploit them and how? Who should profit?'[4] The challenge for universities was to develop a flexible code of practices that would balance the rights of interested parties in ways that encouraged and rewarded innovation and minimised confrontation with creators. IP scholars had valuable knowledge to contribute to the formulation of policy, and some organisations recognised the wisdom in drawing upon that expertise to assist with their deliberations.

The Australian experience recounts the contributions of IP scholars to national policymaking bodies representing universities. Faced with the challenges of managing IP in the early 1990s, universities sought advice from the Australian Vice-Chancellors' Committee (AVCC)[5] on 'how to deal with questions of ownership of IP generated within the institution by staff, students, and under agreements with outside bodies, and under grants of sponsorship'.[6] The preamble to the AVCC's comprehensive 1993 discussion paper, 'Ownership of Intellectual Property in Universities', noted its purpose and intention as 'to provide background information, promote awareness of issues involved, suggest ways to deal with the issues and promote further discussion and consideration within institutions'.[7] Although the foreword to the discussion paper acknowledged the contributions of many academic and administrative staff, 'including academics with expertise in Intellectual Property Law',[8] it was not until the 1995 revision of the paper that specific acknowledgement of those scholars appeared, albeit merged between the two versions.[9] The degree

---

[3] National Academies Policy Advisory Group (NAPAG), *Intellectual Property and the Academic Community* (London: The Royal Society, 1995), p. 57 (app. II: 'Ownership and exploitation of intellectual property generated in academic institutions').

[4] Sir Michael Atiyah OM, 'Foreword' in National Academies Policy Advisory Group (NAPAG), *Intellectual Property and the Academic Community* (London: The Royal Society, 1995), p. i.

[5] Universities Australia replaced this peak body in May 2007.

[6] Australian Vice-Chancellors' Committee (AVCC), 'Ownership of intellectual property in universities', Discussion Paper (AVCC, 1993), 'Preamble', [1.1].

[7] Ibid.

[8] Robert H T Smith, 'Foreword' to Australian Vice-Chancellors' Committee (AVCC), 'Ownership of intellectual property in universities', Discussion Paper (AVVC, 1993).

[9] Australian Vice-Chancellors' Committee (AVCC), 'Ownership of intellectual property in universities', rev. ed., Discussion Paper (AVCC, 1995). The foreword, written by Don McNicol, states: 'The AVCC wishes to express its appreciation to the following people who assisted with the preparation of the original paper and its revision: Chair: Professor Raoul Mortley; contributors: D Dwyer, P Griffith, J McKeough, R McLean, A Monotti, K Puri, S Ricketson'.

of appreciation became yet more expansive when the AVCC published a later revision in 2002 as a policy and good practice guide.[10] Along with acknowledgements to those who assisted with the earlier paper, there is an express acknowledgement of 'the tremendous contribution of then Associate Professor Jill McKeough in shaping the earlier discussion paper into a policy and good practice guide'.[11] Demand for guidance was high from other quarters following the publication in 1993 of the AVCC discussion paper. The matters of ownership and control of IP were of concern for both higher education institutions and academic and general staff. The then National Tertiary Education Industry Union (NTEU) recognised the need for a coherent policy position. Its Intellectual Property Working Party whose members included Professors Andrew Stewart and Chris Arup, both employment law and IP law scholars, developed a policy statement, the Model Intellectual Property Policy and Explanatory Memorandum around 1993–1994.[12]

Another story comes from the UK. The NAPAG,[13] formed in 1992 to grapple with the multitude of complex issues that arise in an environment that encourages commercialisation of academic science, recognised that these issues are not confined to IP or other legal considerations. The Intellectual Property Working Party, made up of scientific, technological, medical, ethical, commercial and legal expertise, published a report in 1995 titled *Intellectual Property and the Academic Community*.[14] Professor William Cornish from the University of Cambridge chaired the working party and several other IP scholars, including Dr Noel Byrne, Professor Gerald Dworkin, and Dr Hector MacQueen,[15] contributed information for the report. Almost a decade later, Professor David Vaver from the University of Oxford contributed to the wider policies involving IP and universities through his membership on the UK Intellectual Property Advisory Committee and the Royal Society working group on intellectual property.[16]

---

[10] See AVCC, 'Ownership of intellectual property in universities: Policy and good practice guide' (AVCC, 2002).
[11] Ibid., 3.
[12] National Tertiary Education Industry Union (NTEU), 'Model intellectual property policy – Higher education' (circa 1994; on file with author).
[13] The NAPAG includes the British Academy, the Conference of Medical Royal Colleges, the British Academy of Engineering and the Royal Society.
[14] NAPAG, *Intellectual Property and the Academic Community* (London: Royal Society, 1995).
[15] Now professor, University of Edinburgh.
[16] The Royal Society, *Keeping Science Open: The Effects of Intellectual Property Policy on the Conduct of Science* (London: Royal Society, 2003).

Contributions of IP scholars in working groups and organisations that promote the interests of the creators are extensive in the US, where freedom of expression and freedom to innovate are themes that necessarily involve questions of ownership of IP created within universities. A recent example is the 2014 report of the American Association of University Professors (AAUP), 'Defending the Freedom to Innovate: Faculty Intellectual Property Rights after *Stanford* v. *Roche*', which was written by a committee that included among its members copyright and labour law scholar Professor Robert A. Gorman from the University of Pennsylvania.[17] A catalyst for the report was the increasing level of institutional claims to own patentable inventions arising from research. The link with the 2011 decision in *Stanford* v. *Roche*[18] was the Supreme Court's affirmation that the faculty inventor was the initial owner of his or her inventions and that the university employer had no mandate under federal law to claim ownership of those inventions. The university's entitlement to own an employee's invention consequently could arise only from the transfer of those rights from the inventor. The other catalyst was:

increasing institutional interest in declaring ownership of faculty intellectual property subject to copyright – most notably evident in demands that faculty members cede ownership of online courses and other instructional materials to their universities.[19]

Some key points in the AAUP report were the need to assert the rights of faculty members as 'independent scholars, teachers, and researchers' and to resist attempts by administrators to treat scholars as 'employees no different from those working in for-profit corporations that exist for the benefit of investors'.[20] The authors concluded that administrative efforts to control the IP in faculty scholarship demanded 'principle-based restoration of faculty leadership in setting policy in this increasingly important area of university activity'.[21] Critically, the call was not to discount any entitlement of universities in the fruits of the scholarship but to ensure policy development proceeds in consultation with those whose rights are affected.

---

[17] Cary R Nelson, Gerald Barnett, Robert A Gorman, Henry Reichman and Eileen Zurgbriggen, 'Defending the freedom to innovate: Faculty intellectual rights after *Stanford v Roche*' (2014) 100 *Academe* 38; see also, Robert A Gorman, 'Intellectual property: The rights of faculty as creators and users' (1998) 84 *Academe* 14.
[18] *Board of Trustees of the Leland Stanford Junior University* v. *Roche Molecular Systems, Inc.* 563 US 776 (2011).
[19] Nelson et al., 'Defending the freedom to innovate', 38.   [20] Ibid.   [21] Ibid.

19.3 Involvement of IP Scholars at the Institutional Level

In addition to contributions to overarching policymaking, IP scholars assisted in the development of institutional IP policies. The individual contributions have been significant. Universities commonly provide for an IP advisory committee within their policy framework. Alternatively, it is common where there are separate policies for patents and copyright for each to provide for a standing committee to address specified issues.[22]

However, the complex issues are not limited to IP and inevitably demand a multi-skilled approach. Universities that retain advisory IP committees in their present governance structures may prescribe among their membership classifications the representation of diverse academic disciplines. This may or may not result in appointment of an IP or any other legal scholar for that matter, but it ensures faculty representation of some kind. The Research and Innovation Committee at the University of Oxford has an IP Advisory Group sub-committee whose terms of reference give it responsibility to report and make recommendations on a wide-ranging scope of issues relating to IP policy and management. Until his retirement at the end of 2007, Professor David Vaver, the former director of the Oxford Intellectual Property Research Centre, chaired this advisory group. Its composition continued to include an IP scholar – namely Professor Graeme Dinwoodie – as the academic representative from the Social Sciences Division until his replacement following his return to the US with a representative from the faculty of management.

Often the IP scholar became involved in institutional committees due to a record of scholarship in this relatively specialised area. A pioneer in the UK, Professor William Cornish, published a seminal paper in 1992 in which he considered the issues facing universities and scholars.[23] In the absence of contractual arrangements that govern rights in IP, Professor Cornish considered the general terms in the employment contract that should apply to ownership of IP created in academia. Should those terms mirror the default principles that operate in employment? Do past conventions warrant consideration of special terms in this employment environment? Professor Cornish drew a distinction between rights that the university should own (those that depend on registration such as patents and designs), and those that exist without the need for any formal application whose ownership should vest in the creator. In broad terms, his rationale for this distinction was its 'advantage of according with the

---

[22] Copyright Standing Committee, 'Copyright policy', Columbia University, 2000, II F.
[23] W R Cornish, 'Rights in university inventions: The Herchel Smith Lecture for 1991' (1992) 14 1 *European Intellectual Property Review* 13.

current understandings which seem broadly to prevail within universities, government and industry in this country'.[24] An essential point in leaving informal rights with the staff member was the need 'to guard the freedom to publish and, if they wish it, to keep control over the exploitation of their concepts'.[25] The express protection for the freedom of academic staff to publish and control the exploitation of their concepts appears in regulation 4 of the University of Cambridge Ordinance on Intellectual Property Rights:

> University staff are entitled to decide that the results of any research undertaken by them in the course of their employment by the University shall be published or disseminated to other persons to use or disclose as they wish in accordance with normal academic practice.[26]

This provision is unusual among university IP policies as it recognises the power of the inventor to choose not to patent an invention (in the absence of an express restriction in a funding or other contract). Other universities may achieve the same goal implicitly by imposing reporting obligations only on inventors who seek to commercialise their inventions. The more common approach is to impose a reporting obligation on all inventors and leave its evaluation to the party who receives the report.

Among other appointments at the University of Cambridge, Professor Cornish chaired the Research Policy Committee of the General Board that developed and reviewed policy on ownership of IP rights (IPRs). The university adopted the model broadly in 2002 and it continues to this day.[27] The Annual Report of the University of Cambridge General Board to the Council in 2003–2004 acknowledged Professor Cornish's 'major contribution to the work of the Board, particularly in relation to the development of policies on Copyright and IPR'.[28]

The complexity of legal issues in this area and the role for both IP and employment law expertise to inform IP policy direction is not always appreciated or easy to demonstrate with practical examples. However, the review of the University of Cambridge Ordinance in 2005 provides such an example. A proposed amendment to regulation 4, quoted earlier, imposed certain obligations of confidentiality on staff who decide to commercialise the results of their research. The perspectives of an IP scholar and an employment law scholar when confronted with this issue

---

[24] Ibid., 16.   [25] Ibid., 18.
[26] University of Cambridge, Statutes and Ordinances, 2018, p. 1058, reg. 4.
[27] Ibid., 1057–60, regs. 5–15.
[28] University of Cambridge General Board to the Council, 'Annual report 2003–04' 5984 *Cambridge University Reporter*, 15 December 2004, [13.3], retrieved from www.admin.cam.ac.uk/reporter/2004-05/weekly/5984/2.html.

can differ and complement each other. An IP scholar may view this change as essential to protect against a premature disclosure of an invention prior to filing a patent application: a potentially catastrophic outcome for a significant invention. An employment law scholar may draw attention to the impact of the introduction of an obligation of confidence on an employee's pre-existing rights and to the enforceability of those changes to the employee's employment contract. Professor Simon Deakin, an employment law scholar at the University of Cambridge, entered the debate on the proposed amendment to regulation 4. When universities make changes to their IP policies, statutes and regulations, they need to be confident that the changes do not amount to a unilateral change to the employment contract that is unenforceable against its employees. Professor Deakin noted that although it is a common provision in the employment contract for university employees to agree to be bound by the statutes, regulations, ordinances and policies in force from time to time, opinions differ on the extent to which changes to IP policy can be made unilaterally. He drew attention to 'the legal uncertainty over the extent to which general rules concerning ownership by an employer of IPR created by employees may have been displaced by past practices in the University'.[29] In response, and following discussion with Professor Cornish, the council and general board removed this obligation and included instead the implications for the inventor of prior publication. They reasoned that there are practical incentives for an inventor who has agreed to seek protection to keep the material confidential.[30]

In Australia, IP scholars were also active in IP policy formulation and implementation at the institutional level – including chairing committees and drafting IP policies for consideration, reviewing draft documents, conducting informal discussions with legal officers and making appointments to working parties and standing intellectual property committees. The consultative process of IP policymaking at Monash University provides one example of welcoming the expertise of the IP scholar and, in particular, that of Professor Ricketson. The story is one of university-wide consultation on policy direction and begins in July 1992 when the then deputy vice-chancellor (research), Professor Robert Porter, convened a university colloquium on IP. In attendance was Professor Ricketson, who had joined the faculty of law in 1991 and was a member

---

[29] 'Third joint report of the council and the general board on the ownership of intellectual property rights (IPRs): Notice', 6008 *Cambridge University Reporter*, 25 July 2005, retrieved from www.admin.cam.ac.uk/reporter/2004-05/weekly/6008/3.html.
[30] Ibid.

of the then patents committee. He played a prominent role in the development of IP policy at this time, his contributions extending to preparation of an issues paper titled 'Intellectual Property Rights in the University Context'[31] to which he appended his Draft University Statute on Intellectual Property as a basis for further discussion. An important outcome of the colloquium was broad support for replacement of the then Patents Statute and Regulations with a more broadly based IP Statute and Regulations as well as replacement of the Patents Committee with an IP advisory committee to deal with all matters concerning IP.[32] The university Solicitor's Office prepared the Monash Intellectual Property Policy Statement in 1992.[33] Professor Porter circulated the statement widely across the university with a proposal 'to establish a working party to examine the responses and comments and to coordinate and superintend the development of University policy and legislation in this area'.[34] The university solicitor, Susan Bath, released the final legislation for comment on 13 April 1994. The university council passed the final legislation following its approval by academic board at its meeting of 8 June 1994. Both Professor Ricketson and I continued to be actively involved in IP policymaking through our lengthy membership of the successor to the Patents Committee, the Intellectual Property Committee (IPC), a committee of the academic board established under the Intellectual Property Statute 11.2.[35]

The experience at Columbia University in the US provides another positive example of a consultative approach to IP policymaking assisted by an IP scholar. A provostial faculty committee, co-chaired by Professors Jane Ginsburg (law) and Ira Katznelson (political science and history), was appointed to prepare a copyright policy. In its introduction to the University Senate in 2000, Professor Ginsburg commented on the benefits of the circulation of a draft policy for comment.

---

[31] Sam Ricketson, 'Intellectual property rights in the university context' (Issues Paper, Monash University, August 1992). See also his article that mapped out the legal and policy issues for all parties to consider: Sam Ricketson, 'Universities and their exploitation of intellectual property' (1996) 8(1) *Bond Law Review* Article 2.
[32] Notes of the university colloquium 'Intellectual Property – Towards a University Statute', held 24 July–3 August 1992.
[33] Karline Ziegler (a senior assistant solicitor) and consultant solicitor, Denise A Kerr.
[34] R Porter, Memorandum: Draft Monash University policy statement – Intellectual property (9 December 1992), 2.
[35] Monash University, Monash University Statute, s. 11.2 (Intellectual Property) ss. 4 & 7 and Intellectual Property Regulations pursuant to Statute 11.2 (1994), reg. 4, both passed in 1994.

Ginsburg said a month-long period of comment and discussion, conducted by e-mail and in numerous meetings, prompted the committee to clarify many points. She also mentioned one significant substantive change in the second draft: the committee abandoned its original requirement of more stringent disclosure requirements for works of software.[36]

This inclusiveness of all stakeholders in the policy-making process need not involve IP scholars: the ownership and exploitation of IP that academic scholars, students and visitors create raise multiple issues, only some of which necessitate the expert contributions of IP scholars and legal experts in general. Nevertheless, it seems self-evident that this expertise must be beneficial in designing policies for IP subject matter where matters of IP law are relevant. The provost acknowledged this in the minutes of a senate meeting and praised the outcomes as 'the most balanced copyright policy in the United States'.[37]

Anecdotal evidence, as well as my own experience at Monash University, suggests that a number of Australian IP scholars who were actively involved in IP policy development from the 1990s have not been involved in IP development in recent years. Some universities have moved away from a governance structure that dictates an IP advisory group or committee with a membership that includes representation from the academy. For instance, the IPC at Monash University was a standing committee of the academic board and established under the Intellectual Property Statute and Regulations.[38] Its meetings became intermittent, revived to consider a revision of the Intellectual Property Statute in 2011, and ceased to exist following extensive university-wide consultation and the eventual enactment of a new Monash University Statute in 2014. The IP regulation-making power now vests in the vice-chancellor. Part 5 of the Monash University (Vice-Chancellor) Regulations (Intellectual Property) replaces the earlier legislation and makes no provision for a standing IP policy advisory committee with a particular composition.[39] Nevertheless, the vice-chancellor may decide to convene a group of people or an individual with appropriate expertise to advise on matters of policy that arise from time to time and relate to IP. However, there is no obligation to do so and no obligation to consult with the academy.

---

[36] Tom Mathewson, 'University senate unanimously adopts new copyright policy in final meeting of the year' (5 May 2000) 25(22) *Columbia University Record* (New York).
[37] Columbia University Senate, 'Meeting of March 31, 2000', notes of senate discussion, retrieved from http://senate.columbia.edu/archives/plenary/99-00/mar99-00.html.
[38] See Monash University, Monash University Statute.
[39] Monash University, Monash University (Vice-Chancellor) Regulations, pt. 5.

19.4 Conclusion

This chapter considers instances where external bodies and universities have welcomed and valued the involvement of IP scholars in assisting with policy development on ownership and exploitation of university IP. There are examples of leading involvement of IP scholars in external collaborations formed to assist each individual university and staff and other creators within them to understand the issues and to offer options for achieving balanced policies for the ownership and exploitation of IP. The contributions at institutional level generally arise from membership of representative committees whose tasks concern IP policy advice and development. While the issues concern all faculty members, IP scholars are in a unique position, as both IP experts and members of the academy, to assist those with ultimate responsibility for policy to explore the myriad choices and to explain the legal consequences of each under IP laws. They can alert all parties to unreasonable claims and to the risks for friction between staff and employers that some policy options might pose in this area of complexity. However, as the reliance upon contributions from both IP and employment law scholars at the University of Cambridge demonstrated, good policy and outcomes benefit from drawing upon the rich expertise that exists within the academy. The US experience that provoked the AAUP 'Defending the Freedom to Innovate' report[40] also highlights that universities risk dissension and bad publicity among their faculty – and potential future faculty – if they fail to recognise the importance of a collegiate and representative process for development of IP policies that affect the rights of the creators. The authors of the AAUP report objected to administrators imposing policies as to ownership of IP without consultation with the creators and sought 'principle-based restoration of faculty leadership in setting policy in this increasingly important area of university activity'.[41]

This may provide a cautionary note for the recent actions at Monash University. The changes that remove the IPC as a standing committee of the academic board and vest leadership of IP policy development with the vice-chancellor followed a process of extensive consultation within the university.[42] Nevertheless, the detail of the policy itself and procedures for policy development were not the subject of this consultation. There is no assurance that an IP policy advisory committee, whenever

---

[40] See Nelson et al., 'Defending the freedom to innovate'.   [41] Ibid., 38.
[42] This is the case also at the University of Melbourne: see Vice-Chancellor Regulation, enacted by Council on 14 December 2015, commenced on 21 July 2016, Pt. 4, reg. 13 (Intellectual Property).

constituted, will include faculty representation. There are clear pragmatic justifications for the removal of a formal IP advisory group or committee and a decline in involvement of IP scholars on matters of law and policy. First, IP policy issues may arise spasmodically and are better dealt with on an ad hoc basis with a committee constituted with the appropriate expertise for the issue under consideration. Second, non-compliance with regulatory obligations for periodic meetings of an IP committee may threaten the enforceability of claims to IP.[43] It is simpler as an administrative matter to convene an appropriate advisory group when a policy issue arises for determination. However, experience suggests that it is unwise to implement major policy change without faculty involvement in setting policy that might adversely affect the existing rights and responsibilities of faculty members. Therefore, a university that relies upon an ad hoc process for constituting an IP policy advisory group or committee for advice is wise to document the broad composition of such a group or committee, to ensure inclusion of stakeholders when policy change may affect their existing IP rights and interests.

Significant contributions of IP scholars, only some of which appear in this chapter, richly adorn the history of IP policy development. The extent to which IP scholars continue to be active in this space remains unclear and it is impossible to express any conclusion of general application. Nevertheless, there is anecdotal evidence that a number of formerly active Australian IP scholars are no longer included in institutional IP policy development and management. Again, there are likely to be pragmatic explanations for this. It may reflect completion of the hard work in the early days of IP policy development. The issues that now arise in universities may no longer require this specialised scholarly expertise but instead require expertise that is relevant for practical implementation of policies. The emphasis upon protecting, managing and exploiting IP in accordance with an agreed policy demands a range of expertise oriented to transactional experience across a range of areas, only one of which is IP. Universities have their legal departments with expertise in licensing and other contractual matters, law firms and patent attorneys provide expert independent advice, and technology transfer or commercialisation units include expert staff to advise and manage the commercialisation process. IP scholars who sit on an IP advisory committee that deals with such matters may find they have little expertise to contribute. However,

---

[43] *University of Western Australia v. Gray (No 20)* (2008) 246 ALR 603, 678 [255]-[256].

policies do not remain stagnant, and there will always remain a critical role for IP scholars when universities propose changes to existing rights and responsibilities under IP law that affect creators. As the AAUP concluded in its 2014 report, it is important not to discount any entitlement of universities in the fruits of the scholarship but to ensure that a process of consultation with the academy and others with existing rights and responsibilities precedes substantive policy development.

20 'Measuring' an Academic Contribution

Mark Davison

> *The only wealth which you will keep forever is the wealth you have given away.*
> Marcus Aurelius
>
> *Count no man happy until the end is known.*
> Solon

20.1 Introduction

Universities, rightly, claim a place in the very centre of the process of the advancement of society. They do so via teaching and research and the nexus between those two activities.[1] While there is considerable evidence to support those claims, those generic claims cannot by themselves justify the various forms of extensive funding that are delivered to universities via government, students, alumni and some generous donors.

In order to continue to justify that funding, the contribution that academics make to society at large and to particular sectors of society concerned with their particular disciplines should be evaluated and assessed. The hard part is working out how to go about that process of evaluation and assessment. Business can be assessed by examining the financial bottom line and still is, although there is a justifiable societal concern with other business outcomes. Health can be assessed by considering increases in life expectancy and success in relation to various medical treatments. Evaluating the contribution of academics is a more complex process.

Those charged with overseeing the performance of universities or, perhaps more accurately in the twenty-first century, those who charge ever-increasing amounts to oversee the performance of universities,[2]

---
[1] See generally a speech to the National Press Club by Margaret Gardner, Chair, Universities Australia, 27 February, 2019, retrieved from https://bit.ly/2kgRhOe.
[2] Julie Hare, 'Uni vice-chancellors average salary package hits $890,000', *The Australian*, 5 August 2017, retrieved from https://bit.ly/2lQqJU9.

have understandably struggled with the challenge of assessing the performance of researchers. This challenge is particularly acute in the humanities and social sciences (HASS), where the optimal means of evaluating outcomes are not so clearly defined and the time frame for accurate evaluation is far wider than it might be in science, technology, engineering and mathematics (STEM) disciplines. For example, the first Chinese premier, Chou En Lai, is alleged to have said that it is 'too early to say' what is the impact of the French Revolution,[3] and the same could also be said of the writings of Aristotle and Plato.[4] It is difficult to imagine a similar time frame being required for assessing the efficacy of a new pharmaceutical drug. Fortunately, a very significant part of the value of Professor Ricketson's writing on intellectual property (IP) can be measured without having to wait many centuries, but the relevant time frame for doing so has probably been longer than the standard time frame for evaluating the efficacy of pharmaceuticals.

As a consequence of and in response to these difficulties, different measures have been put in place from time to time. Measurement of the research performance of legal academics has ranged from, at one end, almost no measurement beyond the point of acquiring tenure, to far more complex systems at the other end.

In Australia, to offer just one example, the government and hence universities have opted for complex systems. Measures have included purely quantitative ones, such as the number of publications in a given period of time. Books have counted as 'five points', articles as 'one point' and so on. Until recently, the Australian government handed out some research income to universities purely on that basis. Those quantitative measures have also included, from time to time, counting the amount of research money earned on the assumption that such research inputs were a useful proxy for outputs, since important outputs were thought to be difficult, if not impossible, without such significant inputs. It is still the case that Australian government research income is awarded on the basis of grant money earned. In other words, winning a grant is itself grounds for giving further research funding. Such an approach may be of considerable relevance in the context of the STEM disciplines, where access to laboratories and other expensive resources is a prerequisite for most

---

[3] Chas Freeman, 'Zhou's cryptic caution lost in translation', *Financial Times* (London), 10 June 2011.
[4] See, e.g., Catherine Nixey, *The Darkening Age: The Christian Destruction of the Classical World* (London: Macmillan, 2017) for a theory about attempts to effectively expurgate Greek philosophy from Western thought.

effective research. Its connection to some HASS disciplines, and law in particular, is more tenuous, although that has not deterred university management from continuing to focus on the issue, partly because of the funding system just described.

More recently, those searching for research excellence have attempted to identify high-quality publications by reference to the journal or the identity of the publisher of the work in question. Again, the thinking is that the quality of the journal or the quality of the publisher is a close proxy for the quality of the article, book chapter or book published by the journal or publisher in question. Given the disruption of the print industry by constant mergers and acquisitions and the digital revolution, this process is an increasingly difficult one to implement. For example, convincing university research departments that online legal services dealing comprehensively with significant areas of law by providing regular re-writing of material that synthesises new case law and legislation with the old is still a work in progress. Some law academics of very great ability have given up on contributing to such works because their understandable desire to keep their jobs outweighs their patience with universities' reluctance to embrace some of the new online realities.

The search for measuring quality has also been expressed in research excellence exercises such as the Excellence in Research for Australia (ERA) in Australia,[5] and the Research Assessment Exercise and its successor, the Research Excellence Framework, in Britain.[6] The Research Assessment Exercise predated and presumably informed the ERA. The former involved consideration of each relevant academic's top four publications in seven years, while the ERA involves consideration of all publications with an emphasis on the top 30 per cent of those publications, as nominated by universities.[7] All publications in the last six years are considered in that exercise although no significant amount of government money is awarded on the basis of the results. Universities have to be content with earning a ranking of their research that is relevant for reputational purposes.

In theory, the process might be a useful one, although in some ways it is an expanded and modified version of the system under which one is judged by one's own faculty members. As with all measurement

---

[5] See Australian Research Council, 'Excellence in research Australia', Australian Government, retrieved from www.arc.gov.au/excellence-research-australia.
[6] See 'About the REF', Research Excellence Framework, retrieved from www.ref.ac.uk/about.
[7] See Australian Research Council, 'Excellence in research Australia'.

processes, it has its drawbacks. For instance, the time frame in which the excellence of publications is measured is relatively immediate, at least in the context of HASS. In addition, while those who generously give their time to undertake the assessment process have both the skills to undertake it and the civic-minded willingness to do so, the sheer volume of publications involved and the time frame in which the publications are to be assessed substantially hinder the undertaking. While the details of the assessment process are not completely transparent, it is difficult to avoid the suggestion that both assessors and those responsible for choosing the top 30 per cent of publications necessarily revert to consideration of matters such as the titles of the journals or the names of the book publishers. All of that is further confused by different concepts of *excellence* as opposed to say *impact* of legal publications.

Finally, one might have regard to citations of works. Such an approach is certainly worthy of some attention although, again, with law, the system for measuring such citations is incomplete at best and possibly misleading at worst. Part of the reason for this inadequacy is that legal writing might be referred to in multiple fora of significance by multiple audiences. In addition the 'referencing' in question may well be referencing in the sense that legal practitioners and judges read it and rely on the principles contained in it without themselves writing publications with formal references to the published works. Alternatively, some practitioners or judges might give imprecise references that are not necessarily caught by automated citation searching. Nevertheless, the views contained have been adopted or at least seriously considered and have influenced the attitude and approach of those practitioners or judges.

The university administrators' dilemma about how to measure research performance in the academic discipline of law is dwarfed by the dilemma that academics face as a consequence of changes in approaches of those administrators. Administrators come and go more quickly than academics, with the consequent pressure on the former to deliver change in order to justify their current position and to increase their prospects of further advancement in due course. Those changes include bona fide but frequent attempts to measure the performance of academics by introducing new measures. While what gets measured usually gets attention, that general proposition is of limited use for an academic who has already written and published their material by reference to a pre-existing assessment regime different to that which might now be adopted with retrospective effect. To put it another way, the position of the goalposts is frequently changed without notice during the very act of academics kicking the ball.

20.2 The IP Treatise and Academia

Given all those circumstances surrounding the attempts to monitor legal academics and thereby influence the nature of their research efforts, it is even more remarkable that Sam Ricketson has written and published his treatises on the law of intellectual property (in Australia),[8] the 100-year history of the Berne Convention,[9] and the Paris Convention.[10]

Hindsight is always 20/20 and – as noted so frequently by the courts when considering inventiveness and what was obvious at a given prior point in time – not only completely useless but thoroughly misleading. Hindsight tells us that Ricketson's decisions to invest so much of his time and energy into writing his treatises were rational and obvious decisions and the outcomes for both himself and the multiple audiences that enjoy the fruits of his labour, equally predictable.

However, if different dates were chosen for considering the priorities that Ricketson may have adopted, a prospective consideration of the work involved in those treatises in the context of most, if not all of the measures referred to earlier, would suggest that perhaps they should never have been written. After all, the 2,778 pages of those 3 treatises, plus indexes, appendices, tables of treaties, legislation and cases, yielded a mere 15 points of publications from a quantitative perspective and a mere 3 books, and the last of those was not published until 2015. Under current Australian research funding guidelines, their monetary value to a university would amount to the princely sum of zero. Even allowing for inflation and economic growth, the sum remains the same.

For British Research Assessment Exercise purposes, they would have constituted only three publications – insufficient to meet the requirement of four in seven years. From an Australian ERA perspective, they would have constituted only three publications and for a discipline required to

---

[8] See Staniforth (Sam) Ricketson, *The Law of Intellectual Property: Copyright, Designs and Confidential Information* (Sydney: Lawbook Co, 1984).

[9] See Sam Ricketson, *The Berne Convention for the Protection of Literary and Artistic Works: 1886–1986* (London: Centre for Commercial Law Studies, Queen Mary College, Kluwer, 1987).

[10] See Sam Ricketson, *The Paris Convention for the Protection of Industrial Property: A Commentary* (Oxford: Oxford University Press, 2015). Other works that Ricketson has co-authored also most certainly qualify as very fine treatises, but this chapter focusses on his sole authored treatises. These include Ann Louise Monotti with Sam Ricketson, *Universities and Intellectual Property: Ownership and Exploitation* (Oxford: Oxford University Press, 2003); the sequel to the Berne Convention treatise, Sam Ricketson and Jane C Ginsburg, *International Copyright and Neighbouring Rights: The Berne Convention and Beyond*, 2nd ed. (Oxford: Oxford University Press, 2006); and Sam Ricketson and Christopher Creswell, *The Law of Intellectual Property: Copyright, Designs and Confidential Information*, 2nd rev. ed. (Sydney: Thomson Reuters, 2015).

identify its top 30 per cent of publications for any six-year period, providing a mere three publications over a period of about thirty-five years, would be sub-optimal. Even allowing for an unnecessarily excessive length of sixty pages per article, about fifty articles could have been produced and published in lieu of those works or, more realistically, at twenty-five to thirty pages per article or book chapter, a minimum of a hundred 'quality' pieces could have emerged and been published regularly throughout the given period of time at about three per year.[11]

In prospect, a well-counselled young academic in the late 1970s and early 1980s might well have been told prior to embarking on the projects that the proposed lengthy works, especially the first two which were published in 1984 and 1987 respectively, might well constitute some of the longest academic suicide notes in history. So it is most fortunate for the IP community, broadly defined, that performance development management processes, quantitative measures, pressure to win national competitive grants and other measures were not so formally entrenched in Australian universities at the time.

Ricketson has drawn an analogy between writing his treatises on the Berne and Paris Conventions with mountaineering. In his preface to his commentary on the Paris Convention he said about his Berne and Paris works, 'climb one mountain, move on to the next'.[12] Of course, the mountaineer's justification for climbing a mountain – namely, 'because it is there' – does not quite fit and should probably be replaced by the justification, 'because it is not yet there but it would be useful if it were and challenging to create it'. For example, the written history of the first 100 years of the Berne Convention was not 'there' or anywhere for that matter. It was written by Sam Ricketson. He not only climbed Mount Everest, he constructed it as he went from materials that had to be sourced and then carefully placed so as to permit the next foothold to be created.

To the extent that the mountaineering analogy is to be used, one should also be cognisant of the equipment available at the relevant time. The point is cogently made in the preface to the new edition of the work on the Berne Convention co-authored with Professor Jane Ginsburg.[13] Personal computers were still not ubiquitous when the research for the first edition was done. More importantly, the digitisation of hard copies of historical documents had not really begun in earnest, and the means of

---

[11] To be clear, Ricketson's output over and beyond that in the three treatises has been prodigious.
[12] Ricketson, *The Paris Convention for the Protection of Industrial Property*, xlix.
[13] See Ricketson and Ginsburg, *International Copyright and Neighbouring Rights*.

distributing those documents electronically either quickly or over significant distances were not yet available to researchers in the legal discipline. In turn, those technological limitations required physical attendance at places such as the World Intellectual Property Organization (WIPO) library in Geneva and the Max Planck Institute Library in Munich and 'long hours of tedious transcription'[14] because conservation concerns prevented photocopying of some original documents. To continue the mountaineering analogies, Everest was climbed without oxygen. Those technological limitations were even more relevant to the prior work on Australian IP law that was published in 1984 – namely Ricketson's *The Law of Intellectual Property: Copyright, Designs and Confidential Information*. There was no Austlii database[15] that would give instantaneous access to relevant Australian cases and legislation.

Of course, with the benefit of hindsight, the wisdom of Ricketson's decisions to undertake those mammoth projects is clear. The works were met with the many accolades that they deserved from within the global and Australian IP law academic community and beyond those communities as well as professional success in the form of professorial appointments (even at a time when such appointments at Australian universities were relatively rare), first at Monash University and later at the University of Melbourne.

20.3 The IP Treatise and Multiple Audiences

That the verdict on Ricketson's major works from academia was unanimously positive can now be identified by the use of the very technology not available to him when the first two of his treatises were written. For example, electronic searching reveals that Google Scholar displays 587 citations of the first edition of Sam's work on the Berne Convention and 275 for the second edition co-authored with Professor Ginsburg. Hein Online, *Westlaw World Journal* and Elgar Online reveal many others. Similar searches of his other works also reveal large numbers of citations and, given the limitations of citation systems relating to legal publications described earlier, we can be confident that the quantitative numbers revealed by such searches do not accurately reflect the actual number of citations of the works.

---

[14] Ibid., vii.
[15] Australasian Legal Information Institute, retrieved from www.austlii.edu.au.

As to qualitative measures, the foreword by Professor Roy Goode to the work on the Berne Convention describes it as 'magisterial';[16] reviews have described it variously as 'a feat of scholarship', 'seminal' and 'one of those universal books destined to become a key point of reference in a particular field, an indispensable volume that could impress any reader'.[17]

The Berne Convention work has clearly had a substantial impact beyond the confines of academia and has deeply affected consideration of copyright matters at both WIPO and the World Trade Organization (WTO). WIPO has commissioned further reports from Ricketson on specific aspects of international copyright law as a direct consequence of the work associated with the treatise on Berne and the reputation derived from it.[18]

Due to its specific application to Australian domestic law, those with an eye trained primarily on the international law perspective can too easily overlook Ricketson's ground-breaking treatise on Australian IP law published in 1984 prior to the Berne Convention work. To write either treatise in a career would be an extremely significant achievement. To have written both within the time frame in question is quite extraordinary. Again, electronic searching of legal databases reveals some of the extent of influence of the work on Australian IP law. A simple search of the Austlii database of Federal Court of Australia decisions reveals the extent to which and the speed at which the Australian judiciary looked to that work to assist it when determining IP disputes.[19]

---

[16] Roy Goode, 'Foreword' in Ricketson, *The Berne Convention for the Protection of Literary and Artistic Works*, p. ii.

[17] For a summary of those reviews, see Jose Bellido, 'Sam Ricketson's *The Paris Convention for the Protection of Industrial Property: A Commentary* (OUP, 2015)' (2016) 7 *IP Law Book Review* 10, retrieved from https://bit.ly/2lQM0wY.

[18] See details of Sam's work for WIPO on limitations and exceptions in the digital environment and a proposed framework for a new treaty on visual artists' resale rights at Sam Ricketson, WIPO Study on Limitations and Exceptions of Copyright and Related Rights in the Digital Environment, WIPO Standing Committee on Copyright and Related Rights, 9th sess., UN Doc SCCR/9/7 (5 April 2003), retrieved from www.wipo.int/meetings/en/doc_details.jsp?doc_id=16805; and Sam Ricketson, Proposed International Treaty on Droit de Suite/Resale Royalty Right for Visual Artists, SG15–0565 (June 2015).

[19] At least seventeen federal court decisions cited the work between 1985 and the end of 1988. There are also at least fourteen citations of works by Ricketson in High Court of Australia decisions and well over twenty citations of his works in the decisions of the Full Federal Court of Australia since 2002, the year that Austlii created a separate database for Full Court decisions. A number of other Full Court decisions refer to him in his capacity as counsel in the relevant cases. Many of those decisions citing his works made multiple references to various works and included extensive quotations from them.

20.4 The Future of the IP Treatise

Given all of the discussion here about the different means by which law academics are assessed and research targets are imposed on them, it is reasonable to ask whether Ricketson's works might be the last of the truly big treatises that effectively start from scratch to comprehensively deal with both a large topic and one with a long history. Other factors that might obstruct such works include the far greater ready availability of historical documents (although that factor may operate in both directions), and the targeted and piecemeal manner in which issues tend to be addressed, making it harder for the treatise writer to provide a sustainable synthesis.

Yet for all of that, an important and possibly overriding consideration will be the nature of the IP academic. A likely scenario is that those who are fortunate enough to have tenured research and teaching positions will not be those who respond immediately to every new means of measuring their performance. If responding to extrinsic rewards was the primary motivator of all legal academics, many more would have entered the private profession and sought the superior financial rewards it offers. Yet it is precisely the intrinsic rewards that flow from doing the time-consuming, tedious work coupled with intellectual insight that drives many academics as well as the degree of independence in working conditions.

Ricketson refers to these intrinsic benefits in the preface to the second edition of the Berne Convention treatise, when he notes:

> some regrets for the rigours (and delights) of earlier times when dusty volumes and documents had to be tracked down and studied in places far from the normal comforts and conveniences of one's desk and office (one should not overstate the difficulties involved in being 'required' to spend time in such places as Geneva and Munich in the pursuit of scholarship!')'.[20]

Even when the process was more digitised, as it was with the Paris Convention work, in acknowledging the support of his family while writing this work, Ricketson notes the 'pleasure and joy that I have had in pursuing this project to fruition'.[21] To put it more bluntly, despite the many reasons not to write these treatises (some of which already existed at the time they were being written), Ricketson was almost certainly going to write them anyway.

---

[20] Ricketson and Ginsburg, *International Copyright and Neighbouring Rights*, vii–viii.
[21] Ricketson, *The Paris Convention for the Protection of Industrial Property*, lxii.

20.5 Conclusion

Regardless of the speculation as to the future of IP treatises of the breadth and depth of those written by Ricketson, we do have three magnificent examples of what can be done by way of a major treatise in the realm of IP, and these have been the focus of this chapter. Some concluding remarks of a slightly more idiosyncratic nature are in order.

First, a particular indicator of Ricketson's thoughtful and scholarly character is his habit of placing interesting and provocative quotes from other authors at the beginning of some of his book chapters and articles as well as his casebook on IP (currently in its fifth co-authored edition, with another under preparation).[22] Perhaps due to the quite formal nature of a legal treatise, few such quotes are contained within the treatises he has written that are discussed here. However, to give but one example from his many less formal writings, chapter 5 of the casebook quotes from Professor Benjamin Kaplan's work that:

> when copyright has gone wrong in recent times, it has been by taking itself too seriously, by foolish assumptions about the amount of originality open to man as an artificer, by sanctimonious pretensions about the iniquities of imitation.[23]

Perhaps my favourite is from chapter 12 of that casebook, where the concept of manner of manufacture in patent law is introduced (and, very arguably, exhaustively defined) by the following quote from Lewis Carroll's 1871 book, *Through the Looking Glass*:

> 'There is glory for you!' 'I don't know what you mean by "glory",' Alice said. ... 'I meant, "there's a nice knock-down argument for you!"' 'But "glory" doesn't mean a "nice knock-down argument",' Alice objected. 'When I use a word,' Humpty Dumpty said in a rather scornful tone, 'it means just what I choose it to mean - neither more nor less.'[24]

I trust that the quotes appearing at the beginning of this chapter meet with Ricketson's approval but, in an attempt to increase that possibility, let me provide some further explanation of their choice on this occasion. Without the need for any specific details of sales volumes, book prices or

---

[22] Sam Ricketson, Megan Richardson and Mark Davison, *Intellectual Property: Cases, Materials & Commentary*, 5th ed. (Chatswood, Australia: LexisNexis Butterworths, 2013). Vicki Huang will join the sixth edition.

[23] Benjamin Kaplan, *An Unhurried View of Copyright* (New York: Columbia University Press, 1967), p. 78, quoted in Ricketson et al., *Intellectual Property: Cases, Materials & Commentary*, 221.

[24] Ricketson et al., *Intellectual Property: Cases, Materials & Commentary*, 638, quoting Lewis Carrol, *Through the Looking-Glass, and What Alice Found There* (London: Macmillan, 1871), p. 81.

royalty rates, those who have contributed to this book and most of those who read it will be sufficiently well informed about the academic publishing process to appreciate that Ricketson's treatises have entailed the giving away of vastly greater intellectual wealth than any financial benefit that may have accrued to him from such publications. The hours, days, weeks, months and years of intensive research, of ferreting out historical documents and then placing selected contents within the context of wider propositions are exhibited within his treatises. So too are the thoughtful and long-considered words about all manner of concepts and propositions both big and small that are raised by the subject matter of those treatises. The gift of intellectual wealth to the world is great. Even with an extended term of copyright to what will hopefully be a very long life plus seventy years, it is inconceivable that the financial returns on those publications will come close to their value to society at large, even taking into account the non-financial rewards to which Ricketson alludes in his epigraph.

Second, Ricketson's generosity in the realm of his research has been replicated in other aspects of his academic and professional work. He has given generous and wise assistance and counsel to many over several decades, judged not just by what is given but the manner in which it is given. It is that generosity which no doubt has contributed to Sam's standing within both academia and the profession more broadly. It also has permitted him to be accepted by those with a wide range of views on IP, as he has always carefully considered the views of others and asserted his own in a respectful manner. Hence Ricketson could and did provide the quote from Kaplan that is set out earlier for the purposes of stimulating debate while maintaining his own views on the importance of copyright and, in particular, the position of authors. Of course, these kinds of academic contributions are very difficult to 'measure' at the institutional level notwithstanding their real significance.

As for the 'end', we are thankfully not speaking of the particular end that Solon had in mind. Nevertheless, looking back over the career (to date) of a remarkable IP law academic, we can now appreciate the contribution of Sam Ricketson to IP scholarship over a period of roughly thirty-five years, and the preceding comments on his IP treatises were designed to do that. But it seems appropriate to finish on a more human note – and to say that, if the purpose of a virtuous scholarly life is to be happy and useful, I trust that this book's acknowledgement of Ricketson's great usefulness is the source of considerable happiness for him.

21 Language and Law
The Role of the Intellectual Property Treatise

David Llewelyn

As an area of legal study and practice, intellectual property law lacks the conceptual coherence of an internally consistent and discrete law subject like 'contract', 'criminal' or 'tort', which has its own normative rules that are applicable throughout the subject (perhaps, to borrow from a Kantian perspective, 'a pure law subject')[1] or even one that describes a category of law which involves the application of different pure laws to a subject matter, like environmental law or entertainment law (an applied field of legal study or practice). For this reason, mixing and matching notions or terms from one area of IP law with those from others can be at best, confusing and at worst, dangerously misleading, however beguiling it may be to do so.

This risk of confusion, or worse, is exacerbated when different languages are used and different legal systems involved. On even such a basic issue as the difference between copyright and *droit d'auteur*, Sam Ricketson raised at the very outset of his treatise on the 1886 Berne Convention,[2] in a note on terminology:[3] 'is copyright the correct name by which to describe the rights covered by the Convention?' He proceeded to explain clearly what he meant by the terms as well as others such as *performing right*, *représentation* and *exécution* (and even Anglo-Saxons as compared to Celts!),[4] where there are risks of comparing apples with oranges.

In all these areas the IP treatise aims to assist and clarify. In this chapter, the term *treatise* is used to describe a systematic and detailed presentation of a whole area of the law (such as patents, trade marks or copyright), or on a particular statute or convention. On the other hand, a

---

[1] It is recognised that there are those who would contend that no field of law, even contract law or property law, can properly be described as discrete and made up of internally consistent, normative rules, but instead all fields of law rely for their coherence on their application in a variety of external, or applied, circumstances. However, the point being made in relation to IP law, that it is a mix of the applied and the pure as explained, remains valid.

[2] Sam Ricketson, *The Berne Convention for the Protection of Literary and Artistic Works: 1886–1986* (London: Centre for Commercial Law Studies, Queen Mary College, Kluwer, 1987).

[3] Ibid., vii.   [4] Ibid., iii.

monograph is a work on a specific aspect of an area of law (such as the three-step test in copyright, the inventive step requirement in patent law or 'the parts played by use in trade mark law). However, it is fair to say that today, at least in the UK and Australia, it is difficult to discern any common understanding of the term *treatise* and it is often used interchangeably with *textbook* or *practitioners' work*.[5]

The IP treatise (or textbook) is a relatively recent arrival on the bookshelves in the UK and Australia. Before the early 1980s, almost a full century after the 1883 Paris Convention and the Berne Convention three years later (on both of which Ricketson has written a treatise),[6] the treatises in the IP field covered only one or more of the individual rights that go to make up what today we call IP law. They were on copyright and related matters, or on patents, or on trade marks and passing off or even on designs: but not on IP law generally.[7]

21.1 On Copyright and Related Matters

In the field of copyright law, Copinger[8] was the one that stood the test of time after its first publication in 1870. Although there were occasional

---

[5] For a detailed historical analysis of the role of treatises in both Roman law and the development of the common law, see A W B Simpson, 'The rise and fall of the legal treatise: Legal principles and the forms of legal literature' (1981) 48 *University of Chicago Law Review* 632.

[6] Sam Ricketson, *The Paris Convention for the Protection of Industrial Property: A Commentary* (Oxford: Oxford University Press, 2015); Ricketson, *The Berne Convention for the Protection of Literary and Artistic Works*. For the second edition of the latter, published this time by Oxford University Press in 2006, Ricketson was joined as author by Jane Ginsburg. The joint authors noted in the preface that 'the world has changed greatly since 1986, the year of Berne's centenary. But while Berne itself has remained unrevised ..., its stature and importance have changed beyond all recognition': Sam Ricketson and Jane C Ginsburg, *International Copyright and Neighbouring Rights: The Berne Convention and Beyond*, 2nd ed. (Oxford: Oxford University Press, 2006), p. ix.

[7] In *Intellectual property: Omnipresent, Distracting, Irrelevant?* (New York: Oxford University Press, 2004), William Cornish notes that: 'As an umbrella term, ['intellectual property'] became common in the 1960s with the setting up of the UN organ, the World Intellectual Property Organization (WIPO to its supplicants and its revilers). Before that, the idea of attributing the quality of property to rights over inventions, aesthetic works, and brands was looked at askance' p. 2.

[8] See Walter Arthur Copinger, *The Law of Copyright in Works of Literature and Art: Including That of the drama, Music, Engraving, Sculpture, Painting, Photography and Ornamental and Useful Designs: Together with International and Foreign Copyright, with the Statutes Relating Thereto, and References to the English and American Decisions* (London: Stevens and Haynes, 1870). Of which, Jose Bellido and Lionel Bently (eds.), *Intellectual Property – Oral History Project* retrieved from www.iporalhistory.co.uk, says: 'Although its first edition was an important milestone in the history of British copyright, the fact is that its different editions throughout the late nineteenth century and across the whole twentieth century were even more crucial for its emergence as the leading text on British copyright.'

pretenders to the crown (some of which are mentioned later), it reigned supreme after World War I until the arrival in 1980 of *The Modern Law of Copyright* by Hugh Laddie, Peter Prescott and Mary Vitoria, barristers all in a competing set of chambers.[9] A review of the latter in the 1982 *Sydney Law Review* by a 'Lecturer (part time) in Principles of Equity and in Industrial and Commercial Property, University of Sydney' proclaimed: 'It should be made plain that this work is destined to be the classic in the field. There has been nothing like it to date.'[10]

On the other side of the Atlantic, the admirable Eaton S Drone[11] had published his *A Treatise on the Law of Property in Intellectual Productions in Great Britain and the United States*,[12] setting out punchily in the preface his view on the role of the treatise writer:

> The maker of a treatise should never lose sight of the fact that his duty is to give the law as it is. But this cannot always be done by simply recording what has been decided by the courts. Jurisprudence is a science based on principles rather than on single decisions. ... Dealing thus with principles, the writer of a treatise may determine with reasonable certainty what the law is where it has not been judicially interpreted. In the case of copyright, there are many important questions concerning which [of?] the statutes are silent or not clear, and which have not arisen in the courts, though they are likely to come up at any time. Not to consider these, simply because they are not discussed in the reports, is to leave a treatise on this subject lacking, without excuse, in thoroughness and usefulness.[13]

Back in the UK, the progress made at Berne at the two diplomatic conferences in 1884 and 1885 led to 'a move for a complete revision of its archaic and chaotic Copyright Acts, but considerations of time

---

[9] See Hugh Laddie, Peter Prescott and Mary Vitoria, *The Modern Law of Copyright* (London: Butterworths, 1980).

[10] W M Gummow, 'Laddie, Prescott, Vitoria: The modern law of copyright' (1982) 9 *Sydney Law Review* 709.

[11] In his '*The Laws of Copyright: An Examination of the Principles Which Should Regulate Literary and Artistic Property in England and Other Countries* (Yorke Prize essay of the University of Cambridge for 1882, revised and enlarged. Artistic and musical copyright added) (London: J Murray, 1883), Thomas Edward Scrutton (later Lord Justice Scrutton) said in the preface, '[Drone is] by far the best book on Copyright in existence', p. vii. In due course, the second edition of Scrutton's treatise, *The Law of Copyright*, published by William Clowes & Sons in 1890 (and now including the Berne Convention), was described by the *Law Quarterly Review* as 'not only the easiest, but the most useful and practical work on copyright'. In the third edition six years later, Scrutton asked plaintively in the preface: 'Is it too much to hope that a strong Government, with time to spare for unambitious but useful legislative reforms, may do something practical to assist the literary workers of the Empire?', p. vii. His pleas were eventually heard.

[12] Eaton S Drone, *A Treatise on the Law of Property in Intellectual Productions in Great Britain and the United States: Embracing Copyright in Works of Literature and Art, and Playright in Dramatic and Musical Compositions* (Boston: Little, Brown, & Co, 1879).

[13] Ibid., vii–viii.

prevented this from occurring'. The subsequent legislative changes were therefore limited to those necessary to enable the UK to sign the convention (signed by the UK after the 1886 diplomatic conference).[14]

Later treatise writers on copyright law did not hold back their criticisms of the legislature and followed in Drone's footsteps in terms of their duty to give the law as it is. For example, hot on the heels of his *Treatise on the Law of Copyright in the United Kingdom and the Dominions of the Crown, and in the United States of America*,[15] the prolific author, Inner Temple barrister and member of the Faculty of Advocates, Evan James MacGillivray,[16] made his views crystal clear in the preface to his 1906 *Digest of the Law of Copyright*:[17]

It is deplorable in the twentieth century, and in the light of rational legislation in the United States of America, Germany, Japan, and many other foreign countries, to find the British legislature passing an Act which insists on defining a book in the curious and ambiguous phraseology employed in the Copyright Act of 1842, and which adheres to the present ridiculous system of registration.[18]

With two major copyright statutes in 1911 and in 1956, the system of registration had gone but the complexity of the subject remained (and it has got no easier since). In his foreword to *Copyright: Modern Law and Practice* by Carter-Ruck and Skone James,[19] another eminent barrister of the time, Kenneth (later Lord) Diplock, commented of the new treatise:

The law of copyright like the law of libel and slander, despite its wide impact on so many members of the community, has come to be regarded by lawyers as well as others as an arcane branch of the law to be comprehended only by the expert. That any branch of the law should be a mystery is a reflection upon those who make and those who administer it. [This work] is comprehensible to layman and Lord Justice alike.

---

[14] Ricketson and Ginsburg, *International Copyright and Neighbouring Rights*, [2.50]. For further fascinating detail, see Ronan Deazley, 'Commentary on International Copyright Act 1886' in Lionel Bently and Martin Kretschmer (eds.), *Primary Sources on Copyright (1450–1900)* (Swindon: Arts and Humanities Research Council, 2008), retrieved from www.copyrighthistory.org.

[15] Evan James MacGilllivray, *Treatise on the Law of Copyright in the United Kingdom and the Dominions of the Crown, and in the United States of America: Containing a Full Appendix of All Acts of Parliament, International Conventions, Orders in Council, Treasury Minute and Acts of Congress Now in Force* (London: John Murray, 1902).

[16] In *Treatise on the Law of Copyright*, MacGillivray admitted at the start of the chapter on copyright, with a refreshing modesty: 'The history of copyright has been exhaustively dealt with by Mr Copinger, Mr Scrutton, and Mr Drone in their respective treatises on copyright law. I feel that I can add nothing useful', p. 3.

[17] Evan James MacGilllivray, *A Digest of the Law of Copyright* (London: Butterworth, 1906).

[18] Ibid., ix.

[19] Peter Frederick Carter-Ruck and E P Skone James, *Copyright: Modern Law and Practice* (London: Faber, 1965).

This is how legal text-books should be written: intelligible to the non-lawyer whose business or vocation is intimately affected by the particular branch of the law, comprehensive for the general lawyer who is called upon from time to time to advise a client upon a problem arising in this special field, a reference book for the specialist lawyer with an opinion to write, an agreement to draft or a case to conduct in the Courts.[20]

The arcane nature had been well described in the preface to an earlier treatise in 1930 on an area of IP law that continues to trouble the student, the practitioner and the courts: *Copyright in Industrial Designs* by Alan Daubeny Russell-Clarke.[21] He explained resignedly:

there are certain things which people invent which fall midway between a patent and a design, which perhaps ought to be protected, as they are protected in Germany under a *Gebrauchsmuster*, but for which there is no real protection in this country. In lieu of anything better, it may be of assistance to persons who have invented such things to register them as designs if they can, as the fact of possessing a registration may serve to deter others from entering the field. But a person who obtains a registration of this description should do so with his eyes open, and should realize the comparative hopelessness of trying to bring an action upon it.[22]

The same author expanded the scope of his treatise twenty years later in *Copyright and Industrial Designs*,[23] mentioning in its preface just one of a number of what he terms 'unnatural' alliances that still bedevil a coherent treatment of the IP law field as a whole:

The desirability of a comprehensive work embracing all branches of copyright law has long been felt. This book covers copyright in literary, dramatic, musical and artistic works, and also copyright in industrial designs.

The reason why no attempt has so far been made to embody all aspects of the subject under one cover is probably attributable to the fact that when in 1875 registration of designs was, for convenience of administration, transferred

---

[20] Ibid., 5–6.
[21] Alan Daubeny Russell-Clarke, *Copyright in Industrial Designs* (London: Sir Isaac Pitman & Sons, 1930). For the cases in which Russell-Clarke appeared, see Bellido and Bently, *Intellectual Property*.
[22] Russell-Clarke, *Copyright in Industrial Designs*, vi. In his treatise *The Law of Copyright in Designs*, published by Sweet and Maxwell thirty-five years earlier, Lewis Edmunds, another barrister, explained in his preface: 'The fact that no work specially devoted to the Law of Designs, and attempting a complete treatment of the subject, has appeared for many years past, makes it unnecessary to offer any excuse for the production of this work. The object is to present an exhaustive exposition': Lewis Edmunds, *The Law of Copyright in Designs: Together with the Practice relating to Proceedings in the Courts and in the Patent Office* (London: Sweet & Maxwell, 1895), p. v.
[23] Alan Daubeny Russell-Clarke, *Copyright and Industrial Designs* (London: Sweet & Maxwell, 1951).

to the Patent Office, industrial copyright came to be associated with patent rather than copyright law. The alliance is, however, in many respects an unnatural one.[24]

21.2 On Patents

Before World War II the field of patent law was not short of treatises. Albeit that it was not an area of the law that attracted many, those it did were all scientifically qualified as well as gentlemen (there were no women in the field at this time) of the law. Indeed, Lincoln's Inn barrister Gerald John Wheeler complained in the preface to his treatise, *Patents and Prolongation*,[25] that the Patent Office was hidden away in Southampton Buildings:[26]

It is also a pity that the Patent Office is not in a more conspicuous building: on a corner site: easily found; and presenting an inviting appearance ... both from patriotic motives, and financial motives, it ought to be made easy to Inventors as a body to quickly perceive where, and how, they can protect their inventive thoughts.[27]

For Kenneth Raydon Swan, barrister of the Middle Temple, the treatment of patents, designs and trade marks together in one treatise arose as a practical matter from their inclusion in a single Act of Parliament in 1883,[28] and when they were separated in the Patents and Designs Act 1907, and the Trade Marks Act 1905,[29] this necessitated no change. He noted in the preface to *The Law and Commercial Usage of Patents, Designs and Trade Marks*:[30]

---

[24] Ibid., x.
[25] Gerald John Wheeler, *Notes on the Prolongation of Letters Patent for Inventions: With the Patents, Designs, and Trade Marks Acts, 1883–8, consolidated; the Board of Trade rules and the Patent Office Rules and Directions; and the New Rules of the Judicial Committee of the Privy Council* (London: Eyre and Spottiswoode, 1898).
[26] For a time, it shared its accommodation with the Secretaries of Bankrupts and Lunatics.
[27] Wheeler, *Notes on the Prolongation of Letters Patent for Inventions*, p. v.
[28] See Patents, Designs and Trade Marks Act 1883.
[29] According to Sir Robin Jacob, 'Fletcher Moulton piloted the Trade Marks Act 1905 through the House of Commons and is said to have drafted much of it himself': Sir Robin Jacob, 'Intellectual Property' in Louis Blom Cooper, Brice Dickson and Gavin Drewry (eds.), *The Judicial House of Lords 1876–2009*) (Oxford: Oxford University Press , 2009), pp. 711, 712. Sir Robin describes Lords Parker and Fletcher Moulton as 'the two IP giants of the early twentieth century', p. 712; on the other hand, the latter's obituary in *The Times* (London), 10 March 1921, p. 13 (mentioned again later in the footnotes) expressed the view that he was 'a man of striking and even extraordinary ability yet it can hardly be said that he was, or would ever have become, a great Judge'.
[30] Kenneth Raydon Swan, *The Law and Commercial Usage of Patents, Designs and Trade Marks* (London: Archibald Constable & Co, 1908).

Though Patents, Designs and Trade Marks cannot be said to be very intimately related to one another from a purely legal point of view – at any rate not to the degree to which their previous collocation in a single act of Parliament would seem to imply – nevertheless they undoubtedly possess affinities of a practical kind, amply justifying their traditional association. Lodged together under the roof of the Patent Office and jointly supervised by the Comptroller general of Patents, Designs, and trade Marks they are not unnaturally linked in the public mind as the three principal forms of monopoly ... No excuse is needed, therefore, for uniting these subjects in the compass of a single volume.

Nor is excuse needed for producing a treatise of this nature at the present time. Patents and Designs Act, 1907 and Trade Marks Act, 1905, have rendered obsolete to a great extent existing works.[31]

Of course, there were also commentaries (again by barristers) on particular statutes. The previous year, one on the Patents and Designs Act 1907 written by barristers James Roberts and Hugh Fletcher Moulton had been published, noting in its preface:

This book does not pretend to be a treatise on Patent Law. There are already many excellent works on the existing Patent Law, and it will not, for a considerable time and until there have been many judicial decisions, be possible to write a treatise on the new Law.[32]

In their preface, the authors cross-referred to James Roberts's earlier treatise, *Grant and Validity of British Patents for Inventions*,[33] and bemoaned the fact that 'no less than 51 per cent of litigated patents are found invalid by the court'.[34]

The coming into force of the Patents Act 1949, was followed closely by the first treatise authored by Thomas Anthony Blanco White, *Patents for Inventions and the Registration of Registered Designs*.[35] He explained in the preface who he was writing for and why:

The passing of the Patents Act, 1949, and the Registered Designs Act, 1949, should sufficiently excuse the publication of a new textbook of patent law. ... A textbook of a subject such as this is necessarily addressed to more than one class

---

[31] Ibid.
[32] James Roberts and Hugh Fletcher Moulton, *The Patents and Designs Act, 1907: With Notes and the Practice Thereunder* (London: Butterworth, 1907). This was the son of Lord (Fletcher) Moulton, who had also had an outstanding practice at the Patent Bar. For a detailed account see his obituary in *The Times* (London), 10 March 1921.
[33] James Roberts, *Grant and Validity of British Patents for Inventions* (London: John Murray, 1903).
[34] Ibid., p. vii.
[35] Thomas Anthony Blanco White, *Patents for Inventions and the Registration of Registered Designs* (London: Stevens, 1950). The treatise cited at the outset: 'The whole trouble is, that the English language is unsuited to patent actions' (per Roxburgh J in *Strachan and Henshaw Ltd v. Pakcel Ltd* (1949) 66 RPC 49, [1]).

of reader: to established practitioners; to members of the legal profession who have no special knowledge of patents; and to students with little previous knowledge either of English law generally or of the English patent system. ... Those practitioners who find the introductory parts tendentious and imprecise are asked to remember that only a broad outline is aimed at there; while those students who find the introductory parts insufficient to prepare them for tackling the main text, would do best to begin with the author's smaller and more popular work [Patents and Registered Designs, Stevens, 'This is the Law' series, priced at 4s.][36]

In the first few years after World War II, Thomas Blanco White had authored three works that were far from being treatises but which were arguably even more influential than any treatise on the development of the IP law scene in the UK and Australia. These were three concise booklets of less than 100 pages each covering what would then have been known as 'industrial and intellectual property law': *Trade Marks and the Law of Unfair Competition* (1947), *Patents and Registered Designs* (1947) and *Copyright* (1949).[37] The role and importance of these booklets in the development of intellectual property law as an academic discipline, in both the UK and Australia, is described by Jose Bellido in his fascinating article, 'The Constitution of Intellectual Property as an Academic Subject',[38] observing of the patents booklet:

Perhaps the most prominent characteristic ... was its attempt to bridge the legal and technical gulfs between the expert and the layman. Instead of trying to close the profession, it opened it up to the uninitiated.[39]

This characteristic remains true of the most recent incarnation of those three booklets: *A Guidebook to Intellectual Property* by Sir Robin Jacob, Daniel Alexander and Matthew Fisher[40] (the sixth edition of what, when it was first published in 1970, was a guidebook that traced its origins to the Blanco White booklets and their subsequent revision and publication by Stevens & Sons as a single textbook *Industrial Property and Copyright* in 1962).[41]

---

[36] Ibid., vii. [37] All published by Stevens & Sons.
[38] Jose Bellido, 'The constitution of intellectual property as an academic subject' (2012) 37 *Legal Studies* 369. Bellido notes that Blanco White read physics at Cambridge where, among no doubt many others, he met Benjamin Britten who described him as 'one of the cleverest boys he ever met', p. 372.
[39] Ibid., 374.
[40] Oxford: Hart Publishing, 2013. The previous five editions were published by Sweet & Maxwell and the sixth edition's (self-styled) 'custodians' comment in the preface: 'A work as idiosyncratic as this did not fit well with Sweet's model of major textbooks and student specific works', p. v.
[41] Bellido, 'The constitution of intellectual property as an academic subject', 376–7, traces the influence of Blanco White's 1962 book on teaching of the subject in the UK and Australia and notes also that such later IP treatises as William Cornish, *Intellectual Property: Patents, Copyright, Trade Marks, and Allied Rights* (London: Sweet & Maxwell,

21.3 The Arrival of the IP Treatise

In the preface to his outstanding 1984 treatise, *The Law of Intellectual Property: Copyright, Designs and Confidential Information* in Australia, a work that more than complied with Diplock's strictures, Ricketson noted:

> To date, the writing on this area of law has tended to be fragmented, with a number of specialist texts dealing with particular branches of the subject. It, therefore, seemed that there was a place for a single text which treated the subject in an integrated fashion.[42]

The timing was perfect: It was a period when a single author could tackle the IP field as a whole in that integrated fashion and produce a single text, albeit that few were sufficiently well read and rounded to do so. Following the publication in 1980 of Jim Lahore's *Intellectual Property in Australia*,[43] which Ricketson acknowledged 'must take first place',[44] and a year later Bill Cornish's groundbreaking[45] treatise on the whole of UK and (then) European Economic Community (EEC) IP law, *Intellectual Property: Patents, Copyright, Trade Marks and Allied Rights*,[46] Ricketson supplied the third IP treatise in four years, and a clean sweep for Australian academics.[47]

In other countries too, the IP treatise (bounded by two covers) surveyed the scene around the same time. In Japan, Teruo Doi, professor at Waseda University in Tokyo authored *The Intellectual Property Law of*

1981)and Lionel Bently and Brad Sherman, *Intellectual Property Law* (Oxford: Oxford University Press, 2001)were aimed at the same three types of readers Blanco had in mind: students, lawyers and business people and overseas specialists who want 'a relatively succinct presentation of United Kingdom law', as explained by Cornish in his preface on p. ix.

[42] Staniforth (Sam) Ricketson, *The Law of Intellectual Property: Copyright, Designs and Confidential Information* (Sydney: Lawbook Co, 1984), p. vii. In his acknowledgements (p. ix), Ricketson expressed his indebtedness to three outstanding figures in the common law IP world: Jim Lahore, Bill Cornish and Des Ryan.

[43] Jim Lahore, *Intellectual Property in Australia* (Sydney: Butterworths, 1980).

[44] Ricketson, *The Law of Intellectual Property*, 3 (fn. 1).

[45] The adjective *groundbreaking* was used to describe it by Lionel Bently and David Vaver in the preface (p. xii), to *Intellectual Property in the New Millennium: Essays in Honour of William R Cornish* (Cambridge: Cambridge University Press, 2004). Indeed, they even suggested that it remained 'the most intellectually sophisticated work of its kind'.

[46] Cornish, *Intellectual Property*. (Gerald Dworkin recollects Bill Cornish telling him that Sweet & Maxwell had its doubts whether there was a market for a treatise on IP!). A lot of the work for the treatise was done by Cornish in 1979 while at what was then the Max Planck Institute for Foreign and International Patent, Copyright, and Competition Law in Munich (founded in 1966), and today is the Max Planck Institute for Innovation and Competition.

[47] See further Chapter 21 in this volume, by Mark Davison.

Language and Law: Role of Intellectual Property Treatise   289

Japan[48] that, with its publication in 1980, made the intricacies of the Japanese system accessible to English-language readers for the first time. As Doi said in his foreword, it was:

> a comprehensive treatise on the intellectual property law of Japan. There are numerous books in the Japanese language in the area of intellectual property law but they deal with either industrial property law or some of its subdivisions or copyright law and do not cover the whole area.[49]

It was around that time, the early 1980s,[50] that the description *intellectual property law* started to acquire acceptability, rather than the earlier divide between *industrial property* and *copyright and related rights*: Even in 1977, Harmut Johannes of the (then) EEC Commission chose as the title of his treatise *Industrial Property and Copyright in European Community Law*.[51] The IP treatises of the Australian professorial trio Lahore (1980), Cornish (1981) and Ricketson (1984) played an important role in this popularisation of the description in the Commonwealth.[52]

From then on, it got immeasurably harder for any one person, however knowledgeable and talented, to cope with and encompass all aspects of the ever-expanding field. When the second edition of his IP treatise was published in 1999,[53] Ricketson acknowledged the problem:

> enormous developments which have made the task of writing a full second edition unusually onerous. Law reform activity has been unending and substantive legislative change has continued unabated in each of the principal statutory regimes of patents, copyright, designs and trade marks, while a number of sui generis regimes have been added ... IP law, in consequence, has become something of a raging torrent.[54]

---

[48] Teruo Doi, *The Intellectual Property Law of Japan* (Alphen aan den Rijn, the Netherlands: Sijthoff & Noordhoff 1980).
[49] Ibid., p. xix.
[50] Of course, there was the occasional use of the term in the 1970s in the sense we now know it. The publication of the thirty-two-page first issue of Hugh Brett's brainchild, the *European Intellectual Property Review* in October 1978 was an important step in the process: In its first editorial, by Hugh Brett, Peter Ford and Mary Vitoria, it proclaimed: 'An understanding of the inter-relationship of intellectual rights is essential if IP is to be successfully protected and exploited', p. 1.
[51] Harmut Johannes, *Industrial Property and Copyright in European Community Law* (Leyden: Sijthoff, 1976).
[52] At the end of the 1980s they were joined by Andrew Brown and Anthony Grant, *The Law of Intellectual Property in New Zealand* (Wellington, Butterworths, 1989).
[53] Sam Ricketson, *The Law of Intellectual Property: Copyright, Designs and Confidential Information*, 2nd ed. (Sydney: Lawbook Co, 1999); revised 2000, 2001, 2002, with Christopher Creswell.
[54] Ibid., 5.

The 'raging torrent' had also swept away one of the other rationales for the 1984 treatise:

> The current work loses one of the original rationales of the first edition which was to contain 'within the space of one volume, all the Australian law relating to intellectual property rights'... The present quarantining of subject matter has been dictated simply by logistical and publishing factors.[55]

21.4 A Broad Range of Rights

Intellectual property rights are all different and thus the author of the IP treatise must systematically explain, compare and contrast. A slapdash or superficial treatment of all the rights as if they were the same not only leads to confusion and disappointment but risks devaluing the importance of each of them in its proper place in a coherent system of law that should provide appropriate and balanced protection against unfair appropriation of the fruits of another's mental labour.

This is not a new problem, as Ricketson commented of the 1883 Paris Convention, which was 'motivated by a fair dash of idealism': 'its subject matter is diverse and apparently only loosely connected'.[56] Apropos the further opacity added by language, he notes that in the official English-language translation of the convention, 'nowhere ... does one find a definition of a patent or even an indication that this is for an "invention"', whereas in the official language of the convention, French, 'the term "brevet d'invention" is rather clearer on this point'.[57]

Of course, intellectual property (which in reality is often not 'intellectual' in any meaningful sense and also often strains at the boundaries of what we understand to be 'property'[58]) and the legal rights to protect it

---

[55] Ibid., vi.
[56] Sam Ricketson, *The Paris Convention for the Protection of Industrial Property: A Commentary* (Oxford: Oxford University Press, 2015), p. 1.
[57] Ibid.
[58] In any coherent analysis, it is difficult to categorise confidential information as an 'intellectual property' right, let alone 'property': see the discussion in William Cornish, David Llewelyn and Tanya Aplin, *Intellectual Property: Patents, Copyright, Trade Marks and Allied Rights*, 8th ed. (London: Sweet & Maxwell, 2013), at paras. [8-01] to [8-08], noting at para. [8-07] the statement by Lord Denning, in *Fraser* v. *Evans* [1969] 1 All ER 8, 11, that the English law approach to such protection is based 'not so much on property or on contract, but rather on good faith'. Of course, for convenience that treatise on intellectual property includes treatment of the action for breach of confidence as a right 'allied' to patents, copyright and trade marks, in the sense that they are often dealt with together in practice or in a commercialisation context such as a patent and know-how licence, but that does not mean that it sits there comfortably. See also, Lionel Bently, 'Trade secrets: "Intellectual property" but not "property"?' in Helena Howe with Jonathan Griffiths (eds.), *Concepts of Property in Intellectual Property Law* (Cambridge: Cambridge University Press, 2013) p. 60.

are essential for the economic development of many countries and the success of many businesses in today's linked world. This is the reason for the groaning bookshelves and e-readers full of tomes on different aspects of the IP laws and practice of almost every country (for they are all different, to a greater or lesser extent), almost all out of date as soon as they are published, so continuous are the developments in the field. On these bookshelves and in these e-readers the IP treatise retains an important place.

21.5 Conclusion

The value of the well written IP treatise cannot be overstated: It is an essential tool for the student, the legislator and the lawyer as well as all the other stakeholders in an ever more important field. A field in which dangers lurk for the unwary participant: the danger of sloppy use of language, the danger of misuse of foreign laws and authorities, the danger of misguided elision of difficult issues that need to be treated with scalpel-like precision. In the end, they all come back to the need to be careful with language: reading, using and interpreting words is much of what a lawyer does, and the IP treatise assists with. After all, even Dick the Butcher's call to 'Kill all the Lawyers!' in *Henry VI Part 2* must be read in context: 'As a careful reading of that text will reveal, Shakespeare insightfully realized that disposing of lawyers is a step in the direction of a totalitarian form of government.'[59]

---

[59] Per Justice Stevens of the US Supreme Court, at fn. 24 in his dissenting opinion in *Walters v. National Association of Radiation Survivors* (1985) 473 US 305.

22 Intellectual Property in the Courtroom
The Role of the Expert

Peter Heerey

I am delighted to join in this Festschrift for Sam Ricketson, who has graced the worlds of academe and the bar with equal aplomb and distinction. This contribution concerns the questions of the relevance, value and management of expert evidence in the context of intellectual property (IP). These are questions academics, lawyers and judges may disagree about, including in Australia. Indeed, as Professor Ricketson has observed (with respect to expert evidence in unfair competition cases), '[w]idely different views have been expressed as to the utility of such evidence in assisting courts in their determinations'.[1] Nevertheless, in my view, experts serve a useful function in IP cases and it makes good sense for judges to design strategies to ensure that the best value can be obtained from their evidence.

22.1 IP Case: Lawyers and Experts Needed

With most forms of property, the primary mode of protection is self-help. You can lock your car in your garage, or your jewellery in your safe. But IP is in essence something intangible and unlockupable. The property is not the physical thing, the trade mark or the product of the invention but rather the right to prevent others from infringing your exclusive rights to use that trade mark or product. Self-help is not available. The aggrieved owner must turn to lawyers and courts. In the court, disputes will often arise as to the nature of the right itself – whether the trade mark is a purely generic term or the patent is novel when compared with the prior art. Again this is different from arguments about non-IP.

So IP lawyers can take some confidence. For the foreseeable future, they are always going to be essential. Their jurisdiction is an endlessly

---

[1] Sam Ricketson, 'The place of expert evidence in unfair competition cases: The Australian experience', in Andrew T Kenyon, Ng-Loy Wee Loon and Megan Richardson, *The Law of Reputation and Brands in the Asia Pacific* (Cambridge: Cambridge University Press, 2012), p. 203.

renewable resource, not vulnerable to legislative destruction or restriction like, for example, personal injuries litigation.

Moreover, commercial wealth is increasingly based on IP. Currently, the top four companies in the world by market value are Apple, Amazon, Alphabet (Google), and Microsoft.[2] All have IP at the core of their operations. Probably twenty or even ten years ago, manufacturing, financial or resources companies would have filled those slots. The importance of IP as a store of commercial value has risen compared with tangible property such as land, buildings, machines and ships. Airbnb and Uber are, respectively, the largest hotel and taxi companies in the world, notwithstanding that they own only software.

Technology advances at an exponential rate and becomes more and more complex and specialised. Contests before the courts fall to be adjudicated by judges who have no technical background, or at least probably not in the particular area of expertise of the dispute. Explanation and advice from experts in the relevant field will be essential.

This chapter looks at some of the practices and procedures which have been developed in Australian courts, and particularly the Federal Court of Australia, regarding the use of expert witnesses.

22.2 The Expert in the Courts

In a paper published a few years ago, Justice Steven Rares of the Federal Court of Australia noted that he had heard cases concerning topics as diverse as accounting, quantity surveying, fire protection, wildlife paths, metallurgy, naval architecture, navigation of container ships in a gale, mechanical engineering, the appropriate flooring for elephant enclosures in zoos and the mating of those mammals.[3] The most polymathic of judges could not be expected to delve unaided into disputes arising in all such fields of human endeavour.

I get the very broad impression that for judges now on the bench, any non-legal tertiary qualifications are likely to be in the humanities. This may be changing with today's practitioners. In the process of researching and writing this chapter, I conducted an informal survey of twenty-two IP counsel at the Victorian Bar. Eight survey respondents (36 per cent) had some scientific or technical tertiary qualifications, such as bachelor

---

[2] 'The 100 largest companies in the world by market value in 2018 (in billion US dollars)', Statista, 11 May 2018, retrieved from https://bit.ly/2kF2jgj.

[3] Justice Steven Rares, 'Using the "hot tub" – How concurrent expert evidence aids understanding issues', Paper presented at the Continuing Legal Education Seminar, University of New South Wales, 23 February 2017, 4 [5].

degrees in pharmacology, biochemistry or genetics. True to say, this may be an unrepresentative sample of the bar as a whole, since lawyers who also have scientific or technical qualifications may naturally be more inclined towards a practice in IP.

Sir Robin Jacob, for many years the leading patent judge on the Court of Appeal of England and Wales, speaks of judges who are 'scientifically numerate but not an expert in the particular technology'.[4] I think that is a valid point. Like all people, different judges have different skills and interests. Some are more at home with questions of language, human character and behaviour than the world of mathematics, physics and chemistry. (Although in my experience, it is notable how often patent cases ultimately turn on issues as to the meaning of words. And sometimes the patent in dispute is not exactly a high-tech discovery. For example, in *Commissioner of Patents* v. *Emperor Sports Pty Ltd*,[5] I was a member of a Full Court considering an invention which consisted of a Velcro strap attached to football shorts for playing touch rugby, the removal of the strap by an opponent providing an equivalent of a tackle.)

22.3 The Expert: Chosen by Parties or Appointed by the Court?

Can an expert witness chosen by one of the parties be truly independent? Would that witness be called at all unless he or she was assessed as favourable to the party's case? Having nailed his or her colours to the party's mast, does the expert not feel an obligation to defend the client's case to the bitter end?

Modern court rules stress the importance of independence and the primacy of the duty owed by the expert witness to the court. For example, Annexure A to the current Federal Court Expert Evidence Practice Note states:

2. An expert witness is not an advocate for a party and has a paramount duty, overriding any duty to the party to the proceedings or other person retaining the expert witness, to assist the Court impartially on matters relevant to the area of expertise of the witness.[6]

---

[4] Sir Robin Jacob, *IP and Other Things: A Collection of Essays and Speeches* (Oxford: Hart Publishing, 2015), p. 51.
[5] (2006) 149 FCR 386.
[6] Federal Court of Australia, Practice Note GPN-EXPT – Expert Evidence, 25 October 2016, Annexure A.

Nevertheless, there is a lingering scepticism. As far back as 1877, Sir George Jessel MR said:[7]

A man may go, and does, sometimes to half a dozen experts. He takes their honest opinion: he finds three in his favour and three against him; he says to the three in his favour: "Will you be kind enough to give evidence?" He pays the three against him their fees and leaves them alone; the other side does the same. It may not be three out of six; it may be three out of fifty. ... I am sorry to say the result is that the court does not get the assistance from experts which, if they were unbiased and fairly chosen, it would have a right to expect.

Sir George went on in that patent case to discuss the possibility of the court appointing an expert of its own. He accepted that such a power exists. But he pointed out the practical difficulties: The court does not know how many of these experts have been consulted by the parties, either in the particular case or a similar patent. And whether a particular expert has been largely employed by the particular solicitor on the one side or the other. He concluded that '[i]t is so extremely difficult to find out a really unbiased expert and a man who has no preconceived opinion or prejudice'.[8]

One might add that the adversarial nature of litigation in common law courts means that, as a matter of human nature, a witness will usually see the acceptance of his or her evidence as an objective coinciding with the ultimate success of the party on whose behalf he or she testifies. Whether fact or opinion, people like to be believed.

In the humble case of an intersection collision, the casual passer-by, called to say that the other party drove through the red light, will want to be believed. On learning of a favourable result, he or she might well say to a friend, 'our side won'. Nelson's sailors wanted to win, notwithstanding that they had been enlisted by way of the press gang.

By way of example, I was involved in a (very civilised) debate over proposed Queensland Supreme Court Rules to provide for court-appointed experts. Initially, the proposal was for a single court-appointed expert to be the norm, with party experts being allowed only by leave. The final version was less restrictive and allowed party experts as of right, subject to certain conditions as to the filing of reports and costs sanctions.[9] In volume 23 of the *Civil Justice Quarterly* (UK), Justice Geoffrey Davies of the Queensland Supreme Court put the case in favour of court-

---

[7] *Thorn* v. *Worthing Skating Rink* [1877] 6 Ch D 415, 416.   [8] Ibid.
[9] See Uniform Civil Procedure Rules 1999 (Qld) Pt. 5. See also Jacob, *IP and Other Things*, 43 fn. 1.

appointed experts.[10] I argued the contrary.[11] In a commentary by Sir Robin Jacob,[12] I can modestly claim a narrow victory on points. In that commentary, Sir Robin observed that:[13]

- Most experts, particularly those who give evidence regularly, genuinely do try to help the court. Anecdotally, since the introduction, following the Woolf Report,[14] of the express duty, most practising lawyers and judges in England and Wales would say the quality of expert evidence has improved.
- There is 'the real sanction of a serious slagging off by the judge if the expert is found to have breached his duty'[15] – compounded of course if the case is one which attracts media publicity.
- There is the risk of losing the respect of one's professional peers.

Some very limited and generalised enquiries I have made among Australian judges suggest a similar conclusion, notwithstanding some spectacular exceptions, such as a case, which attracted much publicity, where the witness cheerfully admitted to plagiarising another report. The witness explained that this was permissible because his report was not for a peer-reviewed publication. On the judge enquiring why court evidence should have a lower status, the witness said that his evidence was only for 'educative' purposes.[16]

Harking back for a moment to Sir George Jessel's *cri de coeur*, there does not appear to be any ground for objection in principle to expert-witness shopping. Experts may, and often do, honestly differ in their opinions. Selecting one whose opinion is helpful to the client's case, albeit after a perhaps extensive search, is not inconsistent with the ethics of an adversarial system.

As Dr Johnson explained to Boswell in the analogous context of the relevance of a lawyer's belief in the merits of the client's case:

---

[10] Justice Geoffrey Davies, 'Recent Australian developments: A response to Peter Heerey' (2004) 23 *Civil Justice Quarterly* 396.
[11] Justice Peter Heerey, 'Recent Australian developments' (2004) 23 *Civil Justice Quarterly* 386.
[12] Sir Robin Jacob, 'Court-appointed experts v party experts: Which is better?' (2004) 23 *Civil Justice Quarterly* 400.
[13] Ibid., 404.
[14] Lord Woolf, 'Access to justice: Final report' (1996), retrieved from https://bit.ly/2m6LD1R.
[15] Jacob, 'Court-appointed experts v party experts', 404.
[16] See *Guy v. Crown Melbourne Limited (No 2)* [2018] FCA 36 (2 February 2018).

An argument which does not convince yourself, may convince the Judge to which you urge it; and if it does convince him why, then, Sir, you are wrong and he is right.[17]

22.4 Expert Assessors

Another technique for obtaining the assistance of experts is the appointment of an assessor. This is someone who is not a witness, but whose role is to assist the judge by explanation and advice. As will be seen, just how that explanation and advice is to be given has become a matter of controversy.

There is a specific power given by section 217 of the Patents Act 1990 (Cth) for courts to 'call in the aid of an assessor to assist it in the hearing and trial or determination of any proceedings under (the) Act'. It is not exactly an everyday experience. In *Genetics Institute Inc* v. *Kirin-Amgen Inc (No 2)*,[18] after a contested hearing, I appointed Professor Ross Coppel, head of microbiology at Monash University, as an assessor in a patent case concerning the hormone erythropoietin (EPO) and genetic engineering. Although that provision had been in the Patents Act since 1903,[19] the only previous example of appointment of an assessor was in the High Court in 1935, and that was by consent.[20]

Counsel opposing the appointment, Annabelle Bennett SC, later a good friend and colleague on the Federal Court, airily asserted that the technology was not all that difficult, was taught in secondary schools and discussed in the mainstream media. However, since Dr Bennett held a PhD in inorganic chemistry, and my scientific education ended with sulphuric acid and iron filings, I thought the appointment of Professor Coppel would at the least do no harm.

There was no indication in the Patents Act, or any court rules, of the procedure to be followed. One possibility was that communications between assessor and judge would be only in writing, with copies made available to the parties. At the other extreme, which I adopted, I discussed the case fully in private with Coppel. He sat with me on the bench and did not participate directly in the hearing, but on occasions would suggest something I could put to a witness or counsel. When writing the judgment, I would discuss drafts with him, so as to avoid scientific solecisms. He told me that when the trial started the genetic technology under dispute in the case was at about third-year

---

[17] James Boswell, *The Life of Samuel Johnson, LLD* (London: John Sharpe, 1830), p. 168.
[18] (1997) 78 FCR 368.   [19] See Patents Act 1903 (Cth) s 86(8).
[20] *Adhesives Pty Ltd* v. *Aktieselskabet Dansk Gaerings-Industri* (1935) 55 CLR 523.

undergraduate level, but by the time it finished we were at post-doctoral stage. Coppel's assistance was hugely valuable, to say the least.

As it turned out, Bennett's client, which had opposed the appointment of the assessor, won the substantive trial. The other side appealed, among other things complaining of breach of natural justice. The Full Court dismissed the appeal.[21] Their Honours noted that the High Court held in *Re JRL; Ex parte CJL*[22] the rule that once a case gets under way 'a judicial officer keeps aloof from the parties (and from their legal advisors and witnesses)'[23] does not debar a judge hearing a case from 'consulting with ... court personnel whose function is to aid him in carrying out his judicial responsibilities'.[24] An assessor, who of course will be only appointed if he or she is, and is seen to be, completely independent of the parties, is in effect, pro tem, an officer of the court and assists the judge just like an associate, research assistant or other court staff.

There is a long-established practice in England of using assessors in admiralty cases as well as in patent and other technical cases, even at appellate level, as in *Biogen* v. *Medeva PLC*.[25] This was another case concerning genetics. The House of Lords had two independent advisors. Lord Goff of Chieveley described their assistance as 'invaluable'.[26] In the United States in *Association of Mexican-American Educators* v. *California*,[27] the US Court of Appeals for the Ninth Circuit approved the appointment of a 'technical advisor'.

Closer to home, a useful analogy is the Australian Competition Tribunal.[28] When constituted for a hearing, the chair is a Federal Court judge and there are two other members, usually an economist and a person with business experience. My experience of working in the tribunal was that it was a great advantage to be able to discuss often highly technical evidence informally in private with fellow tribunal members.

Sometimes there can be a degree of inhibition against asking in open court a question which might expose one as being not too bright. Lawyers may see the introduction of an assessor as lessening their control over the case. The participation of an assessor in the private way I have advocated may be argued to impinge upon the current Holy Grail of

---

[21] *Genetics Institute Inc* v. *Kirin-Amgen Inc* (1999) 92 FCR 106 (Black CJ, Merkel J, Goldberg J).
[22] (1986) 161 CLR 342.
[23] *Re JRL; Ex parte CJL* (1986) 161 CLR 342, 346 (Gibbs CJ), 351 (Mason J), citing with approval *R* v. *Magistrates' Court at Lilydale; Ex parte Ciccone* [1973] VR 122, 127 (McInerney J).
[24] (1986) 161 CLR 342, 351 (Mason J). [25] [1997] RPC 1. [26] Ibid., 31.
[27] 231 F 3d 572 (2000) at 590.
[28] See 'About the tribunal', Australian Competition Tribunal, retrieved from www.competitiontribunal.gov.au/about.

'transparency'. It is critical of course that the assessor has to be, and be seen to be, totally independent as well as appropriately qualified. That said, the judge has to produce a judgment in which facts are properly found on properly admissible evidence and the law properly applied to those facts. If this does not happen, the judgment will not survive the appellate process. Assuming the sine qua non of the assessor's independence, the parties are adequately protected.

After the *Genetics Institute*[29] case discussed earlier, the Rules Committee of the Federal Court, chaired by Justice Kevin Lindgren, drafted a rule which would provide for the use of assessors in the informal way I had followed. However, the proposed rule struck trouble when tabled at the next full meeting of judges. Notwithstanding the explicit ruling of the Full Court in the *Genetics* case itself, some judges complained of the lack of natural justice. Others relayed anecdotes of cases in which they had been able to master the most technical issues, to the unfeigned admiration of the expert witnesses.

The upshot was a new order, 34B, which laid down an elaborate procedure for exchange of written communications with an expert assistant appointed by the court, with copies to the parties.[30] A completely new set of court rules was promulgated in 2011. These rules contain no equivalent to Order 34B, or indeed anything about the use of assessors.[31] So hopefully this useful technique will still be available, at least in patent cases.

22.5 The Hot Tub

Traditionally, expert witnesses give their evidence along with lay witnesses in the course of presentation of the client's case. The plaintiff calls all its witnesses, including experts, and then closes its case. The defendant then does the same.

In more recent years in Australia, a radical departure from this system has evolved. After all lay witnesses from all parties have been called, the parties' experts give evidence together. While referred to in court rules by the somewhat boring title of 'concurrent evidence',[32] the colloquial term *Hot Tub* remains the preferred description. (The witnesses sit at a table.

---

[29] *Genetics Institute Inc* v. *Kirin-Amgen Inc* (1999) 92 FCR 106.
[30] Federal Court Rules 1979 (Cth) O 34B.
[31] Federal Court Rules 2011 (Cth), repealing Federal Court Rules 1979 (Cth).
[32] See, for example, Civil Procedure Act 2010 (Vic) s. 65K, 'Court may give direction about giving of evidence, including concurrent evidence, by expert witnesses'. See also Federal Court Rules 2011 (Cth) r. 23.15.

They do not literally sit in a hot tub. Constraints of propriety and court design dictate a less exciting solution.)

The procedure works basically as follows:[33]

1. After each expert has prepared his or her report, there is a pre-trial order that they confer together, without lawyers, to prepare a joint report on the matters about which they agree and those on which they disagree, giving short reasons as to why they disagree. Often the range of difference between the experts, which had been apparently vast if one put their two reports side by side, reduces to a narrow point or points of principle or the accuracy of a particular assumption. In addition to, or instead of, a joint report, the experts may each produce, a day or so before giving evidence, a brief position paper identifying the critical issues and the witness's position thereon.
2. In the courtroom, at the conclusion of both parties' lay evidence, the experts are called to give evidence together in their respective fields of expertise. First, each expert will be asked to identify and explain the principal issues, as they see them, in their own words. Each can then comment on the other's exposition and ask questions of and engage in conversation with the other – that is to say directly – without the intervention of counsel. There will then be conventional cross-examination and re-examination by counsel. This may follow after all experts have made their statements and questioned each other. Or it may be expert by expert.

One unconventional technique sometimes used is as follows. If cross-examining counsel receives an unfavourable answer to a question, or does not fully understand it, he or she can turn to their own expert and ask what that expert says about the other's answer. But the technique has its hazards. Cross-examining counsel's own expert may say: 'He's right. And let me explain why.' Another possible variation is that the procedure is carried out issue by issue. The issues are settled by the judge beforehand and dealt with by separate experts' expositions and questioning, both of each other and by counsel. In litigation over the Kilmore East bushfire in Victoria, Justice Jack Forrest of the Victorian Supreme Court applied this technique in a Hot Tub with no less than nine experts.[34] I have been told of another case, about escaping gas, in which eighteen experts were retained. The parties retained a facilitator whose task, successfully carried out apparently, was to organise the witnesses into sub-groups and identify issues and competing views.

---

[33] See, for example, Federal Court Rules 2011 (Cth) r. 23.15.
[34] *Matthews* v. *SPI Electricity Pty Ltd (Ruling No 32)* [2013] VSC 630 (18 November 2013).

A great advantage of the Hot Tub is that all the experts on the topic are together in the witness box at the one time, answering the questions on the same basis. This is a world away from a traditional cross-examination of each expert in the various parties' cases, sometimes happening weeks apart, with a raft of other evidence having interposed, perhaps destroying or modifying assumptions on which the first expert's evidence was given.

Another benefit is that the experts feel capable of explaining the matters to the judge and putting their points of view in a way in which they feel free to use their knowledge and experience. At the Australian Legal Conference in Melbourne in 1997, the distinguished scientist Sir Gustav Nossal said of the conventional method of giving expert evidence:

> the formality and seriousness of the proceedings, and their highly structured nature, differ from what scientists usually experience. ... The set piece, stately quality of examination and cross-examination can lead to a sense of incompleteness: If only I had said so and so; if only they'd asked me.[35]

Certainly the Hot Tub procedure can save time and expense. In a competition law case I heard, *Australian Competition and Consumer Commission* v. *Boral Ltd*,[36] the lay evidence took some four weeks, but the expert evidence of two distinguished economists, which was fundamental to the whole case, was disposed of in a day.

One criticism of the Hot Tub procedure sometimes heard is that a particularly articulate or confident or assertive expert may dominate proceedings and over-awe more diffident colleagues.[37] But these personality traits are a fact of life and are equally likely to be present when witnesses, expert or lay, give evidence from the witness box in the conventional way. I must say I have not seen any real evidence of this supposed problem, except perhaps in an accountants' Hot Tub in a share valuation case, where one adopted a rather studied Perry Mason style. It was rather counterproductive as far as I was concerned. Indeed, to the contrary, I think the physical separation of experts from their own camp when they are in the joint conference or at the witness table in the courtroom with (usually) respected colleagues tends to lower any partisan atmosphere and encourage an objective and professional approach.

---

[35] Sir Gustav Nossal, Paper presented at the 30th Australian Legal Convention, Melbourne, 19 September 1997, See Marvin J Garbis, 'Aussie inspired musings on technological issues – Of kangaroo courts, tutorials and Hot Tub cross-examination' (2003) 6 *Greenbag* 141, 144.
[36] (1999) 166 ALR 410.
[37] See, for example, Henry Ergas, 'Reflections on expert economic evidence' (2006–2007) *New South Wales Bar News* 39, 42–3.

22.6 Is This Expert Really Necessary?

Are there any areas of overlap – that is to say, fields the subject of academic and scientific discourse which nevertheless raise questions capable of understanding by lay people? Questions which remain, as lawyers like to say, jury questions?

At common law, as the High Court made clear in *Transport Publishing Co Pty Ltd* v. *Literature Board of Review*:[38]

> Ordinary human nature, that of people at large, is not a subject of proof by evidence, whether supposedly expert or not.

However, section 80(b) of the uniform Evidence Acts changed all that by providing that evidence of an opinion is not inadmissible only because it is about 'a matter of common knowledge'.[39]

It may be doubted whether that change was a good idea. In a case raising the issue of whether consumers were likely to be misled by the colouring of chocolate wrappers of rival producers, the Federal Court was treated to a ninety-page affidavit by an 'expert' discussing the supposed effect of such arcane concepts as 'cognitive dissonance', 'decision-heuristic cues' and 'operant conditioning'.[40]

My view is that expert evidence should be confined to cases where a judge or tribunal cannot make a sensible decision without it. For neurosurgery or oil exploration, fine. For consumers' reliance on chocolate wrappers, I suggest not.

To offer another example, I believe, or at any rate hope, it still to be the law that expert opinion evidence is not admissible on the meaning of non-technical ordinary English words. Cases over the construction of statutes, contracts, wills and other documents are not yet burdened with conflicting opinions from linguists and post-modern literary theorists. Similarly, in other fields, expert opinion evidence should be limited to cases where it is really needed.

Our system of justice is not based on a search for absolute truth. It is rather directed at resolving disputes according to law fairly and rationally and, dare one say, in an economically efficient way.

---

[38] (1956) 99 CLR 111, 119 (Dixon CJ, Kitto and Taylor JJ).

[39] The uniform Evidence Acts consist of the following seven Australian statutes: Evidence Act 1995 (Cth); Evidence Act 2011 (ACT); Evidence Act 1995 (NSW); Evidence Act 2004 (Norfolk Island); Evidence (National Uniform Legislation) Act 2011 (NT); Evidence Act 2001 (Tas); Evidence Act 2008 (Vic). They are substantially similar (although not identical) to the *Evidence Act 1995* (Cth). The uniform Evidence Acts have not been adopted by Queensland, South Australia and Western Australia.

[40] *Cadbury Schweppes Pty Ltd* v. *Darrell Lea Chocolate Shops Pty Ltd* [2006] FCA 363 (31 March 2006), revd (2007) 159 FCR 397.

23 Copyright and the 'Profession' of Authorship

Colin Golvan

Victor Hugo, the creative colossus of the nineteenth century, was one of the great champions of the rights of the author. Speaking in 1878, Hugo said: 'All the old monarchical laws denied and still deny literary property. For what purpose? For the purpose of control. The writer-owner is a free writer. To take his property is to take away his independence.'[1] Hugo's involvement in the discussions leading to the first international copyright convention is the stuff of legend. His focus on the rights of the author shaped the drafting of the Berne Convention, the subject of such considerable scholarship of Sam Ricketson.[2]

Likewise, in national legal systems, the notion of authorship is at the heart of copyright, which is ultimately concerned with the protection of copying of the form of expression of an author.[3] For instance, the concept is simply framed in section 32 of the Australian Copyright Act 1968 (Cth) (Copyright Act) – copyright subsists in an original work, and in section 35(2) of that Act, which provides that the author of a work is the owner of copyright subsisting in it.[4] Yet the term *author* is barely defined in the Copyright Act, and in practice it is a concept which wears many faces.

---

[1] As quoted in James Boyle, 'Victor Hugo: Guardian of the public domain', The Public Domain: Enclosing the Commons of the Mind, 18 July 2014, retrieved from www.thepublicdomain.org/2014/07/18/victor-hugo-guardian-of-the-public-domain.

[2] See Sam Ricketson, *The Berne Convention for the Protection of Literary and Artistic Works: 1886–1986* (London: Centre for Commercial Law Studies, Queen Mary College, Kluwer, 1987); Sam Ricketson and Jane C Ginsburg, *International Copyright and Neighbouring Rights: The Berne Convention and Beyond*, 2nd ed. (Oxford: Oxford University Press, 2006).

[3] *Walter* v. *Lane* [1900] AC 539, 554; *Donoghue v Allied Newspapers Ltd* [1938] Ch 106, 110 (cited as *Donoghue*).

[4] See *IceTV Pty Ltd* v. *Nine Network Australia Pty Ltd* (2009) 80 IPR 451, [33], [34], [47–9], [52] and [54].

In this chapter, drawing on my experience as a practising copyright lawyer,[5] I point out, that the recognition of authorship in copyright law runs from the bland to the sublime. A parts list may be protected,[6] as might a great work of creative genius. It is an aspect of the 'genius' of copyright that the same regime protects the limitless range of human expression all within the rubric of the concept of 'a copyright work'.

23.1 Authorship: Scope and Limits

How does one discern when the moment of authorship commences? Is it, as I am doing, at the time of putting my own words on the page? Does each word and the ordering of the words capture something unique about me as an author? Presumably the formulation of the previous sentence (and indeed this sentence) indicates something about me as the author. Or, by venturing these thoughts (and claiming private ownership in them as expressed pursuant to the Copyright Act), am I here being a mere mouthpiece for the crypto-capitalist quest to enlarge the scope of personal property rights in the limitless empire of intangible private property, which has become so dominant in domestic and international commerce?

And where does authorship end? The concept of author as director is, of course, long and well-established in the making of movies. Alfred Hitchcock, the auteur, is well recognised. There is the much-analysed 'Hitchcock Touch' which distinguishes his movies.[7] How do we understand his authorship? Does one become an author by the crafting of the scene of a film written, photographed and performed by others – in the sense of the lending of a veneer across the entirety of the work? And what of the definitive performance of a piece of music, played with the same notes available to any performer? Is there authorship? How is it to be defined? And then there is the orchestra conductor as author or interpreter. It is surely one of the most unusual and enigmatic acts of authorship in the creative arts – his or her back to the audience, and not a single note is played. And yet, the mere mention of a Rattle, Barenboim or Dudamel will draw a full house, and we won't hear peep from them and will barely get to see their faces. We watch their hands in frenzied movement directing the performances of a large group of highly talented

---

[5] In a number of the cases mentioned in this chapter, I appeared as counsel, and in some of them alongside (or in opposition to) Sam Ricketson who invariably brought considerable authority and scholarship to the approach adopted.
[6] *Autocaps (Aust) Pty Ltd* v. *Pro-Kit Pty Ltd* (1999) 46 IPR 339.
[7] See, e.g., Wieland Schwanebeck (ed.), *Reassessing the Hitchcock Touch: Industry, Collaboration, and Filmmaking* (Cham, Switzerland: Palgrave Macmillan, 2017).

performers. One wonders what would happen if Sir Simon did not turn up? Would disaster and embarrassment on stage ensue? It would be unthinkable for the London Symphony to perform on stage without its conductor. The Copyright Act acknowledges the role of a conductor as 'a performer' in s. 191B, and accordingly grants performers' rights protection to conductors with respect to the sounds made in the conducted performance.

As matters stand, authorship of works involving creative endeavour which is not reduced to material form will be excluded from copyright protection, while a vast array of creative endeavours that do result in material forms are accorded the status of an authored work. This is fundamental to the operation of the Copyright Act with respect to works.[8] And one has to ask why so much latitude is granted to authored works reduced to material form when other types of authorship may be left outside the scope of copyright protection altogether (or only admitted on the most limited terms).[9]

To give some more particular examples:

23.1.1 Arts and Crafts

Auguste Rodin's works continue to be made from moulds presumably produced by the great (and very dead) man. In the art market, works said to be produced by Rodin from the moulds which he made are considered to have a particular special value – and are promoted as Rodin originals. And then there is the controversy of works produced today from the Rodin moulds. Are they genuinely 'works of Rodin', or the product of a form of mass production? The issue is particularly highlighted with the capacity to bypass the mould with the potential use of 3D printing.

The glass craftsman Dale Chihuly makes little himself, but directs a process, which results in the production of complex and beautiful glass pieces. He is typically credited as author of these pieces – without his attribution the value of these works would be significantly reduced. Attribution identifies Chihuly, but he may not have laid a finger on any glass in the course of the creative and manufacturing process.

The Australian artist Patricia Piccinini also directs a complex manufacturing process. Her 'out of this world' and yet often life-like creatures are the product of complex planning and fabrication, involving a creative and manufacturing team which she leads. While she supervises all stages in the realisation of her intended imagery, she needs fabricators to give

---

[8] See Copyright Act 1968 (Cth) s. 22(1).
[9] See, for instance (re performers' rights), Copyright Act 1968 (Cth), Part XIA.

effect to her artistic creations. They are highly expert and she would readily acknowledge that her works would not exist without them.

It would be odd to treat the craftsperson working behind the scenes as 'a mere scribe', in the sense of a transcriber of a speech,[10] and yet the 'authorship' of the highly skilled artisan collaborator is invariably not recognised other than in background materials.

23.1.2 Aboriginal Art

Many larger works of Aboriginal art are the product of group processes. Even smaller works have elements depicted by some unknown person with the defining touches done by the attributed author. Often it is impossible to discern the work of the attributed author or authors.

Aboriginal art often involves no statement of authorship recorded by the artist on the work. In fact, it would be unusual to find a signed work of a traditional Aboriginal artist. In the vast array of rock art found throughout Australia, it would be very difficult to identify one instance of authorial attribution.

I suggest that this practice of not signing works is, at least in part, today concerned with the rejection of the idea of private or individual authorship in a cultural sense. The art market demands attribution, but the artists and their communities can often be indifferent to public declarations of attribution.

While authorship of the works of traditional Aboriginal artists in a conventional Western sense (attracting copyright protection) might be uncontroversial, the artist often understands his or her practice as occurring in a communal environment where artistic expression is recorded for, and on behalf of, the community. Senior artists work in an environment of management, permissions and controls. A particular artist may have the exclusive right to depict an image, such as the Magpie Goose (in the case of the Arnhem Land artist and Ganalbingu elder John Bulun Bulun).[11] He does so as the delegate of the community with special roles and responsibilities which attach to the exclusive right to depict particular images. He functions under the management of clan leaders and is responsible to them for the proper depiction of the imagery which he is entitled to depict exclusively.

In the *Bulun Bulun* case,[12] Justice von Doussa sought to engage with the gulf in the conceptual approach to the issue of authorship and ownership

---

[10] See *Donoghue* [1938] Ch. 106.
[11] *Bulun Bulun* v. *R & T Textiles Pty Ltd* (1998) 41 IPR 513 (cited as *Bulun Bulun case*).
[12] Ibid.

from a Western perspective compared with the traditional Aboriginal approach, likening the position of the traditional Aboriginal artist to that of fiduciary with obligations to the beneficiaries of the fiduciary relationship to properly protect a permitted artwork from wrongful reproduction by bringing an action for infringement.[13] The judge interestingly speculated on the legal standing of the beneficiaries, or tribal owners, in an infringement setting in a case where the fiduciary failed to act:

> had Bulun Bulun merely failed to take action to enforce his copyright, an adequate remedy might be extended in equity to the beneficiaries by allowing them to bring action in their own names against the infringer and the copyright owner, claiming against the former, in the first instance, interlocutory relief to restrain the infringement, and against the latter orders necessary to ensure that the copyright owner enforces the copyright.[14]

23.1.3 Artistic Schools

In an entirely different setting, there is the age-old practice of schools of artists who would work with the great masters, such as in the case of Rembrandt or Caravaggio, with the line being obscured between the work of the master and that of the pupil. Sometimes a work is credited 'of the school', a kind of satellite world in the great universe of the eternal masters of the classical arts. Seemingly never-ending contests are fought out among art experts to determine whether a work was that of the master or a pupil in the style of the master. A determination against attribution in favour of the artist will almost inevitably result in a work being relegated to a lesser place in public exhibition or being removed from public viewing entirely.

Similarly group authorship, even under the command of the master, does not quite carry the same appeal as the unaided hand of the sole genius.

A piece of music of Vivaldi has said to have been 'discovered', which prior to the announcement of the discovery was thought to be the work of a pupil of Vivaldi.[15] Music experts declared the work to be a work of Vivaldi. How? Because it was said to bear the distinctive mark of his musical hand – a kind of assumed DNA that only specially trained ears can hear. The attribution instantly raised the profile of the work to a new status, such is the potency of authorial attribution.

---

[13] Ibid., 529, 531. [14] Ibid., 531.
[15] Dayla Alberge, 'Vivaldi's lost masterpiece is found in library archives', *The Guardian*, 15 July 2012, retrieved from www.theguardian.com/music/2012/jul/15/orlando-furioso-vivaldi-1714-version.

23.1.4 Originality versus Creativity

Copyright is, of course, agnostic about creative input. In the case of works, copyright protection essentially requires an act of authorship by reduction to material form in a manner which involves something more than copying. The threshold for originality is low. There is no requirement of intellectual innovation or any contribution to learning in order to satisfy the requirements of protectable authorship, which opens copyright to the protection of a very wide range of works, and well beyond works of any artistic merit. Though linked as subjects (as sub-categories in the study of intellectual property), copyright and patents could not be further removed on the threshold requirements for subsistence.

The focus for protection in copyright is on form of expression, or the individual voice, which is a very narrow basis for founding protection – that is, based on the particular 'voice' or selection of the author.

The telling of someone else's story can enjoy its own protection under copyright,[16] just as the depicting of an artwork based on ideas supplied by another person.[17] The telling of the same story can have many different fathers or mothers from a copyright perspective. In the more remote corners of copyright protection, an author can be a compiler of data, such as of a price list for car parts – as long as a process of individual selection is made.

Originality can be expressed in quite unusual ways. For instance, *Elwood Clothing Pty Ltd* v. *Cotton On Clothing Pty Ltd*[18] involved the issue of authorship by means of the layer of visual expression beneath the conspicuous placement of visual imagery on a garment. In that case, there was the copying of stylistic features of the design of artworks on Elwood garments, based on the placement of words, numbers and graphic images. Cotton On copied the location of the various features of design on their garments, but changed the words, numbers and graphics. For example, where the number '1' was located on the Elwood garment, Cotton On substituted another number in the same position. The question for infringement purposes concerned the proper identification of the original elements of the Elwood design and implicitly whether the Cotton On works constituted new works though stylistically they were copied from the Elwood designs. Elwood failed at trial to prevent the copying conduct, which was considered to be the copying of ideas rather than form of expression due to the changes in the expressed

---

[16] *Walter* v. *Lane* [1900] AC 539.
[17] Thus, for example, *Kenrick & Co* v. *Lawrence & Co* (1890) 25 QBD 99.
[18] (2008) 80 IPR 566, and on appeal at (2008) 172 FCR 580 (cited as *Cotton On*).

conduct. On appeal, a contrary view was taken which embraced the location of key elements of the garment designs. In argument on appeal, the example was given of the artwork of the famous Australian/New Zealand artist Rosemary Gascoigne, whose work features images showing letters and numbers against road-sign yellow backgrounds. It was argued, by way of analogy, that her work would be infringed by simply changing the numbers and letters but keeping them in the same positions, as occurred in the Cotton On instance. This approach was accepted on appeal.[19]

23.1.5 Modern Art

One of the most celebrated instances in modern times for the low-threshold perspective was highlighted by Andy Warhol's famous Campbell's Soup Can paintings – every soup label and can in the range was lovingly depicted in large-format individual panels.

Warhol was depicting the soup can with its label, in a way to convey the can in three dimensions, and then across the homey range of soups – chicken and vegetable as well as hearty beef. By so doing, he was bringing the skills of high art to the forefront of the authorship debate in contemporary art, closely linking high artistic endeavour with the banal, and thus removing the kind of moral authority or superiority one might otherwise associate with creative authorship.

Here we have one of the great modern artists putting his signature to images of the most mundane and uninteresting products (at least to those who could contemplate affording buying one of the panels). The works are defiantly anti-authorial and deliberately challenge the notion of art as a means of unique and often agonised or ingenious self-expression. The artist has facetiously given way to the sterility of the consumer market and as such has divorced himself from the traditional role of the artist standing above the day-to-day discourse of ordinary people.

These works are an expression of rebellion against traditional notions of authorship, raising in turn the interesting and challenging notion of whether the copyright in Campbell's soup labels was infringed. It is almost inconceivable that Campbell's soups would (or could) sue Warhol for infringement, but, of course, why would they even contemplate something so ridiculous in the face of the immortalisation of the most humble soup label? Notions of authorship, as a statement of creative superiority, were turned on their head.

---

[19] *Cotton On* (2008) 172 FCR 580 at [76]–[80].

In 2017, the UK artist Damien Hirst challenged notions of fakery with his much-noted exhibition of fake 'lost treasures' displayed in Venice.[20] Hirst created his own vast universe of lost treasures supposedly found on a wreck – all of which he created and which he displayed with a litany of deliberately ridiculous attributions to ancient craftsmen. He was clearly the owner of copyright, as author, of a host of works which he falsely attributed to others, raising an interesting issue of what would have happened if one of his so-called ancient finds came to be copied. The pretence of false attribution would no doubt quickly dissipate.

For me, one of the great moments of authorship in contemporary art practice occurred in the remote Australian outback town of Papunya in the early 1970s. The use of the term *remote* is to understate the isolation of Papunya, situated hundreds of kilometres from Alice Springs in the heart of the central desert of Australia.

The story of Papunya and its art movement is fabled. A school teacher in the early 1970s, Geoffrey Bardon, became interested in the possibilities for Aboriginal artists exploring the ancient skills of body painting and drawing in sand. He bought some acrylic paints and encouraged the artists to experiment with oil painting and the colour range permitted by commercial paints. They painted the walls of the school building and some boards – displaying highly coloured dots and lines, transforming the craft of much more simple drawings in sand or on bodies which had great tribal meaning. The artists had themselves never seen the use of acrylic paints in art before. They had never been to art galleries and had no idea about the evolution of art forms in the contemporary art world. They were not meaning to imitate any external artform and yet were using materials otherwise unknown to them in visionary and brilliant ways.

As a moment of authorship, the event was unique. Here was an entirely original artform which did not emerge from the canon of world art, but which was entirely original, and was the starting point for an indigenous movement which had not previously engaged with the colour palate of acrylic paints.

It was a remarkable achievement. While it conveyed the hallmarks of being ancient, it was in fact truly contemporary, and inspired a great wave of painting which now defines the desert art movement of Australia. The great canvasses of this movement adorn the most important art galleries of Australia and a number of the great art galleries of the world. They look timeless, but in fact the form of the depiction is relatively

---

[20] 'Damien Hirst: Treasures from the wreck of the unbelievable', Palazzo Grassi, retrieved from https://bit.ly/2khgjga.

contemporary. And once the range of colours became available, the artists did extraordinary things with colour – depicting their desert country in a way which was previously unseen by the general public. The complete originality of the movement, as distinct from a movement which was derivative and responsive to a predecessor movement, puts these developments in a unique class.

It is not surprising that infringers moved in quickly to take advantage of the new artform and the evolving art movements of Aboriginal Australia which emerged at this time.

An initial challenge in managing the problem of infringement focussed on the issue of subsistence. Were the artists genuinely authorial or mere scribes of an ancient practice? The scribe argument has been overwhelmingly rejected as a view that reflected ignorance of the profound Aboriginal art practice which vividly engaged with the remarkable natural environment of our homeland.[21]

23.1.6 Technical Art and Artificial Intelligence

Climbing down from these heights, the creative neutrality of copyright is a key feature of its universal application. I have mentioned price lists. There is a pantheon of simple works (in the sense of only passing creative interest) which have come to be protected.

In a series of cases, the display home builder Barrett Homes Pty Ltd,[22] trading as Porter Davis, established an entitlement to copyright protection in a section of a display home which featured a series of rooms located around an exterior entertainment area, which was promoted as an al fresco dining area. One of the most contentious issues in the cases was the claim of copyright subsistence in the identified part of the house plan, which came to be referred to as the 'Al Fresco Quadrant'. Barrett established authorship of the part of the plan notwithstanding allegations that it must have been copied from earlier iterations of the al fresco dining concept. Notwithstanding extensive attempts to prove the influence of these earlier iterations, the particular expression of the form of the feature could not be found in any variant said to have been available to the author of the particular variant sought to be protected by Barrett. Findings of subsistence in favour of Barrett were made in a series of cases involving different claims of infringement against competing display

---

[21] *Milpurrurru* v. *Indofurn Pty Ltd* (1994) 30 IPR 209 at 224.
[22] *Metricon Homes Pty Ltd* v.*Barrett Property Group Pty Ltd* (2008) 75 IPR 455 (on appeal), *Barrett Property Group Pty Ltd* v. *Dennis Family Homes Pty Ltd* (2011) 279 ALR 12.

home builders. The claims were also challenged before Full Courts, which confirmed the subsistence of copyright in favour of Barrett.[23]

In *Telstra Corporation Ltd* v. *Phone Directories Co Pty Ltd*,[24] the limits of this creative neutrality were identified in the requirement to at least have a human author at the helm. The issue there concerned a computer generated alphabetic listing of names, addresses and telephone numbers in the white pages telephone directory. While humans contributed individual lines of data, as new telephone connections were made, the compilation (literary work) was produced by a computer ordering the data. The Federal Court denied protection on the basis that a work of authorship, being the compiled list, required human authorship. In essence, the court found that there were human contributors of data but there was no human author of the compilation.

On appeal, Justice Perram stated: 'Whilst humans were ultimately in control of the software which did reduce the information to a material form, their control was over a process of automation and they did not shape or direct the material form themselves (that process being performed by the software). The directories did not, therefore, have an author and copyright cannot subsist in them.'[25] His Honour, adopting the metaphor of an autopilot, said of the making of the compilation that it is 'flying itself'.[26]

This requirement exposed shortcomings in the ambit of the protection of works in an age of automated authorship. In short, works created by artificial intelligence fall outside the notion of authorship as we know it in the Copyright Act. Invariably, there will be a need to address the protection of works of artificial intelligence, but this will require a significant revision of present notions which equate authorship with the 'human hand'.

The UK Copyright, Designs and Patents Act 1988 provides in section 9(3) that: 'In the case of a literary, dramatic, musical or artistic work which is computer-generated, the author shall be taken to be the person by whom the arrangements necessary for the creation of the work are undertaken.'[27]

It is anticipated that future Australian legislation on this issue will follow this approach and, in a similar manner, the approach which

---

[23] *Metricon Homes Pty Ltd* v. *Barrett Property Group Pty Ltd* (2008) 75 IPR 455; *Carlisle Homes Pty Ltd* v. *Barrett Property Group Pty Ltd* [2009] FCAFC 31.
[24] (2010) 264 ALR 617 at first instance and on appeal at (2010) 194 FCR 142, an application for special leave being refused: [2011] HCA Trans 248 (cited as *Telstra Corp*).
[25] *Telstra Corp* (2010) 194 FCR 142, 179 [119].   [26] Ibid., 178–9 [118].
[27] Copyright, Designs and Patents Act 1988 (UK) c. 48, s. 9(3).

applies to producers of a film, in section 98 of the Copyright Act, where the maker of the film for valuable consideration (i.e., the producer) is deemed to be the owner of copyright in it. In other words, the person who causes the making of an automated compilation (for valuable consideration) will be deemed to be the author or owner of copyright in it, with 'owner' being preferred to the artifice of 'author'. Clearly there is a need to address this issue, and invariably in a manner which departs from the threshold requirement of human authorship, which ordinarily applies when regard is had to subsistence.

23.2   Postscript

Copyright has traditionally been agnostic on the issue of authorship, and has eschewed notions of creative authorship. While this approach has held good in the context of human authorship, copyright faces enormous challenges with the emergence of artificial intelligence and the notion of machine-originated authorship, potentially transcending even the notion of there being a person who makes the arrangements necessary for the creation of a work (referred to earlier). It is inevitable that this issue will need to be addressed, and possibly outside of the bounds of conventional copyright. Clearly, the Victor Hugo notions of 'the rights of authors', and ideas of providing incentives for authorship which permits protection for many years after the life of the author, become meaningless in this setting.

In many ways the story of copyright has been a story of 'catching-up' as developments in technology raise considerable challenges to the existing body of copyright law, such as in the case of the need for protection of computer-generated data. The emergence of authorship by artificial means unquestionably raises the need for some fundamental rethinking about the nature of copyright and authorship.

Laudatio

24 Sam Ricketson
Teacher, Scholar, Advocate and Law Reformer

Jill McKeough

An understanding of the balancing of private rewards and public benefit for the results of mental labour, the emergence of intellectual property law as a discrete area of law (at least from the middle of the nineteenth century),[1] and the global governance regime for intellectual property (IP) rights, are topics which remained opaque to most Australians until the last quarter of the twentieth century.[2] Recent scholarship points to the concept of 'coherence' as being 'a fundamental principle in Australian law'[3] explicated by the High Court in (among others) patent cases[4] and in academic literature. It is no exaggeration to say that with the publication of Sam Ricketson's landmark text, *The Law of Intellectual Property*,[5] explication, coherence and understanding of this area of the law, across the board, appeared in Australia for the first time. Adding to this, his

---

[1] See Brad Sherman and Lionel Bently *The Making of Modern Intellectual Property Law: The British Experience 1760–1911* (Cambridge: Cambridge University Press, 1999), p. 61 ff.
[2] With some notable contributions from intellectual property commentators on discrete topics, including the discussion of breach of confidence in Roderick P Meagher, William M C Gummow and John R F Lehane, *Equity Doctrines and Remedies* (Sydney: Butterworths, 1975), now in its fifth edition (ed. John D Heydon, Mark J Leeming and Peter G Turner), and Francis Gurry, *Breach of Confidence* (Oxford: Oxford University Press, 1984), the basis of Tanya Aplin, Lionel Bently, Philip Johnson and Simon Malynicz, *Gurry on Breach of Confidence: The Protection of Confidential Information*, 2nd ed. (Oxford: Oxford University Press, 2012); and of copyright in James C Lahore with Phillip B C Griffith, *Copyright and the Arts in Australia* (Carlton, Victoria: Melbourne University Press, 1975); James C Lahore, *Intellectual Property in Australia* (Sydney: Butterworths, 1977)– the latter being initially focussed on copyright but now covering in loose-leaf form all the main fields.
[3] Andrew Fell, 'The concept of coherence in Australian private law' (2018) 41 *Melbourne University Law Review* 1160, 1161.
[4] Ibid., 1172, 1193.
[5] Staniforth (Sam) Ricketson, *The Law of Intellectual Property: Copyright, Designs and Confidential Information* (Sydney: Law Book Co, 1984).

commentaries on international instruments such as the Berne Convention,[6] and the Paris Convention,[7] a thorough overview of IP law at the domestic and international levels was created. From this basis, Ricketson has been throughout his career an authoritative and respected writer, teacher and commentator on legal doctrine, law reform and public policy across the broad range of IP and, in particular, in the area of copyright, an area in which I have also been involved.

24.1 Scholarship

When I began my professional life at the University of New South Wales, Sam Ricketson was already a youthful member of a pioneering 'band' of Australian law academics, including Jim Lahore, Francis Gurry (now director of the World Intellectual Property Organization), William Gummow (soon to become a judge), Michael Blakeney and Michael Pendleton, who were at the forefront of the definition and description of the field which came to be known as 'intellectual property'. Most of these people were working overseas, notably in the UK, for much or all of the time, and even Ricketson who was mainly in Australia when I was starting out had undertaken his LLM at the London School of Economics and Political Science in 1976. A mentor for many, fellow Australian Bill Cornish, professor of law at the London School of Economics and Political Science, University of London, had in 1981 written the first book which combined the disparate legal fields of registered and unregistered trade marks, copyright, patent, registered designs, trade secrets and in some jurisdictions sui generis regimes such as plant varieties protection, into a single legal genus, exploring the common themes of these hitherto professionally and academically separate areas of law.[8] This theme was taken up in various books on IP published in the early 1980s in various jurisdictions.[9] However, it was not until Ricketson's

---

[6] Sam Ricketson, *The Berne Convention for the Protection of Literary and Artistic Works, 1886–1986* (London: Kluwer for the Centre for Commercial Law Studies, Queen Mary College, University of London, 1987); Sam Ricketson and Jane Ginsburg, *International Copyright and Neighbouring Rights: The Berne Convention and Beyond*, 2nd ed. (Oxford: Oxford University Press, 2006).

[7] Sam Ricketson, *The Paris Convention for the Protection of Industrial Property: A Commentary* (Oxford: Oxford University Press, 2015).

[8] William R Cornish, *Intellectual Property: Patents, Copyright, Trade Marks and Allied Rights* (London: Sweet & Maxwell, 1981), now in its eighth edition, co-authored with David Llewellyn and Tanya Aplin.

[9] See, for instance, Lahore, *Copyright and the Arts in Australia*; Michael Pendleton, *The Law of Intellectual and Industrial Property in Hong Kong* (London: Butterworths, 1984); Michael Blakeney and Jill McKeough, *Intellectual Property: Commentary and Materials* (North Ryde, NSW: Law Book, 1987).

The Law of Intellectual Property appeared in 1984 that the Australian law was definitively chronicled and delineated. Closely afterwards came his definitive *The Berne Convention for the Protection of Literary and Artistic Works, 1886–1986* followed, somewhat later, by *The Paris Convention for the Protection of Industrial Property*.[10]

It is difficult to recall the world before email, the internet and Google, but such a world existed before the 1990s, when commercial internet providers began to offer services to universities and businesses. IP teachers had generally not been offered any subjects on the area of intellectual property in their own legal education and did not know who else was teaching the subject matter in other universities. Putting together a set of materials for students was a rather hit-and-miss affair with no guiding commentary or overview of the area of protection of economic investment in creative effort. Sam Ricketson's books (along with various articles and chapters written around the same period) were, in this environment, like the sun coming out from behind a cloud.

24.2 Teaching and Advocacy

Sam Ricketson was a generous and enthusiastic participant at the inaugural Intellectual Property Teachers Conference held at the University of New South Wales in November 1991, which continues to be a very active network in which virtually all Australian academic IP lawyers have at some stage participated.[11] The conference was put together by writing to deans of law schools and asking 'Do you have anyone teaching intellectual property?' With the collegiality which has been a notable aspect of the academic IP community, many responded positively when the letter was passed on to them, and contributed the $50.00 registration fee (including dinner at a local restaurant) to attend. From the beginning the conference was designed to allow discussion of the teaching, research and scholarship of IP and the challenges of covering the field in a crowded law school curriculum.

Throughout his career, Sam Ricketson has presented his research to a wide variety of audiences, speaking at conferences on topics across the field of IP, international trade, commercialisation of innovation, corporate law and conflicts of law. As a persuasive and authoritative speaker, he has been adroit at communicating complex and detailed material in a

---

[10] See Ricketson, *Berne Convention* and Ricketson, *Paris Convention* and the chapters by Antony Taubman, David Llewelyn and Mark Davison in this book.
[11] The latest conference was held in Hobart, hosted by the University of Tasmania, in February 2019, retrieved from www.utas.edu.au/law/intellectual-property-conference.

clear and cohesive manner, leaving the audience better informed than when they arrived and reassured by not only his vast knowledge but also his mellifluous Melbournian diction. The broad reach of Sam Ricketson's research and his skill at presentation of complex ideas has also enabled him to pursue a successful career as a barrister,[12] earning the respect of the world of industry and commerce for being a 'real-world' scholar.

24.3   Law Reform

In addition to creating the palimpsest upon which IP teaching and scholarship could proceed, Sam Ricketson has been a participant, commentator on and observer of law reform during the most fraught years of discussions of copyright reform in Australia. Indeed, as other commentators have indicated, without him, there would have been little known of the law to critique and reform. His ground-breaking work consists partly in studies of the history and parameters of law, providing the basis of vast understanding from which to participate in discussions of reform.

IP reform discussions take place in an international context; there is a direct link between international trade and intellectual property law. This link was the explicit basis for the Agreement on Trade-Related Aspects of Intellectual Property Rights (TRIPS Agreement).[13] Alongside, and perhaps supplanting, multilateral harmonisation is an emerging environment of bilateral trade negotiations. Ricketson's work on the Berne Convention, in particular, has set the scene for a consideration of the continuing interpretation of that document and its continuing relevance.

A fundamental aspect of the challenges to copyright reform is the development of the digital economy. In 2000, John Perry Barlow argued that copyright cannot be patched or retrofitted to the digital environment and an entirely new way of thinking is required. He describes the United States Digital Millennium Copyright Act of 1998,[14] for example, as 'ludicrously misguided'.[15] Ricketson's scholarship, on the other hand, points the way to evolution of concepts and adaptation of general

---

[12] See the chapters by Peter Heerey and Colin Golvan in this book.
[13] Marrakesh Agreement Establishing the World Trade Organization, opened for signature 15 April 1994, 1867 UNTS 3 (entered into force 1 January 1995) annex 1C (Agreement on Trade-Related Aspects of Intellectual Property Rights; cited as TRIPS Agreement.
[14] Digital Millennium Copyright Act, Pub L No. 105-304, 112 Stat. 2860 (1998).
[15] John P Barlow, 'The next economy of ideas', *Wired*, 10 January 2000, retrieved from www.wired.com/2000/10/download.

principles of copyright protection to the changing milieu and the desirability of finding unifying and underlying principles.[16]

In the contest of globalisation and international trade developments over the past two decades, there has been an increasing opening up and deregulation of the Australian economy. Successive federal governments have pursued a national competition policy in the interests of making Australian business more efficient and productive. In the early 1990s a specific trigger for reviewing the interface between intellectual property and competition law came about with the Hilmer Review (established October 1992). The aim of this independent inquiry into national competition policy was to identify opportunities for micro-economic reform and to enable the Australian economy to blossom in a more open, contestable world forum. The Hilmer report, published in 1993,[17] noted the 'difficulties of determining the proper balance between the exercise of intellectual property rights and the promotion of competition' but did not deal with IP in any substantive way[18] and said there needed to be a separate inquiry. This was the Intellectual Property Competition Review Committee (IPCRC or Ergas Review).[19] More recently, copyright reform has been discussed in the House of Representatives IT Pricing Inquiry 2013,[20] the Harper Review 2014,[21] the Australian Law Reform Commission (ALRC)'s Copyright and the Digital Economy Inquiry 2014 (for which I was the responsible law reform commissioner),[22] the Productivity Commission inquiry into intellectual property arrangements 2016, and in between the Attorney–General Department's Fair Use Review in 2005.[23]

Academic engagement in law reform has been subject to the inherent tensions between competing stakeholders. The tensions are real and

---

[16] See, e.g., Sam Ricketson, WIPO study on limitations and exceptions of copyright and related rights in the digital environment, prepared for the World Intellectual Property Organization Standing Committee on Copyright and Related Rights, 9th sess., WIPO Doc SCCR/9/7 (5 April 2003), 20.
[17] Independent Committee of Inquiry, *National Competition Policy Review* (Canberra: Australian Government Publishing Service, 1993).
[18] Ibid., 150.
[19] Intellectual Property and Competition Review Committee, Review of intellectual property legislation under the Competition Principles Agreement, Parliament of Australia (1993).
[20] House of Representatives Standing Committee on Infrastructure and Communications, 'At what cost? IT pricing and the Australia tax', Parliament of Australia (2013).
[21] Ian Harper, Peter Anderson, Su McCluskey and Michael O'Bryan, 'Competition policy review: Final report', 2015.
[22] ALRC, 'Copyright and the digital economy' (Report No. 122, 2014).
[23] Attorney-General's Department, 'Fair use and other copyright exceptions; An examination of fair use, fair dealing and other exceptions in the digital age' (Issues Paper, 2005).

interesting, particularly in the light of overwhelming political imperatives that face successive governments, and the lobbying campaigns from stakeholders. Academics have played a significant role in law reform and seen it as part of their public intellectual contribution, whether in participating as members of review bodies or in making submissions. Sam Ricketson has been a contributor since well before the current demands to do more 'impact and engagement'.[24] As well as contributing to and advising on law reform (including as a valued member of the Advisory Committee for the ALRC Copyright and the Digital Economy Inquiry report, noted earlier), he has analysed proposals for reform, or the need for reform, from first principles.

This has been especially the case for copyright law, an area of law that has lacked substantial reform in Australia over many years. A new Patents Act was introduced in 1990, and a new Trade Marks Act in 1995, but there has been no new copyright act and no major reform, although there has certainly been no shortage of reviewing of copyright law, with one of the most contentious areas being the boundaries of ownership and use of copyright material. In 1983 the Copyright Law Review Committee (CLRC) was established to consider and report to the attorney-general on specific copyright matters referred to it from time to time. The CLRC undertook a number of seminal inquiries, including into computer software protection (1994), journalists' copyright (1994), moral rights (1988), importation provisions of the Copyright Act (1988), performers' protection (1987) and several others, but none was so bold as the inquiry into simplification of the Copyright Act conducted in 1999.[25]

In its report, written substantially by Andrew Christie, the CLRC adopted a broad view of exceptions to rights under the heading of fair dealing and suggested the creation of two classes of subject matter – creations and productions – instead of the existing eight technology-specific categories. The recommendations on fair dealing were to consolidate the fair dealing provisions into a single section and expand it to an 'open-ended model', not confined to the closed list of fair dealing purposes but applying five 'fairness factors' to all fair dealings.[26] This is very like what we call *fair use* – at the time it was the subject of some controversy (which may help to explain why the CLRC's recommendations were never

---

[24] See current Australian Research Council requirements, retrieved from www.arc.gov.au/engagement-and-impact-assessment.

[25] CLRC, Simplification of the Copyright Act 1968 Part 1: Exceptions to the Exclusive Rights of Copyright Owners (1998); Simplification of the Copyright Act 1968, Part 2: Categorisation of Subject Matter and Exclusive Rights, and Other Issues (1999).

[26] CLRC, Simplification of the Copyright Act 1968 Part 1, 54–5.

implemented). The point was made by various interested parties that 'simplifying' the statute would not make it simpler at all but would create unintended consequences.

For Ricketson's part, while aware of the transaction costs of reform, he was quite open to the changes being proposed. He described the two parts of the final report as recommending 'quite radical departures from the present legislation' and the recommendations on fair dealing might have been seen as 'an Exocet in sheep's clothing – an elegantly coiffured wolf ready to cut through swathes of copyright owners' exclusive rights in the interests of "balance"'.[27] However, the CLRC's model was described as 'a neat and elegant one that will bring the existing multiplicity of exceptions into a coherent and orderly relationship'.[28]

In these comments, Ricketson perhaps foreshadowed a current debate in copyright reform; as to whether exceptions (and statutory licences) in the Copyright Act 1968 (Cth) are adequate and appropriate in the digital environment. The conclusion of the ALRC[29] and subsequently the Productivity Commission,[30] that asking the right questions about use of copyright material, in the context of a broad principles–based approach, is a vastly preferable and technology neutral solution to many of the woes of current copyright law, was to a large extent foreseen by Ricketson in his 1992 article 'New Wine in Old Bottles: Technological Change and Intellectual Property Rights'.[31] At the same time, he has warned against knee-jerk reform, either extending protection or restricting existing rights, without sound empirical evidence – for example, as to extension of the copyright term.[32]

In making the case for introduction of a broad flexible exception of fair use, one of the most lively discussions on law reform in recent times has been that of the three-step test, and its interpretation. Among the most favoured objections to copyright law reform is the lament that the three-step test would be breached (despite the fact that the US has not been challenged on fair use in any international forum).[33] Ricketson's

---

[27] Sam Ricketson, 'Simplifying copyright law: Proposals from down under' (1999) 21 *European Intellectual Property Review* 537, 541.
[28] Ibid., 549.   [29] ALRC, 'Copyright and the digital economy'.
[30] Productivity Commission, 'Intellectual property arrangements' (Inquiry Report No. 78, 2016).
[31] Noting also the contribution of other scholars to this debate, Sam Ricketson, 'New wine in old bottles: Technological change and intellectual property rights' (1992) 10 *Prometheus* 53, 76, citing Michael Pendleton and Grant Hammond at fn. 111.
[32] Sam Ricketson 'The copyright term' (1997) 23 *International Review of Intellectual Property and Competition Law* 758.
[33] See ALRC, 'Copyright and the digital economy', 117 ff; Productivity Commission, 'Intellectual property arrangements', 184.

commentary on the three-step test[34] is universally cited as authoritative on its construction and meaning, along with his work on the history and context of the Berne Convention.[35] He has pointed out that in the initial discussions, members to the Berne Convention wanted to retain their existing national laws permitting exceptions to the right of reproduction and were careful 'to ensure that this provision did not encroach upon exceptions that were already contained in national laws'.[36] Along with other commentators, including Jane Ginsburg, his co-author on the second edition of his Berne Convention book, he is influential on the possibilities of and the extent to which the three-step test allows 'wiggle room' for a fresh look at exceptions.[37] For example, in discussion of the three-step test under Berne article 9(2) and article 13 of the TRIPS Agreement, Ricketson and Ginsburg have traced the drafting history of the concept of 'equitable remuneration' and the adaptability of various forms of exceptions to copyright ownership, and have commented that the test is not a 'bright line rule' but can accommodate over time and format to allow a wide range of practices to comply with the test.[38]

However, given that the three-step test is the 'evil twin' of fair use,[39] Ricketson and Ginsburg have been enthusiastically cited at times in favour of the proposition that the requirement of exceptions applying in 'certain special cases' means that a broad exception, such as fair use, cannot be introduced (at least not in Australia).[40] On the other hand, Ricketson and Ginsburg can also be cited for the proposition that 'certain special cases should not have a normative interpretation'.[41] They have also warned against 'a grim future' with respect to the use of technological protection measures to cut down on existing exceptions to copyright use,[42] arguing that 'even in those countries where there is the most vigorous commitment to the advancement of author's rights, it is recognised that there is a need for restrictions or limitations upon these rights in particular cases'.[43]

---

[34] Ricketson, WIPO study on limitations and exceptions of copyright.
[35] Ricketson, *Berne Convention*.
[36] Ricketson, WIPO study on limitations and exceptions of copyright, 20.
[37] Hugh Hansen (ed.), *Intellectual Property Law and Policy*, vol. 11 (Oxford: Hart, 2010), p. 263.
[38] Ricketson and Ginsburg, *International Copyright and Neighbouring Rights*, [13.25].
[39] Justin Hughes, 'Fair use and its politics – At home and abroad' in Ruth L Okediji (ed.), *Copyright Law in an Age of Limitations and Exceptions* (New York: Cambridge University Press, 2017), p. 235.
[40] See ibid., 243ff.   [41] Ibid., 243 fn. 32.
[42] Ricketson and Ginsburg, *International Copyright and Neighbouring Rights*, [15.23].
[43] Ibid., [756].

As debates on reform of Australian copyright law defences continue, Sam Ricketson's latest word might be his signature in 2018 to a submission to the Department of Communication and the Arts, Copyright Modernisation Consultation review by nine Australian IP academics (myself included),[44] stating that:

> The case for more flexible exceptions to infringement has been made and justified, repeatedly. The government's task at this point is a simple one. In undertaking reform of the Copyright Act 1968, the government should be guided exclusively by the recommendations of the ALRC in its *Copyright and the Digital Economy* report, and the PC in its *Intellectual Property Arrangements* report.
>
> The best option for reform is to introduce a 'fair use' exception to infringement. This should be in the form outlined by the ALRC in its recommendations 5-1, 5-2 and 5-3 (as supported in principle by the PC in its recommendation 6.1).

24.4 In Summary

In summary, Sam Ricketson has made a major and distinctive contribution in the Australian setting through his marshalling of the law of intellectual property into a coherent account, and his communication of an understanding of the competing considerations inherent in protecting intangible property. His elegant explication of the law is placed in an international and ever-evolving context, within which he has explained the past as a guide to the future, and we are all grateful beneficiaries of his work.

---

[44] Isabella Alexander et al., 'Copyright modernisation consultation, Response to consultation paper', Department of Communication and the Arts, 4 July 2018, retrieved from https://bit.ly/2kexC1f, 1.

CAMBRIDGE INTELLECTUAL PROPERTY AND INFORMATION LAW

Titles in the Series (formerly known as Cambridge Studies in Intellectual Property Rights)

BRAD SHERMAN and LIONEL BENTLY *The Making of Modern Intellectual Property Law*
IRINI A STAMATOUDI *Copyright and Multimedia Products: A Comparative Analysis*
PASCAL KAMINA *Film Copyright in the European Union*
HUW BEVERLY-SMITH *The Commercial Appropriation of Personality*
MARK J DAVISON *The Legal Protection of Databases*
ROBERT BURRELL and ALLISON COLEMAN *Copyright Exceptions: The Digital Impact*
HUW BEVERLY-SMITH, ANSGAR OHLY and AGNÈS LUCAS-SCHLOETTER *Privacy, Property and Personality: Civil Law Perspectives on Commercial Appropriation*
CATHERINE SEVILLE *The Internationalisation of Copyright Law: Books, Buccaneers and the Black Flag in the Nineteenth Century*
PHILIP LEITH *Software and Patents in Europe*
GEERTRUI VAN OVERWALLE *Gene Patents and Clearing Models*
LIONEL BENTLY, JENNIFER DAVIS and JANE C. GINSBURG *Trade Marks and Brands: An Interdisciplinary Critique*
JONATHAN CURCI *The Protection of Biodiversity and Traditional Knowledge in International Law of Intellectual Property*
LIONEL BENTLY, JENNIFER DAVIS and JANE C GINSBURG *Copyright and Piracy: An Interdisciplinary Critique*
MEGAN RICHARDSON and JULIAN THOMAS *Framing Intellectual Property: Legal Constructions of Creativity and Appropriation 1840–1940*
DEV GANGJEE *Relocating the Law of Geographical Indications*
ANDREW T KENYON, MEGAN RICHARDSON and NG-LOY WEE-LOON *The Law of Reputation and Brands in the Asia Pacific Region*
EDSON BEAS RODRIGUES, JR *The General Exception Clauses of the TRIPS Agreement: Promoting Sustainable Development*
ANNABELLE LEVER *New Frontiers in the Philosophy of Intellectual Property*
SIGRID STERCKX and JULIAN COCKBAIN *Exclusions from Patentability: How the European Patent Office Is Eroding Boundaries*
SEBASTIAN HAUNSS *Conflicts in the Knowledge Society: The Contentious Politics of Intellectual Property*
HELENA R HOWE and JONATHAN GRIFFITHS *Concepts of Property in Intellectual Property Law*
ROCHELLE COOPER DREYFUSS and JANE C GINSBURG *Intellectual Property at the Edge: The Contested Contours of IP*
NORMANN WITZLEB, DAVID LINDSAY, MOIRA PATERSON and SHARON RODRICK *Emerging Challenges in Privacy Law: Comparative Perspectives*
PAUL BERNAL *Internet Privacy Rights: Rights to Protect Autonomy*
PETER DRAHOS *Intellectual Property, Indigenous People and Their Knowledge*

SUSY FRANKEL and DANIEL GERVAIS *The Evolution and Equilibrium of Copyright in the Digital Age*
Edited by KATHY BOWREY and MICHAEL HANDLER *Law and Creativity in the Age of the Entertainment Franchise*
SEAN BOTTOMLEY *The British Patent System and the Industrial Revolution 1700–1852: From Privileges to Property*
SUSY FRANKEL *Test Tubes for Global Intellectual Property Issues: Small Market Economies*
JAN OSTER *Media Freedom As a Fundamental Right*
SARA BANNERMAN *International Copyright and Access to Knowledge*
ANDREW T KENYON *Comparative Defamation and Privacy Law*
PASCAL KAMINA *Film Copyright in the European Union (second edition)*
TIM W DORNIS *Trademark and Unfair Competition Conflicts*
GE CHEN *Copyright and International Negotiations: An Engine of Free Expression in China?*
DAVID TAN *The Commercial Appropriation of Fame: A Cultural Critique of the Right of Publicity and Passing Off*
JAY SANDERSON *Plants, People and Practices: The Nature and History of the UPOV Convention*
DANIEL BENOLIEL *Patent Intensity and Economic Growth*
JEFFREY A MAINE and XUAN-THAO NGUYEN *The Intellectual Property Holding Company: Tax Use and Abuse from Victoria's Secret to Apple*
MEGAN RICHARDSON *The Right to Privacy: Origins and Influence of a Nineteenth-Century Idea*
MARTIN HUSOVEC *Injunctions against Intermediaries in the European Union: Accountable but Not Liable?*
ESTELLE DERCLAYE *The Copyright/Design Interface: Past, Present and Future*
MAGDALENA KOLASA *Trade Secrets and Employee Mobility: In Search of an Equilibrium*
PÉTER MEZEI *Copyright Exhaustion: Law and Policy in the United States and the European Union*
GRAHAM GREENLEAF and DAVID LINDSAY *Public Rights: Copyright's Public Domains*
OLE-ANDREAS ROGNSTAD *Property Aspects of Intellectual Property*
ELENA COOPER *Art and Modern Copyright: The Contested Image*
PAUL BERNAL *The Internet, Warts and All: Free Speech, Privacy and Truth*
SEBASTIAN FELIX SCHWEMER *Licensing and Access to Content in the European Union: Regulation between Copyright and Competition Law*
DANIELA SIMONE *Copyright and Collective Authorship: Locating the Authors of Collaborative Work*
EMILY HUDSON *Drafting Copyright Exceptions: From the Law in Books to the Law in Action*
GRAEME GOODAY and STEVEN WILF *Patent Cultures: Diversity and Harmonization in Historical Perspective*

Lightning Source UK Ltd.
Milton Keynes UK
UKHW022205060320
359940UK00005B/44